D1536068

FLASH MATH CREATIVITY

Second Edition

DAVID HIRMES
JD HOOGE
KEN JOKOL
PAVEL KALUZHNY
TY LETTAU
LIFAROS
JAMIE MACDONALD
GABRIEL MULZER
KIP PARKER
KEITH PETERS
PAUL PRUDENCE
GLEN RHODES
MANNY TAN
JARED TARBELL
BRANDON WILLIAMS

friendsof

DESIGNER TO DESIGNER™

an Apress® company

Flash Math Creativity, Second Edition

ISBN (pbk): 1-59059-429-0

Printed and bound in China   9 8 7 6 5 4 3 2

Trademarked names may appear in this book. Rather than use a trademark symbol with every occurrence of a trademarked name, we use the names only in an editorial fashion and to the benefit of the trademark owner, with no intention of infringement of the trademark.

Distributed to the book trade in the United States by Springer-Verlag New York, Inc., 233 Spring Street, 6th Floor, New York, NY 10013 and outside the United States by Springer-Verlag GmbH & Co. KG, Tiergartenstr. 17, 69112 Heidelberg, Germany.

In the United States: phone 1-800-SPRINGER (1-800-777-4643), fax 201-348-4505, e-mail orders@springer-ny.com, or visit www.springer-ny.com. Outside the United States: fax +49 6221 345229, e-mail orders@springer.de, or visit www.springer.de.

For information on translations, please contact Apress directly at 2560 Ninth Street, Suite 219, Berkeley, CA 94710. Phone 510-549-5930, fax 510-549-5939, e-mail info@apress.com, or visit www.apress.com.

The information in this book is distributed on an "as is" basis, without warranty. Although every precaution has been taken in the preparation of this work, neither the author(s) nor Apress shall have any liability to any person or entity with respect to any loss or damage caused or alleged to be caused directly or indirectly by the information contained in this work.

The source code for this book is freely available to readers at www.friendsofed.com.

Commissioning Editor
Steve Rycroft

Technical Editor
Keith Peters

Content Architect and Editor (First Edition)
Ben Renow-Clarke

Technical Reviewers (First Edition)
Kristian Besley, John Flanagan, and Matthew B. Hein

Graphic Designer and Compositor
Katy Freer

Editorial Board
Steve Anglin, Dan Appleman,
Ewan Buckingham, Gary Cornell,
Tony Davis, Jason Gilmore,
Chris Mills, Steve Rycroft,
Dominic Shakeshaft, Jim Sumser,
Karen Watterson, Gavin Wray,
John Zukowski

Project Manager
Beckie Stones

Copy Editor
Nicole LeClerc

Production Manager
Kari Brooks

Production Editor
Kelly Winquist

Proofreader
Elizabeth Berry

Cover Designers
Kurt Krames and Katy Freer

Front Cover Content
Glen Rhodes

Manufacturing Manager
Tom Debolski

CONTENTS

CONTENTS

FOREWORD TO THE FIRST EDITION

Most people don't find creating scripted graphics in a regular programming language that easy. I remember starting C at university and being struck dumb with disbelief that the drawing commands that I knew and loved in BASIC just didn't exist any more. The only thing that we had was a sub-simple graphics library built by the lecturers that was intentionally impossible to use. They didn't want us to breathe images, they just wanted us to bubble-sort our dreams. Flash was a godsend because it made this simple again by allowing me to create graphics in a standard drawing interface, code in a standard coding interface, and combine the two by simply placing the code on the graphic. Suddenly it all made sense. This ease of use has led to many other people tinkering with programming who wouldn't normally do so, and many programmers and mathematicians finding better ways of modeling and displaying what's in their heads. It's a scene reminiscent of the bedroom programming craze of the 80s, and a lot of the math that was being explored then is being brought back to life now.

I moved house a while back, and one of the things I uncovered was a box of old Beebug magazines for the BBC Micro computer, and looking through them I found various programs for creating fractal trees, Lorenz attractors, and function modeling in 3D—all things that turn up in this book. Of course now the resolution's a bit better and they don't take six hours to plot, but the basic principles are the same.

But creation's not all that it's about. Once you've fashioned your masterpiece, you have to change it (save it somewhere first if you like). Art is rarely perfect, there's always something more to add, or something more to take out. In Flash this is the easiest thing in the world to do. Change one variable and you change the whole piece, sometimes subtly, and sometimes astronomically. This is really where the whole book started, with the idea of change.

I love tinkering with code, I love the differences I can make with a quick change here or there, and I can spend hours with the simplest things just changing the same variable over and over again and being mesmerized by the results. Call it simple-minded, but that's me. I'd just spent a few hours doing exactly this when I had a Victor Kiam moment: I loved it so much, I wrote the book. Except I didn't, I just had an idea, the hard writing work was done by the 15 fantastic authors whose passion for the project surprised even me. It's changed a bit since its inception (at one stage I just wanted hundreds of experiments and nothing else), but the basic idea has remained the same—a collection of small experiments with a few iterations each to get you started, and an explanation of what the main variables do so that you'll have a good idea of what to change. To be honest though, I'd almost prefer you to ignore all of this, just grab the files from the site, open them in Flash, and do your best to break them. Once you've done that then go to the chapter and work through the iterations there, gaining a better understanding of the processes that make them tick, then finally go back into Flash and break them again—that's where the fun is, and I think where the majority of the learning is.

The book is split informally into two parts. The first part of the book deals with the smaller experiments, each with an average of ten iterations, and each inviting you to delve into the code and start fiddling. The second section of the book consists of the final three authors; these guys' experiments are more complete applications with interfaces to alter the variables within them. That's certainly no reason to not go into the code and adapt it though, it just means that you can try new things without having to go back into Flash every time.

Most of all though, for me this book is about inspiration. I only did Math at the most basic level at school, but that doesn't stop me being amazed and intrigued by the experiments in this book. I think I must have almost spent as much time going into the files and messing with them as I did editing the material, and I now have a lot more Flash knowledge than I started out with. Working on this book has inspired me to create and experiment a lot more in Flash, and given me more of the information that I needed to translate some of my more esoteric ideas into reality.

The book's filled with ideas to get you started, do with them what you will, but when you're done be sure to post them up on the dedicated forum on our site at **www.friendsofed.com/fmc**. There's nothing I like more than having new code to mess about with.

Ben

Birmingham, December 2001

Get all the FLAs from here: www.friendsofed.com/fmc/downloads

Break them in a good way.

FOREWORD

In late 2001, I was contacted by friends of ED and asked if I would like to contribute to a new book called *Flash Math Creativity*. In fact, I had only recently gotten started in ActionScript through friends of ED books, so it was a real honor to be asked to contribute. Then I saw the spec for the book: 15 Flash "creatives," each creating four experiments, with several iterations of each experiment, giving all the code and a little explanation, allowing the reader to go wild. My initial impression was, "That is *exactly* the kind of book I would run right out and buy!"

Apparently I wasn't the only one who thought that way. The last couple of times I was hanging out at the friends of ED exhibition booth at Flash conferences, it seemed there was a steady stream of people asking for "that Flash math book." It was one of the most popular books in the friends of ED line, with a bit of a cult following.

Unfortunately, as is the way with most books of this nature, it got old. Since the original version was published, Flash has gone through two very major changes. Flash MX brought us a real event model and the drawing API, along with lots of other exciting changes. Then MX 2004 came along with ActionScript 2.0 and real object-oriented programming that wasn't painful to work with. Going back through the code and file structure of the various experiments in the original version of *Flash Math Creativity* was an almost scary experience. Code scattered all throughout the movies, no worrying about case-sensitivity, using numbers as variables, "tricks and tips" that would make a best-practices advocate cry. Did we really code like that?

On the other hand, there were some truly amazing pieces in the first edition of this book. Even going through it almost 3 years later, there are experiments in this book that make my jaw drop. It would be a shame to have this book die such an untimely death just because of a serious case of bad syntax!

Luckily, the kind hearts at friends of ED could not bear such a thing and decided to give this patient an emergency session of CPR, ActionScript 2.0 style. And so, for the second time, I was asked to contribute to this book, this time as a technical editor. My mission: to work my way through the book, cover to cover, bringing it up to speed with the latest version of Flash. I quickly agreed and got to work. Then I did some creative math of my own: 15 authors, 4 experiments each, 10 to 20 iterations of each experiment . . . It's a good thing for them that I'd already signed a contract! Anyway, we somehow made it through, and the result is in your hands, a fresh and up-to-date second edition of *Flash Math Creativity*, ready to keep you up late at night exploring new ideas with Flash.

I'll take this opportunity to say a few words on the conversion process from Flash 5 to ActionScript 2.0 in Flash MX 2004. This wasn't an easy process, and I don't mean just technically. Obviously, structure and syntax in the files needed to be updated, but these aren't just dry, stale applications or the kind of sample code you'd find in a how-to book—each experiment was a highly creative piece of digital art, and that creativity usually extended to how it was coded, the techniques that were used, and even the variable names. So, yes, things needed to change, but just how much to change was an exercise in fine judgment.

After a few false starts, I settled on a rough process. The first thing I did was bring all the code in the movie to the first frame of the main timeline. I then handled any scope and case-sensitivity issues, and initialized any required variables. At that point, I did whatever was necessary to get the file working again in its new format and producing exactly the same effect the original artist created. From here, I assigned types to variables and function parameters and returns, swapped any outdated actions with their newer counterparts (`random(x)` to `Math.random()*x`, for instance), and replaced any "bad-practice" or "illegal" code with something more acceptable to achieve the same effect. And finally, any inefficient or confusing sections of code were smoothed out.

For the most part, if the file still functioned and did what the original did, that was the end of my work. However, in some cases I had to look at incorporating an ActionScript 2.0 class or two. For the vast majority of the experiments, this would have obviously been overkill, but some of those in the latter part of the book were sufficiently complex that they did warrant being put into classes. They aren't the best examples of OOP by far, but they do simplify the resulting code, while retaining as much of the author's original style as was technically feasible.

The result that I strove for in every line of the book was what the original author might have done, given the current tools. If I don't get any hate mail from any of those original authors, I'll know that I at least partially succeeded. In all seriousness, though, I'm sure they'll be as thrilled as I am that this wonderful book has been given a new lease on life.

Keith Peters

Boston, August 2004

Inspiration is hard to pin down. More often than not I find it comes from things I come across in daily life, whether that be television, film, music, or just everyday objects or events. Working with Flash I often attempt to reproduce some kind of pattern or graphical effect that I've observed. While I generally start out with an end product in mind, the process of construction sometimes throws up new possibilities and I'll often end up somewhere completely different.

Jamie Macdonald is currently living and working freelance in London.

jamie macdonald
www.nooflat.nu

The basic effect

All of my experiments start from the same base file, so rather than typing out the same thing four times, I'll just do it this once.

The pieces that I've made here are pretty simple. None of them took more than a couple of hours to put together, but I think they all have possibilities, and the effect on each piece of changing a few parameters is striking. What the pieces have in common is that they work with sine and cosine curves to produce various types of motion, so if you're going to work with these files, it's useful to have an idea of how these curves behave. Both curves oscillate. If you look at the two diagrams you'll see that between 0 and 360 degrees they vary between 1 and –1 (for example, sin 90 = 1 and sin 270 = –1). The cosine curve is the same as the sine curve except it's moved along, or translated.

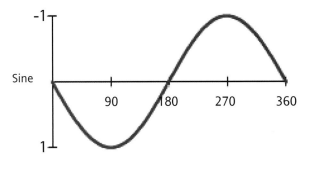

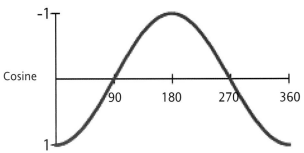

So from this you can say that if you want an oscillation between 10 and –10, you would just multiply the sine degree by 10. For an oscillation between 0 and 40, you would use 20 multiplied by the sine degree, and then add 20 to the result. It's worth noting that these functions accept values above and below the 360-degree range—beyond this, they continue oscillating in the same way, so the numbers 10, 370, 730, and so on will all have the same sine values.

When you're dealing with these functions within Flash, you have to remember that they don't work with degrees, but with radians—a different unit of measurement.

Before you use Flash's math functions, you need to convert your values from degrees to radians, which is a relatively simple procedure:

360 degrees = 2*pi radians
180 degrees = pi radians
1 degree = pi/180 radians

So to convert a value in degrees to radians, you use this formula:

radians = degrees*Math.PI/180

That's the basic math out of the way. Now let's look at making the template file that all the experiments start from. First you need a movie clip called **ball**, which consists of a 42x42 pixel red circle in the center of the stage. This movie clip is exported with the Identifier **ball** from the Library.

That's it for the objects, but one further thing that I added was a function on the main timeline to enable you to dynamically change a movie clip's brightness. This works using the **setTransform** method, and you can use it with any color object that you set up. It's worth noting that this is set up to only accept brightness values above 0. Add this code to the first frame on the main timeline:

```
function setBrightness(col:Color,
➥ brightness:Number):Void {
  var anum:Number = 100 - brightness;
  var bnum:Number = 255/100 * brightness;
  col.setTransform( {ra:anum, ga:anum, ba:anum,
  ➥ rb:bnum, gb:bnum, bb:bnum, aa:100, ab:0} );
};
```

The template file is now complete. The only changes you need to make for each file now are to add actions to the first frame on the main stage.

towardsUs

The first effect involves movie clips that originate in the center of the stage and expand, oscillating around the center point until they appear to hit the viewer's screen and then fade out. The heart of the experiment is made up of two main functions. The main **onEnterFrame** function is used to instantiate the movie clips, and the **expand** function is used to make them grow. Remember that all of the code for these experiments goes on the first frame of the main movie. Here's the code in its entirety:

```
var scaleMax:Number = 800;
var fadeOut:Number = 0.93;
var frequency:Number = 10;
var colMin:Number = 0;
var colMax:Number = 40;
var colVariance:Number = colMax - colMin;

function hRad(Void):Number {
  return 4 + Math.random();
}
```

```
function vRad(Void):Number {
   return 4 + Math.random();
}
function vRadInc(Void):Number {
   return 0.1;
}
function hRadInc(Void):Number {
   return 0.1;
}
function lrSpeed(Void):Number {
   return 5 + Math.random() * 40;
}
function scaleUpSpeed(Void):Number {
   return 1.02;
}
function nooCol(Void):Number {
   return colMin + Math.random() * colVariance;
}
var depth:Number = 0;
onEnterFrame = function () {
   if (Math.floor(Math.random() * frequency) == 0) {
      depth++;
      var noo:MovieClip = _root.attachMovie("ball", "ball"+depth, depth);
      var col:Color = new Color(noo);
      setBrightness(col, nooCol());
      noo._x = -50;
      noo._y = -50;
      noo._xscale = noo._yscale = 10;
      noo.scaleSpeed = scaleUpSpeed();
      noo.lrSpeed = lrSpeed();
      noo.hRad = hRad();
      noo.vRad = vRad();
      noo.hRadInc = hRadInc();
      noo.vRadInc = vRadInc();
      noo.lr = 0;
      noo.onEnterFrame = _root.expand;
   }
}
function expand() {
   this.lr += this.lrSpeed;
   this.hRad += this.hRadInc;
   this.vRad += this.vRadInc;
   this._x = Stage.width / 2 + this.hRad * Math.sin(this.lr * Math.PI/180);
   this._y = Stage.height / 2 + this.vRad * Math.cos(this.lr * Math.PI/180);
   this._yscale = this._xscale *= this.scaleSpeed;
   this.swapDepths(Math.floor(this._xscale));
   if (this._xscale > _root.scaleMax) {
      this._alpha *= _root.fadeOut;
      if (this._alpha < 3) {
         this.removeMovieClip();
      }
   }
}
```

You'll notice that I try and keep a lot of the separate parts of my code wrapped up in functions, as I find that it's easier to find, understand, and modify things when they're in discrete, functionality-driven blocks. It also means that I can return different values depending on the situation, making the math in the main control function a bit neater and easier to digest.

The key variables and functions

scaleMax = The maximum scale before fading out.

fadeout = The speed of the fade-out.

frequency = How often a new movie clip is created.

colMin = The minimum brightness.

colMax = The maximum brightness.

colVariance = The variation in brightness.

lr = The value used to determine where on the sine or cosine curve the ball is. The faster it increases, the faster the oscillation.

hRad = The amount of horizontal oscillation on either side of the center.

vRad = The amount of vertical oscillation on either side of the center.

vRadInc = The speed at which the amount of horizontal oscillation increases.

hRadInc = The speed at which the amount of vertical oscillation increases.

lrSpeed = The left-right speed—the speed of oscillation.

scaleUpSpeed = The speed at which the object expands.

nooCol = The brightness of each movie clip.

noo = The name of the current object.

Now I'll cover the running of the **onEnterFrame** and **expand** functions. The **onEnterFrame** function is executed every frame, and it creates a random number between 0 and the **frequency** variable set earlier. If the random number equals zero, then it creates another movie clip using **attachMovie**. It positions and scales the movie clip, and sets its brightness. It then goes through calling each of the parameter functions and uses the values returned by these functions to set variables inside the **ball** movie clip. The final thing that this function does is set the movie clip's **onEnterFrame** handler to equal **expand**, which is the function that I'll turn to next. As **expand** is now the **onEnterFrame** handler of the movie clip, whenever you refer to **this._x** in the function, you're actually referring to the x position of the instance of whichever ball that it's called from.

The **expand** function is where the main math of the movie is carried out. First, you increment your oscillation variables, **lr**, **hRad**, and **vRad**. The lines that set the _x and _y properties are where the sine and cosine curves come into play. You set these values to be at the middle of the stage plus **hRad** or **vRad** multiplied by the sine or cosine of **lr**. As you saw earlier, the sine of any value will be somewhere between –1 and 1, so here you're setting the **x** position to somewhere between **stage.width** minus **hRad**, and **stage.width** plus **hRad**, and it will move between those two values. You then multiply the scale of the object by **scaleSpeed** to increase the size of the object, and then finally you check whether it has reached its maximum size, in which case you decrease its alpha until the object is transparent enough be removed without noticeably blinking away.

towardsUs2

In this iteration I decided to change the file so that instead of oscillating around the center point, the circles just rush straight at the viewer. I also made them go a bit faster for better effect—the other changes I made were cosmetic. Here's the list of variables that I changed:

```
var scaleMax:Number = 600;
var frequency:Number = 5;
var colMax:Number = 90;
function hRad(Void):Number {
   return 0;
}
function vRad(Void):Number {
   return 0;
}
function vRadInc(Void):Number {
   return 0;
}
function hRadInc(Void):Number {
   return 0;
}
function scaleUpSpeed(Void):Number {
   return 1.2;
}
```

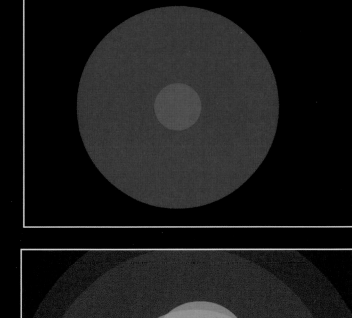

towardsUs3

In this iteration, I gave the circles a set, rather than an incremental, oscillation and shortened the time it takes them to fade out, resulting in a fast, spinning effect.

```
var fadeOut:Number = 0.7;
function hRad(Void):Number {
   return 40;
}
function vRad(Void):Number {
   return 40;
}
```

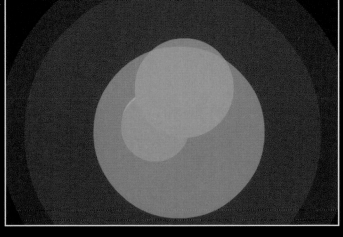

towardsUs4

I changed this one so that the circles begin from nothing, but then rapidly spiral out of the screen.

```
var scaleMax:Number = 400;
function hRad(Void):Number {
   return 0;
}
function vRad(Void):Number {
   return 0;
}
function vRadInc(Void):Number {
   return 5;
}
function hRadInc(Void):Number {
   return 5;
}
```

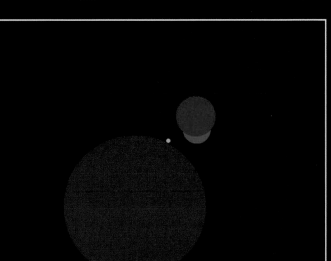

towardsUs5

Here, I decided to just oscillate the movie clips on the horizontal, with a more constant stream of circles appearing from both sides of the screen.

```
var frequency:Number = 2;
function vRadInc(Void):Number {
  return 0;
}
function hRadInc(Void):Number {
  return 20;
}
```

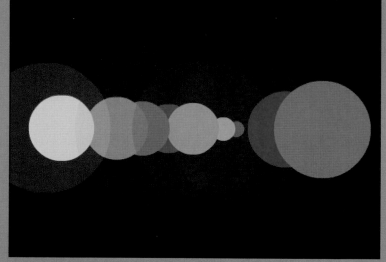

towardsUs6

I decided to reduce the tempo for this iteration. The circles expand at a more leisurely pace, moving from side to side, before "popping" as they approach the screen.

```
function hRadInc(Void):Number {
  return 5 * Math.random();
}
function lrSpeed(Void):Number {
  return 3 + Math.random() * 3;
}
function scaleUpSpeed(Void):Number {
  return 1.05;
}
```

towardsUs7

Back to spiraling again now, but this time with a controlled increment, meaning that all the circles follow more or less the same path.

```
var scaleMax:Number = 900;
var frequency:Number = 10;
var colMax:Number = 20;
function vRadInc(Void):Number {
  return 1.5;
}
function hRadInc(Void):Number {
  return 1.3;
}
function lrSpeed(Void):Number {
  return 10;
}
function scaleUpSpeed(Void):Number {
  return 1.1;
}
```

towardsUs8

Here, the circles oscillate toward us rapidly.

```
var colMin:Number = 70;
var colMax:Number = 90;
function hRad(Void):Number {
  return 5;
}
function vRad(Void):Number {
  return 25;
}
function vRadInc(Void):Number {
  return 0;
}
function hRadInc(Void):Number {
  return 0;
}
function lrSpeed(Void):Number {
  return 40;
}
```

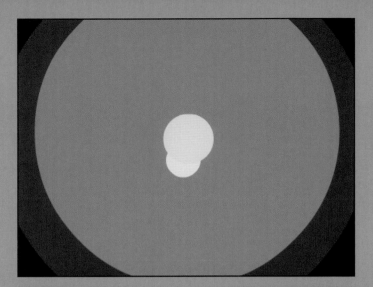

towardsUs9

In this experiment I've increased the speed of the horizontal oscillation to the extent that the circles appear to be emanating from three separate points.

```
function hRad(Void):Number {
  return 300;
}
function vRad(Void):Number {
  return 9;
}
function lrSpeed(Void):Number {
  return 60;
}
```

towardsUs10

In this final experiment, I reduced the horizontal oscillation and changed the increment and oscillation speed to create a gentler, wider spiral.

```
function hRad(Void):Number {
  return 200;
}
function vRadInc(Void):Number {
  return 1;
}
// speed at which horizontal magnitude increases
function hRadInc(Void):Number {
  return 1;
}
// speed of oscillation
function lrSpeed(Void):Number {
  return 10 + Math.random() * 10;
}
```

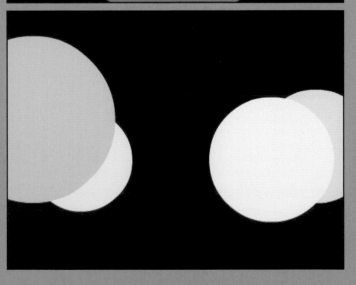

There are a number of ways you could change this movie. First of all, there are a lot of variations that can be created just by changing the parameters, for example, the oscillation could expand on the x-axis, but not the y-axis; the speed of oscillation could vary more wildly; the clips could fade out earlier or scale up slower; and so on. Beyond that, you could try swapping around the sine and cosine methods, or dropping in tan instead and seeing what effect that has.

inLine

For this effect you're going to place the circles in a line, and then each circle is going to expand and contract using a sine curve to set its value. You'll use each circle's distance from the center to determine the degree it starts with (and thus its position on the sine curve), giving the effect of a wave moving along the line from the center—a chain reaction.

Once again I'll start off with all the code on the first frame of the root (following on from the `setBrightness` function):

```
var hsp:Number = 4;
var total:Number = 70;
var twidth:Number = (total-1)*(hsp);
var brmin:Number = 0;
var brmax:Number = 40;

function inc(val:Number):Number {
   return 3;
}
function colinc(val:Number):Number {
   return 4;
}
function yMag(val:Number):Number {
   return 1;
}
function minScale(val:Number):Number {
   return 1;
}
function maxScale(val:Number):Number {
   return 12;
}
function startDegree(val:Number) {
   return 3 * val;
}
for(var i:Number = 0; i<total; i++) {
   var noo:MovieClip = _root.attachMovie("ball", "ball" + i, i);
   var offset:Number = Math.abs((total / 2) - i);
   noo._y = Stage.height / 2;
   noo._x = (Stage.width - twidth) / 2 + hsp * i;
   noo.baseY = Stage.height / 2;
   noo._xscale = noo._yscale = minScale();
   noo.inc = inc(offset);
   noo.colinc = colinc(offset);
   noo.col = new Color(noo);
   noo.brmin = brmin;
   noo.brmax = brmax;
   noo.degree = noo.coldegree = startDegree(offset);
   noo.brvariation = noo.brmax - noo.brmin;
   noo.yMag = yMag(offset);
   noo.minScale = minScale(offset);
   noo.maxScale = maxScale(offset);
   noo.variation = noo.maxScale - noo.minScale;
```

```
    noo.onEnterFrame = oscillate;
}
function oscillate(Void):Void {
    this.degree += this.inc;
    var value:Number = Math.sin(this.degree * Math.PI/180);
    this._xscale = this._yscale = this.minScale + (this.variation/2)
    ➥ + (this.variation/2) * value;
    this.coldegree += this.colinc;
    var value2:Number = Math.sin(this.coldegree * Math.PI/180);
    var brightness:Number = this.brmin + (this.brvariation/2) +
    ➥ (this.brvariation/2) * value2;
    setBrightness(this.col, brightness);
    this._y = this.baseY + value2 * this.yMag;
}
```

The key variables and functions

hsp = The spacing on the x-axis
total = The total number of circles
twidth = The total width of the line of circles
brmin = The minimum brightness
brmax = The maximum brightness
inc = The speed of oscillation in scale
colinc = The speed of oscillation of brightness
yMag = The amount of vertical oscillation
minScale = The minimum scale of an object
maxScale = The maximum scale of an object
variation = The difference between **minScale** and **maxScale**
brvariation = The difference between **brmin** and **brmax**
startDegree = The degree at which each circle starts
offset = How far the current position is from the center position
noo = The name of the current object
degree and **coldegree** = Counters
value = The sine value of **degree**
value2 = The sine value of **coldegree**

You'll notice that some of these functions are passed an argument, **val**, which will represent how many positions away from the center each ball is placed. The variable that is passed as this argument is **offset**, so most of the time you can think of these as being synonymous.

For this experiment, you don't need an **onEnterFrame** function, because you're just setting the clips up at the start and then leaving them to take care of themselves. You just run a loop to position all of the movie clips initially, and then set the clips' **onEnterFrame** to the **oscillate** function at the end. In this function you increment the two counters, **degree** and **coldegree**, and then calculate the sine values of those two values and use them to set the scale and brightness of the ball, respectively.

inLine2

The following changes lessen the gaps between the circles, creating a more solid feel.

```
var hsp:Number = 3;
function inc(val:Number):Number {
  return 10;
}
function colinc(val:Number):Number {
  return 40;
}
function minScale(val:Number):Number {
  return 10;
}
function maxScale(val:Number):Number {
  return 24;
}
```

inLine3

This one is a bit thicker and bouncier; the wave is more pronounced.

```
function yMag(val:Number):Number {
  return 3;
}
function minScale(val:Number):Number {
  return 20;
}
function maxScale(val:Number):Number {
  return 30;
}
function startDegree(val:Number) {
  return 9 * val;
}
```

inLine4

Here, I changed **inc** to give more of a pulsing effect. I also toned down the bounce.

```
function inc(val:Number):Number {
  return 3 * val;
}
function yMag(val:Number):Number {
  return 0;
}
function startDegree(val:Number) {
  return 5 * val;
}
```

inLine5

In this iteration, I increased a lot of the values, including the **startDegree**, so the objects are more spread out and you begin to lose the impression that they form a solid.

```
function inc(val:Number):Number {
  return 10 * val;
}
function yMag(val:Number):Number {
  return 3 * val;
}
function minScale(val:Number):Number {
  return 10;
}
function maxScale(val:Number):Number {
  return 20;
}
function startDegree(val:Number) {
  return 35 * val;
}
```

inLine6

I created another quite different effect here by dividing rather than multiplying **val** to give **startDegree** and also by changing **yMag** similarly.

```
var hsp:Number = 4;
var total:Number = 50;
function yMag(val:Number):Number {
  return 30 / (val / 3);
}
function startDegree(val:Number) {
  return 35 / val;
}
```

inLine7

Back to a straight line again, but with a faster pulsating wave.

```
function yMag(val:Number):Number {
  return 0;
}
function maxScale(val:Number):Number {
  return 30 + 10 / (val / 3);
}
function startDegree(val:Number) {
  return val;
}
```

As with the previous effect, just changing the values of the parameters can produce many variations. You might also try using each ball's distance from the left of the line instead of the center of the line as the value affecting how fast the scale oscillates.

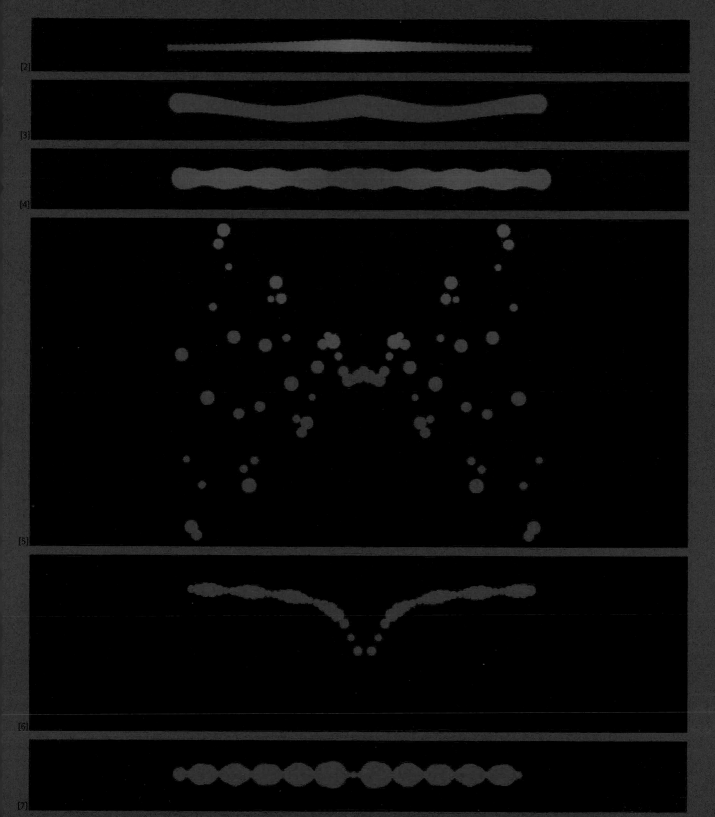

[2]

[3]

[4]

[5]

[6]

[7]

rightToLeft

This effect involves creating circles that orbit a central point that moves across the screen from right to left, while also oscillating up and down. The vertical motion will be taken care of in the same way as with the previous effect: incrementing a value and calculating the sine of that value to create the oscillation. For the orbiting, you need to use sine and cosine in a different way. For any given circle, you can calculate the **x** and **y** positions of a point on the circumference if you're given the radius and the angle at which the point is to the center. You can calculate this by making a right-angle triangle from the center of the circle to the point on the circumference as in this diagram:

So, in Flash the two formulas needed are

```
xposition = radius *
➡ Math.cos(degrees*Math.PI/180)
yposition = radius *
➡ Math.sin(degrees*Math.PI/180)
```

Now you can move on to creating the effect. Here's the code to add to the first frame of the template file:

sine(angle) = opposite / hypotenuse
» opposite = sine(angle) * hypotenuse

cosine(angle) = adjacent / hypotenuse
» adjacent = cosine(angle) * hypotenuse

To find a point on the circumference of a circle we use the properties of a right angle triangle.
So for this circle the x and y positions of the point shown are:

x position = cosine(40) * 100 = 76
y position = sine(40) * 100 = 64

```
var frequency:Number = 30;
var colMin:Number = 0;
var colMax:Number = 50;
var colVariance:Number = colMax - colMin;

function leftRightSpeed(Void):Number {
   return -2;
}
function maxScale(Void):Number {
   return 120;
}
function minScale(Void):Number {
   return 60;
}
function leftRightRadius(Void):Number {
   return 150;
}
function circlingSpeed(Void):Number {
   return 5;
}
function circleStartPoint(Void):Number {
   return 0;
}
function upDownRange(Void):Number {
   return 10;
}
function yFreqInc(Void):Number {
   return 12;
}
function nooCol(val):Number {
   val *= 30;
   return colMin + colVariance * 0.5 + (0.5 * colVariance) * Math.sin(val * Math.PI / 180);
}

var g:Number = 0;
var depth:Number = 0;
```

```
onEnterFrame = function(Void):Void {
  g++;
  if (g > frequency) {
    g = 0;
    depth++;
    var noo = attachMovie("ball", "ball" + depth, depth);
    noo._y = Stage.height / 2;
    noo.fulcrumX = noo._x = Stage.width + 30;
    noo.maxScale = maxScale();
    noo.minScale = minScale();
    var col:Color = new Color(noo);
    setBrightness(col, nooCol(depth));
    noo.variance = noo.maxScale - noo.minScale;
    noo.acrossRadius = leftRightRadius();
    noo.upDownRange = upDownRange();
    noo.degree = circleStartPoint();
    noo.degreeInc = circlingSpeed();
    noo.yFreq = 0;
    noo.yFreqInc = yFreqInc();
    noo.leftRightSpeed = leftRightSpeed();
    noo.onEnterFrame = shootMeAcross;
  }
};

function shootMeAcross(Void):Void {
  this.fulcrumX += this.leftRightSpeed;
  this.degree += this.degreeInc;
  this._x = this.fulcrumX+Math.cos(this.degree * Math.PI / 180) * this.acrossRadius;
  this._xscale = this._yscale = this.minScale+(this.variance * 0.5) + (this.variance * 0.5) *
  ➥ Math.sin(this.degree * Math.PI / 180);
  this.yFreq += this.yFreqInc;
  this._y = Stage.height / 2 + this.upDownRange * Math.sin(this.yFreq * Math.PI / 180);
  this.swapDepths(Math.floor(this._xscale));
  if (this._x < -40) {
    this.removeMovieClip();
  }
}
```

The key variables and functions

frequency = How often circles are created.
colMin = The minimum circle brightness.
colMax = The maximum circle brightness.
colVariance = The range of brightness.
leftRightSpeed = How fast the circles move across the screen.
maxScale = The maximum circle scale.
minScale = The minimum circle scale.
leftRightRadius = The radius of the circle that the ball moves around.
circlingSpeed = The speed at which the ball moves around the circle.
circleStartPoint = The degree at which the ball starts on the circle.
upDownRange = The range of the ball's up/down motion.
yFreqInc = The speed at which the ball moves up and down.
nooCol = The brightness for each ball. Increasing the **val** multiplier means the colors will oscillate more.
noo = The name of the current object.
fulcrumX = The center point that a circle orbits around. By moving this, you move the circle.

The main math goes on in the **shootMeAcross** function, which is called as the **onEnterFrame** handler of each circle. You start off by moving the fulcrum across the screen, and you then increment the **degree** value, which takes the circle around its orbit, and the **yfreq** value, which controls the **y** position of the circle. You set the **x** position of the circle using the cosine of the **degree** value, and then you set the scale using its sine value (you're using this instead of **y** to simulate depth—you've effectively flipped the circle on its side). After that, you set the **y** position using the sine of the **yfreq** variable so that it oscillates up and down. The final thing to do is remove the movie clip when it goes offscreen.

13

rightToLeft2

In this iteration I've made the **upDownRange** much greater, increasing the impression that the balls are moving in a three-dimensional space.

```
function leftRightRadius(Void):Number {
  return 50;
}
function circlingSpeed(Void):Number {
  return 10;
}
function upDownRange(Void):Number {
  return 70;
}
function yFreqInc(Void):Number {
  return 4;
}
```

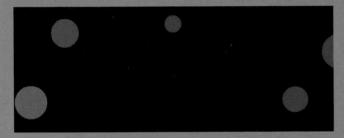

rightToLeft3

In this iteration I increased the number of balls, so it appears almost to be a constant stream. I also changed the path that they oscillate around.

```
var frequency:Number = 3;
function leftRightSpeed(Void):Number {
  return -3;
}
function maxScale(Void):Number {
  return 180;
}
function leftRightRadius(Void):Number {
  return 60;
}
function circlingSpeed(Void):Number {
  return 8;
}
```

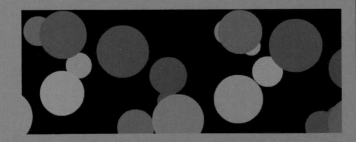

rightToLeft4

Here I altered the scaling and the **upDownRange** to produce a more concentrated, almost flat line with occasional gaps.

```
var frequency:Number = 4;
function minScale(Void):Number {
  return 0;
}
function leftRightRadius(Void):Number {
  return 30;
}
function upDownRange(Void):Number {
  return 20;
}
function yFreqInc(Void):Number {
  return 1;
}
```

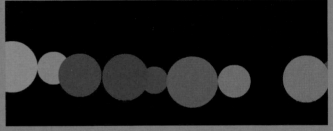

rightToLeft5

I changed the **upDownRange** and **yFreqInc** here to produce a nice looping motion.

```
var colMax:Number = 100;
function maxScale(Void):Number {
  return 60;
}
function upDownRange(Void):Number {
  return 60;
}
function yFreqInc(Void):Number {
  return 10;
}
```

rightToLeft6

This iteration creates another different loop.

```
var colMax:Number = 20;
function leftRightRadius(Void):Number {
  return 50;
}
function upDownRange(Void):Number {
  return 120;
}
function yFreqInc(Void):Number {
  return 5;
}
```

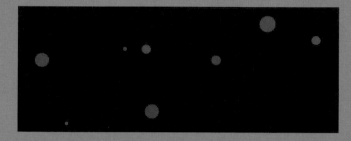

rightToLeft7

Here I've decreased the **upDownRange** significantly and widened the loop to produce this effect with a lot of depth.

```
var frequency:Number = 1;
function leftRightSpeed(Void):Number {
  return -4;
}
function maxScale(Void):Number {
  return 40;
}
function leftRightRadius(Void):Number {
  return 80;
}
function circlingSpeed(Void):Number {
  return 5;
}
function upDownRange(Void):Number {
  return 19;
}
```

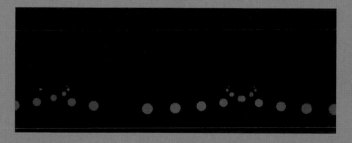

rightToLeft8

In this example I've changed the code to produce a single loop, but with a kink.

```
var frequency:Number = 2;
function leftRightSpeed(Void):Number {
  return -3;
}
function maxScale(Void):Number {
  return 90;
}
function circlingSpeed(Void):Number {
  return 3;
}
function yFreqInc(Void):Number {
  return 10;
}
```

rightToLeft9

The addition of some random elements in this final iteration gives a more chaotic feel.

```
var frequency:Number = 3;
function leftRightSpeed(Void):Number {
  return -2 - Math.random();
}
function maxScale(Void):Number {
  return 120;
}
function upDownRange(Void):Number {
  return Math.random() * 50;
}
```

There are many different effects that you can create here by altering the parameters—for instance, you could vary the speed of circling and the speed of motion across, which can produce a snaking form or various spirals. Also try changing the shape of the object.

sinGrid

This final effect positions a number of circles in a grid and then uses a sine wave to alter their color and brightness. Within this grid, you can create the effect of a wave by starting each circle off with a degree value slightly offset from the one next to it. You can calculate this offset in a number of ways, but the basic thing you need to do is to divide 360 by the total number of circles. Say, for instance, you have ten objects. You can start them off at 36, 72, 108, 144, 180, 216, 252, 288, and 324 degrees, and so on. With these start values, each circle will be placed somewhere between the minimum and maximum scales (as the sine values oscillate between 1 and −1). As each degree value increases, the gap between them will be maintained, and it will appear that a wave is moving across the grid, starting from the bottom right and moving up row by row. If you change this offset so the values vary between 0 and 180, then this will appear as only half of a sine wave.

Once again you'll start off by adding all of the code into the first frame of your template.

```
var across:Number = 10;
var down:Number = 10;
var total:Number = across*down;
var hsp:Number = 20;
var vsp:Number = 20;
var degInc:Number = 360 / total;
var numberOfOscillations:Number = 1;
var bx:Number = (Stage.width - hsp * across) / 2;
var by:Number = (Stage.height - vsp * down) / 2;

function increment(offset):Number {
   return 30;
}
function minScale(Void):Number {
   return 3;
}
function maxScale(Void):Number {
   return 54;
}
function minBrt(Void):Number {
   return 0;
}
function maxBrt(Void):Number {
   return 50;
}
```

```
var row:Number = 0;
var column:Number = 0;

for (i=0; i<total; i++) {
   var noo:MovieClip = attachMovie("ball",
   ➡ "circ" + i, i);
   noo._x = bx + column * hsp;
   noo._y = by + row * vsp;
   noo.col = new Color(noo);
   var offset:Number = Math.abs(total / 2 - i);
   noo.myInc = increment(offset);
   noo.minScale = minScale();
   noo.maxScale = maxScale();
   noo.variance = noo.maxScale - noo.minScale;
   noo.minBrt = minBrt();
   noo.maxBrt = maxBrt();
   noo.colVariance = noo.maxBrt - noo.minBrt;
   noo.onEnterFrame = undulate;
   noo.degree = i * degInc * numberOfOscillations;
   column++;
   if (column == across) {
      column = 0;
      row++;
   }
}

function undulate(Void):Void {
   this.degree += this.myInc;
   var sinVal:Number = Math.sin(this.degree *
   ➡ Math.PI/180);
   this._xscale = this._yscale = this.minScale +
   ➡ (this.variance * 0.5) + (this.variance * 0.5)
   ➡ * sinVal;
   var brightness:Number = this.minBrt + (0.5 *
   ➡ this.colVariance) + (0.5 * this.colVariance)
   ➡ * sinVal;
   setBrightness(this.col, brightness);
}
```

The key variables and functions

across = The number of circles across.
down = The number of circles down.
total = The total number of circles.
hsp = The horizontal spacing.
vsp = The vertical spacing.
degInc = The number of degrees per circle to span one complete oscillation.
numberOfOscillations = How much of a complete curve to display at once.
bx = The starting **x** position.
by = The starting **y** position.
increment = How fast the wave moves across. You pass this an offset value that represents how many positions away form the center the current circle is (you're not using this initially, but it can be implemented).
minScale = The minimum scale.
maxScale = The maximum scale.
minBrt = The minimum brightness.
maxBrt = The maximum brightness.
column and **row** = The current column and row.

The **for** loop sets up the grid initially, and it's then updated constantly by the **undulate** function that contains the majority of the math. This function's fairly simple, just incrementing the **degree** value and then using that to set the scale and brightness as before.

sinGrid02

This simple change gives a diagonal pulse.

```
var numberOfOscillations:Number = 12;
```

sinGrid03

Increasing the value again gives a steeper diagonal pulse.

```
var numberOfOscillations:Number = 21;
```

sinGrid04

Decreasing the value to less than 1 gives a single bottom-to-top pulse.

```
var numberOfOscillations:Number = 0.5;
```

sinGrid05

By changing the **increment** to a random value, the effect starts off with the single pulse, but then rapidly descends into chaos.

```
function increment(offset:Number):Number {
  return 10 * Math.floor(5 * Math.random());
}
```

sinGrid06

Here, I changed the **increment** value again, this time to incorporate the **offset**, to create gradual changes of direction.

```
function increment(offset:Number):Number {
  return 4 + offset;
}
```

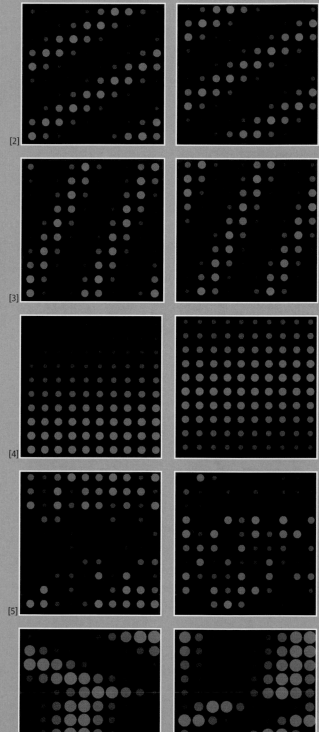

[2]

[3]

[4]

[5]

[6]

sinGrid07

Here the shape of the grid is different: a vertical rectangle.

```
var across:Number = 7;
var down:Number = 14;
var numberOfOscillations:Number = 100;
function increment(offset:Number):Number {
   return 14 + offset / 20;
}
```

sinGrid08

For this iteration, I kept the main formula the same but changed the shape of the grid to a really long, thin rectangle.

```
var across:Number = 5;
var down:Number = 25;
```

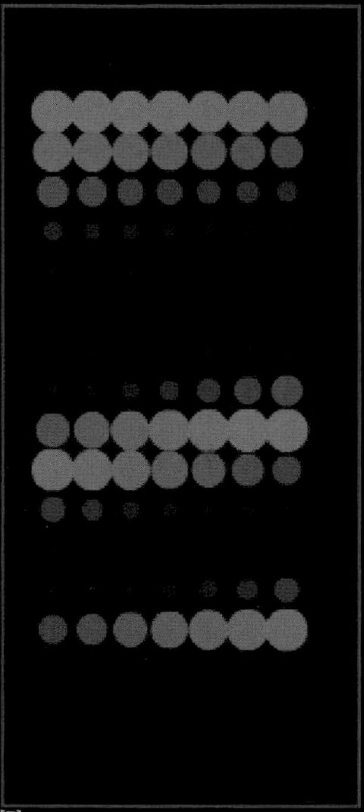

[7]

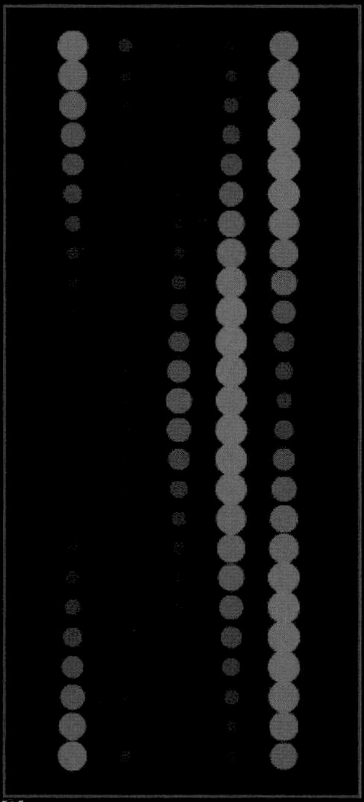

[8]

sinGrid09

Back to the square pulsing grid again, but this time with a different brightness in the pattern.

```
var across:Number = 10;
var down:Number = 10;
var numberOfOscillations:Number = 3;
function minScale(Void):Number {
   return 15;
}
function maxScale(Void):Number {
```

```
   return 60;
}
function maxBrt(Void):Number {
   return 100;
}
```

sinGrid10

Decreasing the spacing between the circles, but at the same time increasing the scale of them, makes the circles begin to lose their individuality and morph into oscillating blocks of color.

```
var hsp:Number = 7;
var vsp:Number = 7;
var numberOfOscillations:Number = .33;
function minScale(Void):Number {
   return 45;
}
function maxScale(Void):Number {
   return 130;
}
```

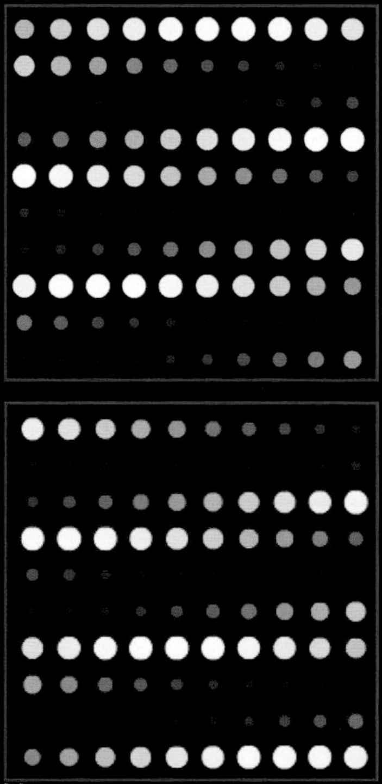

[9]

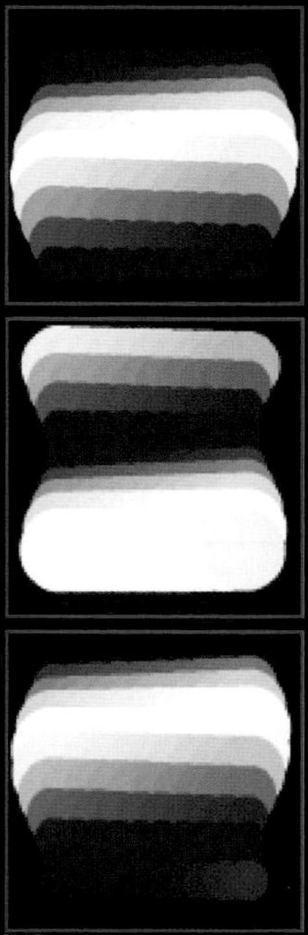

[10]

With this effect, you might try implementing the **offset** value so that the speed of oscillation is determined by how far each ball is from the center, or you could change this so it's affected by how far it is from the corner, and so on. Altering the **numberOfOscillations** variable can produce different types of waves. It's also worth noting that you can reverse the direction of any wave by subtracting the increment from 360, so an increment of 320 will move in the opposite direction from an increment of 40.

When I walk down the street, lie in bed, drive my car, stare at the city skyline or play piano my mind is always running away in a crazy mathematical spiral. I'm always looking for patterns. No, I'm not insane; my mind just works like that.

So, in this particular mathematical quest, I found myself looking for the patterns and beauty in everything I saw. You know what I discovered? That everything is beautiful in some way, or another. The grid of window lights in the city skyline, the streak of after-images left by looking at the sun, the rolling of waves or the swaying of branches; they're all beautiful – and they're all driven by numbers.

Naturally, life isn't a plain grid, so I found myself adding lots of randomization to the mix. Also, as the experiments went on and I modified, shifted, and adjusted the values, I found that I did stray somewhat from the original idea, but that's because the beauty left the real world, and entered the just-as-beautiful digital, numeric, mathematical realm.

I started my mind going early in life when I was about 4 years old. At that age, I began playing the piano, which was sitting unused in our house. I've been playing ever since then. Later, in 1997, I co-wrote a full-length musical called Chrystanthia. Somewhere along the way, I picked up game programming as a hobby, and eventually ended up making games professionally for home console systems. Then, in 1998, I discovered how I could take all my experiences and combine them when I discovered Flash. The rest is history. I share my ideas on my web site, www.glenrhodes.com.

glen rhodes
www.glenrhodes.com

Flowers

The "Flowers" experiment essentially consists very simply of the following code:

```
for(var i:Number=0; i<120; i++) {
  var nm:MovieClip = attachMovie("petal", "petal" + i, i);
  nm._x = Stage.width / 2;
  nm._y = Stage.height / 2;
  nm._rotation = Math.random() * 360;
  nm._xscale = nm._yscale = Math.random() * 100 + 20;
}
```

This code is placed on the main timeline and attaches instances of a movie clip with the linkage name `petal` on the main timeline. The instances are placed in a circle, much like the petals of a rose are arranged. This creates a simple virtual flower.

The key variables

`i` = The main counter variable that is used in a loop to count through the copies as they're made
`nm` = A temporary string variable used to store the name of the new petal (`petal1`, `petal2`, `petal3`, and so on)
`s` = A counter used for scale (this will appear in `flower3.swf`)
`rot` = A counter used for rotation (this will appear in `flower3.swf`)
`dr` = A variable attached to each petal instance, which is used as an increment for increasing the `_rotation` of the petal every frame (this will appear in `flower6.swf`)

Iterations

In `flower2.swf`, I've added one line of code to the main loop:

```
nm.swapDepths(2000 - nm._xscale);
```

This will place petals that are smaller on top of the larger petals in the background. This is a more accurate depiction of the way a real flower's petals are arranged.

[2]

In `flower3.swf`, instead of using random variables for scale and rotation, I'm using a fixed set of variables:

```
nm._rotation = rot += 15;
nm._xscale = nm._yscale = s;
nm.swapDepths(2000 - nm._xscale);
s++;
```

This creates a radial patterned effect, somewhat like a seashell.

[3]

In `flower4.swf`, the code is the same as `flower3.swf`, except `rot` is increased by 7 instead of 15 with each copy. In addition, the flower itself has been changed to a creamy gradient color, creating another cool seashell look.

[4]

In `flower5.swf`, `s` is increased by 2 with each copy instead of 1, and `rot` is increased by 14. The contents of the petal image have been changed to a shape-tweened black-and-white gradient, so that when it's fully formed, the "seashell" has a cool color-scrolling effect.

`flower6.swf` is identical to `flower5.swf`, except that the shape tween is slightly different, and I've added the following code to the main loop:

```
nm.dr = Math.random() * 4 - 2;
nm.onEnterFrame = function(){
   this._rotation += this.dr;
}
```

[5]

This will make each petal rotate on the spot by `dr` each frame.

In `flower7.swf`, the petal has been changed to be long, slim, and oval in shape, and the code used for the petal's `onEnterFrame` handler has been changed to include the following:

```
nm.onEnterFrame = function(){
   this._xscale += 2;
   this._yscale += 2;
   this._rotation++;
   if (this._xscale > 300){
      this._xscale = 10;
   }
};
```

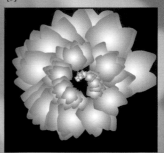

[6]

This will make the flower grow toward us every frame, and eventually, when the petal gets too big to be seen, it will become small again and reappear in the center of the flower with a really cool and strange effect. I also changed the `_rotation` line in the `main loop` back to `Math.random() * 360` to make the flower more random again.

In `flower8.swf`, everything is the same, except the petal is now purple/blue and when `_xscale` is greater than 300, I'm now taking the petal and setting its `_xscale` and `_yscale` to be 10. This creates a perpetual sinking effect—like we're flying into the flower or the petals are flying toward us.

[7]

`flower9.swf` looks very much like fireworks. All the petals start out at a random `_xscale` and `_yscale` between 0 and 10, and then they expand out quickly from the middle. As it expands, each petal's `_alpha` is being decreased, so it's fading out. When the petals have faded out, they're moved back to the middle and shrunk. The process then repeats. To achieve this, I changed `s` in the main loop to

```
s = Math.random() * 10;
```

And I changed the code in petal's `onEnterFrame` handler as follows:

```
nm.onEnterFrame = function() {
   this._xscale += 2;
   this._yscale += 2;
   this._alpha—;
   if (this._xscale>200) {
      this._alpha = 100;
      this._rotation = Math.random()*360;
      s = Math.random() * 20;
      this._xscale = s;
      this._yscale = s;
   }
};
```

[8]

[9]

In `flower10.swf`, the effect is almost that we're flying through space, and stars are streaking past us. It's just like `flower9.swf`, except that the `_xscale` and `_yscale` of each petal begins at a random value between 0 and 100, instead of 0 to 10.

In `flower11.swf`, I'm using the same code as `flower10.swf`, except the graphic has been changed to be a single tear-shaped white dot. This is near where the end of the petal would have been, so now it really looks like stars streaking toward us.

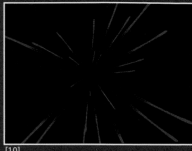

[10]

I've taken the star-field angle to its logical conclusion, so I'll return to the roots of this experiment. `flower12.swf` takes us back to the original code, creating static flower images. The petal image has been changed to be a smooth red gradient with a white tip and a purple base.

`flower13.swf` is identical to `flower12.swf`, except that in the main loop, s is being calculated like this:

```
s = Math.random() * 5;
```

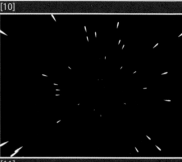

[11]

and the `_xscale`/`_yscale` of each petal is being calculated like this:

```
nm._xscale = nm._yscale= s * s * s + 10;
```

This creates an exponential separation of petals as they move outward—the inner petals are much closer together than the outer petals. This is more consistent with the way real flowers look.

`flower14.swf` is identical, except the shape of the petal has been changed slightly.

In `flower15.swf`, rather than calculate a random s, s is incremented like this:

```
s+=0.04;
```

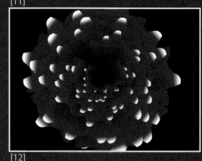

[12]

and the rotation of the instance is calculated like this:

```
nm._rotation = r += 6;
```

This creates an exponential spiral, which fades from red to black in the middle and is lined with a white edge.

In `flower16.swf`, s is incremented by 0.02 with each copy, and `_rotation = r+=27`. Also added is this line:

```
nm._alpha = s -= 0.5;
```

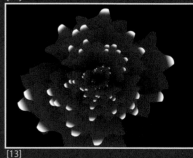

[13]

This creates a tight spiral of copies which fade as they go outward. The effect here looks like an electron micrograph of a pollen spore, with digital coloring.

`flower17.swf` uses the same code, except each petal has an `onEnterFrame` handler, with one line of code in it:

```
nm.onEnterFrame = function(){
    this._xscale--;
}
```

This creates a pollen spore, which implodes and then expands in a cool way. I've also added a spike to the tip of the petal graphic itself. When it implodes, it then expands slowly in the opposite direction and looks like some sort of headless blowfish.

In `flower18.swf`, the code is identical to `flower16.swf`, except the image of the petal has changed, and rather than staying black at the inner end of the petal, it fades to a creamy white. When run, this SWF generates another flowerlike image with a glowing light at the center.

[14]

`flower19.swf` uses the same code as the previous iteration, just with a slightly different image for the flower and therefore a different-looking final image. The effect is somewhat like an alien tropical flower of unknown origin.

[15]

[16]

[17]

[18]

[19]

The effects of this experiment, and its various iterations, can be further expanded to make better use of the random functions, to create wilder and more varied-looking flowers. Perhaps the flowers could be combined with the tree effect to produce completely organic, computer-generated images.

23

Trails

This code is attached to frame 1 of the main timeline in `trails.fla`:

```
_quality = "LOW";
var fade:Number = 0.9;
var counter:Number = 1;
attachMovie("master", "master", 0);
master.dx = 4;
master.dy = 4;
master.dr = 1;
master.onEnterFrame = function() {
  this._x += this.dx;
  this._y += this.dy;
  this._rotation += this.dr;
  if (this._x > 550) {
    this._x = 550;
    this.dx *= -1;
  }
  if (this._x < 0) {
    this._x = 0;
    this.dx *= -1;
  }
  if (this._y > 400) {
    this._y = 400;
    this.dy *= -1;
  }
  if (this._y < 0) {
    this._y = 0;
    this.dy *= -1;
  }
  var copy:MovieClip = attachMovie("master", "copy" + counter, counter++);
  copy._x = this._x;
  copy._y = this._y;
  copy._rotation = this._rotation;
  copy.onEnterFrame = function() {
    this._alpha *= _root.fade;
    if (this._alpha <= 3) {
      this.removeMovieClip();
    }
  };
};
```

In the Library is a movie clip exported with the linkage name **master**, which is a white, rounded square. Now, the master code basically attaches a copy of **master** on the stage, and assigns it a few properties and an **onEnterFrame** handler. This handler moves **master** around the stage and bounces it off the walls. As **master** moves, it spawns copies of itself every frame, with the instance names **copy1**, **copy2**, **copy3**, etc. When a copy is created, it's given the current properties (**_rotation**, **_x**, **_y**, **_alpha**) of **master**. Finally, the copy is given its own **onEnterFrame** handler, which will cause it to stay exactly where it is and fade out. This creates a very smooth set of trails behind the bouncing **master** movie clip. These effects are based on a motion effect.

The key variables

dx = The horizontal speed at which **master** is moving
dy = The vertical speed at which **master** is moving
dr = The speed at which **master** is rotating every frame
fade = The rate at which the copies fade out
counter = A variable that keeps track of which copy of **master** you're creating (so that unique names are given to each copy)

Iterations

For `trails2.swf`, I decided to change the motion of `master` to sine and cosine formulas, like so:

```
this._x = 275 + Math.cos(2 * this.ang) * 200;
this._y = 200 + Math.sin(3.2 * this.ang) * 170;
this.ang += 0.05;
```

The fading copy is the same, except that I set `_yscale` to be equal to `_alpha`, so that the copy will fade out and squash vertically as it does so. With the position now being set by sine and cosine, I'm able to remove all of the code that checks to see if the movie clip has left the screen.

`trails3.swf` is identical to `trails2.swf`, except when the copy fades out, it now squashes horizontally and rotates away as it fades by adding `_rotation += 5` to the `onEnterFrame` handler. The image has also been changed to a rainbow box.

`trails4.swf` is identical to `trails3.swf`, except I have two movie clips on the main timeline, `master` and `master2`. These move with the same sine and cosine formulas, except that `Math.sin(3.2*ang)` is on `_y` on `master` and on `_x` on `master2`. They're opposite so that the two `master` movie clips (and their trails) will dance about in mirroring curves.

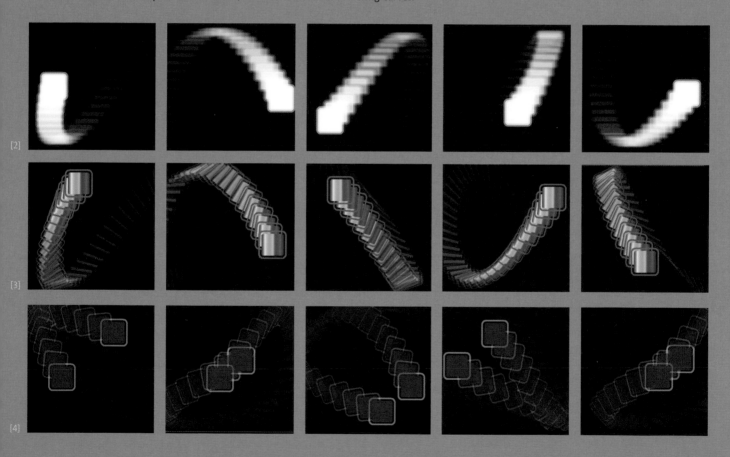

[2]

[3]

[4]

trails5.swf uses the same motion, except the **master** object is rotating as it moves, and it's moving faster. I've also changed the image to be a dumbbell shape, which creates a trail that looks like a DNA strand. I also incorporated code to create a **Color** object and dynamically change the color of the master (and hence the copy) based on its **_x** and **_y** position, like so:

```
this.r = 250 - (this._x / 2);
this.g = this._y / 2;
this.b = 80;
var col:Number = (this.r << 16) +
➥ (this.g << 8) + this.b;
this.c.setRGB (col);
```

I added the **Color** object definition to the actions on frame 1:

```
master.c = new Color(master);
```

trails6.swf is identical to **trails5.swf**, except that the center point of the **master** movie clip has been moved to the left circle on the dumbbell, which creates a cool lopsided swinging effect as it moves around. I also changed the color algorithm a bit—nothing special:

```
this.r = 0;
this.g = 250 - (this._y / 2);
this.b = (this._x / 2);
```

trails7.swf is identical to **trails5.swf**, except the rotation of **master** is now a function rather than a fixed amount:

```
this._rotation += Math.cos(this.ang) * 5;
```

This has the effect of making **master** look like it's swooping like a bird, rather than just spinning haphazardly. I also changed **ang** to **0.03**.

trails8.swf uses the same motion as **trails7.swf**, but the image in **master** has been changed to look like some sort of strange dragon or bird. When run as a trail, it looks like a long flying dragon swooping around the screen—very cool. It also moves slower than **trails7.swf**.

Finally, **trails9.swf** (opposite page) looks like **trails8.swf**, except it uses the **Color** object to make the dragon all black, evil, and ominous-looking. The copies also scale away on **x** and **y** to look like the tail is receding into the distance. To enhance this effect, I added in a background of mountains and an orange sky.

You could easily make the dragon keyboard- or mouse-controlled and create a game of some sort, or perhaps create a fleet (flock?) of dragons.

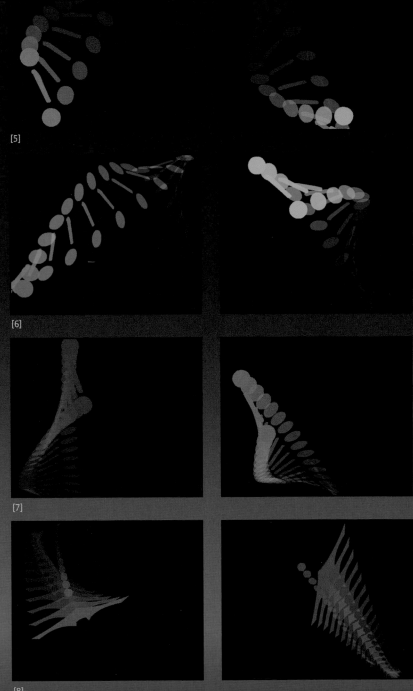

[5]

[6]

[7]

[8]

[9]

Trees

This code is attached to frame 1 of the main timeline in **treemake.fla**:

```
var numsticks:Number = 1;
var maxsticks:Number = 200;
var da:Number = 20;
attachMovie("stick", "stick", 0);
stick._x = Stage.width / 2;
stick._y = Stage.height - 100;
stick.destr = 90;
stick._rotation = 90;
stick.onEnterFrame = tree;
function tree() {
  if (this.destr<-180) {
    this.destr += 360;
  }
  if (this.destr>180) {
    this.destr -= 360;
  }
  if (this._rotation<-180) {
    this._rotation += 360;
  }
  if (this._rotation>180) {
    this._rotation -= 360;
  }
  if (this._rotation>this.destr) {
    this._rotation—;
  }
  if (this._rotation<this.destr) {
    this._rotation++;
  }
  this._rotation = Math.floor(this._rotation);
  if (this._rotation == this.destr && numsticks<maxsticks && this.dead != true) {
    var ra:Number = this._rotation*(Math.PI/180);
    var dx:Number = Math.cos(ra)*20;
    var dy:Number = Math.sin(ra)*20;

    var nm:MovieClip = attachMovie("stick", "st" + numsticks, numsticks++);
    nm._x = this._x - dx;
    nm._y = this._y - dy;
    nm._rotation = this._rotation;
    nm.destr = this._rotation - da;
    nm.onEnterFrame = tree;

    nm = attachMovie("stick", "st" + numsticks, numsticks++);
    nm._x = this._x - dx;
    nm._y = this._y - dy;
    nm._rotation = this._rotation;
    nm.destr = this._rotation + da;
    nm.onEnterFrame = tree;

    this.dead = true;
  }
};
```

In the Library is a movie clip exported with the linkage name **stick**. This is simply a 20-pixel-long horizontal line, with the center point at the right end.

When this movie is started, an instance of **stick** is put on the stage and assigned the function **tree** as its **onEnterFrame** handler. This will cause it to spawn two copies of itself (**st**n, **st**(n + 1)), creating new sticks that branch off at **da** degrees on either side of the parent. Then, those branches will each create two more copies in exactly the same way, and so on, until the shrub is complete. When a new branch is created, it's given a **_rotation** equal to that of its parent. It's also given a **destr** or **destination rotation**. This is where it wants to be when it spawns its own branches. This process has the effect of making the tree appear to grow out of itself. You may also notice that some of the branches have an annoying habit of rotating almost full circle before coming to a rest. I'll deal with this issue later. In the meantime, take a look at **treemake.swf**.

The key variables

destr = The destination rotation that **stick** must be at before it spawns its two child branches. The **_rotation** of the stick will be subtracted from or added to, to slowly get to its destination.

numsticks = A global counter that keeps track of the number of sticks copied. This increments each time a copy is made.

maxsticks = The maximum number of sticks allowed before spawning is halted. Otherwise, the tree would grow infinitely and crash the computer.

dead = A flag that determines whether or not the code of a stick needs to be run anymore. Once a stick has reached its **destr** and it has spawned its child branches, its code no longer needs to be run, so its **dead** value is set to **true**.

nm = A temporary variable used to create the string that is the name of the child stick ("**st**" + **_root.numsticks**).

ra = A variable that is the **_rotation** of this stick converted from degrees to radians, to be used with **Math.cos** and **Math.sin**.

dx = The **x** offset from the base of the stick to the tip, to determine where to place the starting point of the child stick.

dy = The **y** offset from the base of the stick to the tip, to determine where to place the starting point of the child stick.

da = A global variable that is the amount of angle to add to/subtract from the current **_rotation** in order to set the child's **destr**. If the parent is at 60 degrees, and **da** is 20, then the **destr** of the two children will be 40 and 80.

Iterations

treemake2.swf is identical to the original **treemake.swf**, except that the calculation of branch length has been adjusted to look like this:

```
var len:Number = (Math.random() * 10) + 10;
```

so that **len** is going to be a number between 10 and 20. This line goes just before the **dx** and **dy** calculations, and the **dx** and **dy** lines were also changed so that they're now multiplied by **len** instead of 20. Also, another new piece of code has been added:

```
var randa:Number = Math.floor(Math.random()*da);
```

This goes just after the first **var dy:Number = Math.sin(ra) * len;** line. I've also changed the two **nm.destr = this._rotation** lines, replacing the final **da** with the new **randa**. This means that rather than set the **destr** of **stick** to **da**, it will be set to a random number between 0 and **da**. This iteration makes the tree take on a much more random organic appearance. Finally, I changed **da** to 45 to make the tree more open and spread out.

In **treemake3.swf**, I introduced a variable for stick length (called **sticklen**) and set it to 40. So, whereas in the previous example the stick length was between 10 and 20, in this iteration the stick length is between 10 and **sticklen**, by changing this code:

```
var len:Number = (Math.random() * (sticklen -
➡ 10)) + 10;
```

To make this work, I also lengthened the actual graphic of the movie clip to 40 pixels to allow for a length greater than 20 without creating strange gaps between the branches (due to **len** being greater than the actual length of the **stick** graphic, so the child branches are spawned beyond the end of the parent).

In `treemake4.swf`, I decided on a radical change and removed the real-time rotation of the stick (using `destr`). Instead, the `_rotation` of each child is simply set to `_rotation + randa` to start with. This speeds up the process and takes care of some situations where sticks were rotating completely around the circle to get back to their `destr`. To do this, I first removed all of the initial set of `if` statements up to and including the line `this._rotation = Math.floor(this._rotation)`. Then I removed a clause in the long `if` statement (`this._rotation == this.destr &&`). The final pieces I removed are the two lines beginning `_root[nm].destr`, and then I added `–randa` and `+randa`, respectively, to the end of the `nm._rotation = this._rotation` lines. I also added a semitransparent circle at the end of each stick to highlight the joint.

`treemake5.swf` is identical to `treemake4.swf`, except I've added a vertical linear brown gradient to each stick to give it a 3D feel. This makes the tree appear more lifelike.

In `treemake6.swf`, I've added two green leaves to the stick. When the tree is fully grown, this creates a tree that is full of leaves.

`treemake7.swf` is identical to `treemake6.swf`, except the leaves have been turned to pink blossoms, and I've changed `da` to 20 and the `len` from "10 to `sticklen`" to "20 to `sticklen`" (by changing both 10s to 20s), so it's a much more vertical tree.

In `treemake8.swf`, I added two small branches to the graphic of the stick. This creates a tree with a fuller look, with many more branches.

In `treemake9.swf`, I added some greenery to these small branches, creating a lush tree.

`treemake10.swf` shows the removal of all the random elements and a greater concentration on the patterns, so `var len = sticklen – 10` and `randa = da`. Now, you can just as easily take out the line entirely and then replace all occurrences of `randa` with `da`. On the first keyframe, `da` has been set to 25 and `sticklen` has been set to 45. The stick image has also been changed to a gradient-filled blue gem, just for fun.

In `treemake11.swf`, I did a few things. First, I changed the shape to a simple green line with a little white "x" on the end. I also set the background color to black. I set `da` to 45 and `sticklen` to 45. This creates some very interesting mathematical patterns, based on 45-degree angles. Finally, I added code to make each successive generation fade out a bit, with this:

```
nm._alpha = this._alpha - 10;
```

In `treemake12.swf`, I changed `da` to be 66.66 degrees. This creates a lovely hexagonal pattern. I also changed the image on the stick to be a red-to-black gradient, with white tips.

In `treemake13.swf`, `_root.da` is a simple 90 degrees. The image of the stick has been changed to a horizontal brown-to-black gradient, and this creates a cool basket-weave effect.

`treemake14.swf` is the chessboard of the future! `da` is still 90 degrees, but the image has been changed to a radial-filled black-to-white gradient, with a gray square drawn next to it. `sticklen` has been changed to 65.

In `treemake15.swf`, `da` has been changed from 90 to 88. This creates the appearance that the chessboard is starting to collapse chaotically from the middle.

In `treemake16.swf`, the colors have been changed. The background is white and the stick is black with a softened edge. `da` is 75 and `sticklen` is 45. This creates something that looks like an X-ray photograph of a crystallized molecule.

This could be used to create many cool and interesting background images. Try making the image of the stick more or less complicated, and just play around with the different values for `da`, `sticklen`, and `maxsticks`. You could also make some of the position determination a math function, to change the look of the positioning.

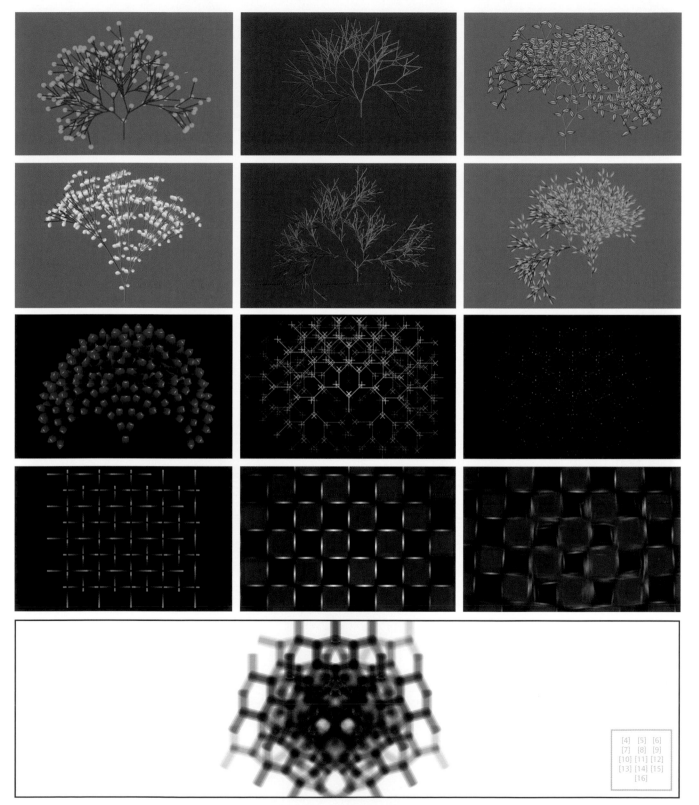

[4] [5] [6]
[7] [8] [9]
[10] [11] [12]
[13] [14] [15]
[16]

Circles

The following code is attached to the main timeline of `circ1.fla`. In the Library is a movie clip exported with the linkage name `circle`. This movie clip consists of a single black circle about 62 pixels in diameter.

```
var num:Number = 0;
for (i=0; i<10; i++) {
   for (j=0; j<10; j++) {
      var nm:MovieClip = attachMovie("circle", "cir"+num, num);
      nm._xscale = 171;
      nm._yscale = 171;
      nm._x = i * 62.5;
      nm._y = j * 62.5;
      nm.sx = nm._x;
      nm.sy = nm._y;
      nm.ang = 0;
      nm.mynum = num;
      num++;
      nm.onEnterFrame = function() {
         this._x = this.sx + Math.sin(this.ang) * this.mynum
         this._y = this.sy + Math.sin(this.ang) * this.mynum;
         this.ang += 0.1;
      };
   }
}
```

The `for` loop in the code is responsible for attaching and laying out the circles. Essentially, what you're doing is creating a grid of circles onscreen. The theory behind this experiment is that you can do different things with the circles in this grid and achieve very cool results.

The key variables

`sx` = The starting `_x` location of each circle.

`sy` = The starting `_y` location of each circle.

`ang` = A variable used as a counter in a circular loop. This is an angle that is fed into various trigonometry functions and then incremented. Each circle copy has its own `ang`.

`mynum` = A unique number given to each circle in the order that it's created.

`i` = An outer counter for the loop that positions the circle. `i` is used to determine the copy's `_x`.

`j` = An inner counter for the loop that positions the circle. `j` is used to determine the copy's `_y`.

`num` = A temporary counter used during the loop to determine which circle you're currently creating.

Iterations

In `circ1.swf`, the grid of circles simply pulses along a diagonal line, with each circle along pulsing a bit more than the previous one. The amount of motion that the grid of circles possesses is determined by the value of each circle's `mynum`. This uses a `Math.sin` function on the `_x` and `_y` of each circle to create this pulse.

In `circ2.swf`, the circles are pulsing along only `_x`, not `_y`. Also, the line that increments `ang` (`this.ang+=0.1`) has been changed to `this.ang += this.mynum / 450;`. This means that each circle will pulse at a slightly different rate, and a very cool wavelike motion is created, as all the circles move of their own accord.

In `circ3.swf`, the line `this._x =` in the `onEnterFrame` handler of each circle movie clip has been changed to `this._yscale = this._xscale = this.sx + (Math.sin(this.ang) * this.mynum);`. Also, `sx` and `sy` have been changed to equal `_xscale` and `_yscale`. This means that each circle won't pulse in position, but rather in size. This creates a very cool set of patterns as areas of light and dark move across the screen, as if you're looking at a printed newspaper close up. Watch this one for a while and you'll be entranced.

In `circ4.swf`, I've added the `this._x = this.sx + (Math.sin(this.ang) * this.mynum);` back in, which creates a cool horizontal lava-lamp effect as the circles resize and move left and right.

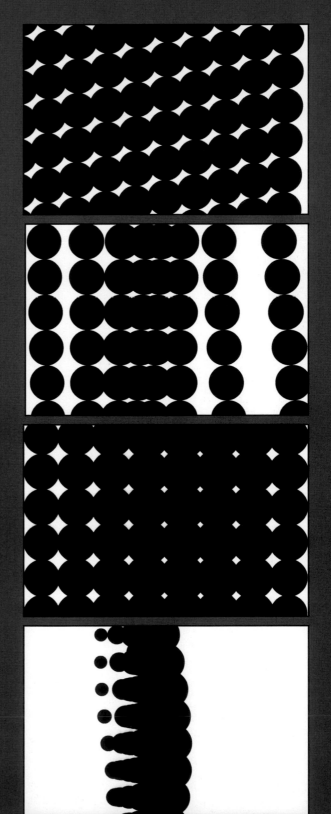

33

In `circ5.swf`, I've added a `Color` object to each circle, with the following lines of code:

```
var c:Color = new Color(nm);
var r:Number = nm._x;
var g:Number = 0;
var b:Number = nm._y;
c.setRGB((r << 16) + (g << 8) + b);
```

As you can see, I'm setting the `r` and `b` components of the circle based upon the circle's `_x` and `_y` position (note that the `g` component is set to 0). I've also rewritten the `onEnterFrame` event so only this code remains in it:

```
this._x = this._yscale = this._xscale = this.sx +
➥ (Math.sin(this.ang) * (this.mynum * 2));
this.ang += this.mynum / 450;
```

This creates a different horizontal lava-lamp effect, which uses a rainbow of blues and reds.

Next, in `circ6.swf`, I set each circle with the following:

```
this._y = this.sy + (Math.sin(this.ang) *
➥ this.mynum);
this._xscale = this.sy + (Math.cos(this.ang) *
➥ (this.mynum * 2));
```

This effect creates the appearance of a hanging wind chime or something similar that's twirling and bobbing in a strong breeze.

In `circ7.swf`, I've added the color code to the `onEnterFrame` handler, so the colors of the circles change based on the position of each circle as it moves, and I've altered the colors slightly to this:

```
this.r = this._x / 3;
this.g = 127 + (Math.cos(this.ang) * 127);
this.b = this._y / 2;
```

The motion of each circle is also now based on a very simple `_x = sin`, `_y = cos` equation:

```
this._y = this.sy + (Math.sin(this.ang) *
➥ (this.mynum));
this._x = this.sx + (Math.cos(this.ang) *
➥ (this.mynum));
```

This means that each circle moves in a circular motion. The overall effect is that of a large wave, which eventually descends into chaos.

In `circ8.swf`, I've added this line of code to the `onEnterFrame`:

```
this._alpha = 50 + (Math.cos(this.ang) * 50);
```

This means that some circles will vanish and reappear in a sweeping motion.

In `circ9.swf`, I changed the shape from a circle to a square with the circle hidden behind. This has a neat flowing-changing-morphing grid effect.

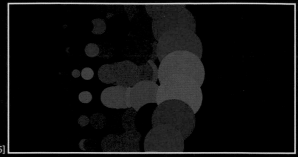

[5]

[6]

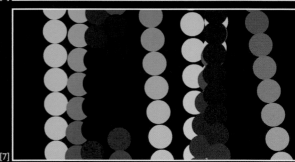

[7]

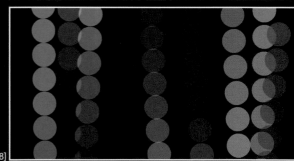

[8]

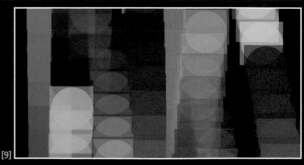

[9]

In **circ10.swf**, there's a stunning visual difference, but a very small code difference. Rather than use **sx** and **sy** as the pivot point for the circle, I'm using 275 and 200, like this:

```
this._x = 275 + (Math.cos(this.ang) * (this.mynum));
this._y = 200 + (Math.sin(this.ang) * (this.mynum));
```

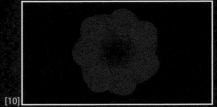

[10]

This creates a really cool spiraling effect. Watch it for a few minutes and you'll see some amazingly mesmerizing patterns emerge. Also try taking out the alpha-changing line to make it run quicker and playing with the colors.

In **circ11.swf**, I've changed the incrimination of **ang** to this:

```
this.ang += this.mynum / 100;
```

[11]

This means **ang** will increment quicker. Above that, though, I've also added this line of code:

```
this.mynum += Math.cos(this.ang);
```

This has the effect of changing the **mynum** value of each circle up and down in a wave.

circ12.swf has one modification:

```
this.mynum += Math.cos(this.ang2 += 0.1) * 7;
```

This crazy line of code makes the spiraling shape expand and shrink, as if it were breathing. I also changed the color code to make the circle blue.

[12]

In **circ13.swf**, I changed the **_x** code to look like this:

```
this._x = 275 + (Math.cos(this.ang) * (this.mynum * 2));
```

By multiplying **mynum** by 2, the spiral takes on a horizontally stretched look. It looks like a spiraling blue galaxy.

[13]

In **circ14.swf**, I've replaced 275 in the **_x** code with **this.mynum * 2**, changed the final **this.mynum** in the **_y** code to **this.mynum * 2**, and taken out the **this.mynum+=** line and added this line instead:

```
this._alpha = 100 - this.mynum;
```

This makes the circles fade out depending on their number. I also changed **ang** to equal **mynum/450** rather than 100 and altered the color code to make it a purple shade:

```
var r:Number = num;
var g:Number = 0;
var b:Number = num * 2;
```

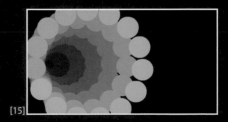

[14]

In **circ15.swf**, I added the following line:

```
this.mynum += Math.cos(this.ang2 += 0.2) * 7;
```

This is similar to the code used in **circ12.swf**, and it creates a pulsing, spiraling look. The colors are now green.

[15]

In **circ16.swf**, I put **sx** and **sy** back into the **_x** and **_y** code:

```
this._x = this.sx + Math.cos(this.ang) * this.mynum * 2;
this._y = this.sy + Math.sin(this.ang) * this.mynum * 2;
```

I also took out the **_alpha** line to make the shapes more visible. The color has been changed to a kind of peach. This looks like a slew of strange dancing snakes.

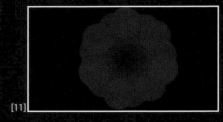

[16]

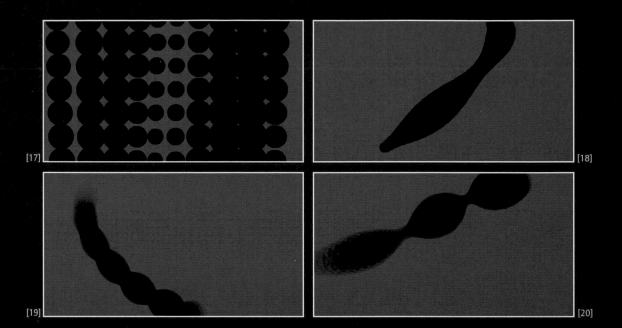

[17]

[18]

[19]

[20]

In `circ17.swf`, the grid effect is revived by changing `sx` and `sy` back to equaling `_xscale` and `_yscale`, and replacing the `onEnterFrame` code with this:

```
this._yscale = this._xscale = this.sx + (Math.sin(this.ang) * ((this.mynum + 40) / 2));
this._x += (Math.sin(this.ang));
this.ang += this.mynum / 450;
```

The circles now pulse in `_xscale`, `_yscale`, and along `_x`. The effect is mesmerizing and organic.

In `circ18.swf`, I've changed the position and scale code slightly to this:

```
this._yscale = this._xscale = this.sx + (Math.sin(this.ang) * ((this.mynum + 40) / 2));
this._x = 275 + (Math.cos(this.ang2 * 1.2) * 200);
this._y = 200 + (Math.sin(this.ang2 += 0.1) * 200);
```

And I've added the following line to the code that sets the `nm` properties:

```
nm.ang2 = num / 50;
```

With this, I've created a strange-looking worm that flies around the screen and has a lumpy, segmented look.

`circ19.swf` is identical to `circ18.swf`, except that I've added this code after setting `nm.ang2`:

```
nm._alpha = (num + 1) / 4;
```

This makes the worm fade out toward the ends.

In `circ20.swf`, I've changed the `_x` code to look like this:

```
this._x = 275 + (Math.tan(this.ang2 * 1.5) * 200);
```

Using the `Math.tan` function, the worm will appear to loop around from right to left, creating the appearance of lots of worms swimming past the screen.

The three main effects here—the spirals, the grid, and the worm—all have emerged out of the same experiment. You could try changing some more of the variables or try different functions. For example, `tan` and `sqrt` can produce interesting effects.

First I wanted to be a fireman, then an astronaut, then a car mechanic, then an architect. Then I wanted to make dioramas for the Museum of Natural History. Then I wanted to be a rock star, then a writer, a 3D animator, a carpenter, and then a writer again. Then for a while all I wanted to do was ride the F train drinking Tecate from a can. Then I wanted to be a web designer, then an artist, then a roof gardener. Now I'm back to fireman.

Like many things in the universe, I try to get the most done with the least amount of work. Creating simple instructions like "1. Draw a line for a while, and then change direction. 2. Repeat 1000 times" is easy to say, but might give you a hand cramp if you actually tried it. This may have been why the artist Sol LeWitt had the bright idea to just write up instructions and then have other people actually produce the artwork. I have a tough time telling people what to do, so I prefer to boss a computer around.

I almost always start out with a specific goal in mind and fail at it miserably. Luckily, the detritus I wind up with is often more interesting than my original goal. Today's discarded failure is tomorrow's friends of ED book chapter.

(Oh, and you might notice that I often take an idea, algorithm, or function from one set of experiments and try to apply it to other sets. Cross-pollination is a great productivity tool, it's not because I'm lazy.)

david hirmes
www.hirmes.com

Lines

The idea behind this piece is pretty simple: Draw a series of connected lines of random length within the bounds of a rectangular area. As the movie plays out, both the random patterns and the rectangle that bounds the patterns are revealed. I think that this piece is a useful place to start exploring the wide world of algorithmic drawing—that is, random and/or semi-intelligent pattern formation.

The following code goes on frame 1 of the main timeline (see `lines 01.fla`):

```
var leftBounds:Number = 20;
var topBounds:Number = 20;
var x:Number = leftBounds;
var y:Number = topBounds;
var rightBounds:Number = 380;
var bottomBounds:Number = 380;
var baseMax:Number = 20;
var randomMax:Number = 10;
var maxLines:Number = 2000;
var counter:Number = 0;
onEnterFrame = function () {
  counter++;
  var line:MovieClip = createEmptyMovieClip("line" + counter, counter);
  line.lineStyle(1, 0, 100);
  line._x = x;
  line._y = y;
  var maxDistance:Number = baseMax * Math.random() * randomMax;
  var minDistance:Number = 2;
  var direction:Number = Math.random() < 0.5 ? -1 : 1;
  var xEnd:Number = x + (direction * (minDistance + Math.random() * maxDistance));
  direction = Math.random() < 0.5 ? -1 : 1;
  var yEnd:Number = y + (direction * (minDistance + Math.random() * maxDistance));
  //
  if (xEnd < leftBounds) {
    xEnd = leftBounds;
  }
  if (xEnd > rightBounds) {
    xEnd = rightBounds;
  }
  if (yEnd < topBounds) {
    yEnd = topBounds;
  }
  if (yEnd > bottomBounds) {
    yEnd = bottomBounds;
  }
  //
  line.lineTo(xEnd - x, yEnd - y);
  x = xEnd;
  y = yEnd;
  if (counter > maxLines) {
    delete onEnterFrame;
  }
};
```

The key variables

Bounds = Sets the boundaries that the lines will be drawn within. My movie is a 400x400 square, so I set **Bounds** to be just within this square.

x and **y** = The current starting position of the line.

baseMax = The base length of a line.

randomMax = A random number that **baseMax** is multiplied by to obtain the final possible line length.

maxLines = The maximum number of lines drawn.

maxDistance = The final possible line length.

minDistance = The minimum line length.

direction = A direction flag, either 1 or −1, used as a multiplier to reverse the direction. This is worked out quite cleverly by taking a random number between 0 and 1, and using this to determine a Boolean state check with the little-employed **?:** conditional operator. If the Boolean check is true, then the first expression (following the **?**) is returned, and if it's false, then the second expression (following the **:**) will be returned.

xEnd and **yEnd** = The target end position of the line to be drawn.

All righty, let's take this thing apart.

The **onEnterFrame** function is where it all happens. First you add 1 to the counter, which keeps track of the number of lines you've created, and then you use **createMovieClip** to create a new empty **line** clip. The name of the clip is set to be **"line" + counter**, and its depth is set to **counter**. To make the code clearer, set the variable **line** to point to the clip you've just created. Next, set a **lineStyle** to be 1-pixel wide, black, and 100 percent opaque. Then, you set the **_x** and **_y** values of the line clip. You start to determine how long the line will actually be and in what direction it will go, first by setting the minimum and maximum line length variables, then by choosing whether the direction will be left or right and up or down, and finally by randomly choosing a distance within these parameters and adding that distance to the existing **x** and **y** positions.

The set of four **if** statements make sure that the line doesn't go past the bounds that you've set up. To finish drawing the line, you use **lineTo** to draw a line to the end positions (**xEnd** and **yEnd**) minus the starting positions (**x** and **y**). Finally, you set the **x** and **y** variables to equal the end positions so the next time you run this function, the line will start where the last one ended, thus creating the illusion of a single continuous line.

The last part of the function checks to see if you've gone over the limit of the total number of lines you set out to create. If you have gone over the limit, the **onEnterFrame** function is deleted. Why? This makes it so this code is no longer called on each **enterFrame** event, freeing up your CPU to do other tasks.

lines 02

Here I've introduced a new simple movie clip of a filled circle and exported it from the Library with the linkage name **circle**. By adding the following code to **onEnterFrame**

```
var circle:MovieClip = attachMovie("circle", "circle" +
➥ (counter + maxLines), counter + maxLines);
```

I've created the circle and ensured that it appears above the lines by adding **maxLines** to the depth count. I've also changed the two **line._** lines to this:

```
line._x = circle._x = x;
line._y = circle._y = y;
```

These set the circle to be at the same position as the start of each line.

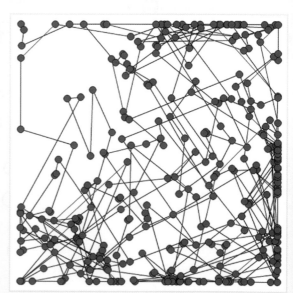

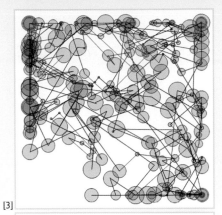

[3]

lines 03

This time I've changed the code to make the circles appear beneath the lines. Here's the new **line** and **circle** positioning code:

```
var line:MovieClip = createEmptyMovieClip("line" + (counter +
➥ maxLines), counter + maxLines);
line.lineStyle(1, 0, 100);
var circle:MovieClip = attachMovie("circle", "circle" + counter,
➥counter);
line._x = circle._x = x;
line._y = circle._y = y;
```

I also changed the size of the **circle** clip with the following new lines:

```
circle._xscale = maxDistance * .4;
circle._yscale = maxDistance * .4;
```

lines 04

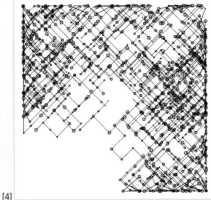

[4]

Here I've reduced the length of the lines by changing **baseMax** and **randomMax** to 6. I also removed the random element in determining the line distance by changing the following lines to

```
var xEnd:Number = x + (direction * (minDistance + maxDistance));
var yEnd:Number = y + (direction * (minDistance + maxDistance));
```

By doing this, I've reduced the possible angles to four. You'll notice that there's a slight exception to this rule at the corners because of the position being overridden by the bounds-checking code.

lines 05

I created this interesting effect by adding just one line of code to the end of the function, just before the **if** statement:

```
this["line" + (counter + maxLines - 10)].removeMovieClip();
```

Now the lines are continuously removed, leaving only ten on the screen at any one time, but the circles remain.

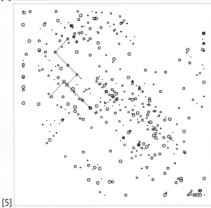

[5]

lines 06

I decided to go right back to the original code again and play with some different effects. Here I added a basic alpha component with the following new lines in the function:

```
alpha++
if ( alpha > 100 ) {
  alpha = 0;
}
line._alpha = alpha;
```

This creates a simple illusion of depth.

lines 07

I went back to the base file again and changed the **lineStyle** from a single pixel width to the following:

```
line.lineStyle(maxDistance / 4, 0x006699, 24);
```

I also added a piece of code to allow the user to pause and then restart the drawing by pressing any key:

```
Key.addListener(this);
onKeyDown = function(){
  onEnterFrame = (typeof(onEnterFrame) == "function") ? null :
  ➥ makeLine;
};
```

[6]

This required a slight change in defining the **onEnterFrame** originally. Rather than simply using `onEnterFrame = function(){…`, the following two lines are needed:

```
onEnterFrame = makeLine;
function makeLine() {
```

followed by the rest of the original function.

lines 08
Returning to the original file, I decided to play around with masking. I added a circular movie clip named **mask**, and in another layer over the top of that, I added a line around the edge of the mask so that the boundary is visible. I created an empty movie clip called **lines** and used the **mask** clip as its mask:

```
createEmptyMovieClip("lines", 0);
lines.setMask(mask);
```

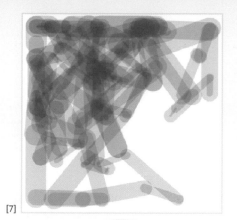

[7]

I then created all the individual line movie clips within the **lines** clip:

```
var line:MovieClip = lines.createEmptyMovieClip("line" + counter,
➥ counter);
```

I changed the **lineStyle** again to this:

```
line.lineStyle(maxDistance / 20, 0x006699, 20);
```

I also changed the **Bounds** and starting position of the line to keep it more within the confines of my mask:

```
var x:Number = 150;
var y:Number = 150;
var rightBounds:Number = 315;
var bottomBounds:Number = 315;
```

[8]

lines 09
Here I changed the shape of the mask again, altered **Bounds** to keep the bounds within my new shape, and reduced **maxLines** to 300 to stop the movie from slowing down too much. I also set the movie quality to low for the same reason. To further enhance the mask effect, I added in an **onEnterFrame** handler to the **lines** clip:

```
lines.onEnterFrame = function(){
  this._rotation++;
};
```

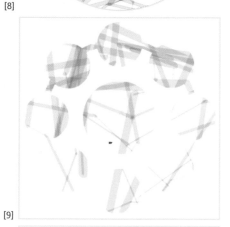

[9]

lines 10
Returning to the original file again, I decided to go down a completely different route. This time I wanted to try and draw curves instead of just straight lines. I achieved this by using sine and cosine to determine the line endpoint, but the addition of the random element in the **maxDistance** variable gives the whole thing a strangely childlike appearance. Here are the new endpoint lines:

```
var xEnd:Number = x + (Math.cos(counter * 0.1) * maxDistance);
var yEnd:Number = y + (Math.sin(counter * 0.1) * maxDistance);
```

I also changed the initial constants to keep the line size small and to set it to start drawing from the middle:

```
var leftBounds:Number = 20;
var topBounds:Number = 20;
var x:Number = 200;
var y:Number = 200;
var baseMax:Number = 4;
var randomMax:Number = 4;
```

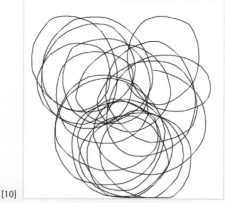

[10]

lines 11

I went back to the original file once more and decided to animate the line drawing. To do this, I started by scaling the individual **line** clips to 0 when they're created, and assigning them a **steps** property and an **onEnterFrame** handler.

```
line._xscale = 0;
line._yscale = 0;
line.steps = 20;
line.onEnterFrame = grow;
```

I then created the **grow** function with the following code:

```
function grow(){
  if(this.steps > 0){
    this._xscale = this._yscale = 100/this.steps;
  } else {
    delete this.onEnterFrame;
  }
  this.steps—;
}
```

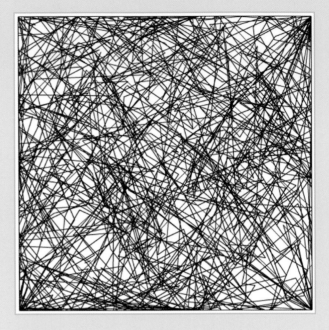

lines 12

In this iteration, the code is largely the same, but I added an **x** and **y** value to make the lines grow at an even rate:

```
line.x = 100 / 20;
line.y = 100 / 20;
```

And in the **grow** function:

```
function grow(){
  if(this.steps > 0){
    this._xscale += this.x;
    this._yscale += this.y;
  } else {
    delete this.onEnterFrame;
  }
  this.steps—;
}
```

lines 13

I wanted to try and get the lines to draw one at a time, so it would look like they were being hand-drawn in one continuous line. To achieve this, I had to add an **if** statement around the code in **onEnterFrame**:

```
if(line.done || counter < 1){
```

This sets a flag to tell the program whether or not the current line has finished drawing, and then I pick up and act on this flag in the **grow** code:

```
function grow(){
  if(this.steps > 0){
    this._xscale += this.x;
    this._yscale += this.y;
  } else {
    this.done = true;
    delete this.onEnterFrame;
  }
  this.steps--;
}
```

lines 14

Here, in addition to having the scale of each line growing, I made it rotate 360 degrees as it grew. This was done by adding an **r** property:

```
line.r = 360 / 10;
```

and using that in the **grow** function:

```
this._rotation += this.r;
```

lines 15

This file uses exactly the same code as the last file—I just changed the amount it rotates to 180 degrees.

lines 16

I changed the code again, switching the **r** property to an **a** property and using it to control the line's **_alpha**. This gives the line the appearance of sliding into place from nothingness.

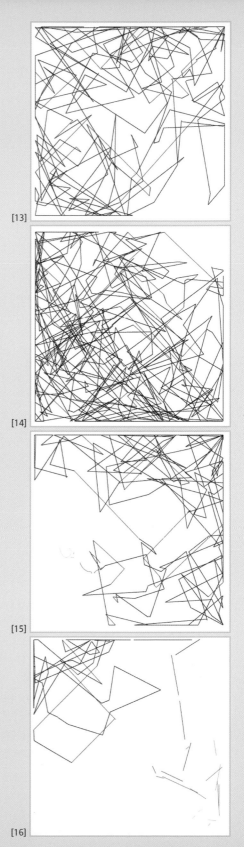

[13]

[14]

[15]

[16]

In and out of the grid

Why a grid? Why "in and out of the grid"? Well, for one thing, I often find it useful to start with a simple structure and play off it, eventually getting so far away that the original structure is barely recognizable. I think there's just a pleasure in seeing a form dissolve into chaos and back to a form.

Let's take a look at the first piece, `grid01.fla`. It has a single clip in the Library. The **atom** clip is a simple translucent rectangle exported with the linkage name **atom**. The alpha is kept down around 25 percent, so that more complex patterns can emerge when many clips are overlapping. The other important thing to notice about the clip is that its registration point is at one end of the rectangle.

All of the code lives on the main timeline, in frame 1:

```
_highquality = false;
var xNumber:Number = 7;
var yNumber:Number = 7;
var total:Number = xNumber * yNumber;
var gridSpacing:Number = 21;
var rotationAmount:Number = 3;
var counter:Number = 0;
createEmptyMovieClip("container", 0);
container._x = 150;
container._y = 150;
for (y=0; y < yNumber; y++) {
  for (x=0; x<xNumber; x++) {
    counter++;
    var atom:MovieClip = container.attachMovie("atom", "atom" + counter, counter);
    atom._x = x * gridSpacing;
    atom._y = y * gridSpacing;
    atom._rotation = Math.random() * 180;
    atom._xscale = 100;
    atom._yscale = 10 + Math.random() * 90;
  }
}
container.onEnterFrame = function() {
  var counter:Number = total + 1;
  while (counter—) {
    this["atom"+counter]._rotation += rotationAmount;
  }
}
```

The key variables

xNumber = The number of clips you'll create on the x-axis (horizontal)
yNumber = The number of clips for the y-axis (vertical)
total = The total number of objects
gridSpacing = How far apart the clips will be from each other
rotationAmount =The amount that the clips rotate every frame

You use a similar method to that described in the "Lines" experiment to create each object. Use a **counter** variable to keep track of the number of clips, and use the same variable to name them and set their depth. You also set a random **rotation** and **yscale** value for each object.

Everything is set up, so now for the most difficult part: putting it in motion. For every **onEnterFrame** event, you cycle through all of the clips and increase the **rotation** parameter by the amount specified in the **rotationAmount** variable.

OK, so I lied about the difficulty—that's all there is to it.

grid 02

After running the first example, you'll probably wonder what this has to do with grids—hopefully, this will make it a bit clearer. In this iteration, things get a little more *griddy*. I started with the addition of two new variables to hold the values of my stage size:

```
var canvasWidth:Number = Stage.width;
var canvasHeight:Number = Stage.height;
```

I then changed the **xNumber**, **yNumber**, and **gridSpacing** to 20. I removed the **rotationAmount** variable and changed the **for** loop to look like this:

```
for (y=0; y < yNumber; y++) {
  for (x=0; x<xNumber; x++) {
    counter++;
    var atom:MovieClip = container.attachMovie("atom",
    ➥ "atom" + counter, counter);
    atom._x = x * gridSpacing;
    atom._y = y * gridSpacing;
  }
}
```

[2]

Lastly, I removed the whole **onEnterFrame** code and changed the position of the **container** clip:

```
container._x = (canvasWidth - (gridSpacing * xNumber)) / 2;
container._y = (canvasHeight - (gridSpacing * yNumber)) / 2;
```

By subtracting the size of the grid by the size of the stage and dividing it by 2, I'm able to center the whole grid on the stage. I also changed the **atom** graphic to be a simple 20x20 filled circle.

grid 03

Now things start to get more interesting. In this iteration I added a few lines to the end of the **for** loop:

```
var scale:Number = Math.random() * 150;
atom._xscale = scale;
atom._yscale = scale;
```

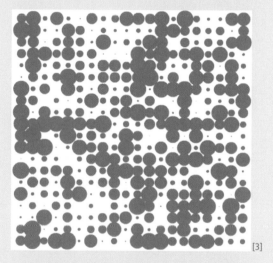

[3]

This creates a complex pattern by simply randomly setting the scale of each circle.

grid 04

In this iteration I started to add some animation with a new **onEnterFrame** function:

```
container.onEnterFrame = function(){
  var counter:Number = total + 1;
  while(counter--) {
    var atom:MovieClip = this["atom" + counter];
    if(atom._xscale < 200 ) {
      atom._xscale++;
      atom._yscale++;
    }
  }
};
```

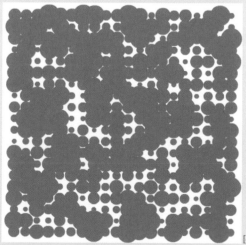

[4]

Here I created a simple animation by incrementing the scale of each circle, stopping when the scale equaled 200. In effect, I'm going from a random pattern back into a standard, uniform grid.

grid 05

I played around a bit with the animation again to create this interesting effect that starts off looking a bit like one of those old flashing-light computers in 1970s sci-fi shows and morphs through strange optical illusions (look out for the white dots that appear inside the circles after you stare at it too long) and into a wobble-skinned square before coming to rest as the grid of circles that we all know and love. How did I achieve this? Quite simply, really.

First I removed the initial random factor, taking out the **scale = Math.random** line and replacing the following two lines with these:

```
atom._xscale = 1;
atom._yscale = 1;
```

Next, I altered the **onEnterFrame** code to this:

```
container.onEnterFrame = function(){
  var counter:Number = total + 1;
  sizer++;
  while(counter—) {
    var atom:MovieClip = this["atom" +
    ➡ counter];
    if(atom._xscale < 200 ) {
      var scale:Number = sizer +
      ➡ Math.random() * 40;
      atom._xscale = scale;
      atom._yscale = scale;
    }
  }
};
```

Rather than steadily increasing the scale here, I've added a random element. The key is that the **sizer** variable is constantly increasing, so that ultimately the scale of every circle will be 200.

grid 06

The code is exactly the same as that in the previous file, but I changed the graphic from a filled circle to an empty one with just an outline to create new patterns.

grid 07

In this example, the grid structure itself becomes much harder to identify because of the rotation of the circles, but it's still there. I moved the circle away from its registration point to give the movie a semi-chaotic orbital feel. The first things I did were change **xNumber** and **yNumber** to 10 and bring back the old **rotationAmount = 3** line. I brought the scaling code back into the **for** loop as well:

```
for (y=0; y < yNumber; y++) {
  for (x=0; x<xNumber; x++) {
    counter++;
    var atom:MovieClip = container.attachMovie
    ➡ ("atom", "atom" + counter, counter);
    atom._x = x * gridSpacing;
    atom._y = y * gridSpacing;
    var scale:Number = Math.random() * 150;
    atom._xscale = scale;
    atom._yscale = scale;
    atom._rotation = Math.random() * 360;
    atom.rotation = rotationAmount;
    atom.rotation *= Math.random() < .5 ? -1
    ➡ : 1;
  }
}
```

Here I've given each circle a random starting rotation and a random rotation direction. I also changed the **onEnterFrame** code to this:

```
container.onEnterFrame = function(){
  var counter:Number = total + 1;
  while(counter—) {
    var atom:MovieClip = this["atom" +
    ➡ counter];
    if(atom._xscale < 200 ) {
      atom._rotation += atom.rotation;
    }
  }
};
```

grid 08

In this iteration I decided to try using letters instead of shapes. I changed **atom** into a dynamic text box and set the instance name to **letter**, with a capital "A" in it initially. I then added the following code to the **for** loop:

```
Key.addListener(atom);
atom.onKeyDown = atomKeyDown;
```

And this is the **atomKeyDown** function:

```
function atomKeyDown(){
  this.letter.text =
  ➡ String.fromCharCode(Key.getCode());
}
```

This code waits for a keypress and then changes the dynamic text field to show the character that was just typed. Try it out to see what I mean—different characters can produce some wildly different patterns. You may also want to remove the random element from the scale of each clip to allow for more uniform patterns.

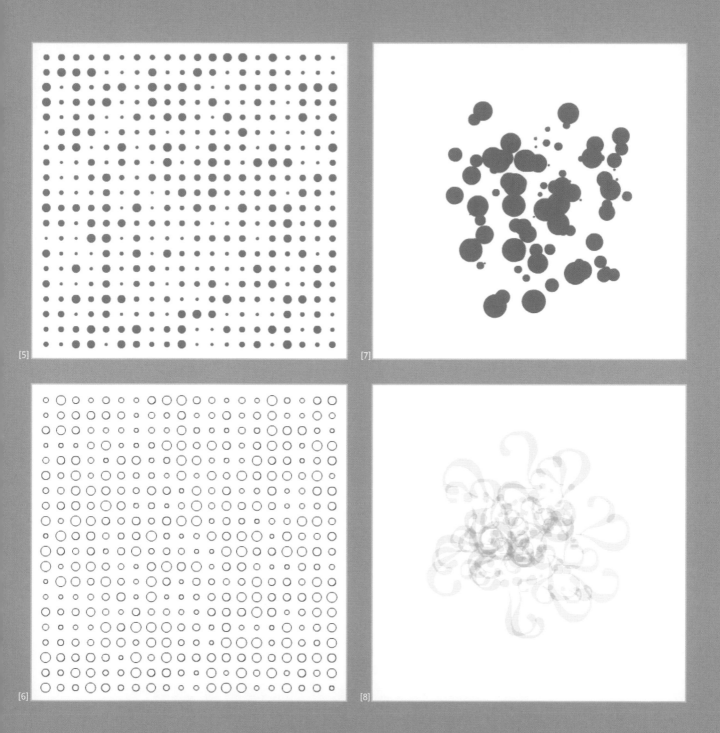

[5]

[7]

[6]

[8]

grid 09

This experiment gives completely different results, but it's based on exactly the same code. By changing a few lines, I've now got a movie that reacts to mouse movements and attaches an almost antimagnetic effect to the mouse pointer. To start with, I changed the graphic back to a simple off-center circle and removed the script for keypresses. Then I turned back to the **container** code. First, I took all of the code relating to rotation out of the **for** loop. Next, I added a line to the end of the **onEnterFrame** function and changed the following line to get this:

```
container.onEnterFrame = function(){
  var counter:Number = total + 1;
  while(counter—) {
    var atom:MovieClip = this["atom" + counter];
    if(atom._xscale < 200 ) {
      var rotation:Number = Math.atan2(this._ymouse - atom._y, this._xmouse - atom._x) /
      ➥ Math.PI * 180;
      atom._rotation = rotation;
    }
  }
};
```

This finds the rotation value that would be used to point the clip to the mouse position, but because the clips are off-center, they instead appear to recoil from the mouse. Try this with different shapes and positions, as it can create some very strange patterns.

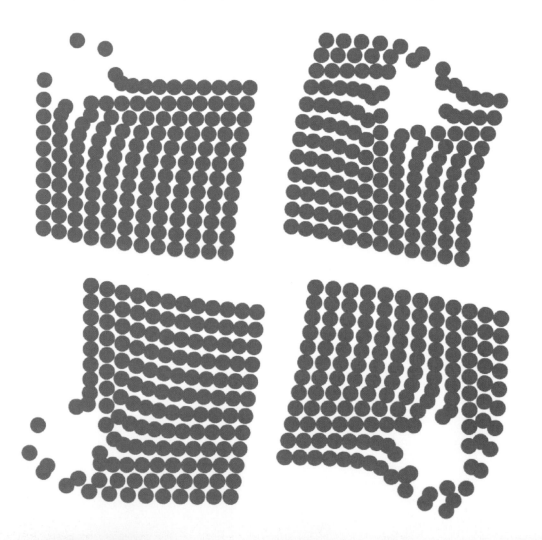

grid 10
Back to basics again for this one, removing all of those mouse-activated shenanigans. I've reduced the **xNumber** and **yNumber** to 5, and raised the **gridSpacing** to 40 to allow for the larger circles that I'll be making. The main change is in the new **move** function, but I also changed the main **container.onEnterFrame** handler to this:

```
container.onEnterFrame = function(){
  i++;
  mamaSin = Math.sin(i * Math.PI / 180);
};
```

In this code I'm just continuously running a sine wave and storing the value in a variable on the root called **mamaSin**. I assign each **atom** clip an **onEnterFrame** handler, setting it to the function **move**. The **move** function then picks up the **mamaSin** value:

```
function move(){
  var v:Number = this.permV * mamaSin;
  this.i += v;
  var angle:Number = Math.cos(this.i * Math.PI / 180);
  // turn value from -1 to 1 range into 0 to 1 range
  angle++;
  angle *= 0.5;
  this._xscale = angle * 100;
  this._yscale = angle * 100;
}
```

Here I start off by initializing a new variable, **permV**, which is my random factor that makes each circle different from the others. I then multiply the random number by the current **mamaSin** and use this to set the scale of **atom**. Try experimenting with different shapes with this one—it can produce some exceptionally interesting results.

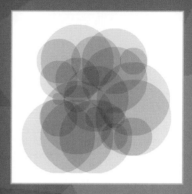
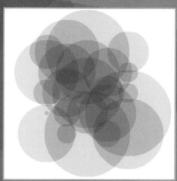
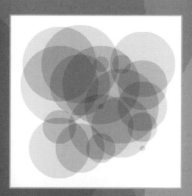

49

Springs

People seem to take some sort of inherent pleasure in watching objects oscillating. There's something about that chaos coming to rest in harmony and structure that fits with the human psyche. Humans like to find patterns in things, and it's even better when those things find patterns for themselves. In this set of pieces, you'll create and explore a simple implementation of spring motion.

The movie, **spring01.fla**, consists of two clips: **container** (dynamically created) and **atom**, which is the actual clip that you'll see in motion. This structure may seem a little convoluted at first, but you'll see later on how useful it can be.

Let's first look at the code on the main timeline that creates the grid of objects:

```
var canvasWidth:Number = Stage.width;
var canvasHeight:Number = Stage.height;
var xNumber:Number = 5;
var yNumber:Number = 5;
var total:Number = xNumber * yNumber;
var gridSpacing:Number = 40;
var counter:Number = 0;
createEmptyMovieClip("container", 0);
container._x = (canvasWidth - (gridSpacing * xNumber)) / 2;
container._y = (canvasHeight - (gridSpacing * yNumber)) / 2;
for (y=0; y < yNumber; y++) {
  for (x=0; x<xNumber; x++) {
    counter++;
    var atom:MovieClip = container.attachMovie("atom", "atom" + counter, counter);
    atom._x = x * gridSpacing;
    atom._y = y * gridSpacing;
    atom.xHome = atom._x;
    atom.yHome = atom._y;
    atom.zHome = 100;
    atom.x = 0;
    atom.y = 0;
    atom.z = 0;
    atom.onEnterFrame = spring;
    Key.addListener(atom);
    atom.onKeyDown = keyDown;
    atom.onMouseDown = mouseDown;
  }
}

var springiness:Number = .2;
var decay:Number = .8;
function spring(){
  this.y = ((this.yHome - this._y) * springiness) + (this.y * decay);
  this._y += this.y;
  this.x = ((this.xHome - this._x) * springiness) + (this.x * decay);
  this._x += this.x;
  this.z = ((this.zHome - this._xscale) * springiness) + (this.z * decay);
  this._xscale += this.z;
  this._yscale += this.z;
  this._alpha = this.z + 100;
}
function keyDown() {
  this._x += Math.random() * 550 - 225;
  this._y += Math.random() * 400 - 200;
  this.z += Math.random() * 200 - 100;
}
function mouseDown() {
  this._x += Math.random() * 550 - 225;
  this._y += Math.random() * 400 - 200;
  this.z += Math.random() * 200 - 100;
}
```

Much of the preceding code has already been described in the "In and out of the grid" section.

The key variables

xHome and **yHome** = The coordinates that this clip will always come back to. Since you've set up the grid already, the place this clip resides is where you want it to always come back to, so you'll set **xHome** and **yHome** to the current **x** and **y** position of this clip.
zHome = The "depth" of the clip, or how far forward and backward the clip will travel in space.
springiness = How tightly wound the spring action will be, and therefore how quickly the spring will move.
decay = How quickly the spring will get back to its original position (**xHome** and **yHome**)—that is, the number of oscillations it will make. Note that **decay** must be a number less than 1 or the spring motion will go on forever (not necessarily a bad thing, but I just thought you should know).

Now we get to the meat of the code. For every **onEnterFrame** event, you determine the new **x**, **y**, and **z** coordinates of the object. Since the computer screen is a 2D surface, you have to fake a **z** or **depth** coordinate by scaling the clip as well as altering its alpha setting—the further back you send the object, the more you'll reduce the scaling and alpha settings of the clip.

The formula you use to create the spring motion is the same for each dimension. Before I explain the formula, let's take a quick look at the **keyDown** and **mouseDown** functions, which are handlers for each atom's **onKeyDown** and **onMouseDown** events. They both have the same code in them. When you click your mouse or press a key, the object is sent to a random destination in every dimension. This is the equivalent of pulling the end of a spring and letting go. Now you're ready to see how the formula works. It looks like this:

```
change = ((home position - current position) * springiness) + (last change * decay)
```

Once the change is determined, you add it to the current position. By the nature of the formula, the current position will eventually wind up back at the home position.

If you feel like the formula is too complicated to understand, don't freak out. I've included an extra Flash file for download (**springgraph.fla**) to help you visualize how the formula works.

spring 02

Here I changed the shape of the **atom** clip to be a square instead of a circle. The **for** loop is the same with the addition of the line

```
atom.rotationDirection = Math.random() < .5 ? -1 : 1;
```

I made a few alterations to the rest of the code to allow for some rotation. I removed the **x** and **y** code from the **spring** function, leaving only **z**, **xscale** and **yscale**, and **alpha**. I then added this line:

```
_rotation = rotationDirection * z;
```

This means that when the user starts the oscillations going, instead of the shape moving in a pendulous manner, it now rotates back and forth on the spot. I also changed the **springiness** to **.3** and the **decay** to **.9** for aesthetic effect.

spring 03

For this experiment I changed the graphic again, this time to a pentagon. I also added a **Color** object to give each atom a random color when it first appears. I set **gridSpacing** to 45 to give a larger gap between the shapes. The main change, though, is the addition of the color object code to the end of the inner **for** loop. I also added a line to set the initial rotation to a random value:

```
atom.rotation = Math.random() * 360;
var c:Color = new Color(atom);
c.setRGB(Math.floor(Math.random() * 0x1000000));
```

The last line of this code is a little tricky. **Math.random** produces a number between 0 and 1. Since **setRGB** expects a six-digit hex value, then to get a random color from the entire range of colors available, I multiply the random value by a hex value equal to the max color value.

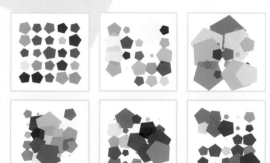

spring 04

Back to circles again. In this iteration, I decided to lose the grid altogether and instead placed all of the objects at the same x and y position. I removed the lines that set the **container** clip's position, so that it stays at 0,0, and I replaced the **for** loop with the following **while** loop:

```
while(counter < 25){
  counter++;
  var atom:MovieClip = container.attachMovie
  ➥ ("atom", "atom" + counter, counter);
  atom._x = canvasWidth / 2;
  atom._y = canvasHeight / 2;
  atom.xHome = atom._x;
  atom.yHome = atom._y;
  atom.zHome = 100;
  atom.x = 0;
  atom.y = 0;
  atom.z = 0;
  atom.onEnterFrame = spring;
  Key.addListener(atom);
  atom.onKeyDown = keyDown;
  atom.onMouseDown = mouseDown;
}
```

For the **atom** code, I returned to the original **spring01** code but made a couple of small alterations. I removed the **alpha** line, and I changed the key and mouse handlers so that everything equals **Math.random() * 200 - 100**.

spring 05

I spiced up the graphic a bit more again, and this time I rotated it by a set amount each time to give it a bit of variety. I changed the code by altering the **counter** line to read

```
var total:Number = 25;
```

I also added this line to the **while** loop to set the initial rotation of the clips:

```
atom._rotation = (360/total)*counter;
```

The only change that I made to the **spring** code was to put the **alpha** line back in.

spring 06

Following on the gridless theme, I decided to try adding in the "Blobs" code and structure, described more fully in the next section. The **while** loop now has the following code in it:

```
while(counter < 25){
  counter++;
  var edge:MovieClip = container.attachMovie
  ➥("edge", "edge" + counter, counter);
  var atom:MovieClip = container.attachMovie
  ➥("atom", "atom" + counter, counter+total);
  atom.edge = edge;
  atom._x = canvasWidth / 2;
  atom._y = canvasHeight / 2;
  atom.xHome = atom._x;
  atom.yHome = atom._y;
  atom.x = 0;
  atom.y = 0;
  atom.onEnterFrame = spring;
  Key.addListener(atom);
  atom.onKeyDown = keyDown;
  atom.onMouseDown = mouseDown;
}
```

I also changed **decay** to be 0.9 and removed the last three lines of **z** code from the **spring** function. In addition, I have the new **edge** symbol in this version.

spring 07

In this iteration I simply commented out the first two lines of the **spring** code that control the **y** positioning. Everything else is the same:

```
//   this.y = ((this.yHome - this._y) *
//   springiness) + (this.y * decay);
//   this._y += this.y;
```

This gives the whole thing a nicely different vertical column effect.

[4]

[5]

[6]

[7]

spring 08

In this experiment I returned to the same code from **spring02.fla**. I changed the graphic to add a dynamic text box over the square with the name **tf**. The only amendments that I made to the main code were to set the **gridSpacing** to **50** and to change the **springiness** to **.2**. Most of the rest of the changes all come in the **spring** code. I removed both of the rotation lines and changed the **alpha** to **z+50**. I added the following:

```
this.tf.text = Math.ceil(this._xscale);
```

This simply sets the dynamic text boxes to show the scale of their parent squares. The other big change I made was to the behavior of the squares themselves. Rather than returning back to their original size when the user takes an action, they now go to a random size set in **zHome**. I achieved this by altering the code in the **key-** and **mouseDown** functions to equal this:

```
this.zHome = Math.random() * 250 - 175;
```

spring 09

Here I decided to go in a completely different direction again, but I follow the same theme of reusing old code from my earlier experiments. This time I decided to use some of the code from the "Lines" experiment, but the structure is exactly the same. Here's the main code:

```
_highquality = false;
var counter:Number = 0;
createEmptyMovieClip("container", 0);
container._x = 200;
container._y = 200;
var x:Number = 0;
var y:Number = 0;
function paint() {
  counter++;
  var lineContainer:MovieClip =
➥ container.attachMovie("lineContainer",
➥ "lineContainer" + counter, counter);
  var maxDistance:Number = 15 * Math.random()
➥ * 10;
  var minDistance:Number = 2;
  var dir:Number = Math.random() < .5 ? 1 : -1;
  var xEnd:Number = x + (dir * (minDistance +
➥ Math.random() * maxDistance));
  dir = Math.random() < .5 ? 1 : -1;
  var yEnd:Number = y + (dir * (minDistance +
➥ Math.random() * maxDistance));
  lineContainer._xscale = xEnd - x;
  lineContainer._yscale = yEnd - y;

  var line:MovieClip = lineContainer.line;
  line.xHome = line._x;
  line.yHome = line._y;
  line._xscale = 0;
  line._yscale = 0;
  line.zHome = 100;
  line.x = 0;
  line.y = 0;
  line.z = 0;
  line.onEnterFrame = spring;
  Key.addListener(line);
  line.onKeyDown = keyDown;
```

```
  line.onMouseDown = mouseDown;
  x = xEnd;
  y = yEnd;
  if (counter > 50) {
    delete onEnterFrame;
  }
}
onEnterFrame = paint;
onMouseMove = function () {
  container._rotation = _root._xmouse;
};
var springiness:Number = .2;
var decay:Number = .8;
```

I won't go over this code again, as I already explained it in the "Lines" section. The **spring** code is exactly the same as that in **spring 01**. The final change to note is the alteration of the positioning code in the key and mouse functions, which are both set as follows:

```
this._x = Math.random() * 550;
this._y = Math.random() * 400;
this.z = Math.random() * 200 - 100;
```

spring 10

There's no code difference in this example, but by changing the graphic from a rectangle to a small, off-center circle, you get an effect that's almost like a pseudo-reflective pool.

spring 11

Here I went back to the original code once more and then added the ability to draw patterns with the mouse. Play around with it to see what I mean. The main change to the code is in the new **onEnterFrame** function, where I added all of the extra functionality:

```
onEnterFrame = function() {
  if(down) {
    container["atom" + record].xHome =
➥ container._xmouse;
    container["atom" + record].yHome =
➥ container._ymouse;
    record++;
    if ( record > total) {
      record = 1;
    }
  }
};
onMouseUp = function() {
  down = false;
};
onMouseDown = function() {
  down = true;
};
```

This code simply places the atom at the current cursor position when the mouse is clicked and cycles around replacing old clips when it reaches the **total** limit. The only other modification that I made was in removing the atom's **onMouseDown** handler because I was already using the mouse to draw with, and I didn't want it springing all over the place while I was trying to draw. All of the spring triggering is now done with the keyboard.

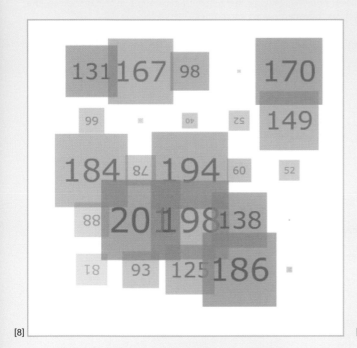

[8]

[9]

[10]

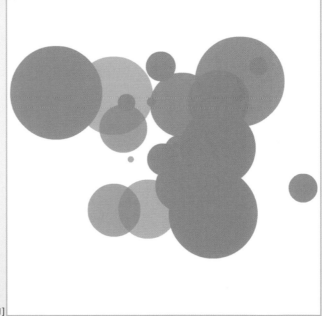

[11]

Blobs

In this experiment, I used a relatively simple technique to create the illusion of individual clips merging with each other. In this first piece, the circular objects move horizontally in fits and starts, creating "new" objects as they merge with each other.

The piece consists of three clips: the now familiar **container**; **ball**, which is simply a white circle; and **edge**, which is a slightly larger circle, the edge of which will become the "visible" portion of the piece.

As ever, all of the code lives on the main timeline:

```
var canvasWidth:Number = Stage.width;
var canvasHeight:Number = Stage.height;
var total:Number = 20;
createEmptyMovieClip("container", 0);
container._x = 0;
container._y = canvasHeight / 2;
for (var i = 1; i <= total; i++) {
  var ball:MovieClip = container.attachMovie("ball", "ball" + i, i + total);
  ball._x = Math.random() * canvasWidth;
  ball._y = Math.random() * canvasHeight / 2 - canvasHeight / 4;
  ball.vx = Math.random() * 60;
  var edge:MovieClip = container.attachMovie("edge", "edge" + i, i);
  edge._x = ball._x;
  edge._y = ball._y;
}
var leftBounds:Number = -edge._width;
var rightBounds:Number = edge._width + canvasWidth;
onEnterFrame = function () {
  for (var i = 1; i <= total; i++) {
    ball = container["ball" + i];
    ball._x += ball.vx;
    if (ball._x > rightBounds) {
      ball._x = leftBounds;
    }
    container["edge" + i]._x = ball._x;
    ball.vx *= 0.8;
    if (ball.vx < 0.00001) {
      ball.vx = Math.random() * 60;
    }
  }
};
```

After setting up the width and height of the canvas and determining how many clips you'll use, you create the clips inside a **for** loop. Notice that the **ball** clip is created at a higher depth than the **edge** clip, and then the **edge** clip is placed in the same **x** and **y** position as the **ball** clip. This is the main component to creating the "blobs" effect—because all the **ball** clips are at a higher depth than all the **edge** clips, the **ball** clips will always cover any of the edges that they come in contact with.

Notice the unique **vx** variable (short for "velocity of **x**") that's created for each ball. This random value determines how quickly the clip will travel. Looking at the **onEnterFrame** function, you see that for every ball object, you increase its **x** value by its own **vx** variable and then check to see if it's offscreen. (When the left and right boundaries were set up , the width of the object was taken into account so that the object is fully offscreen before it's moved to the other edge of the screen.) Once the bounds are checked, the **edge** clip is moved to the same position as the **ball**. Finally, the velocity variable is multiplied by a number smaller than 1 (.8 in this case) so as to create a cheap ease-out motion effect. The **if** statement checks to see when **vx** gets very low, and when it does, it sets a new velocity for the clip.

blobs 02

In this iteration I introduced some new shapes for the blobs. I did this by creating new frames in the **ball** and **edge** clips with the new shapes in them, and then randomly choosing a frame in the code to display the different shapes. This is a really easy way to experiment with new shapes and forms without having to go in and change any of the code. I changed both instances of the **vx** variable to equal **Math.random() * 100** rather than **Math.random() * 60**, so that the shapes shift quicker across the screen. The only additions that I made to the code are in the **for** loop, where I added the shape selection script and also some code to give the shapes a random rotation.

```
ball._rotation = Math.random() * 360;
ball.gotoAndStop(Math.floor(Math.random() * ball._totalFrames)+1);
edge._rotation = ball._rotation;
edge.gotoAndStop(ball._currentframe);
```

You can play around and add as many different shapes as you like now, and the code will automatically accommodate this and randomly select them to display. The only thing to remember is to set the edge for each new shape (as well as the shape itself).

blobs 03

Here I decided to go a different way and allow the shapes a complete run of the screen rather than just letting them go from left to right. I also went back to only using circles, so I removed the rotation and frame selection code that I added last time. I'll go through the changes that I made to the code. First of all, in the **for** loop, I changed **total** to 25 because I was using more of the screen so I wanted more shapes to fill it with. Next, in the **for** loop, I changed **ball._y** to equal **Math.random() * canvasHeight** because I wanted them to occupy the whole screen rather than just a fixed portion of it. Following this, I altered the **ball.vx** line and added a new **ball.vy** line to get this:

```
ball.vx = Math.random() * 3 + (Math.random() < .5 ? -1 : 1);
ball.vy = Math.random() * 3 + (Math.random() < .5 ? -1 : 1);
```

Here I simply give each ball a random **x** and **y** speed. The next changes that I made came right after the **for** loop, where I added top and bottom boundaries to the existing left and right ones:

```
var topBounds:Number = -edge._height;
var bottomBounds:Number = edge._height + canvasHeight;
```

Now on to the **onEnterFrame** code. Here I simply added **y** code the same as the existing **x** code and new bounds-checking code for the balls' new movement. I also removed the lines that changed the ball speed, giving it a smooth, rather than an easing, motion. The new **onEnterFrame** code looks like this:

```
onEnterFrame = function () {
  for (var i = 1; i <= total; i++) {
    ball = container["ball" + i];
    ball._x += ball.vx;
    ball._y += ball.vy;
    if (ball._x > rightBounds) {
      ball._x = leftBounds;
    }
    if (ball._x < leftBounds) {
      ball._x = rightBounds;
    }
    if (ball._y > bottomBounds) {
      ball._y = topBounds;
    }
    if (ball._y < topBounds) {
      ball._y = bottomBounds;
    }
    container["edge" + i]._x = ball._x;
    container["edge" + i]._y = ball._y;
  }
};
```

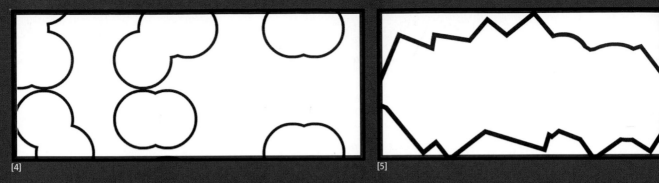

[4]   [5]

blobs 04

In this experiment I made all the balls start from the center of the canvas and explode out of it at a greater speed than the last time. Here are the simple changes that I made—they're all in the **for** loop:

```
ball._x = canvasWidth / 2;
ball._y = canvasHeight / 2;
ball.vx = Math.random() * 6 + (Math.random() < .5 ? -1 : 1);
ball.vy = Math.random() * 6 + (Math.random() < .5 ? -1 : 1);
```

blobs 05

I radically changed the code in this iteration to distribute the clips evenly in a line across the canvas and have them rotate depending on mouse position. This gives the effect of two morphing lines where the shapes themselves begin to become indistinct. This effect can be intensified by covering one half of the canvas with a blank shape on a higher level, leaving only one line morphing away merrily. Here's the complete code for this experiment:

```
var canvasWidth:Number = Stage.width;
var canvasHeight:Number = Stage.height;
var total:Number = 25;
createEmptyMovieClip("container", 0);
container._x = 0;
container._y = canvasHeight / 2;
for (var i = 1; i <= total; i++) {
  var ball:MovieClip = container.attachMovie("ball", "ball" + i, i + total);
  ball._x = i * 20;
  ball._y = Math.random() * 100 - 50;
  ball.direction = Math.random() < .5 ? -1 : 1;
  ball._rotation = Math.random() * 360;
  ball.gotoAndStop(Math.floor(Math.random() * ball._totalFrames)+1);
  var edge:MovieClip = container.attachMovie("edge", "edge" + i, i);
  edge._x = ball._x;
  edge._y = ball._y;
  edge._rotation = ball._rotation;
  edge.gotoAndStop(ball._currentframe);
}
var leftBounds:Number = -edge._width;
var rightBounds:Number = edge._width + canvasWidth;
var topBounds:Number = -edge._height;
var bottomBounds:Number = edge._height + canvasHeight;
onEnterFrame = function () {
  for (var i = 1; i <= total; i++) {
    ball = container["ball" + i];
    ball._rotation += (((_root._xmouse - 200) * .05) * ball.direction);
    edge = container["edge" + i];
    edge._rotation = ball._rotation;
  }
};
```

Most of this code should be self-explanatory, and you'll notice that I brought back the frame selection code for choosing new shapes from **blobs 02**. One new addition worth pointing out is the new **ball.direction** code, which just sets the direction of the shape rotation depending on which side of the center of the canvas that the mouse cursor is in.

blobs 06

This is similar to the last experiment, but rather than having the clips in a line, I distributed them randomly around the screen, and they now spin uniformly rather than being based on mouse position. I also added a new feature where the user can just click the mouse to reposition the shapes instead of having to rerun the entire movie. The only changes that I made to the **for** loop were to remove the **ball.direction** code, and to change the **x** and **y** lines to set a random starting position:

```
ball._x = Math.random() * canvasWidth;
ball._y = Math.random() * canvasHeight;
```

Again, there was very little change to the **onEnterFrame** clip event, where I simply set the shape rotation to an increment rather than having it be mouse based:

```
ball._rotation++;
```

The major change comes with the addition of a new function for when the user presses the mouse button. The code in here is very similar to the **for** loop code, so it shouldn't need explaining:

```
onMouseDown = function() {
   for (var i = 1; i <= total; i++) {
      ball = container["ball" + i];
      ball._x = Math.random() * canvasWidth;
      ball._y = Math.random() * canvasHeight;
      ball._rotation = random(360);
      edge = container["edge" + i];
      edge._x = ball._x;
      edge._y = ball._y;
      edge._rotation = ball._rotation;
   }
};
```

blobs 07

In this iteration I decided to leave rotation and motion, and play around with scaling instead. The shapes now constantly grow in fits and starts. To stop them from just growing out of proportion and out-growing the canvas, I added a toggle so that when the user clicks the mouse the shapes begin to shrink instead, then grow again when the user next clicks the mouse, and so on, and so on. There's one thing to note here: When the shapes shrink into negative numbers, they will start to grow again, because a negative shrink is a grow. I decided to leave this in, as I liked the effect of the pulsing to nothing, and then back out again. The other user control that I added was that instead of having random shapes, every clip is now the same shape and the user swaps between shapes by pressing a key on the keyboard.

With all this new functionality, there are some major changes to the code. I'll start with the relatively little-changed setup code, and then I'll move on to the major new stuff. I changed **total** to 20 to cut down on overcrowding, and below it I added this new line:

```
var grow:Number = 1;
```

This new variable is the toggle for whether the shapes are growing or shrinking. I begin with it set to 1, making all the shapes grow. I changed the **y** position of the shapes to be within a smaller band rather than the whole canvas. They still spread over quite a large area, but the whole thing feels somehow much more manageable and less chaotic like this:

```
ball._y = Math.random() * canvasHeight / 2 -
➡ canvasHeight / 4;
```

Under this, I brought back the old **vx** variable, but this time rather than controlling motion speed, it will control the speed at which the shapes scale.

```
ball.vx = Math.random() * 70;
```

I removed the rotation code from the loop and altered the shape selection code so that it started from the first frame instead of a random one:

```
ball.gotoAndStop(1);
edge.gotoAndStop(1);
```

Now on to the big changes. The **onEnterFrame** function had a major overhaul and now looks like this:

```
onEnterFrame = function () {
    for (var i = 1; i <= total; i++) {
        ball = container["ball" + i];
        ball._xscale += ball.vx * .1;
        ball._yscale += ball.vx * .1;
```

```
        if ( ball._xscale > 400 ) {
            ball._xscale = 400;
            ball._yscale = 400;
        }
        if ( ball._xscale < 1 && ball.vx < 0 ) {
            ball._xscale = 1;
            ball._yscale = 1;
            ball.vx = 0;
        }
        edge = container["edge" + i];
        edge._xscale = ball._xscale;
        edge._yscale = ball._yscale;
        ball.vx *= 0.8;
        if ( Math.abs(ball.vx) < 0.001 ) {
            ball.vx = Math.random() * 70 * grow;
        }
    }
};
```

Here I've replaced the motion/rotation code with scale code and added some similar code to my original easing motion code to make the shapes grow in random spurts.

The **onMouseDown** function has been reduced to just this one line:

```
grow *= -1;
```

This simply toggles the variable **grow** between 1 and –1 whenever the mouse is clicked, which is then used in the previous easing code to make the shape grow or shrink.

Finally, there's another new function to change shapes whenever a key is pressed:

```
Key.addListener(this);
onKeyDown = function(){
    for (var i = 1; i <= total; i++) {
        ball = container["ball" + i];
        if ( ball._currentframe == ball._total
        ➡ frames ) {
            ball.gotoAndStop(1);
        } else {
            ball.nextFrame();
        }
        edge = container["edge" + i];
        edge.gotoAndStop(ball._currentframe);
    }
}
```

This uses fairly straightforward code, just moving along the frames when a key is pressed until it reaches the final frame, and then it loops back to the beginning and starts again.

   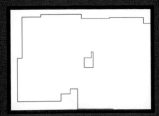

blobs 08

This iteration is very similar to the last one, but I've added some simple tweening animation to a couple of the shapes and started them off set to a random rotation again with these lines at the end of the initial **for** loop:

```
ball._rotation = Math.random() * 360;
edge._rotation = ball._rotation;
```

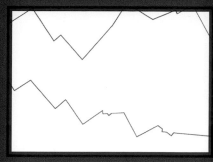

blobs 09

This piece should look familiar if you've been through some of my other experiments, as the code is based on (and is very similar to) the first piece in the "Grids" section. It's basically the same, but with the added code to control the **edge** clip as well as the main shape. Here it is in full:

```
var canvasWidth:Number = Stage.width;
var canvasHeight:Number = Stage.height;
createEmptyMovieClip("container", 0);
container._x = 150;
container._y = 150;
var xNumber:Number = 5;
var yNumber:Number = 5;
var total:Number = xNumber * yNumber;
var gridSpacing:Number = 21;
var rotationAmount:Number = 3;
var counter:Number = 0;
for(var y = 0; y < yNumber; y++) {
  for (var x = 0; x < xNumber; x++) {
    counter++;
    var atom:MovieClip = container.attachMovie("atom", "atom" +
    ➥ counter, counter + total);
    atom._x = x * gridSpacing;
    atom._y = y * gridSpacing;
    atom._rotation = Math.random() * 360;
    atom._xscale = 100;
    atom._yscale = 70 + Math.random() * 30;
    atom.velocity = Math.random() * 4 + 1;
    var edge:MovieClip = container.attachMovie("edge", "edge" +
    ➥ counter, counter);
    edge._x = atom._x;
    edge._y = atom._y;
    edge._xscale = atom._xscale;
    edge._yscale = atom._yscale;
    edge._rotation = atom._rotation;
  }
}
onEnterFrame = function () {
  for (var i = 1; i <= total; i++) {
    atom = container["atom" + i];
    atom._rotation += atom.velocity;
    edge = container["edge" + i];
    edge._rotation = atom._rotation;
  }
};
```

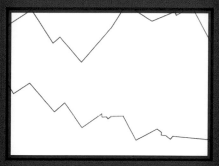

blobs 10

This final experiment is a mix of most of the experiments we've been looking at. It uses a grid structure with a **spring** function on each clip, and the "Blobs" technique to display it all. This is the code:

```
var canvasWidth:Number = Stage.width;
var canvasHeight:Number = Stage.height;
createEmptyMovieClip("container", 0);
var xNumber:Number = 5;
var yNumber:Number = 5;
var total:Number = xNumber * yNumber;
var gridSpacing:Number = 60;
container._x = (canvasWidth - gridSpacing * xNumber) / 2;
container._y = (canvasHeight - gridSpacing * yNumber) / 2;
var counter:Number = 0;
for(var y = 0; y < yNumber; y++) {
  for (var x = 0; x < xNumber; x++) {
    counter++;
    var atom:MovieClip = container.attachMovie("atom", "atom" + counter, counter + total);
    atom._x = x * gridSpacing;
    atom._y = y * gridSpacing;
    atom.xHome = atom._x;
    atom.yHome = atom._y;
    atom.x = 0;
    atom.y = 0;
    atom.onEnterFrame = spring;
    Key.addListener(atom);
    atom.onKeyDown = keyDown;
    atom.onMouseDown = mouseDown;
    var edge:MovieClip = container.attachMovie("edge", "edge" + counter, counter);
    edge._x = atom._x;
    edge._y = atom._y;
    atom.edge = edge;
  }
}
onEnterFrame = function () {
  for (var i = 1; i <= total; i++) {
    atom = container["atom" + i];
    atom._rotation += atom.velocity;
    edge = container["edge" + i];
    edge._rotation = atom._rotation;
  }
};
var springiness:Number = .2;
var decay:Number = .9;


function spring(){
  this.y = ((this.yHome - this._y) * springiness) + (this.y * decay);
  this._y += this.y;
  this.x = ((this.xHome - this._x) * springiness) + (this.x * decay);
  this._x += this.x;
  this.edge._x = this._x;
  this.edge._y = this._y;
}
function keyDown() {
  this._x += Math.random() * 200 - 100;
  this._y += Math.random() * 200 - 100;
}
function mouseDown() {
  this._x += Math.random() * 200 - 100;
  this._y += Math.random() * 200 - 100;
}
```

The **spring** function is pretty much the same as the code in the "Springs" section, and you can find an explanation of it there.

Andrés Sebastián Yáñez Durán (Lifaros)

I'm an ActionScript developer from Chile. There aren't many of us ActionScript coders here, and there aren't many ActionScript jobs either, so I started searching for clients on the Internet, developing some applications, and participating in Flash forums.

I have a lot of hobbies. Sometimes I work as an electronics engineer on satellite communications and networking, and sometimes I work as a painter and sculptor—I love both math and art. Nowadays I'm working on projects as a freelance developer for people in the United States and the United Kingdom. For instance, I'm collaborating as an ActionScript developer for the Economic Commission for Latin America and Caribbean (ECLAC) with the United Nations, integrating Flash with XML, server-side script, and so on. More specifically, I developed a content management system (CMS) to show conferences and their associated documents and assets (images, PDFs, SWFs, etc.), using Flash as the GUI. I'm also developing some e-learning content using Macromedia RoboDemo. In collaboration with Fundación Chile (www.fundacionchile.cl), I've helped to develop an advanced virtual homework machine that's being used both by Chilean teachers and pupils.

Last year I was lucky enough to work with Jonathan Kaye from Amethyst Research (www.amethyst-research.com), a friend of mine and author of *Flash MX for Interactive Simulation*—a real Flash guru! We developed "Fire Scene Command" for the Orange County firefighters, using FlashComm. Finally, I'm also working as an ActionScript instructor (a very nice job!), trying to teach the magic of code, as well as the usual bag of tips and tricks, to my students.

I enjoy playing with math, and I'm always trying to simulate physical phenomena using ActionScript. The main source of inspiration for me is nature—physical parameters such as sound, light, temperature, and pressure, all different natural energies that can be measured and plotted, all heavily centered in math.

Other sources of inspiration are online Flash math forums and math and electronics books. I have a lot of books, some of them concerning satellite communications, signals and systems, digital circuits, microprocessors, and so on, and some covering algebra, vectors, geometry, and Fourier transformations. I only have to pick up and dip into any of them to be inspired.

As you already know, ActionScript is a powerful tool that you can use to develop cool interactive websites and applications by successfully combining science and design. You don't have to be an engineer to deal with engineering concepts—it just takes a little patience and passion. One person's "boring" math problem is another person's amazing creation.

Since the first edition of *Flash Math Creativity* was published, I've been extremely busy with my job. Nevertheless, I still found time to coauthor a number of other books for friends of ED: *Flash Video Creativity*, *Flash MX Components Most Wanted*, and *Fresh Flash: New Design Ideas with Flash MX*. I'm very thankful to friends of ED, because these books have allowed me to show my artistic side and have a really cool creative experience.

lifaros
www.actionscript.cl

Alien message

This application combines randomization and symbol design to generate a strange alien message. To accomplish this task, you're going to develop a tiled pattern on the screen, where each alien letter will fit together perfectly with every adjacent letter.

There are three basic types of letters, lateral, corner, and inner, in movie clips with those names in the Library. You can see all of these shapes in the FLA (`alienmessage.fla`). Notice that I created them all as tessellating shapes, with different shapes as different frames within each of these three main movie clips.

After creating all of the shapes, the code is used to position them on the stage and to change them when the user moves the mouse over them. All of the following code just goes on the first frame of the root.

```
var columns:Number = 14;
var rows:Number = 8;
var xpos:Number = 50;
var ypos:Number = 60;
var width:Number = 39;
var cornersymbols:Number = 8;
var lateralsymbols:Number = 15;
var innersymbols:Number = 9;
var q:Number = 1;
for (var row = 0; row <= rows-1; row++) {
  for (var column = 0; column <= columns - 1; column++) {
    var alien:MovieClip = attachMovie("inner", "alien" + q, q);
    alien.gotoAndStop(Math.random() * innersymbols + 1);
    alien.onRollOver = function() {
      this.gotoAndStop(Math.random() * innersymbols + 1);
    };
    if (row == 0) {
      var alien = attachMovie("lateral", "alien" + q, q);
      alien.gotoAndStop(Math.random() * lateralsymbols);
      alien.onRollOver = function() {
        this.gotoAndStop(Math.random() * lateralsymbols+1);
      };
    }
    if (row == rows-1) {
      var alien = attachMovie("lateral", "alien" + q, q);
      alien._rotation = 180;
      alien.gotoAndStop(Math.random() * lateralsymbols + 1);
      alien.onRollOver = function() {
        this.gotoAndStop(Math.random() * lateralsymbols + 1);
      };
    }
    if (column == 0) {
      var alien = attachMovie("lateral", "alien" + q, q);
      alien._rotation = -90;
      alien.gotoAndStop(Math.random() * lateralsymbols + 1);
      alien.onRollOver = function() {
        this.gotoAndStop(Math.random() * lateralsymbols + 1);
      };
    }
    if (column == columns-1) {
      var alien = attachMovie("lateral", "alien" + q, q);
      alien._rotation = 90;
      alien.gotoAndStop(Math.random() * lateralsymbols + 1);
      alien.onRollOver = function() {
        this.gotoAndStop(Math.random() * lateralsymbols + 1);
      };
    }
    if (row == 0 && column == 0) {
      var alien = attachMovie("corner", "alien" + q, q);
      alien._rotation = 0;
      alien.gotoAndStop(Math.random() * cornersymbols + 1);
      alien.onRollOver = function() {
        this.gotoAndStop(Math.random() * cornersymbols + 1);
      };
```

```
    }
    if ((row == rows-1) && column == 0) {
      var alien = attachMovie("corner", "alien" + q, q);
      alien._rotation = -90;
      alien.gotoAndStop(Math.random() * cornersymbols + 1);
      alien.onRollOver = function() {
        this.gotoAndStop(Math.random() * cornersymbols + 1);
      };
    }
    if (row == 0 && column == columns - 1) {
      var alien = attachMovie("corner", "alien" + q, q);
      alien._rotation = 90;
      alien.gotoAndStop(Math.random() * cornersymbols + 1);
      alien.onRollOver = function() {
        this.gotoAndStop(Math.random() * cornersymbols + 1);
      };
    }
    if (row == rows-1 && column == columns-1) {
      var alien = attachMovie("corner", "alien" + q, q);
      alien._rotation = 180;
      alien.gotoAndStop(Math.random() * cornersymbols + 1);
      alien.onRollOver = function() {
        this.gotoAndStop(Math.random() * cornersymbols + 1);
      };
    }
    alien._xscale = 40;
    alien._yscale = 40;
    alien._x = width * column + xpos;
    alien._y = width * row + ypos;
    q++;
  }
}
```

After each movie clip is attached, it is assigned an **onRollOver** event handler with the following code:

```
alien.onRollOver = function() {
  this.gotoAndStop(Math.random() * innersymbols + 1);
};
```

Note that you'll have to enter the name of the correct movie clip, so if it's a **lateral** movie clip, then it's **lateralsymbols + 1**; if it's the **corner** clip, then it's **cornersymbols + 1**; and if it's the **inner** clip, then it's **innersymbols + 1**. This code just means that when the user runs his mouse over the shape, then another random shape will be chosen to replace it.

The key variables

columns = The number of columns of letters.
rows = The number of rows of letters.
xpos and **ypos** = The starting position in the top-left corner of the screen.
width = The width of each shape. My shapes are 40 pixels (actually, they're 100 pixels scaled down to 40 percent), and they fit together perfectly if I set this variable to 39.
cornersymbols = The number of different frames of corner symbols to choose from.
lateralsymbols = The number of different frames of lateral symbols to choose from.
innersymbols = The number of different frames of inner symbols to choose from.
q = A loop counter.

After setting the initial variables, the main code is found within the two nested **for** loops—one for rows and one for columns. These loops will then assign a random shape of the correct type in the correct place.

alien01

First of all, I experimented with different layouts. Here I made a thin vertical message.

```
var columns:Number = 2;
var rows:Number = 8;
```

alien02

Then I went the other way and made a thin horizontal message.

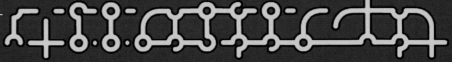

```
var columns:Number = 14;
var rows:Number = 2;
```

alien03

I settled on a good-sized shape that I've kept for all of the rest of the experiments and set about playing with the numbers of different letters. To start with, I set them all to having only one of each, which gave a nice static pattern.

```
var columns:Number = 14;
var rows:Number = 4;
var cornersymbols:Number = 1;
var lateralsymbols:Number = 1;
var innersymbols:Number = 1;
```

alien04

I decided to continue just slowly increasing the number of symbols to see what the different effects were. This one's with two of each symbol. You can make some nice long lines that remind me of those steady-hand coordination games where you have to move a metal ring along a piece of twisting wire with an alarm that goes off if the ring and wire make contact.

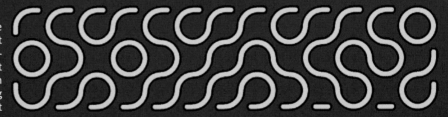

```
var cornersymbols:Number = 2;
var lateralsymbols:Number = 2;
var innersymbols:Number = 2;
```

alien05

This one's with three of each symbol.

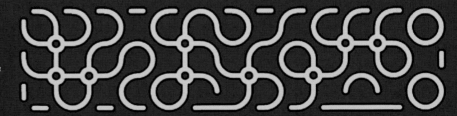

```
var cornersymbols:Number = 3;
var lateralsymbols:Number = 3;
var innersymbols:Number = 3;
```

alien06

And this one's with four of each symbol.

```
var cornersymbols:Number = 4;
var lateralsymbols:Number = 4;
var innersymbols:Number = 4;
```

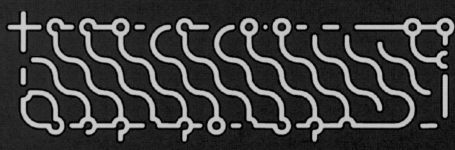

alien07

For the next three experiments, I tried setting two of the letter types to their maximum numbers, but keeping the third at 1, and therefore unchangeable. First, I tried it with the **innersymbols** set in stone.

```
var cornersymbols:Number = 8;
var lateralsymbols:Number = 15;
var innersymbols:Number = 1;
```

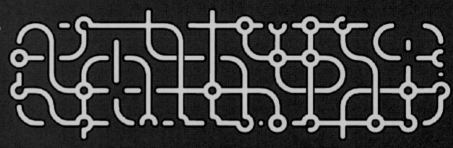

alien08

Next, I tried the effect with the corners set so they always remained curved.

```
var cornersymbols:Number = 1;
var lateralsymbols:Number = 15;
var innersymbols:Number = 9;
```

alien09

Finally, I tried leaving the outer lines as curves and letting the user change the inner characters and the corners.

```
var cornersymbols:Number = 8;
var lateralsymbols:Number = 1;
var innersymbols:Number = 9;
```

Other things you could do with this are play around with some of the other parameters and, of course, modify the shape and color of the letters and background to create some cool designs.

Flag effect

In this set of experiments, you're going to use masking to cut a source image into slices so that you can then control those slices independently. If you use a lot of slices, then you can obtain a soft wave movement like a flag flapping in the wind.

The basic setup is this: In the Library, there's a movie clip with the linkage name `image`. Inside this clip are two layers: a mask layer containing a simple square graphic and a masked layer that contains a movie clip with the instance name `picture`. The `picture` clip simply contains the image that you're going to be working with. Back in the `image` clip, the mask has its center at the center point of the clip, and the `picture` clip has its top-left corner at the center point of the clip. Now that the main parts are in place, the only other thing to add is the code.

By the way, I've also added a couple of sliders to my movie to dynamically control the frequency and amplitude. These are simply tied to the `fx` and `fy`, and `ampx` and `ampy` variables on the main stage. They aren't essential to the running of the movie, but you can find the code for them in the FLA if you'd like to add them yourself.

Here's the main code that sits on the first frame of the root (see `flageffect.fla`):

```
var ycenter:Number = 200;
var xcenter:Number = 275;
var scale:Number = 1;
var mode:Number = 0;
var slices:Number = 30;
var w:Number = 10;

var fx:Number = 1;
var fy:Number = 1;
var ampy:Number = 20;
var ampx:Number = 20;

if (mode == 0) {
    var columns:Number = slices;
    var rows:Number = 1;
} else {
    var columns:Number = 1;
    var rows:Number = slices;
}
for (var n=0; n < rows * columns; n++) {
    var myname:MovieClip = attachMovie("image", "image_"+n, n);
    var row:Number = Math.floor(n / columns);
    var column:Number = n % columns;
    var width:Number = scale * myname.picture._width;
    var height:Number = scale * myname.picture._height;

    var cellxsize:Number = width / columns;
    var cellysize:Number = height / rows;

    myname.picture._width = 100 * columns;
    myname.picture._height = 100 * rows;
    myname.picture._x = -100 * column - 50;
    myname.picture._y = -100 * row - 50;

    myname.row = row;
    myname.column = column;

    myname._x = xcenter + (-width / 2) + cellxsize * column + width / (2 * columns);
    myname._y = ycenter + (-height / 2) + cellysize * row + height / (2 * rows);
    myname.y0 = myname._y;
    myname.x0 = myname._x;

    myname._xscale = cellxsize + 0.3;
    myname._yscale = cellysize + 0.3;

    // degrees to radians constant
    myname.dtr = Math.PI / 180;
```

```
  // counter
  myname.t = 0;

  myname.onEnterFrame = function() {
    if (mode == 0) {
      this.f = fx * this.column * (360 / columns);
      this._y = this.y0 + ampy * Math.sin(this.dtr * (this.f + w * this.t++));
    } else {
      this.f = fy * this.row * (360 / rows);
      this._x = this.x0 + ampx * Math.sin(this.dtr * (this.f + w * this.t++));
    }
  };
}
```

There's additional code on the main timeline of the FLA to make the sliders work with the rest of the code.

The key variables

ycenter = The vertical center of the stage.
xcenter = The horizontal center of the stage.
scale = The scale of the image onscreen. Setting this variable to 2 will double the size of the image, and so on.
mode = The mode flag. A setting of 0 gives horizontal waves, and 1 gives vertical waves.
slices = The number of sections that the image is sliced into.
w = The speed of oscillation.
width = The source image width.
height = The source image height.
columns = The number of columns.
rows = The number of rows.
cellxsize = The slice width.
cellysize = The slice height.
fx and **fy** = The wave frequency.
ampx and **ampy** = The wave amplitude.
dtr = A degrees-to-radians conversion constant.
t = A counter to increment the sine curve parameter.

The code works by attaching many copies of the image and the mask, and then positioning and sizing them, respectively. The code then dynamically positions the clip along the sine curve to give a wave effect.

flag01

First of all, I experimented with the number of slices. Initially, I dropped it to 10 to see what difference a smaller number would make, and I got this chunky effect:

```
var slices:Number = 10;
```

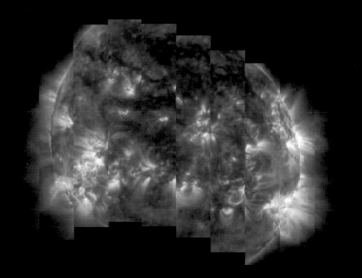

Amplitude

Frequency

69

flag02

Next, I set the number of slices to double its initial value to see how it would run and show how smooth the wave was.

```
var slices:Number = 60;
```

flag03

Seeing how smoothly the last experiment ran, I decided to double the number of slices again and check the effect. This gave a beautifully smooth curve, but the animation was too slow, and Flash began to drop frames.

```
var slices:Number = 120;
```

flag04

This time I decided to go the other way, changing to a horizontal wave and increasing the speed.

```
var mode:Number = 1;
ar slices:Number = 30;
var w:Number = 30;
```

flag05

In the next series, I played around with the frequency variable to see what difference that made.

```
var fy:Number = 2;
```

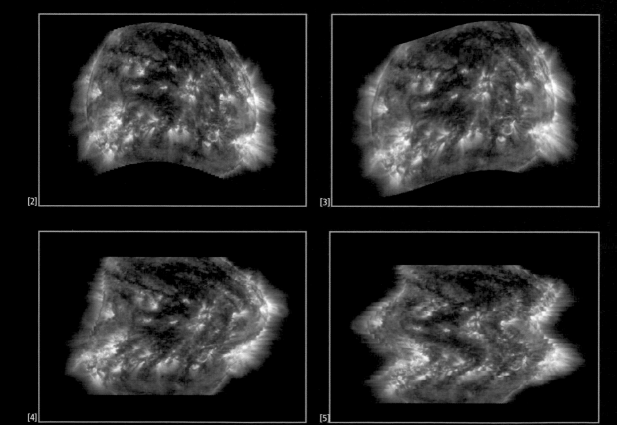

[2] [3] [4] [5]

flag06

I continued with the frequency experiment by gradually incrementing to see the effect of an increased number of waves.

```
var fy:Number = 3;
```

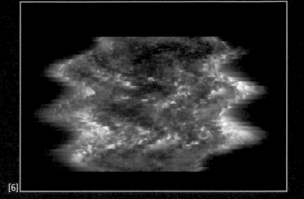

[6]

flag07

Here I set the frequency to 4 and begin to really lose the shape of the image..

```
var fy:Number = 4;
```

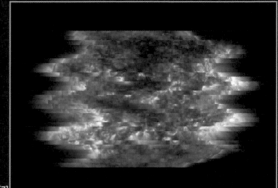

[7]

flag08

After playing with the frequency, I decided to finish by seeing the effect of changing the amplitude. Setting it to a low value gives the impression of a flag flapping in a gentle breeze.

```
var mode:Number = 0;
var slices:Number = 60;
var fy:Number = 1;
var ampx:Number = 5;
```

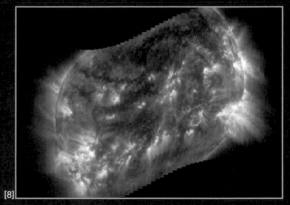

[8]

flag09

Setting the amplitude to a much higher value gives the impression of a stronger gale or someone shaking out a carpet.

```
var ampx:Number = 40;
```

There are many more things you can change in this experiment. For example, try altering the shape of the mask or the image—you can get some really interesting effects from skewed parallelograms. Another thing to try is changing the formula on the **onEnterFrame** handler. By using **tan** instead of **sin**, you can achieve some interesting results, almost like pages flipping.

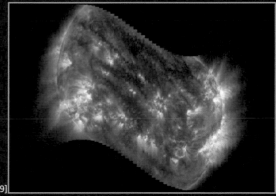

[9]

Rainbow flower

This series of experiments combines two effects, random shape generation and color cycling, to produce some interesting psychedelic flowers. These radial shapes were developed using a Fourier series and then adding sine waves to achieve a smooth, random shape. You then apply a series of color transforms to it to enable the cyclical hue change. You create the strange shapes by using two triangles, resizing them, and placing them next to each other to give a smooth outline.

The movie consists of three sections. The first creates the shape, the second sets up the color information, and the third is an **onEnterFrame** function to cycle the colors. Take a look at **rainbowflower.fla**. If you wish to, you can remove the **onEnterFrame** if you want to create only the shapes and not include the color cycling.

This experiment has a single keyframe with all of the code on it. As mentioned earlier, the graphics consist of two simple 100×100-pixel right-angle triangles inside their own movie clips, one with the linkage name **rainbowtriangle** (the inner triangle) and the other called **redtriangle** (the outer triangle). That's it for the graphics—now for the code. The code in the first section looks like this:

```
// section 1
var points:Number = 120;
var N:Number = 10;
var frequency:Number = 2;
var dtr:Number = Math.PI/180;
var y:Array = new Array();
var x:Array = new Array();
var amplitude:Array = new Array();
var phase:Array = new Array();
var xcenter:Number = 275;
var ycenter:Number = 175;
var df:Number = 360 / (points - 1);
var sum:Array = new Array();


amplitude[0] = 120;
for (var i=1; i <= N; i++) {
  amplitude[i] = 50 / i;
  phase[i] = -180 + Math.random() * 360;
}
for (i=0; i < points; i++) {
  var angle:Number = (i * df - 180);
  var pointangle:Number = frequency * angle;
  sum[i] = amplitude[0];
  for (var j=1; j <= N; j++) {
    sum[i] += amplitude[j] * Math.sin(dtr * (j * pointangle + phase[j] ));
  }
  sum[i] = -sum[i];
  x[i] = sum[i] * Math.cos(dtr * angle);
  y[i] = -sum[i] * Math.sin(dtr * angle);
}
for (i=0; i < points - 1; i++) {
  var mybtriangle:MovieClip = attachMovie("redtriangle", "mybtriangle" + i, i);
  var myatriangle:MovieClip = attachMovie("rainbowtriangle", "myatriangle" + i, i+1000);
  var sk:Number = Math.abs(sum[i]) > Math.abs(sum[i+1]) ? 1 : -1;
  var sj:Number = Math.abs(sum[i]) > Math.abs(sum[i+1]) ? 1 : 0;
  myatriangle._x = xcenter;
  myatriangle._y = ycenter;
  myatriangle._xscale = -sum[i+sj] * Math.cos(dtr * df);
  myatriangle._yscale = -sk * sum[i + sj] * Math.sin(dtr * (df + 0.2));
  myatriangle._rotation = -df * (i + !sj);
  mybtriangle._xscale = sum[i + !sj] - sum[i + sj] * Math.cos(dtr * df);
  mybtriangle._yscale = -sk * sum[i + sj] * Math.sin(dtr * df);
  mybtriangle._rotation = -df * (i + !sj);
  mybtriangle._x = x[i + !sj] + xcenter;
  mybtriangle._y = y[i + !sj] + ycenter;
}
```

That's all of the clip duplication, data calculation, and drawing done. The second section has this code:

```
// section 2
var redstep:Number = 10;
var greenstep:Number = 15;
var bluestep:Number = 5;

var redoffsetstep:Number = 5;
var greenoffsetstep:Number = 10;
var blueoffsetstep:Number = 15;

var red:Number = Math.random() * 100;
var green:Number = Math.random() * 100;
var blue:Number = Math.random() * 100;

var redoffset:Number = Math.random() * 255;
var greenoffset:Number = Math.random() * 255;
var blueoffset:Number = Math.random() * 255;
```

This just sets up the initial color values. The third section contains this:

```
// section 3
onEnterFrame = function(){
  for (var i=0; i < points - 1; i++) {
    var myColor:Color = new Color(this["myatriangle"+i]);
    var myColorTransform:Object = new Object();
    myColor.setTransform({ra:red, rb:redoffset, ga:green, gb:greenoffset, ba:blue, bb:blueoffset});
    myColor = new Color(this["mybtriangle"+i]);
    myColorTransform = new Object();
    myColor.setTransform({ra:red, rb:redoffset, ga:green, gb:greenoffset, ba:blue, bb:blueoffset});
  }
  red += redstep;
  redstep *= (red > 100 || red < 0) ? -1 : 1;
  redoffset += redoffsetstep;
  redoffsetstep *= (redoffset > 255 || redoffset < 0) ? -1 : 1;
  blue += bluestep;
  bluestep *= (blue > 100 || blue < 0) ? -1 : 1;
  blueoffset += blueoffsetstep;
  blueoffsetstep *= (blueoffset > 255 || blueoffset < 0) ? -1 : 1;
  green += greenstep;
  greenstep *= (green > 100 || green < 0) ? -1 : 1;
  greenoffset += greenoffsetstep;
  greenoffsetstep *= (greenoffset > 255 || greenoffset < 0) ? -1 : 1;
};
```

which updates the colors using the values that were initialized in the previous section. This just loops continuously to continue updating the colors.

The key variables

points = The number of segments
N = The number of waves along the outside of the shape
frequency = The number of "petals" that are repeated to make the shape
dtr = The degrees-to-radians conversion constant
y = The vertical coordinate array
x = The horizontal coordinate array
amplitude = The size array
phase = The phase array, used in calculating the shape
xcenter = The horizontal center
ycenter = The vertical center
df = The angular amount of drawn shape, so 360 is the full shape, 180 is half the shape, and so on
sum = An array for holding various calculations for the drawing of the shape

rainbowflower01

I decided to try a few different sets of settings at different frequencies. First off, I kept everything the same and just altered the frequency. With a setting of 1, you just get a random shape.

```
var frequency:Number = 1;
```

rainbowflower02

By increasing the frequency to 3, you can see how each of the petals of the flower repeats itself.

```
var frequency:Number = 3;
```

rainbowflower03

Setting the frequency to 5, you begin to get something resembling a flower, rather than just a blob.

```
var frequency:Number = 5;
```

rainbowflower04

I played around with another set of variables, decreasing the number of waves along the edge of the shape and setting **amplitude[0]** to a negative figure, meaning that the flower goes back on itself.

```
var N:Number = 5;
var frequency:Number = 1;

amplitude[0] = -30;
amplitude[i] = 120 / i;
```

rainbowflower05

I then tried these settings again with different frequencies to create some interestingly spiky overlaps.

```
var frequency:Number = 3;
```

rainbowflower06

Here I used the same settings, but this time with a greater number of petals.

```
var frequency:Number = 5;
```

rainbowflower07

In this final series, I changed **amplitude** and **N** again, and then ran through another set of **frequency** changes. With **N** and **frequency** set to 1, you get a shape like a kidney bean.

```
var N:Number = 1;
var frequency:Number = 1;

amplitude[0] = 80;
  amplitude[i] = 60 / i;
```

rainbowflower08

By setting **frequency** to 3, you get a simple trifoliate shape, like a clover.

```
var frequency:Number = 3;
```

rainbowflower09

Finally, with a frequency of 5, you get a nice, basic, five-petaled rainbow flower.

```
var frequency:Number = 5;
```

This is just a taste of the shapes you can create by fiddling with these algorithms. Try experimenting with some of the other variables or, more simply, just changing the shape and color of the two triangles to give some radically different results.

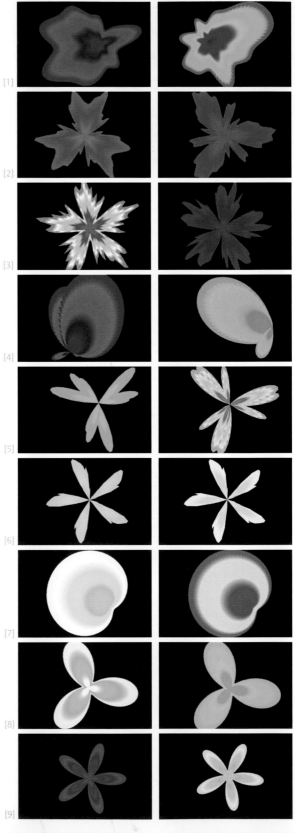

[1] [2] [3] [4] [5] [6] [7] [8] [9]

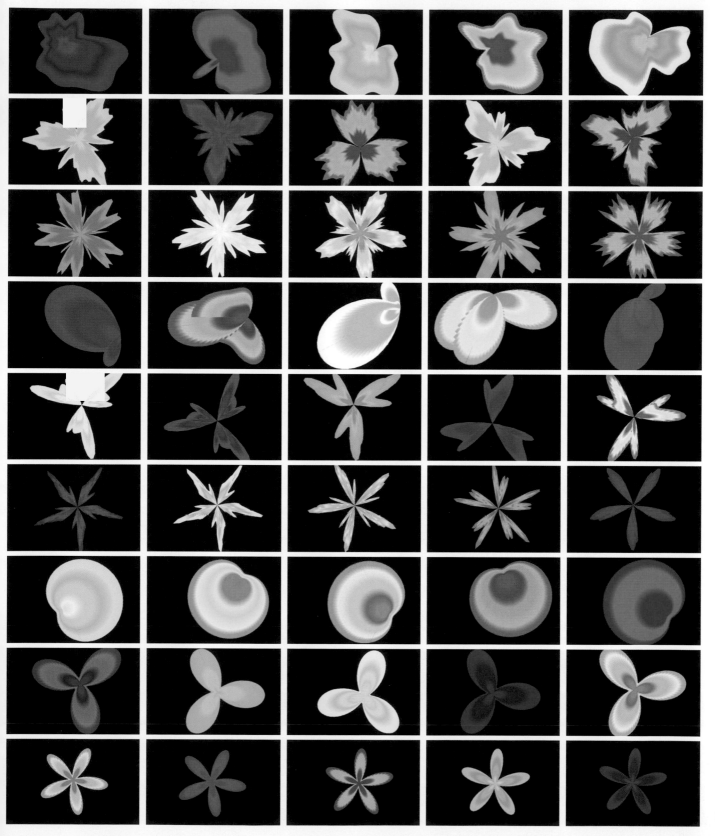

Stem generator

This is a nice stem generator, which was developed to simulate natural backgrounds. Rather than using a branching algorithm to create a tree, this generates nice, leafy climbers or bamboo shoots. Take a look at **stemgenerator.fla**. There are two movie clips to make up the effect, and they have the linkage names **myline** and **myleaf**. **myline** is what you'll use to create the stems, and it consists of the oft-used 100×100-pixel diagonal line with its registration point in the top-left corner, but the line has been replaced with a thin leaf shape to give the stem more structure. **myleaf** is a similarly shaped leaf, but this time it's horizontal with its registration point on the far-left side. There's also a dynamically created movie clip called **mybranch**. This is just a container used to attach the other two movie clips.

The following script is placed on the first frame of the root:

```
var branches:Number = 10;
var xcenter:Number = 275;
var xoffset:Number = 225;

for (var i=0; i<branches; i++) {
  var mybranch:MovieClip = createEmptyMovieClip("mybranch" + i, i);
  mybranch._x = xcenter + Math.random() * 2 * xoffset - xoffset;
  mybranch._y = 400;
  var points:Number = 30 + Math.floor(Math.random() * 40);
  var leaves:Number = 13;
  var y:Array = new Array();
  var x:Array = new Array();
  var dy:Number = 5;
  var offset:Number = 0.007;
  y[0] = 0;
  x[0] = 0;

  for (var j=1; j <= points; j++) {
    y[j] = -dy * j;
    x[j] = x[j - 1] + j * offset * (Math.random() * 21 - 10);
  }
  for (j=0; j < points; j++) {
    var myline:MovieClip = mybranch.attachMovie("myline", "myline" + j, j);
    myline._x = x[j];
    myline._y = y[j];
    myline._xscale = x[j + 1] - x[j];
    myline._yscale = y[j + 1] - y[j];
  }
  for (j=0; j < leaves; j++) {
    var myleaf:MovieClip = mybranch.attachMovie("myleaf", "myleaf" + j, j + 1000);
    var myColor:Color = new Color(myleaf);
    var myColorTransform:Object = new Object();
    myColorTransform.ga = 70 + Math.random() * 30;
    myColorTransform.ba = 0;
    myColorTransform.ra = 0;
    myColor.setTransform(myColorTransform);
    myleaf._x = x[points - 2 * j];
    myleaf._y = y[points - 2 * j];
    myleaf._xscale = 30 + 1 * j;
    myleaf._yscale = 10 + 1 * j;
    myleaf._rotation = Math.random() * 180 - 180;
  }
}
```

The first few lines set up some initial variables and use them to create and position the branches on the screen, governing the number of separate plants. The remaining code is used to create each individual plant. It contains several loops, for the number of points that make up the stem and for the number of leaves on each plant. These loops contain number, position, scale, and color information for leaves and stem.

The key variables

branches = The number of separate plants
xcenter = The horizontal center of the screen
xoffset = The maximum distance from the center that branches will be placed
points = The number of segments making up each stem
leaves = The number of leaves on each branch
dy = The distance between each point, and thus the length of each segment
offset = A multiplier used to determine the width (and therefore also the zigzag) of each segment

[1]

stem01

First of all, I experimented with a couple of iterations of just increasing the number of branches to see the difference in appearance and loading time. Increasing the number to 30 gives a nicely populated screen with a manageable loading time.

```
var branches:Number = 30;
```

stem02

Here I increased the number of branches again to 60. This gives a much denser jungle, but it takes a little too long to load.

```
var branches:Number = 60;
```

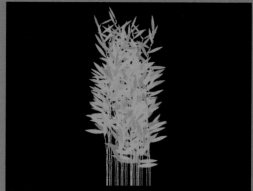

[2]

stem03

I settled on 30 branches as the best medium and moved on to experimenting with different variables. First I looked at the **xoffset**, and I tried a much smaller value to achieve a tight shrub in the center of the screen.

```
var branches:Number = 30;

var xoffset:Number = 50;
```

stem04

I preferred a more spread-out plant, so I tried an **xoffset** of 100, which gave some space between stems, but also still allowed a good sense of depth and cluster from the overlapping leaves. This is the value that I decided to stay with for the rest of the iterations.

```
var xoffset:Number = 100;
```

[3]

[4]

stem05

Next, I turned my eye to the number of leaves on the plant. First, I tried a much smaller number, giving a simpler plant.

```
var leaves:Number = 5;
```

stem06

I quite liked this simplicity, so I tried adding just a couple more leaves to see the effect.

```
var leaves:Number = 7;
```

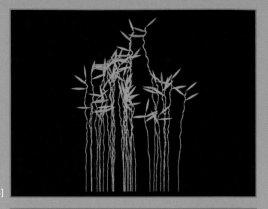

[5]

stem07

Next, I decided to increase the number of leaves to 30 to see what difference that would make. By including leaves all the way down the plant, it completely changed its appearance. Now I have a much heavier shrub.

```
var leaves:Number = 30;
```

stem08

I set the number of leaves back to its original 13, and experimented instead with the **points** value and the scale of the leaves. This gives a nice creeper with well-distributed, wide leaves.

```
var leaves:Number = 13;

var points:Number = Math.floor(Math.random() * 70);

myleaf._yscale = 40 + 1 * j;
```

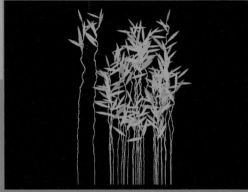

[6]

stem09

I liked the effect of the stubbier leaves, so I played with the scale a bit more to accentuate it.

```
myleaf._xscale = 15 + 1 * j;
myleaf._yscale = 45 + 1 * j;
```

There are numerous things you can do here to create different plants. First of all, the actual graphical elements can be changed to suit your botanical tastes. You can also experiment with different amounts for the variables I've covered here or others that I haven't, such as the **Color** object or the **dy** and **offset** values.

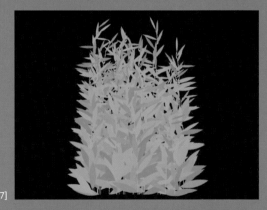

[7]

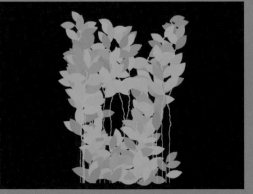

[8]

[9]

I was born last century in southern Germany and currently live in Berlin. I work as a freelance media/motion designer, and at the moment, this means working a lot with Flash on conceptual designs. I also lecture on occasion, and write a bit sometimes too.

I started playing with "programming" as a child – first of all on a computer that didn't even have a monitor, but was connected to an outdated Teletype printer instead. My skills were very limited and the results weren't too impressive, and I quickly got bored with it.

A computer or so later on, I learned how to move blocks and sprites around on the screen, and things became more interesting. Also around this time people started showing me other fascinating stuff, like fractals and their like, which were very popular then. Playing around with these and other things helped my understanding and influenced the way I approached problems.

Today this drawing and moving things by math and programming is part of my job – but I still don't consider myself a programmer or a math whiz. I just need this stuff to bring my designs and visions to life. Not that I do everything in code; the beauty of Flash is that it also lets me animate things manually whenever the feeling takes me, but sometimes when I'm working on scripted animations or games, things seem to take on a strange life of their own, and this is what absolutely fascinates me.

gabriel mulzer
www.voxangelica.net

Fibonacci flower

If you're a designer, you've probably heard of the golden section, golden ratio, or Fibonacci series before—ratios that are common in nature and therefore regarded as divine proportions for things since time began. They're also very useful to provide an appearance of natural harmony when applied on programmed images.

A **Fibonacci series** runs like this:

1, 2, 3, 5, 8, 13, 21, 34, 55, 89, 144, 233, 377, 610, 987, 1597, 2584, 4181 . . .

Each number in the series is the sum of the previous two. The further you go, the more the ratio between two successive numbers will converge to the **golden ratio,** which is approximately 1:1.6180339.

What's special about this ratio is that if you divide anything by it, the ratio between the bigger part and the original is the same as the ratio between the smaller section and the bigger section—the **golden section.** The diagram here illustrates this principle: if you cut the white plane *a* at the dotted line (the golden section), *c* is in a golden ratio to *b*, *b* is in a golden ratio to *a*, and *a* is in a golden ratio to *a+b*.

This gets really interesting if you divide the 360 degrees of a circle this way and use this **golden angle** to repeatedly offset something. Due to the nature of the golden section, you can use either the bigger or the smaller resulting angle.

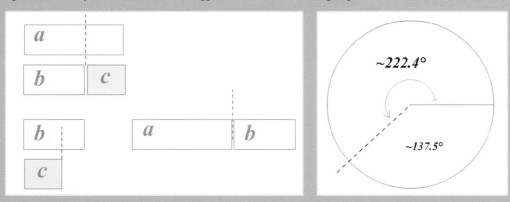

Here you're going to create a movie that consists of two movie clips. The first is the **viewer** movie clip that will act as the stage. This is blank, or with an outline rectangle to show the stage. The second is called **leaf** and consists of a black dot in the example file **fibon0.fla**. The linkage properties of the **leaf** movie clip are set to export, and the clip has been given the identifier name **leaf**. Attach the following code to the main timeline:

```
Stage.scaleMode = "noScale";
var maxleaves:Number = 300;
//
var G:Number = 1 / 1.618033989;
var GA:Number = 360 - 360 * G;
//
var rad:Number = 20;
var rgrowth:Number = 1.005;
//
var cur:Number = maxleaves;
var rot:Number = 0;
onEnterFrame = function () {
  if (cur) {
    cur--;
    //
    rot += GA;
    rot -= int(rot / 360) * 360;
    //
    rad *= rgrowth;
    var x:Number = Math.cos(rot * Math.PI / 180) * rad;
    var y:Number = Math.sin(rot * Math.PI / 180) * rad;
```

```
//
var mc:MovieClip = viewer.attachMovie
➥ ("leaf", "l" + cur, cur);
//
mc._x = x;
mc._y = y;
mc._rotation = rot;
//
}
};
```

The key variables

maxleaves = The number of iterations and of leaves or grains you're going to attach. Here I use 300, which may be quite a lot, but it's necessary to see the effect with these settings. You'll see that a smaller number will be enough later with other values.

G = The golden ratio.

GA = The golden angle in degrees.

rad = The initial radius.

rgrowth = A factor by which the radius will grow with each iteration.

cur = The current iteration. In this case, I start counting backward, because I want to use this iterant as the depth levels for the attached movie clips, and I want the clips attached first to be on top always.

rot = The angle the clip should be offset and rotated. For each iteration, **rot** is increased by the golden angle **GA**.

You start by defining initial values and constants. In the **onEnterFrame** handler, you check if the value of **cur** is greater than 0. If it is, the **if** statement is run. If the value is greater than 0, it means that there are still iterations to be done. Each frame cycle does one iteration. The value of **cur** is decreased by 1 at the start of the **if** statement. This means that the value will eventually reach 0 and the effect will be finished.

After the **rot** value has been increased by the golden angle, the following line ensures that the **rot** value is in the range of 0 to 360:

```
rot -= int(rot / 360) * 360;
```

This is done because results might be less accurate if **rot** gets really high when there are a large number of iterations.

After defining the new radius, you calculate an **x** and **y** location rotated by **rot** and with a distance of **rad** from the center, attach a new movie clip to **viewer**, and place it on this location. The clip is also rotated by the same angle. The latter will result in a visual effect only if your graphic is something other than a perfect round dot in the clip's center. With this code, you'll find the effect in **fibon0.swf**.

If you're the doubting kind, you can quickly prove that this sunflower-type distribution is due only to the special angle. For instance, add 2 or 3 degrees to or subtract 2 or 3 degrees from **GA** in the initialization code and you'll find that even with such slight changes, the even distribution disappears.

fibon0a

To prove the golden ratio, go ahead and try subtracting 3 from **GA**. The sunflower-type symmetry is gone and you're left with a swirl.

```
var GA:Number = 360 - 360 * G - 3;
```

fibon0b

This time, by adding 0.5 to **GA**, you still have a swirl but with a smaller angle resulting in more "prongs."

```
var GA:Number = 360 - 360 * G + .5;
```

fibon0c

Adding 0.3, you still have a swirl rather than the sunflower-type symmetry, but you can see how the pattern gets closer to the original as the value added gets closer to 0.

```
var GA:Number = 360 - 360 * G + .3;
```

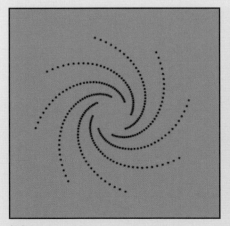

[0a]

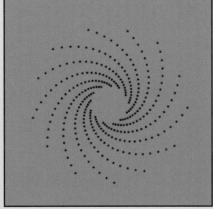

[0b]

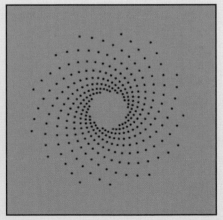

[0c]

fibon1a

To create a more flowerlike pattern, you need to replace the dot graphic with a leaflike one and add growth factors for the **_xscale** and **_yscale** of the clip. Add these variables to the initialization code:

```
var growx:Number = 1.0001;
var growy:Number = 1.018;
var xscl:Number = 45;
var yscl:Number = 19;
```

And then add the following code into the **if** loop that creates the iterations:

```
xscl *= growx;
yscl *= growy;

mc._xscale = xscl;
mc._yscale = yscl;
```

You can make some slight aesthetic modifications to the initial **rad** and **rgrowth** values.

It's also possible to make some changes to vary the golden angle over time. Add the following code to the initialization:

```
var degenerate:Number = 1.001;
```

And add this line to the iteration loop:

```
    GA *= degenerate;
```

Depending on **degenerate**, the golden angle will alter over time in different speeds (for comparison, setting **degenerate = 1** won't alter the angle). Let's now alter the variables in a few more examples to see what the impact is.

fibon1b

To start with, leave the golden angle as it was originally, but decrease the **degenerate** value so that this affects the golden angle in each iteration. Note that you make the y-scaling bigger than the x-scaling this time. You also modify the various growth values slightly.

```
var GA:Number = 360 - 360 * G;
var degenerate:Number = .9998;
var rad:Number = 10;
var rgrowth:Number = 1.013;
var growx:Number = 1.008;
var growy:Number = 1.015;
var xscl:Number = 30;
var yscl:Number = 100;
```

fibon1c

In this iteration of the experiment, you alter both the golden angle (**GA**) and the **degenerate** variable. You also make the scaling equal on both the x-axis and the y-axis.

```
var GA:Number = 360 - 360 * G + 5;
var degenerate:Number = .9999;
var rad:Number = 10;
var rgrowth:Number = 1.013;
var growx:Number = 1.008;
var growy:Number = 1.015;
var xscl:Number = 60;
var yscl:Number = 60;
```

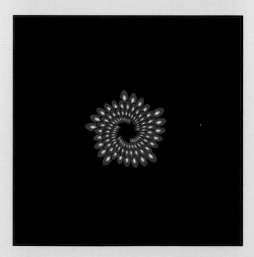

These are just a couple of examples of what you can do. Try changing some more variables on your own. Also, try changing the petal shapes and colors to see what different and vibrant flowers you can achieve.

Particles

A **particle system** consists of a set of tiny objects that all behave under the same set of physical or mathematical laws. These can be additional external forces, such as general gravity, as well as behaviors inherent to the particles themselves. A particle system can get very complex and need a lot of calculating power where particles influence other particles, but even a simple model can develop complex and unpredictable behaviors. Particle systems are used to emulate physical models such as clouds, gasses, rain, and crowds, with each purpose needing specific behaviors and laws.

In this experiment, you'll create a basic particle system consisting of an "emitter" where the particles are generated and a "collector" that attracts the particles. The particles will wander from one to the other, and there will be one additional perturbing force that you can think of as a kind of "wind." The particles will also have their own individual behavior.

If you look at the `particles.fla` file, you'll see that this experiment has four key movie clips. There is the **dot** movie clip that acts as a particle. In the example, the graphic consists of two small lines, but a dot would be just as good if that's what you'd rather use. This clip has its linkage properties set to export, and it has been given the logical identifier **dot**. The **viewer** movie clip acts as the stage for the experiment and has the final two movie clips, **emitter** and **collector**, placed within it.

Let's look at the main code of the experiment, on frame 1 of the root timeline:

```
var emitter:MovieClip = viewer.emitter;
var collector:MovieClip = viewer.collector;
var particles:Number = 38;
//
var pminlife:Number = 20;
var pmaxlife:Number = 50;
var pmass:Number = 40;
var pinitspd:Number = 5;
// emitter
var em_x:Number = emitter._x;
var em_y:Number = emitter._y;
var em_a1:Number = -Math.PI / 180*45;
var em_a2:Number = Math.PI / 180*30;
// collector
var coll_x:Number = collector._x;
var coll_y:Number = collector._y;
var coll_m:Number = 15000;
var coll_r:Number = 50;
// wind
var wind_v:Number = 9;
var wind_a:Number = Math.PI / 180 * (-45);
var wind_vx:Number = Math.cos(wind_a) * wind_v;
var wind_vy:Number = Math.sin(wind_a) * wind_v;
var wind_fq:Number = Math.PI / 180 * 2;
var wind_ph:Number = 0;
//
function reset(mc) {
  mc._x = em_x;
  mc._y = em_y;
  mc.vx = Math.cos(em_a1 + Math.random() * em_a2) * pinitspd;
  mc.vy = Math.sin(em_a1 + Math.random() * em_a2) * pinitspd;
  mc.m = pmass;
  mc.life = random(pmaxlife - pminlife) + pminlife;
}
for (i=0; i<particles; i++) {
  viewer.attachMovie("dot", "p" + i, i);
  reset(viewer["p" + i]);
}
emitter.btn.onPress = function(){
  this._parent.startDrag();
}
emitter.btn.onRelease = function(){
  this._parent.stopDrag();
```

```
      em_x = this._parent._x;
      em_y = this._parent._y;
    }
    collector.btn.onPress = function(){
      this._parent.startDrag();
    }
    collector.btn.onRelease = function(){
      this._parent.stopDrag();
      coll_x = this._parent._x;
      coll_y = this._parent._y;
    }
    onEnterFrame = function () {
      wind_ph += wind_fq;
      wind_f = Math.sin(wind_ph);
      wind_x = wind_vx * wind_f;
      wind_y = wind_vy * wind_f;
      for (i=0; i<particles; i++) {
        var mc:MovieClip = viewer["p" + i];
        if (mc.life) {
          mc.life--;
          //
          var dx:Number = coll_x - mc._x;
          var dy:Number = coll_y - mc._y;
          //
          var d:Number = Math.sqrt(dx * dx + dy * dy);
          var grav:Number = (mc.m * coll_m) / (d * d);
          //
          mc.vx += (wind_x-mc.vx+(dx/d)*grav)/mc.m;
          mc.vy += (wind_y-mc.vy+(dy/d)*grav)/mc.m;
          //
          mc._x += mc.vx;
          mc._y += mc.vy;
          if (d < coll_r) {
            mc.life = 0;
          }
        } else {
          reset(mc);
        }
      }
    };
```

The key variables

particles = The number of particles. This is very much dependent on the speed of your machine and the complexity of code needed.

pminlife, **pmaxlife** = The minimum and maximum number of frames a particle will live. Afterward, it will be reset and represent a new particle.

pmass = The virtual mass of a particle.

pinitspd = The initial speed of a particle.

em_x, **em_y** = The location coordinates of the emitter. This is read from the **emitter** clip's properties, so that you can change these more intuitively.

em_a1, **em_a2** = Two angles (in radians) at which particles will leave the emitter. The first is absolute, and the second will mark a range within which a random number is added to this angle. **Math.PI/180** is the ratio between common degrees and radians, so you can conveniently type in your numbers in degrees and multiply by the ratio.

coll_x, **coll_y** = The location coordinates of the collector.

coll_m = The mass for the collector. With the gravitational force of this mass, it will attract the particles.

coll_r = A radius around the collector. If a particle falls into this range, it will disappear. It will be reset and start as a new particle from the emitter.

wind_v = A maximum velocity for the "wind" that will affect the particles and interfere with their motion toward the collector.

wind_a = An angle at which the wind blows.

wind_vx, **wind_vy** = Vectors calculated from the wind angle and velocity. If the angle of the wind should change, you need to recalculate these every time in the **onEnterFrame** function, but you'll start with a fixed direction in this exercise.

wind_fq = The frequency at which the wind will increase and decease in a tidal manner. The wind will actually blow back and forth in the direction you specify, with periodical increasing and decreasing force. The frequency for this is specified as an angle and will later be added to the wind phase for each frame (**wind_ph += wind_fq;**).

There is a short function in the first section of code, after initializing the variables, that resets the particles: **reset(mc)**, where **mc** is a shortcut reference to the **dot** movie clip instances named **p0**, **p1**, and so on (this shortcut is created in the **onEnterFrame** handler: **var mc:MovieClip = viewer["p" + i];**). Let's take a quick look at some new variables created here.

mc.vx, **mc.vy** = A horizontal and vertical vector resulting from the wind's initial speed and the angle at which it is emitted. The angle is the angle **em_a1** plus a random value from 0 up to the angle **em_a2**. If **em_a2** is set to 0, all particles will leave at the same angle. If it's a full circle, the particles will leave randomly in any direction, and if it's a quarter circle, the particles will be emitted randomly within a quarter circle.

mc.life = The lifespan in frames for each particle, set to a random value between **pminlife** and **pmaxlife**.

The initial section of code ends with a loop that attaches the defined number of particles and initializes them using the **reset** function:

```
for (i=0; i<particles; i++) {
  viewer.attachMovie("dot", "p"+i, i);
  reset(viewer["p"+i]);
}
```

Up to this point, the code would leave all the clips on one spot. You need to use the **onEnterFrame** code that follows to make them move. There are three new variables set at the start of this handler in addition to the wind phase angle (**wind_ph**) already mentioned.

wind_f = An amplitude value calculated using the wind phase that periodically changes between 1 and –1 in a sinusoidal way

wind_vx, **wind_vy** = The actual horizontal and vertical velocities for this phase

The next step in the code is the `for` loop that moves the particles. If the `life` value isn't equal to 0, the `if` statement runs. If the `life` value is 0, the `reset` function is called. The `if` statement starts by decreasing the `life` value by 1. The horizontal, vertical, and absolute distances to the collector are then calculated and stored as `dx`, `dy`, and `d`. The gravitational force is then calculated. You end up with `var grav:Number = (mc.m * coll_m) / (d * d)` using the principle that

```
gravity = (mass1*mass2)/(distance*distance)
```

The horizontal and vertical components of the gravity on the particle (`dx/d*grav` and `dy/d*grav`) are used toward the x and y velocities of the particle (`mc.vx` and `mc.vy`). The wind is also a contributing factor here, so you add the difference between the wind speed and the particle speed to the gravitational force. Finally, you take inertia into account:

```
inertia = force/mass
```

Equated into the variables, for the horizontal speed you're left with

```
mc.vx += (wind_x-mc.vx+(dx/d)*grav)/mc.m;
```

The horizontal speeds are added to the clip's former x and y locations to represent its new location. The final check in the loop is to see if the distance is smaller than the collector's radius, in which case the particle is reset.

In the example file, you'll see that I've added the ability for the emitter and collector to be draggable. If you're interested in this effect, take a look at `particles.fla`. You'll see that a button has been added over the `emitter/collector` graphics within their movie clip, and there's some additional code on the main timeline to set up drag-and-drop functionality using this button.

The motion in this experiment can vary greatly depending on the masses: higher masses on the particle will increase gravity, but they also increase inertia, so the wind doesn't move them that much, and so on. You'll find that gravity decreases very fast with distance. And at certain angles, gravity can speed up the particles so much that they escape the collector completely.

If you need only vertical gravity, you can skip all the collector details, distances, and individual gravity, and use a much simpler model instead:

```
mc.vx +=(wind_x-mc.vx)/mc.m;
mc.vy +=(wind_y-mc.vy)/mc.m+grav;
mc._x += mc.vx;
mc._y += mc.vy;
```

Here `grav` is simply set to a constant such as 1 in the beginning. You can also randomly set the mass of the particles, or reset them at a random position, scale them, or fade them dependent on any of their properties.

Let's now try some variations to see the effects of simple changes. In the example SWFs, you'll see that I've changed the graphics slightly on some of them, and set the emitter and collector in different places to get different effects (keep in mind that the emitter and collector are draggable). Remember to go back to the original `particles.fla` code if you create each variation from scratch.

p1

For this experiment, the particles have a shorter minimum life but the same maximum life. The angles of projection from the emitter also change. The maximum wind speed decreases, so the impact of the wind isn't as great. The wind also hits the particles from a different angle. The tidal motion in which the wind increases and decreases has been increased, though.

```
var pminlife:Number = 5;

var em_a1:Number = -Math.PI / 180 * 60;
var em_a2:Number = Math.PI / 180 * 180;
```

[1]

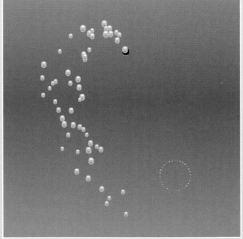

[2]

```
var wind_v:Number = 3;
var wind_a:Number = Math.PI / 180 * (-30);
var wind_fq:Number = Math.PI / 180 * 5;
```

p2

The initial mass of the particles is much heavier, which affects the gravitational force on the particles. The mass of the collector is much lighter, which affects its gravitational pull. The maximum wind speed is faster here. You're also adding variance to the mass when the reset function is called.

```
var pminlife:Number = 40;
var pmaxlife:Number = 120;
var pmass:Number = 4800;
var pinitspd:Number = -3;

var em_a1:Number = -Math.PI / 180 * 45;
var coll_m:Number = 3000;
var wind_v:Number = 180;
var wind_a:Number = Math.PI / 180 * (-30);
var wind_fq:Number = Math.PI / 180 * 5;

mc.m = Math.random() * pmass / 2 + pmass / 2;
```

p3

Here you're making the angle that the particles leave the emitter change from left to right and back again. The collector has a strong gravitational pull due to an increased mass.

```
var pmaxlife:Number = 100;
var pmass:Number = 10;
var pinitspd:Number = 0;
var em_a1:Number = -Math.PI / 180*65;
var em_a2:Number = Math.PI / 180*90;
var coll_m:Number = 20000;
var wind_v:Number = 4;
var wind_a:Number = Math.PI / 180 * (10);
var wind_fq:Number = Math.PI / 180 * 3;
```

p4

In this iteration, the particles move in a circle around the collector. Note the changes to **em_a1** and **em_a2**, which have a big impact in the effect.

```
var pminlife:Number = 40;
var pmaxlife:Number = 120;
var pmass:Number = 2000;
var pinitspd:Number = 10;
var em_a1:Number = Math.PI / 180 * 90;
var em_a2:Number = Math.PI / 180 * 5;
var wind_v:Number = 10;
var wind_a:Number = Math.PI / 180 * (-30);
var wind_fq:Number = Math.PI / 180 * 5;
```

p5

In this final experiment, the fading and color change are simply animated in the movie clip, not scripted. This animation also contains a change in size. The initial particle speed and maximum wind speed here are low, and particle mass is high, which helps create a smoke effect.

```
var pminlife:Number = 55;
var pmaxlife:Number = 80;
var pmass:Number = 180;
var pinitspd:Number = 2;
var em_a1:Number = -Math.PI / 180 * 65;
var em_a2:Number = Math.PI / 180 * 10;
var coll_m:Number = 1000;
var wind_v:Number = 3;
var wind_a:Number = Math.PI / 180 * (60);
var wind_fq:Number = Math.PI / 180 * 1;
```

These experiments demonstrate the ways you can make artificial environmental and climatic conditions, such as wind, gravity, and mass, affect the movement of objects. The principles could be very useful in creating a real-life scene in Flash, and they provide you with control over the elements that you'll never have in real life.

[3]

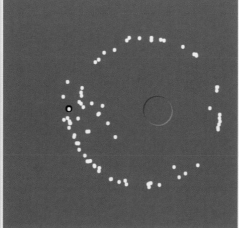

[4]

[5]

Recursive pattern

Recursion is often needed when you have to calculate approximations for limits, like the golden section, or in fractal sets, or for algorithms that need repetitive steps until a condition is met. Besides a loop, these functions can also splice and call several instances of their own in some cases.

More specifically, a **recursive** function is one that returns its output to the very same function again. It's a function that calls itself from within the function. The function needs a condition for whether it should call itself again or stop the recursion.

In this experiment, you'll use recursion to create some simple, self-repetitive patterns where you'll just attach movie clips, and then rotate and scale them relative to each other, over and over.

For the following code, you'll need a movie clip with a linkage identifier name **dot**. This clip is preferably a simple graphic, such as a 100×100 pixel dot that can easily be percentage-scaled. You'll link the **dot** movie clip to a second movie clip, **viewer**, which is just a rectangle outline within which the recursive effect will occur. As usual, the relevant script resides on frame 1 of the root timeline:

```
var angmax:Number = 360 * Math.PI / 180;
var dimin:Number = .382;
var maxchild:Number = 3;
var maxrec:Number = 4;
var dep:Number = 1;
function addthing(x, y, scl, ang, child, sub) {
  dep++;
  var mc:MovieClip = viewer.attachMovie("dot",
  ➥ "d" + dep, dep);
  mc._x = x;
  mc._y = y;
  mc._yscale = mc._xscale = scl;
  mc._rotation = ang / (Math.PI / 180);
  if (sub) {
    var cang:Number = angmax / child;
    while (child) {
      var nx:Number = x + Math.cos(ang) *
      ➥ scl;
      var ny:Number = y + Math.sin(ang) *
      ➥ scl;
      var nscl:Number = scl * dimin;
      var nang:Number = ang + cang * child;
      //
      addthing(nx, ny, nscl, nang, maxchild,
      ➥ sub - 1);
      child--;
    }
  }
}
//
for (i=0; i<maxchild; i++) {
  var ang:Number = angmax/maxchild*(i+1);
  var nx:Number = Math.cos(ang) * 50;
  var ny:Number = Math.sin(ang) * 50;
  addthing(nx, ny, 50, ang, maxchild, maxrec);
}
```

The key variables

angmax = The maximum angle, which is the total maximum angle that subsequent clips will be rotated and placed at. Dependent on the amount of subsequent clips, this angle will be divided by the number of clips.
dimin = A factor to scale subsequent clips by.
maxchild = How many subsequent "children" or "offspring" clips will be added to each clip.
maxrec = The maximum recursion depth, or how many generations of subsequent clips will be added before the function quits.
dep = The depth level at which a new clip is placed.

As you'll see, you have to be a bit careful with the **maxchild** and **maxrec** values, as alterations will affect the total number of clips and recursions.

The bulk of the code consists of the **addthing** function, so let's take a look at what this function consists of. You'll see that the function has six parameters:

x = The _x location of the clip
y = The _y location of the clip
scl = The scale of the clip
ang = The rotation angle of the clip
child = How many offspring will be added for the clip
sub = How many generations will occur, as in the number of times the function will be called from within itself

The function starts by increasing the depth that the new clip is to be placed on by 1 (**dep++**). Each clip will be placed at a different depth. You then attach an instance of the **dot** movie clip and name it in relation to its depth. For example, a clip where the depth is equal to 2 will be called **d2**.

For simplicity and typing convenience, you assign the return value of **attachMovie** to a variable, **mc**, that acts as a shortcut to reference the new attached clip. The clip's properties are set to the location, scale, and rotation of **x**, **y**, **scl**, and **ang**. The function will then use an **if** statement to check if there's another generation to follow—that is, whether **sub** is set to any value other than 0.

If the **sub** value isn't 0, a **while** loop will run after a new variable, **cang**, is defined. **cang** is the child angle and is used for subsequent clips that are produced. If you look at the **while** loop, you'll see that the main action is to call the **addthing** function again from within itself—this is how the recursive pattern occurs. The rest of the loop creates some new variables that are then passed as parameters when the function is called. You'll see that these variables have the same names as the original function parameters, except that they have an **n** prefix at the beginning to show that they're new. The loop will run forever if you don't decrease the value of **child** by 1 every time the statement is looped (**child--**). When the value of **child** is equal to 0, the loop will stop.

Finally, to evoke the nested repetition, you add a line that calls the function once with the initial values:

```
addthing(0, 0, 100, 0, maxchild, maxrec);
```

You can find this effect in **recurs_1.fla**.

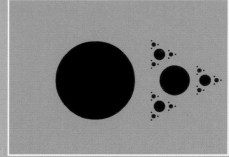

recurs_1a

By replacing the last line that calls the function with a **for** loop that uses the **maxchild** value, you can call the function more than once and with different values:

```
for (i=0; i<maxchild; i++) {
  var ang:Number = angmax / maxchild * (i + 1);
  var nx:Number = Math.cos(ang) * 50;
  var ny:Number = Math.sin(ang) * 50;
  addthing(nx, ny, 50, ang, maxchild, maxrec);
}
```

Let's now play around with the initial values and see what effects can be created.

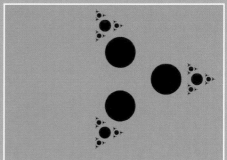

recurs_1b

Here you'll have fewer children, but more recursions. You'll also increase the scaling factor and alter the angle. You'll see that the end effect is very different from the last experiment.

```
var angmax:Number = 520 * Math.PI / 180;
var dimin:Number = .6;
var maxchild:Number = 2;
var maxrec:Number = 5;
```

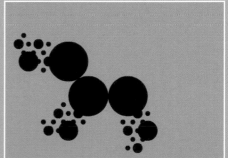

recurs_1c

Now make the number of children and recursions the same. Make the angle so that the clips are within 180 degrees. You'll see in the SWF that they're all located in a semicircle of the dot they're based around.

```
var angmax:Number = 180 * Math.PI / 180;
var dimin:Number = .5;
var maxchild:Number = 3;
var maxrec:Number = 3;
```

Changing the shape of the **dot** symbol in this last example to a triangle can produce star shapes.

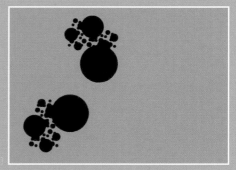

recurs_1d

You might notice that the offset of the next generation always follows one direction, as you're always adding to the angle. For a more homogenous appearance, add an offset angle. Add the following line after the **var cang:Number = angmax / child** declaration:

```
var angoff:Number = -(angmax + cang) / 2;
```

Also modify the **nang** variable so that the child clips aren't placed in a range from the maximum to 0, and are instead using the range of half the maximum to minus half the maximum.

```
var nang:Number = ang + angoff + cang * child;
```

recurs_2

For the next examples, you're going to modify the **dot** symbol. The symbol you're going to use can be found in **recurs_2.fla**. You're going to revert back to a single call of the function and an angle of –90 degrees. Replace the **for** loop that you've been using with the following line:

```
addthing(nx, ny, nscl, nang, maxchild, sub - 1);
```

If you turn to **recurs_2.fla**, you'll see that this change has already been made. This file has the variables set to

```
var angmax:Number = 270 * Math.PI / 180;
var dimin:Number = .618;
var maxchild:Number = 3;
var maxrec:Number = 4;
```

Let's play with the variables again and see what tree effects can be created.

recurs_2a

Here you're decreasing the number of children in each clip. This will give the tree fewer branches and a more realistic tree form. You're also limiting the angle of the branches. This looks like a bare tree in the winter:

```
var angmax:Number = 138 * Math.PI / 180;
var dimin:Number = .618;
var maxchild:Number = 2;
var maxrec:Number = 4;
```

recurs_2b

You're increasing the angle here, and the tree looks more like a conifer or evergreen. A greater angle is filled by more branches, and each branch is more populated. You do this through the recursion and child values. If you look at the tree stump, it has three branches going off it. There are three branches going off each of those, and so on. This is where the number of children comes in. If you look at the number of times a branch splits off into three, you'll see that it is five times—the number of recursions.

```
var angmax:Number = 720 * Math.PI / 180;
var dimin:Number = .5;
var maxchild:Number = 3;
var maxrec:Number = 5;
```

recurs_2c

You restrict the angle again in this next experiment. You also go back to two children. This time, you increase the number of recursions to seven. So, while the branches are thinly populated by children, there are more of them.

```
var angmax:Number = 220 * Math.PI / 180;
var dimin:Number = .618;
var maxchild:Number = 2;
var maxrec:Number = 7;
```

recurs_2d

The next tree is tall, but its branches are all at the top within a small angle, which is set to 90 degrees. Because of the small angle and a higher number of children than in the last experiment, the tree looks densely populated with branches.

```
var angmax:Number = 90 * Math.PI / 180;
var dimin:Number = .5;
var maxchild:Number = 3;
var maxrec:Number = 5;
```

recurs_2e

You can add some slight random value to the new **nang** angle and **nscl** scale, and create a natural-looking tree:

```
var nscl:Number = scl * dimin + Math.random() * 5;
var nang:Number = ang + angoff + cang * child
➥ + Math.random() * 38 * Math.PI / 180;
```

recurs_2f

A final idea is to use a graphic clip that already contains a self-repetitive pattern for a more complex look.

You can see from these files how easy it is to make complex-looking objects from the simplest start point of the basic **dot** movie clip. Try playing around with other shapes and see what objects you can create.

[2a]

[2b]

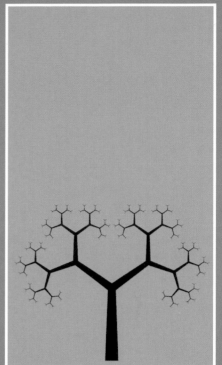

[2c]

[2d]

[2e]

[2f]

Sine & Co.

I use trigonometric functions in nearly every Flash movie I create. You need them whenever you want to translate angles and vectors to and from a Cartesian coordinate system like the stage of Flash. However, they can also be useful for harmonic value changes of any kind.

I've often heard people complaining that they only faintly remember trigonometry from school and claiming that they never really understood it. The basic relation between the most needed functions, sine and cosine, and their corresponding angles can be easily shown and understood with Flash.

The Flash movie for this experiment consists of two movie clips. The first is a container movie clip that acts as the stage for the experiment. In the **trig1.fla** example file, you'll see that this clip, **viewer**, consists of an outline rectangle to define the viewer area and a circle with a 100-pixel radius that is centered on the stage. The second movie clip, **dot**, consists of a small circle, and I've also added a horizontal and vertical line through the center. The linkage properties of this clip are set to export, and the clip has been given the identifier name **dot**.

Here's the code for this experiment. It should be put on the main timeline:

```
var ang:Number = 0;
var angstep:Number = Math.PI / 180 * 1;
var rad:Number = 100;
//
for (i=0; i<3; i++) {
  viewer.attachMovie("dot", "dot" + i, i);
}
onEnterFrame = function () {
  ang += angstep;
  viewer.dot0._x = viewer.dot1._x = Math.cos(ang) * rad;
  viewer.dot0._y = viewer.dot2._y = -Math.sin(ang) * rad;
  //
  viewer.dot0._rotation = -ang * 180 / Math.PI;
};
```

The key variables

ang = An angle measured in radians. Measured in radians, a full circle (360 degrees) is 2xPi. Pi indicates a half circle (180 degrees); Pi/2 indicates a right angle (90 degrees).
angstep = A value that increases the angle step by step. Here it's equal to 1 degree. Use **Math.PI/180** to convert radians to degrees and vice versa. **Math.PI/180*degrees** gives the radians equivalent for degrees; **radians/(Math.PI/180)** or **radians*180/ Math.PI** gives degrees equivalent for radians.
rad = The radius.

The first section of code defines the variables and then goes on to attach the **dot** movie clip three times by means of a **for** loop and the **attachMovie** action. The dots are named **dot0**, **dot1**, and **dot2**.

In the **onEnterFrame** handler, **ang** is increased by **angstep** in each frame. The x locations of **dot0** and **dot1** are set to the cosine of **ang**, multiplied by the radius, and the y locations of **dot0** and **dot2** are set to the sine, once again multiplied by the radius.

Finally, the rotation of **dot0** is set to equal the negative value of **ang** in degrees.

Note that I negated the values for **_y** and rotation, because in Flash **_y** increases downward, while in math it usually increases upward. You don't have to do this—just skip the negative signs if they bother you, and the animation will be flipped.

So, **dot1** changes only its horizontal position, dependent on the angle's cosine value, while **dot2** moves only horizontally, dependent on sine. **dot0** combines both and moves horizontally like **dot1** and vertically like **dot2**, and it moves in a circular line of the radius you specify.

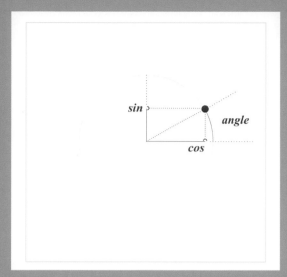

Test **trig1.fla** and watch the effect that this simple code creates. Changing **rad** will change the circle's size. Changing **angstep** will change the speed and the direction if **angstep** is decreasing **ang**.

If you scale the sine and cosine values with two different values, instead of a uniform radius, it will result in an elliptical motion. Add the following lines and remove the **rad** variable:

```
var xscl:Number = 100;
var yscl:Number = 50;
```

Now use this scaling to affect the radius. Modify the **onEnterFrame** handler by replacing **rad** with your scaling factors:

```
viewer.dot0._x = viewer.dot1._x =
➡ Math.cos(ang) * xscl;
viewer.dot0._y = viewer.dot2._y = -
➡ Math.sin(ang) * yscl;
```

You can see this effect in **trig1a.swf**.

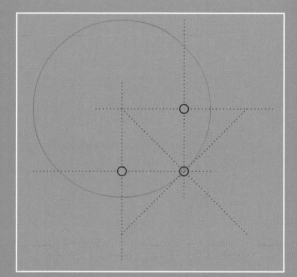

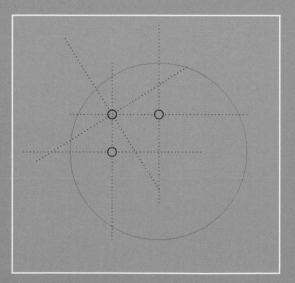

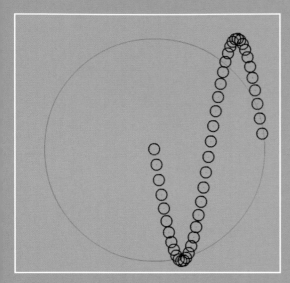

trig1b

Let's start by plotting the sine wave. First, modify the **dot** movie clip by removing the horizontal and vertical lines. You just want the dot here. You won't need the **onEnterFrame** handler for now, and this will have one new variable, **steps**, which is the number of times the loop will run.

```
var ang:Number = 0;
var steps:Number = 45;
var xscl:Number = 100;
var yscl:Number = 100;
//
for (i=0; i<steps; i++) {
  var dot:MovieClip = viewer.attachMovie("dot", "dot" + i, i);
  ang = 2 * Math.PI / steps * i;
  dot._x = xscl / steps * i;
  dot._y = Math.sin(ang) * yscl;
}
```

trig1c

You can animate this effect by now adding an **onEnterFrame** handler and a new variable, **phaseoffset**.

```
var phaseoffset:Number = 0;
onEnterFrame = function(){
  phaseoffset += Math.PI / 180 * 5;
  for(i=0;i<steps;i++){
    ang = 2 * Math.PI / steps * i + phaseoffset;
    viewer["dot" + i]._x = xscl / steps * i;
    viewer["dot" + i]._y = Math.sin(ang) * yscl;
  }
};
```

trig1d

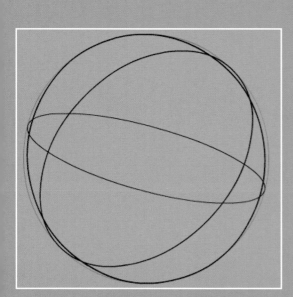

The next experiment requires a couple of changes to the **dot** movie clip. You want to make the graphical element an outline circle with a radius of 100 pixels. You can set this in the Info panel by making the width and height 200 pixels. The circle then needs to be centered in the movie clip. The effect you're going to create hinges on changes to the **_xscale** and **_rotation** in the code:

```
var ang:Number = 0;
var steps:Number = 3;
var xscl:Number = 100;
var yscl:Number = 100;
var angstep:Number = Math.PI / 180 * 1;
var rad:Number = 100;
var phaseoffset:Number = 0;
//
for (i=0; i<steps; i++) {
  var dot:MovieClip = viewer.attachMovie("dot", "dot" + i, i);
}
onEnterFrame = function(){
  phaseoffset += Math.PI / 180 * 3;
  for(i=0;i<steps;i++){
    ang = 2 * Math.PI / steps * i + phaseoffset;
    viewer["dot" + i]._xscale = Math.cos(ang) * xscl;
    viewer["dot" + i]._rotation = ang * 180 / Math.PI;
  }
};
```

trig1e

The next example creates a similar effect, but with different-sized circles. To achieve the `trig1e.swf` effect, you make use of the **_yscale** property:

```
var ang:Number = 0;
var steps:Number = 7;
var xscl:Number = 100;
var yscl:Number = 100;
var angstep:Number = Math.PI / 180 * 1;
var rad:Number = 100;
var phaseoffset:Number = 0;
//
for (i=0; i<steps; i++) {
  var dot:MovieClip = viewer.attachMovie("dot","dot"+i,i);
  dot._yscale = yscl / steps * i;
}
onEnterFrame = function(){
  phaseoffset += Math.PI / 180 * 5;
  for(i=0;i<steps;i++){
    ang = 2 * Math.PI / steps * i + phaseoffset;
    viewer["dot" + i]._xscale = Math.cos(ang) *
    ➥ viewer["dot" + i]._yscale;
    viewer["dot" + i]._rotation = ang * 180 / Math.PI;
  }
};
```

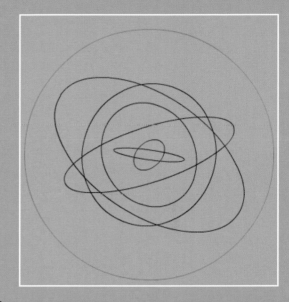

trig1f

Here's the code for the final variation, the effect of which you can observe in `trig1f.swf`:

```
var ang:Number = 0;
var steps:Number = 7;
var xscl:Number = 100;
var yscl:Number = 100;
var angstep:Number = Math.PI / 180 * 1;
var rad:Number = 100;
var phaseoffset:Number = 0;
//
for (i=0; i<steps; i++) {
  var dot:MovieClip = viewer.attachMovie("dot","dot"+ i,i);
}
onEnterFrame = function(){
  phaseoffset += Math.PI / 180 * 1;
  for(i=0;i<steps;i++){
    ang = 2 * Math.PI / steps * i + phaseoffset;
    viewer["dot" + i]._xscale = Math.cos(ang) * 100;
    viewer["dot" + i]._yscale = Math.sin(ang) * 100;
    viewer["dot" + i]._rotation = ang * 180 / Math.PI;
  }
};
```

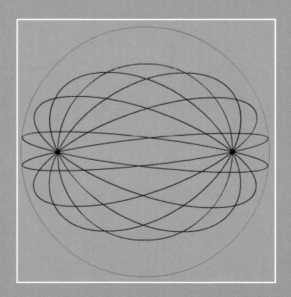

That's the end of our brief look at Sine & Co. You can see how some great effects can be achieved with very basic modifications of the code. You might even understand some of that school trigonometry now!

Paul Prudence was born, lives, and works in London, UK. Early years were spent drafting fantastical landscapes in pen and ink. The most formative experience was undoubtedly the stealing of an encyclopedia of surrealism from the local library as a young teenager. Later on a mistake was made studying fine art at Goldsmiths College in London.

After trashing the idea of being part of the 'art world' and being in the enviable position of being unemployable, he spent a few years travelling, then voluntary working as an art therapist in a mental hospital. Spare time was spent staying up until morning painting pictures influenced by altered states of consciousness.

In the last few years he's traded the traditional mediums of paint and paper for photons and the qwerty mnemonic. Since then he's had some graphic work published in magazines and a video work commissioned by UK TV.

The modular nature of Flash lends itself well to the way I like to work. The combined power of ActionScript with the way nested movieclips work gives us a tool that can make an animated system that with a few tweaks can be radically altered from one state to another. This makes it ideal for artistic experimentation. Old code and clips can be reused in new experiments and built into new and often surprising forms; all modules made in Flash remain alive.

Flash is a uniquely beautiful program that allows a perfect merge of both aesthetic concerns and math. One of my ongoing interests is the relationship between art and math or science, and how the two seemingly disparate disciplines can affect and influence one and another. Flash is a brilliant program for examining this relationship.

I've always been interested in self-replicating and repeating systems such as those found in nature, because often simple iterative processes, repeated over and over, can bring about highly complex forms. The building blocks of life, DNA itself, arise out of replication of other DNA strands. Many of the most beautiful forms in nature, shells, radiolarians, plant structures, and nervous systems come into existence through a repeating core element.

Looking through history it's easy to see a huge amount of art and artifacts that also employ repetitive motifs to great effect. They're often geometric, and sometimes paying homage to the kind of repetition found in nature. For example, in Tibet religious paintings called tankas adorn temples, and are often a swirl with repeating motifs. In Islamic art repetition is taken to its zenith. Complex geometric designs, as well as intricate patterns of vegetal ornament (such as the arabesque), create the impression of unending repetition, which is believed by some to be an inducement to contemplate the infinite nature of God. Often when I go to bed after staring at the screen for hours, I close my eyes and continue to see 3D patterns twisting and moving through space!

paul prudence
www.transphormetic.com

Recursive

For this experiment, you'll need a simple graphic symbol that has its linkage properties set to export. Give it the identifier name **unit**. With this identifier, you can call the clip using the **attachMovie** command. The basic code for the experiment is attached to frame 1 of the main timeline in a new movie. The code is as follows:

```
var a:Number = 0;
var i:Number = 0;
onEnterFrame = function () {
   a++;
   i++;
   var unit:MovieClip = attachMovie("unit", "unit" + a, i);
   unit._y = Math.sin(i) * 300;
   unit._x = Math.cos(i) * 600;
   if (a > 1000) {
      delete onEnterFrame;
   }
};
```

This simple piece of code duplicates the **unit** clip in positions across the screen according to a trigonometric function of the variable **i**. When a certain amount of duplications have passed, the movie stops. The trigonometry plots the duplicates of the clip in sequences that give the final configuration a curved shape. The code is contained in an **onEnterFrame** function to create a loop. The effect that is created can be seen in **recursive_01.fla**.

The key variables

a = A counter to attach individual instances of the clip onto the screen. As each loop passes, 1 is added to the value of **a**, and one new duplication of the clip is added to the screen.

i = Another simple counter with 1 being added to its value on each loop. The x and y positions of the newly added clip are then set according to the sin/cosine value of argument **i**.

Let's look at some examples of how you can modify and build on this starting point. Note that in many of these examples, the graphic has been altered to achieve a different effect. Remember to go back to the base file **recursive_01.fla** to start each experiment.

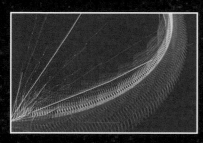

[2]

[3]

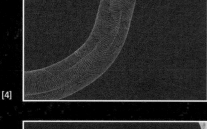

[4]

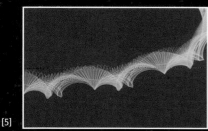

[5]

recursive_02

For the first experiment, you'll increase number of clips attached by replacing 1000 with 2000 in the **if** statement. The value used to calculate the **_x** value has also been changed from 600 to 500. Here are the lines to modify:

```
unit._x = Math.cos(i) * 500;
if (a > 2000) {
    delete onEnterFrame;
}
```

Also add scaling to the clips in both the x and y directions. The **_xscale** value is based on the counter **i**, which also represents a clip's depth. The greater the value of **i**, the larger the scaling factor. Consequently, the later in the effect a clip is drawn, the wider it is on the x-axis. The y-scaling will be the **tan** value of **i**. You'll add rotation to the clips as well. Again, this will be based on the **i** value, and it increases as more clips are attached. Here's the code to add in the **onEnterFrame** function to create this effect:

```
unit._xscale = i / 100;
unit._yscale = Math.tan(i);
unit._rotation = i / 20;
```

recursive_03

Here you modify the **_x** property again, but this time from 600 to 300. The higher this value is, the greater the area across the screen the effect occurs. All the effects start at the left of the screen, but how far across they span is dependant on the value you use here. By decreasing the value, you limit the effects to a smaller area on the left of the screen. Try changing the value that the **cos** output is multiplied by to see the effect of high and low values. Here's the modification you're making in this experiment:

```
unit._x = Math.cos(i) * 300;
```

Also add a rotation value again. By using a sine equation, the value of rotation will move up and down in the same way that the sine curve does. Add the following rotation code:

```
unit._rotation =  Math.sin(i) * 600;
```

recursive_04

In this movie, you'll again change the **_x** property to 300 and add the same rotation value as in the last experiment. The difference between this experiment and the last is that you're increasing the number of clips attached. Here's the code to add/modify:

```
unit._x = Math.cos(i) * 300;
unit._rotation =  Math.sin(i) * 600;
if (a > 1500) {
    delete onEnterFrame;
}
```

recursive_05

For the next experiment, change the **_y** value and once again add rotation. When you changed the **_x** value by multiplying the cosine result by different values, you discovered that the higher the value, the further across the stage the span of the effect. All the effects started on the left, and how far across they went was determined by the multiple value. With the **_y** value, the principle is similar. All the effects start at the top of the screen, but how far down the screen they span is affected by the multiple you use on the sine value. You base the rotation factor on a multiple of the cosine value this time. Add/modify the following lines:

```
unit._y = Math.sin(i) * 200;
unit._rotation = Math.cos(i) * 1000;
```

recursive_06

Now you'll add an alpha effect to the existing variables to add a transparent effect. You'll also add another new variable that changes the color. You'll use the color object to set the RGB transformation value, which is determined by the value of **a**. Here's the code to add/modify to create the **recursive_06.swf** effect:

```
unit._y = Math.sin(i) * 200;
unit._rotation = a;
unit._alpha = 60;
var newcol:Color = new Color(unit);
newcol.setRGB(a * (0xffffff / 2) );
```

recursive_07

Let's now make the rotation conditional. It will only happen when the value of **a** gets over 750. If you watch the effect, you should be able to see where this occurs. Here's the code that deviates from the base clip:

```
if(a > 750){
    unit._rotation = Math.cos(i) * 60;
}
if (a > 1500) {
   delete onEnterFrame;
}
```

recursive_08

Here you're replacing the cosine value with the sine value to calculate the **_x** value, and you're making a smaller number of instances by limiting the **if** statement to 200. Add or modify this code:

```
unit._x = Math.sin(i) * 600;
unit._rotation = i;
unit._yscale = Math.sin(i) * 200;
if (a > 200) {
   delete onEnterFrame;
}
```

recursive_09

This file reintroduces the **_yscale** factor. Once again, you use the sine function to calculate the **_x** positioning with the following code:

```
unit._y = Math.sin(i) * 900;
unit._x = Math.sin(i) * 600;
unit._rotation = i;
unit._yscale = Math.sin(i) * 300;
if (a > 900) {
   delete onEnterFrame;
}
```

recursive_10

Let's now make the math used to calculate the **_x** and **_y** positions a bit more complex. You'll use the square root value in addition to the sine and cosine functions that you've used previously to calculate these values.

```
unit._y = Math.cos(a) * (200 - Math.sqrt(a) *
➥ 30) + Math.cos(a) + 400;
unit._x = Math.sin(a) * (100 - Math.sqrt(a) *
➥ 30) + Math.sin(a) + 200;
if (a > 900) {
   delete onEnterFrame;
}
```

recursive_11

You'll again make use of the code in the last example with slight changes in the numbers. Now also add in the other variables that you've made major use of: **_rotation**, **_yscale**, and **_xscale**.

```
unit._y = Math.cos(a) * (200 - Math.sqrt(a) *
➥ 30) + Math.cos(a) + 150;
unit._x = Math.sin(a) * (200 - Math.sqrt(a) *
➥ 30) + Math.sin(a) + 250;
unit._rotation = i;
unit._yscale = i / 2;
unit._xscale = i / 2;
if (a > 150) {
   delete onEnterFrame;
}
```

recursive_12

This final example is the same as the last, except that you multiply the square root value before putting it to use.

```
unit._y = Math.cos(a) * (200 - Math.sqrt(a) *
➥ 7)+ Math.cos(a) + 150;
unit._x = Math.sin(a) * (200 - Math.sqrt(a) *
➥ 3) + Math.sin(a) + 150;
unit._rotation = i;
unit._yscale = i / 2;
unit._xscale = i / 2;
if (a > 700) {
   delete onEnterFrame;
}
```

It might be interesting to incorporate an alpha change over time to give an impression of three-dimensionality in some of these FLAs. The last three FLAs suggested a new avenue of exploration with circular patterns evolving from the trigonometric functions. It might also be interesting to break into an oval or spiral configuration with the introduction of a new counter variable such as this:

```
unit._y = Math.cos(a) * ( 200 - Math.sqrt(a) * newcounter of small increments ) + Math.cos(a) + 275;
```

It would be nice to subtly animate the **unit** clip, bringing the whole animation alive, or perhaps size the unit according to the relative position of the mouse.

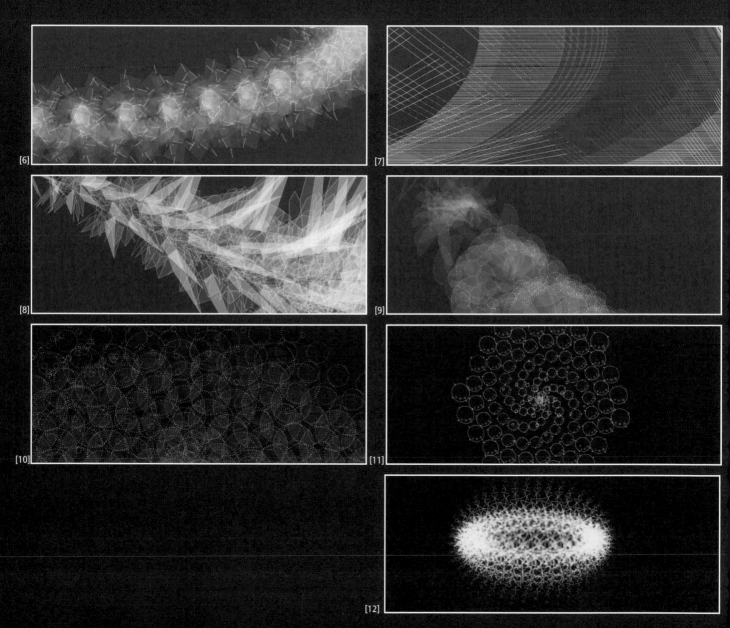

[6]

[7]

[8]

[9]

[10]

[11]

[12]

Swooping

For this experiment, the code will again sit on the first frame of the movie on layer 1. In the Library is a movie clip named **line** exported with a linkage ID of the same name. The code will create initial variables and then have an **onEnterFrame** function to attach the new movie clips. The result of the code is that movie clips are placed along a Bezier path. A Bezier curve is produced mathematically using a minimum of four points. Note that the final animation will depend on the processor speed of the computer running it. You can find the code of the base FLA in **swooping_01.fla**.

Here's the code that sets up the initial variables.

```
// sp
var x0:Number = 0;
var y0:Number = 0;
// dp
var x3:Number = 0;
var y3:Number = 300;
var count:Number = 0;
var start:Number = getTimer();
var speed:Number = 5000;
//bezpoint
var x1:Number = 300;
var y1:Number = 30;
var x2:Number = 30;
var y2:Number = 30;
// Bezier trajectory
var cx:Number = 3 * (x1 - x0);
var cy:Number = 3 * (y1 - y0);
var bx:Number = (3 * (x2 - x1)) + (cx);
var by:Number = (3 * (y2 - y1)) - cy;
var ax:Number = x3 - x0 - cx - bx;
var ay:Number = y3 - y0 - cy - by;
```

And here's the **onEnterFrame** code that follows the initialization:

```
onEnterFrame = function () {
    var elapsed:Number = getTimer() - start;
    if (elapsed > speed) {
        delete onEnterFrame;
    } else {
        count = count + 1;
        var cube:Number = elapsed / speed;
        var square:Number = square * square;
        cube = cube * cube * cube;
        square = cube;
        var line:MovieClip = attachMovie("line", "line" +
 ➥ count, count);
        line._x = (ax * cube) + (bx * square) +
 ➥ (cx * elapsed / speed) + x0;
        line._y = (ay * cube) + (by*square) +
 ➥ (cy * elapsed / speed) + y0;
        line._rotation = count;
        count = count + 1;
    }
};
```

The key variables

x0 = The starting anchor **x** position for the Bezier
y0 = The starting anchor **y** position for the Bezier
x3 = The final anchor **x** position for the Bezier
y3 = The final anchor **y** position for the Bezier
count = The counter
speed = A variable that changes the length and speed of the plot
x1 y1 x2 y2 = The Bezier handle coordinates

All the other variables are used to calculate the Bezier trajectory, and the **onEnterFrame** code serves to place duplicate clips on the Bezier curve. So, there's the base FLA. You'll now alter some variables and observe the effect changes. Each experiment starts at the base FLA unless otherwise indicated.

swooping_02

For this FLA, you'll modify three of the variables. Change the starting anchor position of the Bezier (**y0**), which will move the starting position down. Also change the **x** Bezier handle coordinates. If you look through the code, you'll see what an impact changing just three variables can have due to the math involved in calculating the Bezier curve. For example, **y0** goes toward the Bezier trajectory (**cy** and **ay**) and toward the **_x** and **_y** positions of the duplicate movie clips. In the initial code, here are the changes to make:

```
var y0:Number = 600;
var x1:Number = 200;
var x2:Number = 0;
```

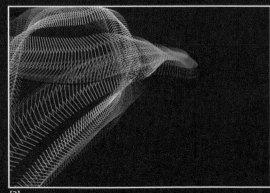

[2]

swooping_03

In this FLA, you'll again play with the basic variables in the initial code. This time you're going to modify the final anchor positions for the Bezier ($x3$ and $y3$) as well as the starting anchor positions. You'll also increase the **speed** variable to change the length and speed of the curve. In **onEnterFrame**, you'll add rotation to the **duplicateMovieClip** action. The rotation will be governed by the **count** value. In other words, it will increase by 1 with each clip that is duplicated. Here are the variable modifications:

```
var y0:Number = 150;
var x3:Number = 150;
var y3:Number = 0;
var speed:Number = 20000;
var x1:Number = 150;
var y1:Number = 150;
var x2:Number = 300;
var y2:Number = 900;
```

And here's the rotation code to add to **onEnterFrame**:

```
line._rotation = count;
```

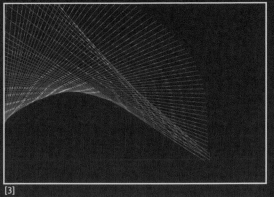

[3]

swooping_03a

This experiment is the same as the last one, except for two modifications. This time, you'll set **x3** to 600, and you'll add **_yscale** to **onEnterFrame** rather than rotation. As the value of **count** increases, the size of the scaling on the y-axis increases. Here's a recap of the variable changes for this experiment:

```
var y0:Number = 150;
var x3:Number = 600;
var y3:Number = 0;
var speed:Number = 20000;
var x1:Number = 150;
var y1:Number = 150;
var x2:Number = 300;
var y2:Number = 900;
```

Here's the scaling code for **onEnterFrame**:

```
line._yscale = count / 10;
```

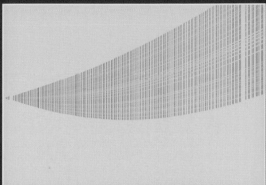

[3a]

swooping_03b

This time, you'll start with **swooping_03a** rather than going back to the base FLA. You'll make three modifications to the variables. You'll also add the rotation back into **onEnterFrame**. This time it will have the same value as the scaling. Here are the variable changes:

```
var x0:Number = 300;
var y0:Number = 200;
var y3:Number = 150;
```

Add this to **onEnterFrame**:

```
line._rotation = count / 10;
```

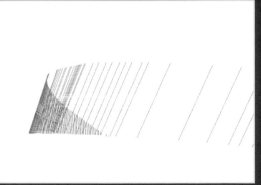

[3b]

swooping_03c

This experiment starts with the code in **swooping_03b**. Here you'll make changes to the scaling and rotation values in **onEnterFrame**. The scaling value of the clip will be the same as the **count** value (which equates to the number of clips duplicated at that point), and the rotation value will be twice that figure.

```
line._yscale = count;
line._rotation = count * 2;
```

There are many interesting spatial convolutions to be had from changing these two lines. I could go on and on. . . .

[3c]

swooping_04

Now let's return to the base FLA (**swooping_01.fla**) for the next experiment. You'll make modifications to the variables as you did in previous experiments. The main change here occurs in **onEnterFrame**, where you add rotation again, but this time it has a more complex formula based on the Bezier handle coordinates. A motion tween has been added to the **line** movie clip for this experiment. Here's the code to alter in the first part of the frame:

```
var y0:Number = 50;
var x3:Number = 150;
var y3:Number = 0;
var speed:Number = 10000;
var x1:Number = 150;
var y1:Number = 150;
var x2:Number = 300;
var y2:Number = 900;
```

Here's the new rotation formula for **onEnterFrame**:

```
line._rotation = (ax * cube) + (bx * square) +
➥ (cx * elapsed / speed) + x0;
```

swooping_05

In this experiment, you're once again going to change the base FLA's handle coordinates and start and final anchor positions. The main changes, though, will be to the **onEnterFrame** code. You're going to halve the **_x** position of the duplicate clips and set the **_y** position to the value of **count**. Also note that rotation and alpha, again linked to the **count** value, have been added. The movie clip has had motion tweens added once more. Let's start with the variable modifications:

```
var y0:Number = 150;
var x3:Number = 150;
var y3:Number = 0;
var x1:Number = 150;
var y1:Number = 150;
var x2:Number = 100;
var y2:Number = 300;
```

Here are the **onEnterFrame** changes:

```
line._x = ((ax * cube) + (bx * square) +
➥ (cx * elapsed / speed) + x0) / 2;
line._y = count;
line._rotation = count * 15;
line._alpha = 80 - (count / 5);
```

Finally, you're going to add rotation to the new movie clip as well:

```
line.onEnterFrame = function(){
    this._rotation++;
}
```

swooping_06

As usual, you start by altering the variables:

```
var x3:Number = 150;
var y3:Number = 150;
var speed:Number = 1000;
var x1:Number = 150;
var y1:Number = 150;
var x2:Number = 100;
var y2:Number = 300;
```

Then, add rotation to **onEnterFrame**, this time using a more complex formula based on the Bezier handle coordinates:

```
line._rotation = ((ax * cube) * (bx * square)
➥ + (cx * elapsed / speed) + x0) * 5;
```

As in the last experiment, you'll add code to the movie clip's **onEnterFrame** handler. This again contains rotation, but you're also adding a random scaling based on the mouse position on the x-axis. This code makes the movie "freak out" when the clip is touched with the mouse:

```
line.onEnterFrame = function(){
    this._rotation += 5;
    if(_xmouse > 0 && _xmouse < 300){
        this._yscale = Math.random() * 100;
    }
}
```

swooping_07

Here are the variables that deviate from the base FLA in this experiment:

```
var x0:Number = 120;
var y0:Number = 50;
var y3:Number = 150;
var speed:Number = 2000;
var x1:Number = 250;
var y1:Number = 150;
var x2:Number = 100;
var y2:Number = 1;
```

In **onEnterFrame**, you add rotation, alpha, and scaling:

```
line._rotation = count * 3;
line._alpha = 80 - count;
line._yscale = cx * elapsed / speed;
```

This time, the movie clip's **onEnterFrame** handler uses the mouse's **_x** position to vary rotation. The code makes the 3D object twist and turn as it's touched:

```
line.onEnterFrame = function(){
    this._rotation++;
    if(_xmouse > 0 && _xmouse < 300){
        this._rotation += _xmouse / 50;
    }
};
```

I really liked the way **swooping_07** looked, appearing as a 3D structure turning in space (a flat shape extruded along a Bezier!), the twist being affected by the mouse pointer. It would be interesting to develop this further with scaling control and perhaps introduce the **Color** object to subtly change the hues of each of the elements depending on the relative position of the mouse. To give this cocoon/dragonfly organism even more life, it would be great to introduce the **Sound** object, perhaps playing loops/drones again depending on the behavior of the organism.

[4]   [5]   [6]   [7]

Circling

The base FLA for this experiment is `circling_01.fla`. This movie is based around the `line` clip, which is exported with the linkage name `line`. The `line` clip has a motion tween over 80 frames. It rotates once over 40 frames, shrinking in size, and then returns to its original size, rotating once back out in the opposite direction. The code for this experiment is placed in frame 1 of the main timeline. The first section contains the variables and a simple function to transform degrees into radians:

```
var alphdev:Number = 1;
var kolorcycle:String = "on";
var curve:Number = Math.floor(Math.random() *
➡ 100) + 1;
var ydist:Number = Math.floor(Math.random() *
➡ 10) + 1;
// this function is used to calculate a point
// on circle
var radius:Number = 1000;
var centerX:Number = 225;
var centerY:Number = 150;
var rotAngleDeg:Number = 0;
var rotAngleRad:Number;
function degreesToRadians(degrees) {
  return (degrees / 180) * Math.PI;
}
var x:Number = 0;
```

The next section is an `onEnterFrame` function with the actions to attach the `line` movie clip. A counter `x` is also set here:

```
onEnterFrame = function () {
  var line:MovieClip = attachMovie("line",
  ➡ "line" + x, x);
  rotAngleDeg += 5;
  rotAngleRad = degreesToRadians(rotAngleDeg);
  line._y = centerY - Math.sin(rotAngleRad) *
  ➡ _ymouse / 10;
  line._x = centerX + Math.cos(rotAngleRad) *
  ➡ _xmouse / 10;
  if (kolorcycle == "on") {
    var newcol:Color = new Color(line);
    newcol.setRGB(x * (0xffffff / 11));
  }
  line._alpha = x * alphdev;
  line._yscale = x / 15;
  line._xscale = x / 15;
  if (x > 70) {
    _root["line" + (x - 70)].removeMovieClip();
    x = 1;
  }
  x++;
};
```

This code basically plots multiple copies of a movie clip with the instance name `line` on a circular path. However, the path is also dependent on the mouse position, so the final plot can be oval in the x or y directions. Each newly plotted duplicate is also individually colored using the **Color** object, its alpha and x/y scale set according to a variable. There is a maximum of 70 duplications on the screen at any one time, and the duplications are plotted on the fly, creating quite complex animations.

The key variables

`alphadev` = The variable used to control the `_alpha` values of duplicated clips.

`kolorcycle` = A switch to control whether the **Color** object is set for individual duplicated clips, and therefore whether they are individually colored.

`centerX` = The `x` position of the center of the circular path.

`centerY` = The `y` position of the center of the circular path.

`rotAngleDeg` = A variable used in the plotting of the circular path at a later stage.

`rotAngleRad` = The rotation increment of the circular path for the next plotted position. It is measured in radians and is calculated from the `degreesToRadians` function.

Let's now experiment with the basic FLA and see what effects we can achieve.

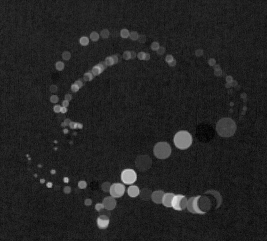

circling_02

In the first variation you're simply going to add rotation to the **onEnterFrame** code. This rotation is based on a multiple of the counter variable **x**. The higher the counter value, the higher the rotation value.

```
line._rotation = x*50;
```

circling_03

Now modify that rotation for the next experiment. Instead of basing the multiple of **x** on a fixed value, base it on the **curve** variable, which gives a random value.

```
line._rotation = curve*x;
```

Also add an **onEnterFrame** handler to the **line** movie clip. These actions will increment the rotation value and use the mouse position to alter the **_x** and **_y** positions of the clips.

```
line.onEnterFrame = function(){
  this._rotation++;
  if(this._y < _ymouse) {
    this._y += 2;
  } else {
    this._y -= 1;
  }
  if(this._x < _xmouse){
    this._x += 2;
  } else {
    this._x -= 1;
  }
};
```

circling_04

In this example, you'll again make positioning affected by the mouse by attaching code to the **line** clip, as you did previously. You'll also modify a few values in the **onEnterFrame** function of the main timeline. The alpha value of the clip will now be reached by multiplying the counter by 10 rather than **alphadev**. The scaling of the clip is being increased by using the value of the counter rather than dividing it by 5. Rotation is added again and is calculated as a multiple of the counter.

```
line._alpha=x*10;
line._yscale=x;
line._xscale=x;
line._rotation = 100*x;
```

circling_05

This experiment changes the color slightly in **onEnterFrame** by changing the number that the larger integer is divided by.

```
if (kolorcycle == "on") {
    var newcol:Color = new Color(line);
    newcol.setRGB(x * (0xffffff / 30));
}
```

The scaling and rotation are all set to the value of **x** for this experiment:

```
line._yscale = x;
line._xscale = x;
line._rotation = x;
```

You'll also increase the period that a clip is present by increasing the counter value at which clips are removed:

```
if (x > 300) {
    _root["line" + (x - 300)].removeMovieClip();
    x = 1;
}
```

circling_06

The deviations from the base file in this experiment start at the top of the frame this time. Halve the value of **alphdev** and turn off the **kolorcycle** variable:

```
var alphdev:Number = .5;
var kolorcycle:String = "off";
```

In **onEnterFrame**, change the scaling factors from **x/15** to **x/10**, making the clips larger. You'll increase the life-time of the clips again, this time to 200. Here are the changes:

```
line._yscale = x / 10;
line._xscale = x / 10;
if (x > 200) {
    _root["line" + (x - 200)].removeMovieClip();
    x = 1;
}
```

circling_07

This time you'll start where the last example left off rather than going back to the base file. First, alter the **alphadev** value again and turn the **kolorcycle** variable back on.

```
var alphdev:Number = .3;
var kolorcycle:String = "on";
```

In **onEnterFrame**, once again change the value that the large integer is divided by to create the new color variable. Finally, re-add rotation and set it to the value of the counter.

```
if (kolorcycle == "on") {
   var newcol:Color = new Color(line);
   newcol.setRGB(x * (0xffffff / 27));
}
line._rotation = x;
```

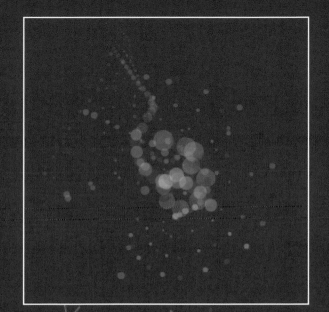

circling_08

Now return to the base FLA for this final example, and change the **alphadev** value:

```
var alphdev:Number = .7;
```

In **onEnterFrame**, add rotation and set that and the scaling using the counter value. Here are the changes:

```
line._yscale = x / 8;
line._xscale = x / 8;
line._rotation = x * 50;
```

Looking back at this sequence, I think my favorite iteration is **circling_05**. It might be interesting to add a more dynamic mouse control environment to some of the other experiments in this sequence similar to the way **circling_05** works.

Still

This experiment revolves around a movie clip in the Library with the linkage name **line**. If you look at **still_01.fla**, you'll see that all the code for this experiment lives on one frame. Here it is:

```
var kolorcycle:String = "on";
var replikants:Number = 500;
var xpos:Number = 2;
var ypos:Number = 3;
var curve:Number = 1;
var ydist:Number = 1;
var xdist:Number = 1.2;
for (var i = 1; i<=replikants; i++) {
  var line:MovieClip = attachMovie("line",
  ➥ "line"+i, i);
  line._x = xpos;
  line._y = ypos;
  line._xscale = 34;
  line._yscale = 34;
  line._rotation = xpos*curve;
  line._alpha = i/(replikants/35);
  if (xpos>600) {
    xpos = 1;
  }
  if (ypos>300) {
    ypos = 1;
  }
  if (kolorcycle == "on") {
    var newcol = new Color(line);
    newcol.setRGB(xpos*(0xffffff/50));
  }
  ypos += ydist;
  xpos += xdist;
  i++;
}
```

Here you'll use a simple **for** loop to duplicate the **line** clip and place instances on the stage. A couple of conditionals check to make sure the next duplication in the loop doesn't appear off the screen, and another checks to see if color cycling is switched on or off.

The key variables

kolorcycle = A switch to control whether the color object is set for individual clips, and therefore whether they are individually colored

replikants = The number of replications to be created

xpos = The starting **x** position for the first duplication

ypos = The starting **y** position for the first duplication

curve = A variable used to give a curved appearance to rows of duplication

xdist = The incremental **x** distance between each duplication

ydist = The incremental **y** distance between each duplication

Now let's play with some variations of this base code and see what the results of particular changes are.

still_02

Start by altering some simple variables, such as the number of replications, positioning, curve, and distribution. Notice that the value divided by in the `if` loop has been altered, but this will have no effect as you have the color cycle turned off here. Here are the changes you can find in the FLA:

```
var replikants:Number = 1000;
var ypos:Number = 70;
var curve:Number = 10;
var ydist:Number = .2;

if (kolorcycle == "on") {
   var newcol = new Color(line);
   newcol.setRGB(xpos * (0xffffff / 50));
}
```

still_03

Starting where you left the last example, now turn the color cycle on so that the change you made in the last example will now occur. Play with some of the other variables, too, to examine the impact. Make the number of **replikants** smaller than you've used before, and make the curve value larger and the **y** distribution much bigger. Here's the code that's been changed in the file:

```
var kolorcycle:String = "on";
var replikants:Number = 300;
var xpos:Number = 150;
var curve:Number = 50;
var ydist:Number = 50;
```

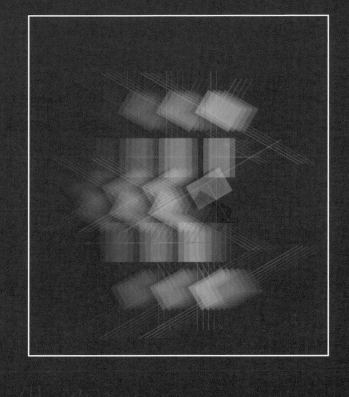

still_04

Now increase the value of the curve by just 1 from its value in `still_03.fla`. This is only a small change, but the configuration of the final replication is completely different. The only other change is to alter the divider used to calculate the color. Make the following changes:

```
var curve:Number = 51;
newcol.setRGB(xpos * (0xffffff / 4));
```

still_05

Continuing from where you left off in `still_04.fla`, turn the color cycle off again. Also alter the number of replications, both the **x** and **y** starting positions and distribution. Here's what's different in the file from the last example:

```
var kolorcycle:String = "off";
var replikants:Number = 100;
var xpos:Number = 300;
var ypos:Number = 140;
var ydist:Number = .1;
var xdist:Number = .1;
```

still_06

In the next example, you'll once again continue where you left off rather than returning to the base FLA. You'll alter the curve and number of replications, but the main change is the addition of scaling to the **for** loop. This scaling is calculated using the counter value **i**. Here's the code I've modified:

```
var replikants:Number = 300;
var curve:Number = 15;
line._xscale = i / 10;
line._yscale = i / ydist;
```

still_07

Let's continue to the next example by modifying the start of the **for** loop. You're going to now use sine and cosine values to calculate the **_x** and **_y** positioning. Remove the scaling and rotation from this example. The loop will now start as follows:

```
for (var i = 1; i <= replikants; i++) {
  var line:MovieClip = attachMovie("line", "line"
  ➥ + i, i);
  line._x = Math.sin(i) * (xpos - i) + 300;
  line._y = Math.cos(i) * (ypos - i) + 150;
  line._alpha = i / (replikants / 35);
```

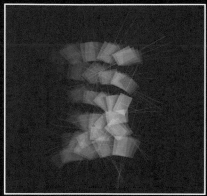

[4]

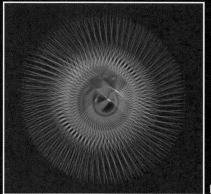

[5]

[6]

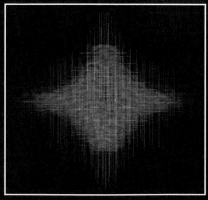

[7]

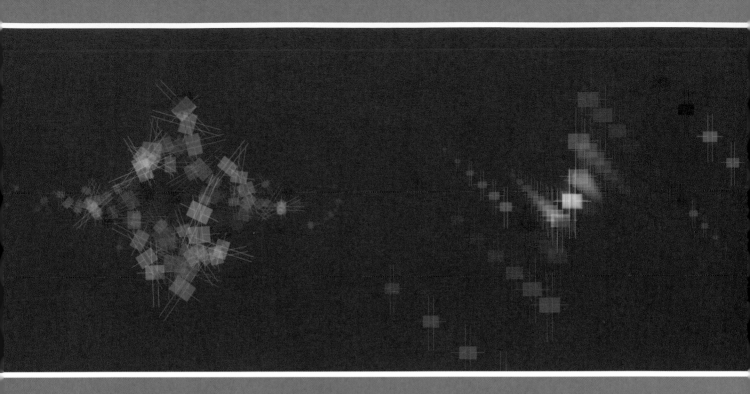

still_08

For this iteration you'll take the previous example and build on it. Turn the color cycle on once again. Also increase the divider used to calculate the color in the **for** loop. Increase the curve value as well. Add the rotation and scaling in again, and slightly alter the math relating to the **_y** position. Here are the modifications:

```
var kolorcycle:String = "on";
var curve:Number = 99;
for (var i = 1; i <= replikants; i++) {
  var line:MovieClip = attachMovie("line",
  ➥ "line" + i, i);
  line._x = Math.sin(i) * (xpos - i) + 300;
  line._y = Math.cos(i) * (ypos - i) + 140;
  line._rotation = ypos * curve;
  line._alpha = i / (replikants / 35);
  line._xscale = i / 10;
  line._yscale = i / 10;
  if (xpos > 600) {
    xpos = 1;
  }
  if (ypos > 300) {
    ypos = 1;
  }
  if (kolorcycle == "on") {
    var newcol = new Color("line");
    newcol.setRGB(xpos * (0xffffff / 36));
  }
  ypos += ydist;
  xpos += xdist;
  i++;
}
```

still_09

For the final example, you'll alter the curve value and the divider used to get a color. The main change in this file is that you're using the **tan** value to calculate both the **_x** and **_y** positions rather than **sin** and **cos**. Here are the final changes:

```
var curve:Number = 99;
line._x = Math.tan(i) * (xpos - i) + 300;
line._y = Math.tan(i) * (ypos - i) + 140;
newcol.setRGB(xpos * (0xffffff / 35));
```

With some of these files I would have liked to have made a slide show, moving though each different FLA and randomizing various elements on each cycle. Later, I might add a mask layer above the **line** clip to slowly reveal the configurations as opposed to them suddenly appearing on the screen.

Born: 31.01.73
Live: London

Having previously worked as a van driver, nanny, ice cream seller, sandwich maker, and band manager, I started making websites in 1997. I'm self-taught and have managed to avoid getting qualifications for anything, though I do have a clean driver's license. I now work through my own company, Hi-Rise Limited, and in collaboration with Anthony Burrill as Friendchip, which was established by accident in 1998. Friendchip's first commercial job was for the inventors of electronic music, Kraftwerk, and we've gone on to work largely with bands and music companies. Friendchip also exhibits in art galleries, as well as making an occasional interactive installation. Hi-Rise Limited does a wide range of work, from children's spelling games to large and serious database driven sites. In all my work, I try to condense ideas into something simple and playful.

Creating sound and graphics with code allows you to be surprised by your own work.

The longer that you write code, the more you realize that you're one of the few groups of people that actually have a use for the algebra they learned at school. Math is obviously the basis of all computer code, and you can only avoid it for so long.

Computers put things together in a way that no human would, occasionally creating something un-expectedly beautiful or, more often, surprisingly humorous. I'm a strong believer in humor in websites. We are, after all, in the business of entertainment, and allowing computers to make the choices leads to a lot of humorous situations. At least they often make me laugh.

kip parker
www.friendchip.com

Composeur

This project was inspired by a few lines in *Gödel, Escher, Bach: An Eternal Golden Braid*, the Douglas Hofstadter book loved by geeks everywhere and also a fine source of interesting mathematical ideas. While discussing computer-generated music, Hofstadter mentions the idea that a combination of Brownian and random movement produces lines of music closest to those humans write. Brownian motion relates to movement in steps, as in plus or minus 1. This piece proves that while that theory may occasionally produce interesting pieces of music, the vast majority is utter drivel!

Take a look in `composeur.fla` to see how this experiment is structured. In the Library you'll see that the movie has just two graphical movie clip symbols and twelve sound symbols. The movie clips have linkage identifiers of `one` and `line`, and the sounds are linked by numbers from 12 (low) to 1 (high). All the code is on frame 1 in the main movie. After a couple of `for` loops, I have defined two functions, `compose` and `getSound`. The code then calls `compose` and sets up an `onEnterFrame` function to call `getSound` once each frame. Let's take a look at the full code listing from frame 1 before I describe it further:

```
var range:Number = 300;
var pitches:Number = 12;
var height:Number = 400;
var notes:Number = 16;
var tone:Number = range / pitches;
var unit:Number = 600 / (notes + 1);
var notesArr:Array = new Array();

//set up movies
for (var i=0; i < notes; i++) {
  var mv:MovieClip = _root.attachMovie("one", "note" + i, i + pitches);
  mv._x = (i + 1) * unit;
  mv._y = height / 2;
  notesArr[i] = mv;
}
for (var j = 1; j <= pitches; j += 2) {
  var line:MovieClip = _root.attachMovie("line", "line"+j, j);
  line._x = 300;
  line._y = (j * tone) + (height - range) / 2;
}
function compose() {
  //a starting point
  var currPoint:Number = Math.floor(Math.random() * pitches + 1);
  for (var i = 0; i < notes; i++) {
    var volume:Number = Math.floor(Math.random() * 3 + 1);
    notesArr[i]._y = (currPoint * tone) + (height - range) / 2;
    notesArr[i]._width = volume * 10;
    notesArr[i]._height = volume * 10;
    notesArr[i].pitch = currPoint;
    notesArr[i].volume = volume;
    if(Math.random() < .5) {
      //random movement
      currPoint = Math.floor(Math.random() * 12 + 1);
    } else {
      if (currPoint == pitches) {
        currPoint--;
      } else if (currPoint == 1) {
        currPoint++;
      } else {
        //50% 50% chance
        if (Math.random() < .5) {
```

```
            currPoint++;
        } else {
            currPoint—;
        }
      }
    }
  }
}
var currentNote:Number = 0;
function getSound() {
  var aNote:Sound = new Sound();
  aNote.attachSound(notesArr[currentNote].pitch);
  aNote.setVolume(33 * notesArr[currentNote].volume);
  aNote.start();
  notesArr[currentNote].gotoAndStop(2);
  if (currentNote > 0) {
    notesArr[currentNote-1].gotoAndStop(1);
  }
}
compose();
onEnterFrame = function(){
  getSound();
  currentNote++;
  if(currentNote > 16){
    currentNote = 0;
    compose();
  }
};
```

The key variables
pitches = The number of "staves"
height = A variable used to help determine the **_y** coordinates of the clips
notes = The number of notes

Let's now examine how the code works. The two **for** loops at the beginning just set up the movie, looping through once to lay out the number of notes specified by **notes** and then again to lay out the staves. The notes are all stored in an array called **notesArr**.

The movie then starts by calling the **compose** function, which randomly chooses a point at which to start in the range of notes. Then it loops through for the number of **notes**, each time randomly setting a volume that determines the volume of the sound and the width/height of the note. The pitch for the note is then set, which determines the pitch it plays and its position on the stave. Finally, the next note is chosen, using the preceding theory. It has a 50/50 chance of either moving randomly to any note in the 12-note range or moving up or down by one.

Earlier I mentioned that the final **onEnterFrame** function contains a call to **getSound**. It also increments the **currentNote** variable once each frame; **getSound** works out which beat is calling it by looking at this variable. When **currentNote** reaches 16, it is reset to 0 and the **compose** function is called again. It then gets the pitch from that clip and creates a new sound object based on this pitch, sets the volume, and then plays the sound. Finally, the movie clip is told to go to frame 2, which just turns it to white, and the last clip is told to go back to the default state in frame 1.

Test the effect, which you can find in **composeur.swf**. It will play some decent tunes from time to time!

composeur2

To improve the likelihood of something tuneful, I changed the plus or minus one motion to include the possibility of no movement:

```
if (Math.random() < .5) {
   currPoint += Math.floor(Math.random()
   ➡ * 2);
} else {
   currPoint—;
}
```

This code replaces the following from the end of the **compose** function:

```
if (Math.random() < .5) {
   currPoint++;
} else {
   currPoint—;
}
```

composeur3

If you like things a little more spiky, you can increase the likelihood of random movement by replacing the original `if (Math.random() < .5)` condition with

```
if(Math.random() < .9)
```

To go a little further with this experiment, it might be worth giving different lengths for each note. This could be achieved by using loops in the sound object.

There are many different ways that the movement of the notes could be graphically displayed; there's no real reason to do it as traditionally as I have.

Another good feature of the sound object is that you can set panning. It might be nice to have the notes bouncing about from ear to ear, or maybe even work out how to produce a two-part harmony.

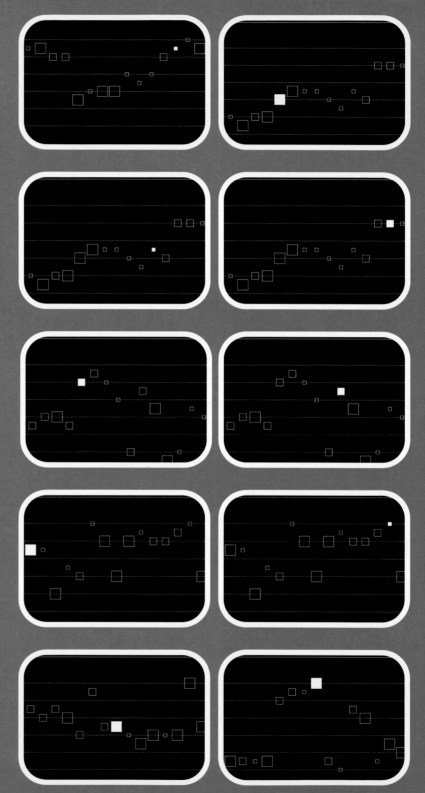

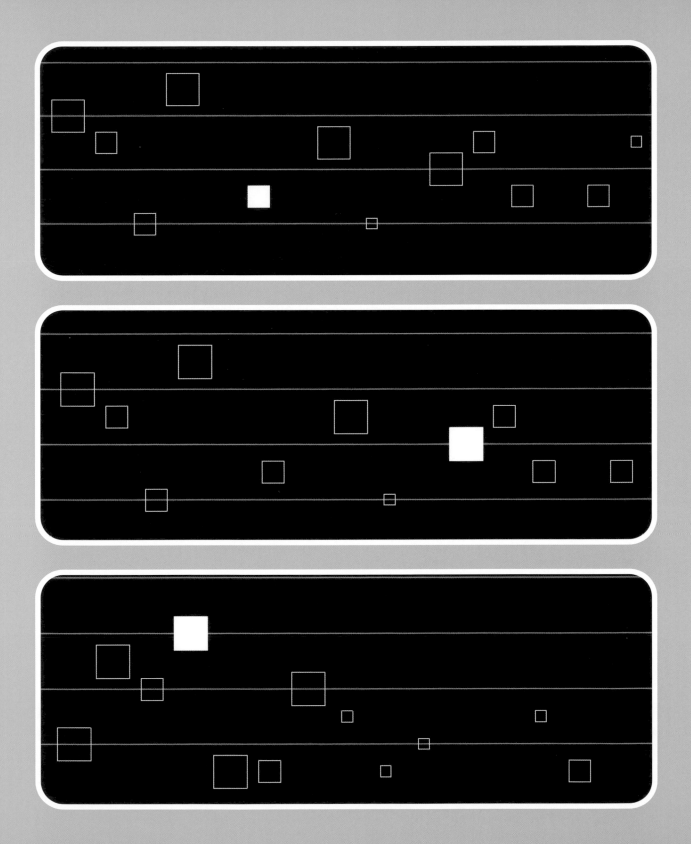

Pause

This piece is heavily inspired by Bridget Riley's *Movement in Squares* (1961). The painting was inspired by Riley's desire to record her impressions of when a squall obscured the black-and-white marble pattern of the paving in a piazza.

I wanted to see how well I could copy the piece programmatically. The following code produced something close to what I was after (see `grid1.fla`):

```
var height:Number = 30;
var width:Number = 30;
var across:Number = 600;
var down:Number = 400;
var min:Number = width / 20;
var max:Number = width - min;
var k:Number = 0;
var aimAt:Number = 28;
var xPos:Number = 0;
var grey:Number = 0;
var i:Number = 0;

while(xPos < across) {
  width = min + (adjusted(aimAt - i));
  for (var j=0; j < down / height; j++) {
    k++;
    var clip = attachMovie("sq", "sq" + k,
    ➥ k);
    if ((k + i) % 2 == 1) {
      hex = 0x000000;
    } else {
      hex = 0xffffff;
    }
    var colour = new Color(clip);
    colour.setRGB(hex);
    clip._x = xPos + width;
    clip._y = j * height;
    clip._width = width;
    clip._height = height;
  }
  xPos += width;
  i++;
}
function adjusted(num) {
  num = Math.abs(num);
  num = Math.min(num, max);
  return (num);
}
```

In essence, this code simply attaches numerous instances of the `sq` image movie clip from the Library into a grid using the `attachMovie` method. The clip is given the linkage identifier `sq` and set to export. The code adjusts the width as it moves across each column to create the valley effect. There are two nested loops that do all the work. The first is a `while` loop, which keeps creating columns until the picture has reached the width set by the variable `across`. It also defines the width for each new column, thereby creating the required effect. The second is a simple `for` loop, which creates the squares inside each column. It's also responsible for creating the checked pattern of the squares, which is achieved using a modulus calculation. Checking for `k%2==1` gives an alternating pattern because the equation evaluates as 1,0,1,0 repeatedly. Adding `i` to the equation (`(k+i)%2==1`) means that the pattern starts at alternating points on each column.

The key variables

`height` = The height of the square to be drawn.
`width` = The width of the square to be drawn. If you set either the height or the width too low (<10), your computer might well crash.
`across` = The horizontal size of the picture.
`down` = The vertical size of the picture.
`min` = The smallest the squares can get.
`max` = The largest the squares can get.
`k` = The counter that is used to name images and set which level to duplicate into.
`aimAt` = The column you wish the effect to happen in. As the counter for the outside loop (`i`) moves closer to `aimAt`, the squares become smaller.

The function `adjusted(num)` is used in working out the width. Squares aren't allowed to get wider than `max`, and negative numbers are returned as positive.

Using the preceding values for the variables gives something fairly close to Riley's original. There are a couple of variations, which are very simple to try. Let's start with the `grid1.fla` file and build on it with every new variation.

grid2

Let's start by changing the **aimAt** variable a couple of times. With the current square size (as defined by the **width** variable), setting **aimAt** to 10 will create a fold on the far left of the screen.

```
var aimAt:Number = 10;
```

grid3

Setting **aimAt** to 30, the fold will be on the far right side.

```
var aimAt:Number = 30;
```

grid4

You can also use different sizes for the squares. However, when the width and height are changed, **aimAt** needs to change too, as this variable refers to column widths. Change the following variable to see this effect:

```
var height:Number = 10;
var width:Number = 10;
var aimAt:Number = 50;
```

grid5

When the grid gets smaller as in the last example, it can start to look a little boring. I decided to add in a few more "folds." You can do this by adding the following line inside the **while** loop just before the **for** loop starts:

```
if(i == aimAt + 17){
    aimAt = 50;
}
```

The following variables are also changed for this experiment:

```
var height:Number = 20;
var width:Number = 20;
var aimAt:Number = 15;
```

The movie now gives itself another target when it is 17 columns past the first **aimAt**.

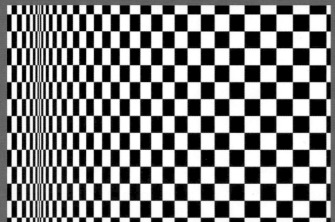

[2]

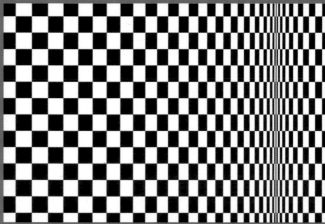

[3]

[4]

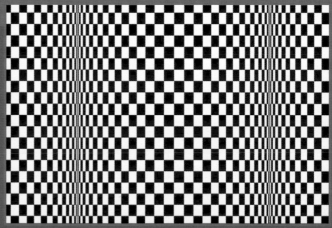

[5]

grid6

It's also possible to put in a number of folds. Let's replace the **if** statement just created with this:

```
if(i == aimAt + 10){
    aimAt = i + 10;
}
```

Every time the program gets ten columns past its target, it puts its target ten columns ahead. Also change the **aimAt** variable to 10 for this experiment.

grid7

Let's now go back to the original **grid1.fla** file and play with the colors. In the code, change the color setting lines to

```
if ((k + i) % 2 == 1) {
    hex = 0x000066;
} else {
    hex = 0xffffcc;
}
```

This change results in a deep blue and pale yellow effect.

grid8

I used the color object to set colors in the last example. It's also quite easy to shift the color as it moves. Add a new variable inside the **for** loop after where the clip properties are set:

```
var dark:Number = j * 18;
```

Also change the color selection:

```
if ((k + i) % 2 == 1) {
    hex = dark;
} else {
    hex = 0xffffff;
}
```

grid9

How about fading out as columns become thinner? Returning once again to the original base FLA, **grid1.fla**, entering the following code with the rest of the clip properties will do this:

```
clip._alpha = 10 + (width*3);
```

grid10

Finally, the rotation of the clip can also be adjusted to create more complex patterns. Add this line to the base FLA's clip properties to create the final effect:

```
clip._rotation = j*4;
```

One idea I wanted to try is to have points on both the horizontal and vertical axes that the squares move toward. It would, however, make the code more complex.

It's not too hard to convert the code to show the lines horizontally instead of vertically.

It would be possible to animate this effect so that the line appears as a ripple across the squares. It could be achieved by storing all the squares in an array and then periodically updating the settings.

122

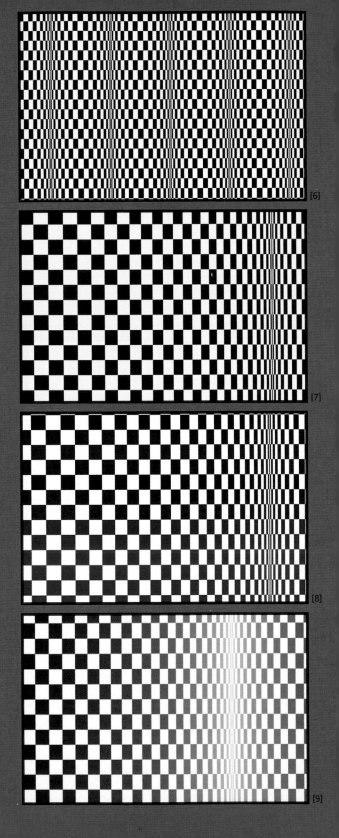

[6]

[7]

[8]

[9]

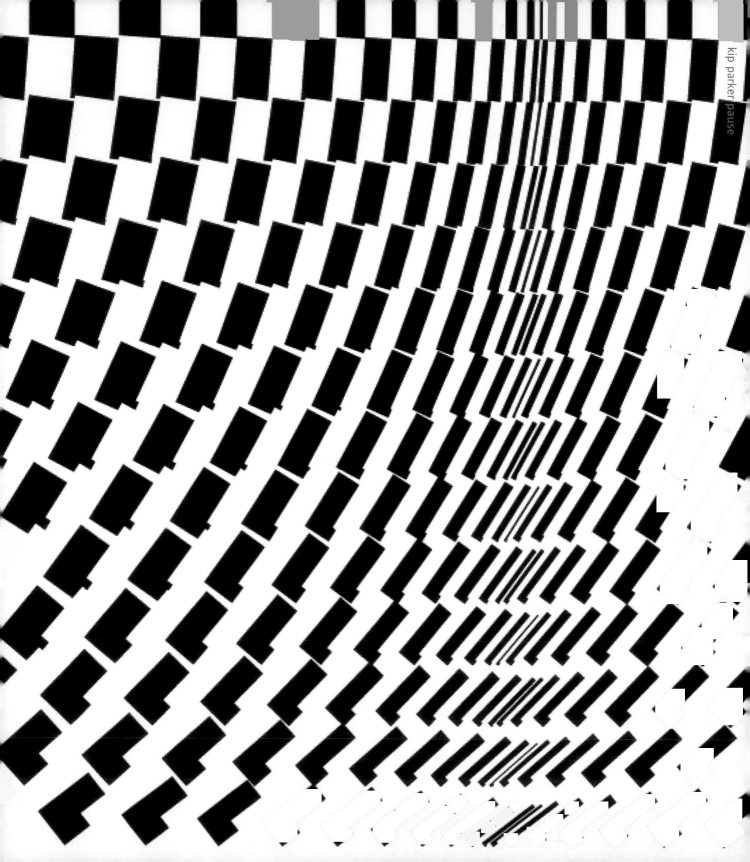

Polygon

This experiment uses an old school favorite, the Pythagorean theorem, to calculate a polygon of any given number of sides. Let's jump straight into some code that dynamically constructs a five-sided polygon (or, more specifically, a pentagon). This code can be tested in **polygon1.fla**:

```
function mixer(r:Number, g:Number, b:Number):Number {
  return r << 16 | g << 8 | b;
}
function rad(deg:Number):Number {
  return (Math.PI / 180 * deg);
}
function drawLine(xStart:Number, yStart:Number,
➡ xStop:Number, yStop:Number, col:Number):Void {
  lineStyle(1, col, 100);
  moveTo(xStart, yStart);
  lineTo(xStop, yStop);
}
function circulate(r:Number, segments:Number, centreX:Number,
➡ centreY:Number) {
  var counter:Number = 0;
  var pointArr:Array = new Array();
  var unit:Number = 360 / segments;
  var yTop:Number = centreY - r;
  for(var i=0; i<=360; i+=unit) {
    var x:Number = centreX + Math.sin(rad(i)) * r;
    var y:Number = yTop + (r - Math.cos(rad(i)) * r);
    pointArr[counter] = new Array(x, y);
    if (counter >= 1) {
      drawLine(pointArr[counter-1][0], pointArr[counter-1][1], pointArr[counter][0],
      ➡ pointArr[counter][1], 0xffffff);
    }
    counter++;
  }
  counter = 0;
}
circulate(100, 5, 300, 200);
```

This code uses the drawing API functions **lineStyle**, **moveTo**, and **lineTo** within a function called **drawLine**. The **drawLine** function allows you to set the beginning and end points of the line as well as a color each time you want to draw a line, rather than make repeated calls to each of those built-in functions.

The key variables

`segments` = The number of sides
`r` = The radius

The `circulate` function uses the Pythagorean theorem (I found some "math for kids" web pages that told me what I needed to know here!) to plot all the points of a polygon with the `segments` value as the number of sides and the radius `r`. These x and y points are stored in an array `pointArr`. As soon as there are at least two pairs of coordinates, the function starts making calls to the `drawLine` function to draw the shape.

In the sample file, the `circulate` function is called with the following parameters:

```
circulate(100,5,300,200);
```

This will draw a pentagon with a radius of 100 in the center of the screen. You can see the results in `polygon1.swf`.

polygon2

The base file works but isn't very interesting. Let's loop the call to **circulate** to get a spirograph-esque effect and use the counter **k** to set the radius parameter. Modify the function call so that it has the following loop:

```
for(k=10;k<=400;k+=10){
   circulate(k,5,300,200);
}
```

polygon3

Here, the x-axis is moved along:

```
for(k=10;k<=200;k+=10){
   circulate(k,8,100+(k/2),200);
}
```

polygon4

Shifting both axes can give an almost 3D effect:

```
for(k=10;k<=200;k+=5){
   circulate(k,4,100+(k/5),300-(k/3));
}
```

polygon5

Let's now set a shape to repeat across the screen. Add a new variable, **interval**, and create a second loop:

```
var interval:Number = 150;
for (v=0; v<400; v += interval) {
   for (var h = 0; h<600; h += interval) {
      circulate(interval, 5, h, v);
   }
}
```

polygon6

Indeed, you can make groups of the shapes across the screen with the following code:

```
var interval:Number = 150;
for(v=0; v < 400; v += interval){
   for(var h=0; h < 600; h+= interval){
      for(var k=0; k<150; k+=10){
         circulate(k, 5, h, v);
      }
   }
}
```

polygon7

This is my favorite effect and is one of the simplest. Set the loop as follows:

```
for(k=10;k<200;k+=5){
   circulate(k,4,300,200);
}
```

Let's also set the color by creating a new variable called **depth**, initializing it to 0, and incrementing it once each time the **circulate** function is called. This is then passed to the **mixer** function, which calculates a 24-bit number to be used as a color value. You can pass that to the **drawLine** function like this:

```
drawLine(pointArr[counter-1][0],
➡ pointArr[counter-1][1],
➡ pointArr[counter][0], pointArr[counter][1],
➡ mixer(depth, depth, depth));
```

This little bit of code has everything you need to make far more complex images. Perhaps turn the image each time it is drawn, to give a real spirograph effect.

[2]

[3]

[4]

[5]

[6]

[7]

Sine

The sine wave is one of the most beautiful and simplest forms in mathematics, and it's also at the foundation of sound theory. If you look at the sample file **sine1.fla**, you'll see that I have code only on frame 1. I'm using the **square** movie clip with its linkage name set to export with an identifier name of **sq**. The result will be a sine curve plotted from the attached clips. Here's the code from frame 1:

```
//distance set along the x axis
var inc:Number = 12;
//initialize x axis
var x:Number = 0;
var a:Number = 120;
var b:Number = 8;
var p:Number = 12;
var v:Number = 200;
var len:Number = 600 / inc;

//width and height of each clip
var w:Number = 5;
var h:Number = 5;
var trans:Number = Math.PI / 180;
for (var i = 0; i<len; i++) {
   var clip:MovieClip = attachMovie("sq", "sq" + i, i);
   // increment independent variable
   x += inc;
   clip._x = x;
   // y-position of object — calculated with sine wave equation
   clip._y = a * Math.sin((b * i + 12) * trans) + v;
   clip._width = w;
   clip._height = h;
}
```

The key variables
a = Amplitude
b = Period
p = Phase shift
v = A value used to display the wave in the center of the movie
x = The x position of the clips
trans = A constant to translate from degrees to Flash's preferred radians
w = The width of each clip
h = The height of each clip
len = A variable used to stop the duplication of the movies when the right edge is reached

Let's now look at some basic variations of the sine curve.

You can also put the main sine creation loop inside another loop and iterate the sine wave all over the place. Add this code in place of the current single loop:

```
var counter:Number = 0;
for(var v = -100; v<500; v+=30){
    for (var i = 0; i<len; i++) {
        var clip:MovieClip = attachMovie("sq", "sq" + counter,
        ➥ counter);
        // increment independent variable
        x += inc;
        clip._x = x;
        // y-position of object — calculated with sine wave equation
        clip._y = a * Math.sin((b * i + p) * trans) + v;
        clip._width = w;
        clip._height = h;
        counter++;
    }
    x = 0;
}
```

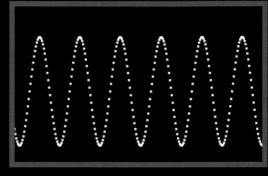

I've used **v**, the vertical adjust property, as the loop variable. I've started it off the page at –100, and it goes past the edge of the page to 500 to make sure the whole stage is covered. To see exactly how this code fits in, turn to **sine3.fla**.

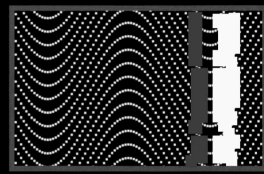

sine4
Instead of just copying the sine wave everywhere, you can alter it slightly on each iteration. For example, add the following code to the end of the outer loop created in the last example (on the line after **x = 0**):

```
a += 10;
```

Also, in the initial variables, set **a** to 10 and **inc** to 9.

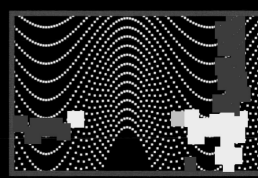

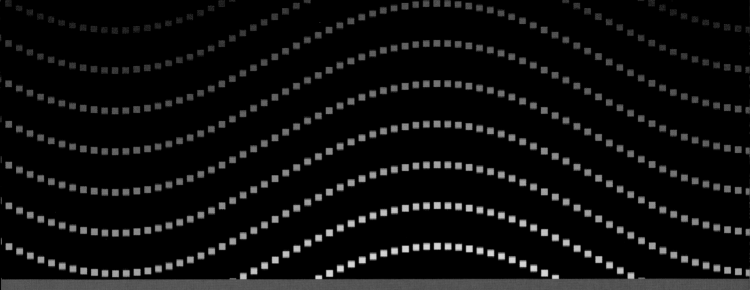

sine5

Let's now use some color transformations on the effect just created. Before the initial variables, right at the start of the script, add the same **mixer** function used in the **polygon** experiments:

```
function mixer(r:Number, g:Number, b:Number):Number {
   return r << 16 | g << 8 | b;
}
```

In this example, you're going to use the **mixer** function to gradually fade from white to darker grays. The grayscale to use is calculated as **256/400 *256**, so you should be able to get from 0 to 256 over the course of the movie. Remove the **a += 10;** line added in the last example and replace it with this:

```
var greyVal:Number = 256 / 400 * v;
var thisColor:Number = mixer(greyVal, greyVal, greyVal);
```

To complete the effect, add the following lines to set the color of each clip (add them to the inner loop on the lines below **counter++**):

```
var newColor:Color = new Color(clip);
newColor.setRGB(thisColor);
```

One final thing to do is set the initial **a** variable to 40. If you get a bit confused with the code placement here, don't worry. You can find the full code in **sine5.fla**.

sine6

The phase setting in the sine equation sets the position at which the sine curve begins to be displayed. By drawing two sine waves on the same vertical adjustment but with different phase settings, you get two waves weaving in and out of each other. The following code creates two waves in one loop:

```
for (var i=0; i<len; i++) {
    var clip:MovieClip = attachMovie("sq", "sq" + counter, counter);
    var clip2:MovieClip = attachMovie("sq", "mirror" + (counter + len), counter + len);
    // increment independent variable
    x += inc;
    clip._x = x;
    clip2._x = x;
    // y-position of object — calculated with sine wave equation
    clip._y = a * Math.sin((b * i + p1) * trans) + v;
    clip2._y = a * Math.sin((b * i + p2) * trans) + v;
    clip._width = w;
    clip._height = h;
    clip2._width = w;
    clip2._height = h;
    counter++;
}
```

Place this code into the base FLA (`sine1.fla`), replacing the original **for** loop that is in that file. In the new file's initial variables, you're going to replace **p** with **p1** and **p2** because you now have two mirrored curves. Also change the **inc** and **a** values. Here's the code you need to alter:

```
var inc:Number = 5;
var a:Number = 40;
var p1:Number = 1;
var p2:Number = 180;
```

To make something more complex, you could introduce the outer loop you used earlier to this effect.

131

sine7

For the final effect, you'll combine the different techniques you've learned along the way. You can find the code for this file in `sine7.fla`. This time, instead of just using grays, you'll add different colors. You'll also see that you're incrementing the altitude from within the inner loop.

Here's the code in full:

```
//distance set along the x axis
var inc:Number = 8;
//initialize x axis
var x:Number = 0;
var b:Number = 6;
var p1:Number = 1;
var p2:Number = 180;
var v:Number = 200;
var len:Number = 600 / inc;

//width and height of each clip
var w:Number = 10;
var h:Number = 10;
var trans:Number = Math.PI/180;
var counter:Number = 0;
for (var v=-100; v<500; v+=20) {
  var a:Number = 10;
  var grey1:Number = 256 - 256 / 400 * v;
  var grey2:Number = 256 / 400 * v * 16;
  var c1:Number = mixer(grey1, 0, 0);
  var c2:Number = mixer(0, 0, grey2);
  for(var i=0;i<len;i++){
    var clip:MovieClip = attachMovie("sq", "sq" + counter, counter);
    var clip2:MovieClip = attachMovie("sq", "mirror" + counter, 1000 - counter);
    // increment independent variable
    x += inc;
    clip._x = x;
    clip2._x = x;
    // y-position of object — calculated with sine wave equation
    clip._y = a * Math.sin((b * i + p1) * trans) + v;
    clip2._y = a * Math.sin((b * i + p2) * trans) + v;
    var colour1:Color = new Color(clip);
    var colour2:Color = new Color(clip2);
    colour1.setRGB(c1);
    colour2.setRGB(c2);
    clip._width = w;
    clip._height = h;
    clip2._width = w;
    clip2._height = h;
    counter++;
    a += 5;
  }
  x = 0;
}
function mixer(r:Number, g:Number, b:Number):Number {
  return r << 16 | g << 8 | b;
}
```

So, the sine curve isn't as boring as it first appears. Try using some of the techniques you've learned here to modify the cosine or tangent curves. You can use and extend the techniques I've shown to achieve many varied Flash effects.

When I was eighteen, I decided to buy a computer instead of a car. That was back in 1991. I did this also in 1993, 1995, and again this year. To me, this is an absolutely brilliant thing to do - at least until cars can fly.

Even before I owned a computer, in some form or another, I have been borrowing CPU time on other people's computers. I was initially motivated to use computers through the text-based adventure games my father would write while I was asleep. It became clear to me that a programmer truly could create something from nothing, and this idea intrigued me.

I completed the ten year program at New Mexico State University and was rewarded a Bachelor of Science in Computer Science for my participation in their experiment. During this time I learned the value of abstracted programming and why I never want to program at a micro level.

My intrigue with the visualization of mathematical processes arises in my eye's inability to discern certain patterns. I enjoy watching the results of computation unfold before me. I see beauty in repeatable patterns and behavior. I take power in seeing a perfect representation of my imagination propagate across networks and lie stored in perfect stasis, for retrieval at any time.

The bulk of these experiments are geometric constructions created with one of two methods: the iterated method, which renders new movieclips one after another in a loop with defined limits, and the recursive method, in which a single instantiation of a movie clip renders itself repeatedly.

Throw in a couple of trigonometric functions and a few gentle geometric shapes, and you have the beginnings of a wondrous universe.

jared tarbell
www.levitated.net

Iterative inspiration

My first set of experiments uses simple iteration to build some beautiful pieces of computational art. I have four layers in my movie, **about**, **logic**, **button**, and **background**, but the only one that you really need is **logic**. Each of these layers has a single frame. The **about** layer just contains some basic information about the file so that when I come back to it in 10 years, I'll understand what it was for. The **button** layer contains, as you'd think it would, a button in its second frame. This means that when the movie has finished running, a regenerate button will appear that you can click to start the whole process again. The **background** layer simply contains a square consisting of dots to give the image a frame. Lastly, but most important, the **logic** layer contains all the code for our movie, all the generative script, and a simple **stop** action.

There are two other important elements to my movie (comp001a.fla). One is a button that sits on the **button** layer, which just starts the generative process off again once it has finished. The other element is a movie clip called **dapoint**, which is the graphic that you'll duplicate on the screen to create the images. This clip is exported from the Library with the linkage name **dapoint**. The graphic is made up of five frames, each with exactly the same crescent shape on it, but filled with a different color, allowing you to create unique images by randomly choosing a frame to give a new color for each movie clip duplication. Here's the code that works the magic. It lives on frame 1 of the **logic** layer.

```
var jlim:Number = 5;
var klim:Number = 5;
regen();
function regen() {
  var depth:Number = 0;
  for (j=0; j<jlim; j++) {
    for (var k=0; k<klim; k++) {
      for (var l=0; l<j+k+1; l++) {
        var newmc:MovieClip = attachMovie("dapoint", "mc" + depth, depth++);
        newmc._x = j * 420 / jlim + 210 / jlim;
        newmc._y = k * 420 / klim + 210 / klim;
        newmc._xscale = 100 + Math.random() * (j + k * 20);
        newmc._yscale = 100 + Math.random() * (j + k * 20);
        newmc._rotation = l * 360 / (jlim + klim);
        newmc.gotoAndStop(Math.floor(Math.random() * newmc._totalframes+1));
      }
    }
  }
}
regenBtn.onRelease = regen;
stop();
```

The key variables

depth = The depth at which the current clip will be placed. You reset the depth to 0 so that when the image is regenerated, it will replace the existing one.

jlim = The number of columns of shapes.

klim = The number of rows of shapes.

Using three nested loops, a single movie clip is attached to the stage a great number of times. The outside two loops (variables **j** and **k**) iterate a fixed number of times as defined by the row and column dimensions. The inside loop (variable **l**) iterates a variable number of times, directly dependent on the current progress through the outside loops. The more times the inside loop iterates, the greater the number of movie clips placed at that particular row and column. Of course, the exact number of attached movie clips, excluding any conditional exceptions, can be computed through **j*k*l**.

With each instantiation, the new object is given unique attributes computed at random and according to the progress of the iteration. This gives you plenty of room for experimentation. You place and rotate each object in the grid space using a multiple of the loop index and a small increment. The small increment is calculated using the limit definitions of each iterative loop for automatic adjustment in loop count changes. Scale is set randomly. At the moment, I'm using a range that increases in proportion to the progress through the loop (groups near the bottom-right corner are more jumbled than groups near the top left). As a final and important step, you set the instantiated movie clip to randomly **gotoAndStop** on one of its frames. This allows a palette of unique graphic shapes to be a part of the construction while keeping the code simple. One other thing to note is that I have my stage set to 420×420 pixels, so if you see the numbers 420 or 210 (420/2) appearing frequently in my scripts, that's why.

comp001b

First off, I changed the following lines of code:

```
for (l=0;l<j+k+5;l++)

newmc._xscale = 100;
newmc._yscale = 100;
newmc._rotation = Math.random() * 360;
```

I also changed the graphic to a section of a circular pipe. Because of the set scale and random rotation, it creates some nice patterns of broken circles.

comp001c

For this iteration I changed the number of duplications again, and I also added in a line to set a fixed alpha.

```
for (l=0;l<j+k+1;l++)

newmc._alpha = 40;
```

I changed **dapoint** to a simple pale square to get these alpha and color-blended images.

comp001d

For this experiment, I went a slightly different way by using letters instead of shapes. I increased the amount of duplications considerably to get a good range of letters, so I reduced the number of rows and columns to keep a good generation speed. I set a fixed rotation to get a good spread of letters, and I added a new line to give a random letter each time. I also removed the alpha line that I added last time.

```
var jlim:Number = 3;
var klim:Number = 3;

for (l=0;l<18;l++)

newmc._rotation = l * 20;
newmc.gf.text = String.fromCharCode(Math.random() * 26 + 92);
```

The big change comes in **dapoint**. This now has only a single frame with a dynamic text box on it with an instance name **gf**.

comp001e

Moving on, I removed the letter code and went back to my shapes. This time, I decided to add a progressive scale to the shapes so that they would grow larger with each successive duplication. To do this, I added a new line at the start of the **regen** function to initialize the scale and a new line in the inner **for** loop to update it. Here are the changes that I made:

```
var jlim:Number = 7;
var klim:Number = 7;

var proscale:Number = 100;

for (l=0; l<j+k+1; l++)

proscale += Math.random() * 14 - 7;
newmc._xscale = proscale;
newmc._yscale = proscale;
newmc._rotation = l * 360 / (jlim + klim);
```

I also changed the graphic back to five frames, but this time with a totally different shape in each frame. It produces some strange, random-looking patterns.

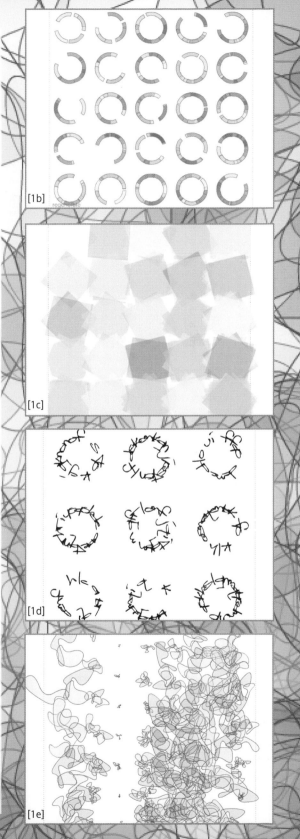

[1b]

[1c]

[1d]

[1e]

135

[1f]

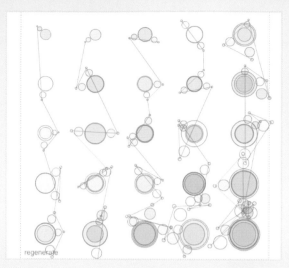

regenerate

[1g]

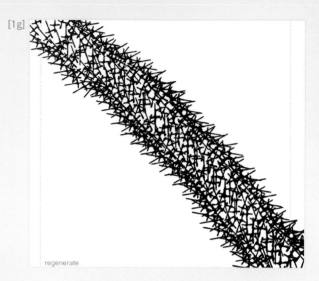

regenerate

comp001f

Another radical change for this one. I used the drawing API to add some lines to the drawing. I changed **dapoint** to be three successively smaller circles with a different color in each of the five frames. There are exactly 100 pixels between the center of the largest circle and the center of the smallest. The movie works by positioning **dapoint**, remembering its position, and then drawing a line to join it to the next copy of **dapoint**. Here's the code in full:

```
var lastpoint:Object = new Object();
var jlim:Number = 5;
var klim:Number = 5;
regen();
function regen() {
  clear();
  var depth:Number = 0;
  for (j=0; j<jlim; j++) {
    for (var k=0; k<klim; k++) {
      for (var l=0; l<(j+k+2)/2; l++) {
        var newmc:MovieClip =
        attachMovie("dapoint", "mc" +
        ➥ depth, 1000+depth++);
        newmc._x = j * 420 / jlim + 210 /
        ➥ jlim;
        newmc._y = k * 420 / klim + 210 /
        ➥ klim;
        var scale:Number = 10 + (j + k) * 4 +
        Math.random() * 20;
        newmc._xscale = scale;
        newmc._yscale = scale;
        newmc._rotation = Math.random() * 360;
        newmc.gotoAndStop(Math.floor(
        ➥ Math.random() *
        ➥ newmc._totalframes+1));
        if(k>0 || l>0){
          lineStyle(1,0,50);
          moveTo(lastpoint.x, lastpoint.y);
        }
```

```
        lastpoint.x = newmc._x + scale *
        ➥ Math.cos(Math.PI / 180 *
        ➥ newmc._rotation);
        lastpoint.y = newmc._y + scale *
        ➥ Math.sin(Math.PI / 180 *
        ➥ newmc._rotation);
        if(l>0 || k>0){
          lineTo(lastpoint.x, lastpoint.y);
        }
      }
    }
  }
}
regenBtn.onRelease = regen;
stop();
```

comp001g

Next, I went back to the original code, removing the drawing code and all of its trappings. This time I added some new script that completely hides the grid pattern, instead producing an odd stream of shapes. I changed **dapoint** to a single frame containing a simple cross. I added three new variables at the start of the function to initialize the position of **dapoint**, and then I added some lines to the inner loop to update these variables and the position and rotation of the shape.

```
var xi:Number = 5;
var yi:Number = 5;
var si:Number = 100;

for (l=0;l<18;l++)

xi += Math.floor(Math.random() * 3);
yi += Math.floor(Math.random() * 3);
si += Math.random() * 8 - 4;
newmc._x = xi;
newmc._y = yi;
newmc._xscale = si;
newmc._yscale = si;
newmc._rotation = l * 20;
```

136

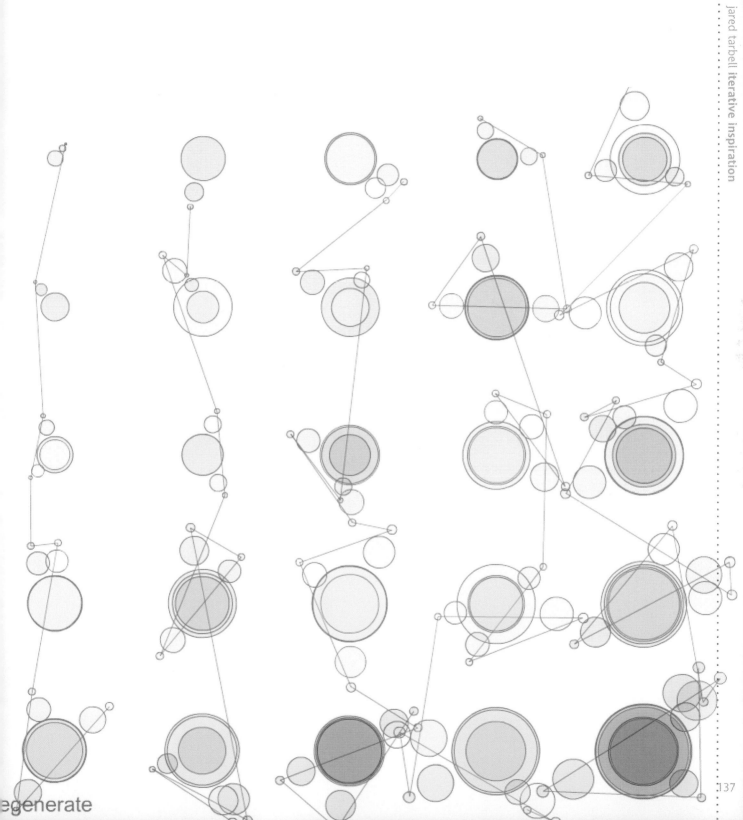

egenerate

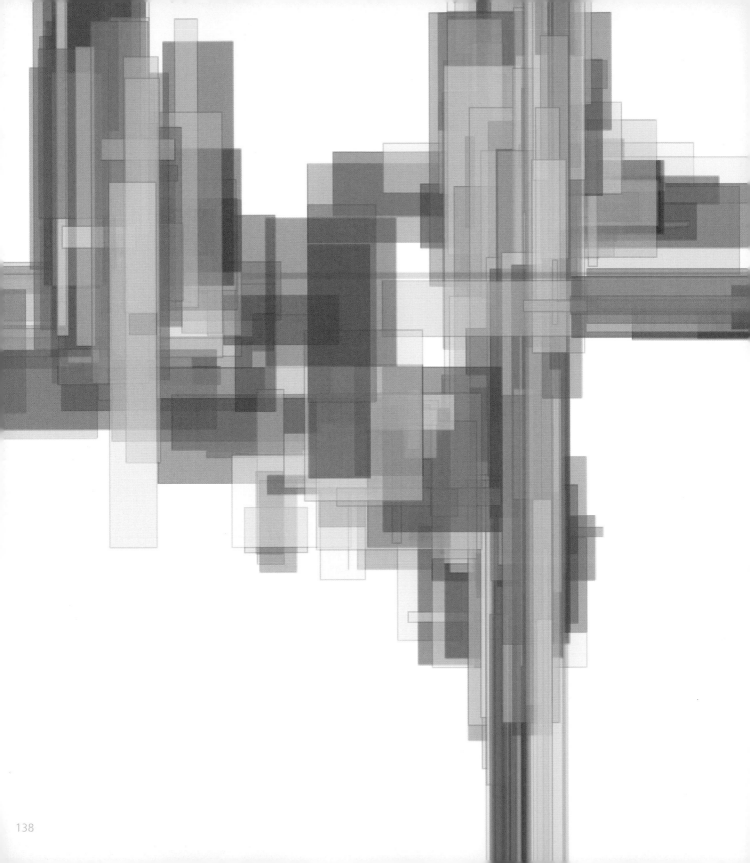

[1h]

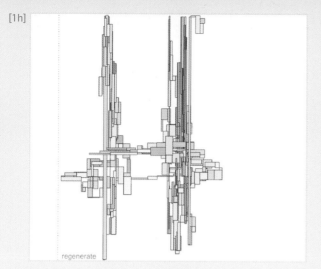

regenerate

[1i]

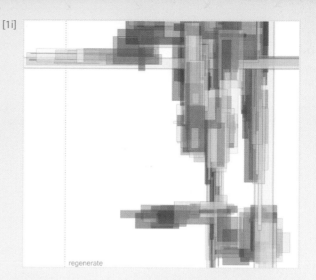

regenerate

comp001h

I removed the **xi**, **yi**, and **si** lines from the last iteration and replaced them with some new code. This time, I added some script to scale and position **dapoint** next to the previous copy of **dapoint**. **ox** and **oy** are the old **x** and **y** positions, and **nx** and **ny** are the new ones. I changed **dapoint** to contain 11 frames of the same 100✕100 pixel square with its registration point in the top-left corner, but I filled it with a different color in each frame. Here are the initial settings:

```
var jlim:Number = 3;
var klim:Number = 7;

var ox:Number = 210;
var oy:Number = 210;
```

And here's the inner **for** loop in full:

```
for (var l=0; l<18; l++) {
    var newmc:MovieClip = attachMovie("dapoint",
    ➥ "mc" + depth, depth++);
    var nx:Number = ox + (j + 1) *
    ➥ (Math.random() * 40 - 20) / (k + 1);
    var ny:Number = oy + (k + 1) *
    ➥ (Math.random() * 40 - 20) / (j + 1);
    nx = Math.abs(nx);
    ny = Math.abs(ny);
    nx %= 420;
    ny %= 420;
    newmc._x = nx;
    newmc._y = ny;
    newmc._xscale = ox - nx;
    newmc._yscale = oy - ny;
    newmc._alpha = 100;
    newmc.gotoAndStop(Math.floor(Math.random()
    ➥ * newmc._totalframes+1));
    ox = nx;
    oy = ny;
}
```

comp001i

Lastly, I made a slight modification to the code and changed **dapoint** to a much larger rectangle so that the rectangles overlap and produce blended colors. The code change I made was just to reduce the alpha:

```
newmc._alpha = 50;
```

The iterative model for generating graphic structures is quite effective when the specifics are known. With a series of repeated steps, you can construct some truly amazing things using simple rules. I believe that this particular set of rules allows for some beautiful effects because of the commonality between the groupings. Common multiples allow the user to see changes in individual structure, as well as the structures themselves.

My suggestion for immediate gratification is to change the basic graphic object. When you do this, keep in mind the degrees to which the object will be rotated, how variations in scale and color might affect the overall appearance, and how individual objects might look when grouped into multiples. Of course, another good change to make is to the number of rows and columns. The placement code has been written in such a way that changing the limits of the grid space will automatically scale and size the objects to fit within it. A change that would be rather tricky to implement, but enjoyable to observe, would be the proportional displacement of each object grouping according to some persistent variable.

Lorenz attractors

Any system expressed in coupled nonlinear differential equations is bound to produce some interesting results. There are many such systems, either invented or discovered. One such system is the so-called Lorenz attractor, the results of which produce beautiful butterflylike results.

For this movie, you have only one frame that contains all of the code. The other element is a movie clip called **line** that is exported from the Library with the name **line**. This clip consists of a 300✕300 pixel square, with its registration point set one-third of the way in from the top-left corner at 100✕100 pixels. Here's the code for the first frame of the main movie:

```
var x0:Number = Math.random() * 10 / 10;
var y0:Number = Math.random() * 20;
var z0:Number = Math.random() * 10;
var h:Number = 0.01;
var a:Number = 10.0;
var b:Number = 28.0;
var c:Number = 8.0 / 3.0;
var depth:Number = 0;

for (var n = 0; n<1000; n++) {
  var x1:Number = x0 + h * a * (y0 - x0);
  var y1:Number = y0 + h * (x0 * (b - z0) - y0);
  var z1:Number = z0 + h * (x0 * y0 - c * z0);
  var newmc:MovieClip = attachMovie("line", "newmc" + depth, depth++);
  newmc._x = x0 * 10 + 210;
  newmc._y = y0 * 10 + 210;
  newmc._xscale = (x1 - x0) * 10;
  newmc._yscale = (y1 - y0) * 10;
  x0 = x1;
  y0 = y1;
  z0 = z1;
}
stop();
```

The key variables

x0, **y0**, and **z0** = The initial starting point, and subsequently the previous point values.
x1, **y1**, and **z1** = The new point values.
h, **a**, **b**, and **c** = The Lorenz constants. It's best not to change these or you'll no longer have a Lorenz attractor.

It works like this. You take an initial set of values, run them through some equations, and use the results for the next seed of values. Then you repeat this process thousands of times, each time marking the progress of the transformation with the instantiation of a new movie clip. The end result is the visualization of transformation over time.

Of course, doing this with random equations usually results in a point that hovers around for a bit and then shoots off the screen toward some infinity (or zero). The trick, then, is to find a set of equations that produce a deterministic result, while remaining chaotic in nature. Systems of this class possess basins of attraction.

So here's the formula, as applied to Flash. Start with some initial random values in 3D space (**x0**, **y0**, **z0**). Specify and calculate all constants to be used in the iteration. For this example, you'll use the Lorenz constants. Notice that one of the constants is an irrational number (variable **c**). Changing these may produce some interesting results, but it is not recommended.

Next, and as a massive, swooping step, calculate the first 1,000 points of the system and render them to the stage. To do this, you begin by making the first transformation, calculating new values for **x**, **y**, and **z**, and assigning them to temporary variables **x1**, **y1**, and **z1**. Next, you name and create a new movie clip, and then finally position and scale the new movie clip to stretch from the last point (**x0**, **y0**, **z0**) to the newly calculated point (**x1**, **y1**, **z1**). In this example, you must multiply the **x** and **y** values by 10 to more fully fill the stage. Also, you offset the point so that the entire system is centered on the stage. Finally, you assign the newly calculated value to the seed values for the next iteration. In this process, old values are discarded but not forgotten (they live now as movie clips on the stage).

comp002b

For this first iteration, I changed the initial starting point and increased the number of iterations. I also commented out the lines that set the scale of the movie clip. I changed **line** to a small black circle with a dotted outline. This gives an effect where you can easily trace the path of the attractor.

```
var x0:Number = -12.1
var y0:Number = -22;
var z0:Number = 28.7;

for (var n=0;n<1500;n++)
```

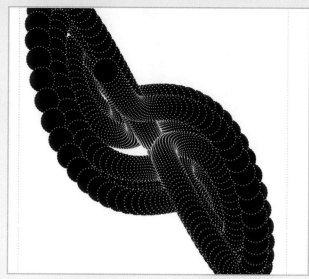

comp002c

This time I changed the start point back to a random value, reduced the number of iterations, and brought back the scale. I changed **line** to a simple outline of a circle, so that you can see an almost wire-frame representation.

```
var x0:Number = (Math.random() * 50 - 25) / 2;
var y0:Number = (Math.random() * 50 - 25) / 2;
var z0:Number = Math.random() * 25 / 2;

for (var n=0;n<750;n++)

newmc._xscale = z0 * 5;
newmc._yscale = z0 * 5;
```

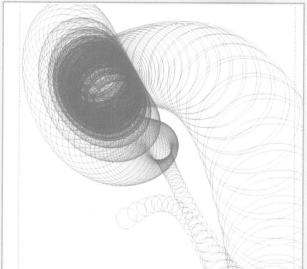

comp002d

I kept exactly the same code in this iteration but changed the shape of **line** to make a cross filled with white. This produces some amazing, seemingly 3D shapes.

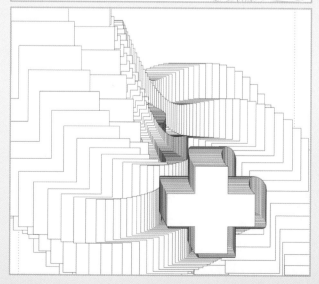

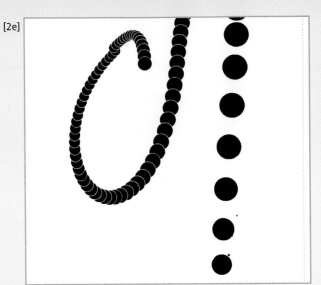

[2e]

comp002e

I hardly changed the code again for this one—I just decreased the number of iterations and added one other line. The main change is to the graphic, where this time I chose to animate it with a simple tween. **line** now contains a small, off-center circle that rotates 360 degrees around the center point over 60 frames. The new line goes just after the scale lines. It is used to start each successive duplication of the movie clip at the next frame, so that they appear to follow each other rather than starting from the same point.

```
for (var n=0;n<100;n++)

newmc.gotoAndPlay(1  + (n % 60));
```

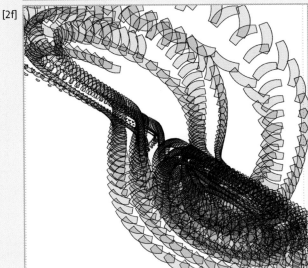

[2f]

comp002f

I removed the new line from the previous iteration and went back to just changing the existing code. The shape is back to being only one frame and in this case is a split circle.

```
var x0:Number = (Math.random() * 50 - 25) / 4;
var y0:Number = (Math.random() * 50 - 25) / 4;
var z0:Number = Math.random() * 25 / 4;

for (var n=0;n<500;n++)

newmc._x = x0 * 12 + 210;
newmc._y = y0 * 12 + 210;
newmc._xscale = z0 * 5;
newmc._yscale = z0 * 5;
```

[2g]

comp002g

Here, as I've done in previous experiments, I changed the graphic to be a random letter. **line** now contains a dynamic text box with the instance name **ch**, and a new line is added to the code to generate a random letter each time.

```
newmc._xscale = z0 * 7;
newmc._yscale = z0 * 7;
newmc.ch.text = String.fromCharCode(Math.random() *
➥ 26 + 96);
```

comp002h

In this iteration, I removed the letter code, replacing the text box with a simple circle, and went for something completely different. Instead of just drawing one attractor, why not draw three? I just copied the duplication and positioning code another couple of times, but changed the positioning. I also added a magnitude variable to use as a multiplier. This is initialized at the beginning of the code with this line:

```
var mg:Number = 8;
```

I then used this value to control the scale and position of the attractors. Try setting it to a smaller number, say 2, to see the difference. Here are the three duplication and positioning code blocks in full (which reside in the main **for** loop):

```
var newmc:MovieClip = attachMovie("line", "newmc" +
➡ depth, depth++);
newmc._x = x0 * mg + 210;
newmc._y = y0 * mg + 210;
newmc._xscale = (z0 + 5) * mg;
newmc._yscale = (z0 + 5) * mg;

newmc = attachMovie("line", "newmc" + depth, depth++);
newmc._x = y0 * mg + 210;
newmc._y = z0 * mg + 210;
newmc._xscale = (x0 + 5) * mg;
newmc._yscale = (x0 + 5) * mg;

newmc = attachMovie("line", "newmc" + depth, depth++);
newmc._x = z0 * mg + 210;
newmc._y = x0 * mg + 210;
newmc._xscale = (y0 + 5) * mg;
newmc._yscale = (y0 + 5) * mg;
```

comp002i

For the final iteration, I kept the **mg** variable, but I used it only to draw one attractor. I removed two of the code blocks and left the last one looking like this:

```
var newmc:MovieClip = attachMovie("line", "newmc" +
➡ depth, depth++);
newmc._x = z0 * mg;
newmc._y = y0 * mg + 210;
newmc._xscale = 50;
newmc._yscale = (x0 + 5) * mg;
```

I changed **line** to a long, thin rectangle.

You may have noticed that the **z** value is completely ignored during the creation of the new movie clip. While the current process renders quite beautiful and complex paths, it is actually an inadequate 2D representation of the system. For further exploration, you may choose to use the **z** value as an attribute effecter. The most obvious use of the **z** value is as a scaler, so that objects with higher **z** values appear larger and closer to the user, while objects with lower **z** values appear smaller and farther away. You could also apply it to the alpha of a movie clip, or rotation. You might even use the **z** value as an index into a many-framed movie clip, for unusual changes in color, shape, or behavior.

If you're comfortable with this attractor, I suggest you next attempt to implement the Ikeda attractor, which is a fantastic, painterly system.

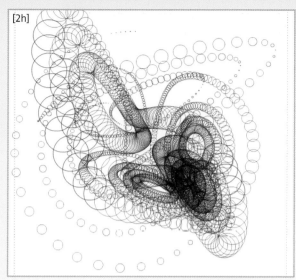

[2h]

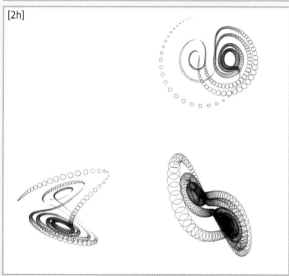

[2h]

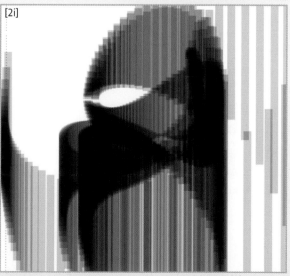

[2i]

Recursive inspiration

This is a lightweight computational piece that creates a number of braided, looping, ropelike structures. The synchronized twisting and looping is a unique effect achieved through elementary trigonometry and a function of variable flow.

This experiment is slightly more complicated to create than the previous two because there is code in multiple functions. The layer structure of the movie is similar to that of the first experiment, with a background and a **logic** layer that contains the code. Also, the movie clip that you're duplicating is a bit more complicated. The actual graphic is held in a clip called **icon**. This is, in turn, held in another movie clip called **nug**, which is made up of two layers with five frames in each of them. The top layer holds code, and the bottom layer holds **icon**. **icon** is tweened over the first four frames so that it increases in size, giving the impression of growth when a new clip is duplicated. Now that the movie is set up, let's go back to the main stage and look at the code.

```
var jlim:Number = 3;
var depth:Number = 0;
for(var j=0; j<jlim; j++) {
  var newmc:MovieClip = attachMovie("nug",
  ➥ "newmc" + depth, depth++);
  newmc._x = j * 420 / jlim + 210 / jlim;
  newmc._y = 210;
  newmc._xscale = 20 - Math.abs(5 *
  ➥ (j - (jlim - 1) / 2));
  newmc._yscale = 20 - Math.abs(5 *
  ➥ (j - (jlim - 1) / 2));
  newmc.depth = depth;
  newmc.frame = 0;
  newmc.onEnterFrame = iterate;

  newmc = attachMovie("nug", "newmc" + depth,
  ➥ depth++);
  newmc._x = j * 420 / jlim + 210 / jlim;
  newmc._y = 210;
  newmc._xscale = -20 + Math.abs(5 *
  ➥ (j - (jlim - 1) / 2));
  newmc._yscale = -20 + Math.abs(5 *
  ➥ (j - (jlim - 1) / 2));
  newmc.depth = depth;
  newmc.frame = 0;
  newmc.onEnterFrame = iterate;
}
var theta:Number = 0;
var v:Number = 0;
var rot:Number;
onEnterFrame = function () {
  rot = -30 * Math.sin(Math.PI / 180 * theta);
  theta += v;
  v += Math.random() * 2 -1;
  v = Math.max(v, -5);
  v = Math.min(v, 5);
};
function iterate() {
  if (this.frame++ > 2) {
    if (this.depth < 80) {
      var newnug:MovieClip =
      ➥ this.attachMovie("nug", "newnug", 2);
```

```
      newnug._y = -100;
      newnug._xscale = 98;
      newnug._yscale = 98;
      newnug._rotation = _root.rot;
      newnug.depth = this.depth + 1;
      newnug.frame = 0;
      newnug.onEnterFrame = iterate;
      delete this.onEnterFrame;
    }
  }
}
stop();
```

The key variables

jlim = The number of ropes on the screen
rot = A value that controls the coil of the rope
theta = An incremental factor used in calculating the rotation
v = A random velocity factor used to increase **theta**

The bulk of the computational work is performed within the **iterate** function. Each long rope is the result of the instantiation of a single, recursive **nug**. **Recursion** is the process of movie clips making copies of themselves. **nug** uses recursion to make itself into a rope.

Recursion is always a tricky business, and if you're not careful it will quickly consume all available memory resources until the computer goes insane. If left unchecked, the **nug** movie clip would replicate itself into eternity, so in this project, the conditional is determined by the variable **depth**, which is increased with each successive **nug**. If the depth is less than 80, it's OK to make another copy; if not, then you stop it.

Admittedly, the code used eventually builds a giant parent/child chain that grows up into absurd levels of hierarchy, which some might say is a bit flaky. My justification is that Flash handles it exceptionally well, and the advantages of nested transformations make it worth the expense.

You position the new movie clip at the end of the current one and reduce its size by only a bit. Remember that all transformations will have exponential effects due to the nested nature of this assembly. You then use a variable at the root level to determine the change in rotation. This allows the user or a separate function to guide the building process somewhat. The unique twisting and looping effect is achieved by referencing the variable **rot** within the root level. At any given time, **rot** is a sinusoidal function of a randomly accelerating position value. Using a system such as this, many variations of growth can be derived by simply modifying the number magnitudes.

One of the most important steps of the replication is incrementing **depth** so that you don't replicate to infinity. Take it out if you really want to understand why (after you save your work, of course).

The rest of the project is merely the initial instantiation of a few **nugs** to start the show. This could have really been anything, but for this project, I decided to use an iterative loop to create six **nugs**, arranged in pairs, backs against each other, facing in opposite directions. I enjoy watching self-similar braids unfold in multiple scales.

comp003b

First of all, I changed the code so that there was only one braid, and it now loops in a different way. I also changed the graphic. All of these code changes are in the **for** loop:

```
var jlim:Number = 1;

// make original
newmc._x = 210;
newmc._y = 210;
newmc._xscale = 20;
newmc._yscale = 20;
newmc._rotation = 90;

// make opposite
newmc._x = 210;
newmc._y = 210;
newmc._xscale = -20;
newmc._yscale = 20;
newmc._rotation = -90;
```

[3b]

comp003c

This time I removed the block of code that creates the reflection and just duplicated the original one at three different angles. Here's the loop:

```
var jlim:Number = 3;

for(var j=0; j<jlim; j++) {
  var newmc:MovieClip = attachMovie("nug", "newmc" +
  ➥ depth, depth++);
  newmc._x = 210;
  newmc._y = 210;
  newmc._xscale = 20;
  newmc._yscale = 20;
  newmc._rotation = 120 * j;
  newmc.depth = depth;
  newmc.frame = 0;
  newmc.onEnterFrame = iterate;
}
```

[3c]

comp003d

For this iteration, I increased the number of arms to seven and changed the graphic slightly to get these spirals that remind me of ancient Greek patterns.

```
var jlim:Number = 7;

newmc._rotation = 360 / 7 * j;
```

[3d]

comp003e

I made another couple of small changes to the code here, but the major visual difference comes from the **icon**. It is now a long, thin, vertical bar with a ball at each end. This produces some wildly different results compared to the previous iterations. Here are the code changes to frame 1:

```
var jlim:Number = 1;

newmc._y = 420;
newmc._xscale = 30;
newmc._yscale = 30;
```

Notice that I've changed to a single braid that grows up from the bottom of the screen. I've also removed the rotation line and changed the **onEnterFrame** slightly to increase the rotation of the braid:

```
rot = -60 * Math.sin(Math.PI / 180 * theta);
```

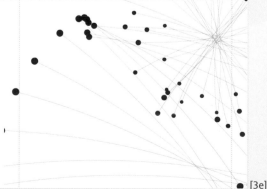

[3e]

comp003f

This effect is similar to the last, but I tightened the velocity, among other things, to give an overlapping alpha effect. The shape has been changed to a simple rectangle. These are the changes to the **for** loop:

```
newmc._y = 400;
newmc._xscale = 20;
newmc._yscale = 20;
```

And these are the changes to the **onEnterFrame**:

```
rot = -10 * Math.sin(Math.PI / 180 * theta);
v += Math.random() * 6 - 3;
```

Finally, I changed the scaling in the **iterate** function to 96 so that it scales away a bit quicker.

comp003g

For this iteration, I went back to having multiple braids, this time four moving away from the center. I also changed **icon** to 11 frames of the same square, but with a different color in each one. To randomly choose one of these frames, I added the following line to the **for** loop:

```
newmc.icon.gotoAndStop(Math.floor(Math.random()
➥ * newmc.icon._totalframes) + 1);
```

Make sure that **icon** has an instance name of **icon** within **nug**. I changed some in the **for** loop as well, to give different rotation and scaling. Here are the rest of the changes:

```
var jlim:Number = 4;

newmc._y = 210;
var scl:Number = Math.random() * 30 + 20;
newmc._xscale = scl;
newmc._yscale = scl;
newmc._rotation = 90 * j + 40 + Math.random() * 20;
newmc._alpha = 50;
```

I also changed the rotation in **onEnterFrame**:

```
rot = -50 * Math.sin(Math.PI / 180 * theta);
```

comp003h

This time I made some major changes. The code now starts with this:

```
var depth:Number = 0;
var n:Number = 0;
var v:Number = 0;
```

This is followed by a new **makeNew** function, which contains the duplication and positioning code:

```
function makenew() {
  // make original
  var newmc:MovieClip = attachMovie("nug",
  ➥ "newmc"+depth, depth++);
  newmc._x = (n+1)*420/6;
  newmc._y = 105;
  var scl:Number = 20;
  newmc._xscale = scl;
  newmc._yscale = scl;
```

```
  newmc._rotation = 180;
  newmc.depth = depth;
  newmc.frame = 0;
  if (Math.random()>.1) {
    newmc.icon.petal._visible = false;
  }
  newmc.onEnterFrame = iterate;
  n++;
}
```

The **onEnterFrame** function now starts with some code that will place five new **nugs** at random intervals, by calling the **makeNew** function:

```
onEnterFrame = function() {
  if(Math.random() < .4 && n < 5){
    makenew();
  }
```

I also made some major changes to **nug**. I created a new movie clip called **petal**. This is a long, thin, horizontal bar with a ball at each end. This clip sits inside **icon** with the instance name **petal**. **icon** itself is a larger circle with the left-hand ball of **petal** centered in it. You'll notice in the **makeNew** function the following code:

```
if (Math.random()>.1) {
  newmc.icon.petal._visible = false;
}
```

This means that there is a 1 in 10 chance of a petal appearing. The rest of the code in **iterate** is similar, but there are some changes to allow the loops to follow their own paths. Here's the code:

```
function iterate() {
  if (this.depth<120) {
    var newnug:MovieClip =
    ➥ this.attachMovie("nug", "newnug", 2);
    newnug._y = -100;
    newnug._xscale = 98.7;
    newnug._yscale = 98.7;
    newnug._rotation = _root.rot +
    ➥ Math.random() * 10 - 5;
    newnug.depth = this.depth+1;
    newnug.frame = 0;
    if (Math.random()>.1) {
      newnug.icon.petal._visible = false;
    }
    newnug.onEnterFrame = iterate;
    delete this.onEnterFrame;
  }
}
```

comp003i

This code is similar to the previous code, but with a few notable changes. First of all, the following changes have been applied to the **makeNew** function:

```
newmc._x = 210;
newmc._y = 210;
var scl:Number = 12;
newmc._rotation = 180 * (n % 2);
```

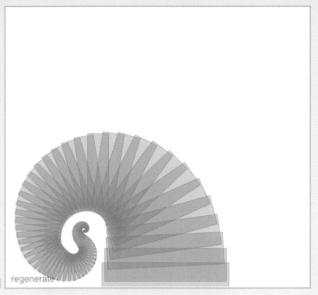

[3f] regenerate

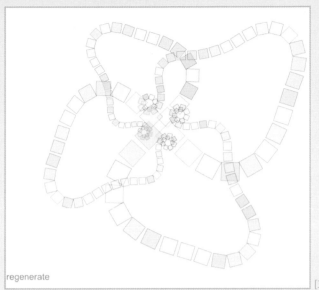

regenerate [3g]

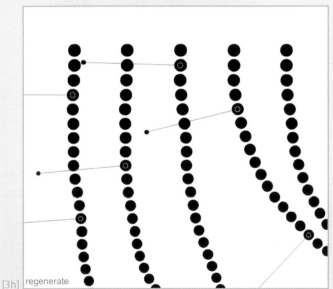

[3h] regenerate

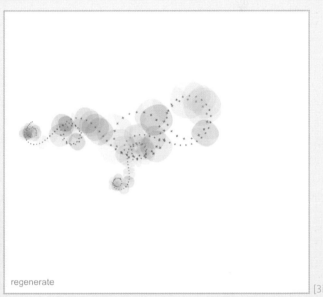

regenerate [3i]

The graphics have also changed radically again. **icon** is now a simple cross, but it contains a clip called **node** that has 33 frames of different colored circles affected by the following code in **iterate**:

```
newnug.icon.node._alpha = 20;
newnug.icon.node.gotoAndStop(Math.floor(Math.
➥ random() * newnug.icon.node._totalframes) + 1);
```

I also changed the **if** statement in **iterate** so that petals appear much more frequently.

To really bring the beauty out from this piece, I suggest making a few quick changes to the braid object's graphic.

Try adding thorns, or horizontal lines, or anything large and transparent for some really interesting effects. Another point of modification might be the magnitude of the constants used in the referenced sinusoidal equation. This will cause all kinds of strange growth behavior, as only slight numerical changes will bring about wild effects in recursive constructs. One change to be cautious of is modifying the maximum depth value for each rope. This value is initially at 80, and changing it to be much larger than 100 will result in some very slow rendering times and memory-intensive object structures. Plus, since by default the rope's scale decreases, objects beyond the depth of 80 aren't much bigger than 1 pixel once they're rendered.

Recursive circles

This is another great example of recursion: a set of concentric circles, each just touching the one below it. Run **comp004a.swf** to see it in action. I'm often more inspired by the end result of a piece than I am to make the piece in the first place, so sometimes I force myself to build something with simple rules that I've used in other projects, while introducing some new bit of randomness. The first few iterations are usually shapes that I expect, while after some tinkering time, they slowly (but sometimes quite suddenly) mutate in constructions I never knew possible. The driving motivation I use in creating pieces such as this is "maximum effect with minimum graphic composure." I view computational art much the same way I do furniture fabric: if I can stare at it day after day and still not recognize the machine that produced the pattern in it, it's a good piece of work.

I think with its subdued color increment and sea creature–like spiraling nature, this computational piece is a good example of what I'm trying to achieve.

This movie has a similar construction to the previous one, with a single frame of code on the root and a movie clip called **nug** containing some graphics. There are a couple of differences, though. The graphic is placed directly in its own layer in **nug** rather than in a separate movie clip, and there is an instance of **nug** attached to the main stage with code as a first action. This clip is scaled to fit the screen and has been given the instance name **mothernug**. The graphic on **nug** itself is just a dotted outline of a circle. **nug** is exported from the Library with the linkage name **nug**.

The code is split into two functions. Here's the code in the first function:

```
regen.onRelease = init;
init();
function init() {
  rscale = Math.random() * 50 + 47;
  rrot = 2 * Math.random() * 7 - 3;
  attachMovie("nug", "mothernug", 0);
  mothernug._x = Stage.width / 2;
  mothernug._y = Stage.height / 2;
  mothernug._width = Stage.width;
  mothernug._height = Stage.height;
  mothernug._rotation = Math.random() * 360;
  mothernug.depth = 0;
  mothernug.onEnterFrame = iterate;
}
```

The first line links the **init** function to the regenerate button, which is on the stage with an instance name **regen**. The **init** function then simply initializes some random scale and rotation values. Next is the **iterate** function, which should look familiar by now:

```
function iterate() {
  if (this.depth<80) {
    var newnug:MovieClip = this.attachMovie("nug", "newnug", 1);
    var rot:Number = this._rotation + rrot;
    var scale:Number = rscale;
    newnug._x = (100 - scale) * Math.cos(Math.PI / 180 * rot);
    newnug._y = (100 - scale) * Math.sin(Math.PI / 180 * rot);
    newnug._xscale = scale;
    newnug._yscale = scale;
    newnug._rotation = rot;
    newnug.depth = this.depth + 1;
    newnug.onEnterFrame = iterate;
  }
  delete this.onEnterFrame;
}
```

Again, it has a **depth** check to prevent the code from escaping from the computer and taking over the world! (OK, so it won't really do that, but you know what I mean.)

The key variables

rscale = A random value used to alter the scale of successive recursions.
rrot = A random value used to alter the rotation of successive recursions.
depth = The limit of new recursions. Once this limit is reached, the movie stops.
rot = The rotation value for the current clip.
scale = The scale value for the current clip.

It's basically a simple inward-growing recursive construction. The intersecting strokes of consecutive copies of the same object create subtle spirals inward toward an unknown point.

Initially, a single instance of a recursive movie clip, named **mothernug**, is dynamically placed onto the stage as a base for the recursion. This copy then begins the same growth process by adding instances of **newnug** within itself, until a maximum of 80 copies has been made. You use a couple of trigonometric functions to place each copy so that its perimeter lies flush with the perimeter of its parent. With a little rotation added, this provides you with the satisfying "spiraling" effect that you see in completed recursions.

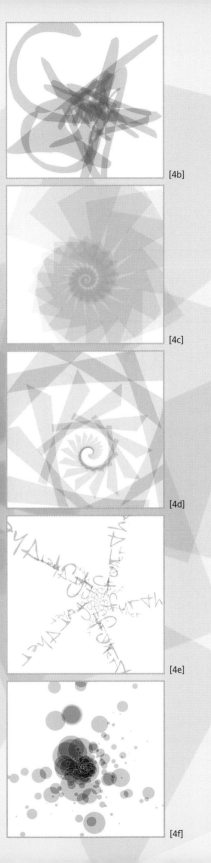

[4b]

[4c]

[4d]

[4e]

[4f]

comp004b

For the first iteration, I decided to try out a trick that I find interesting: replacing the shapes with random letters. This is done by adding the following code to the end of **iterate**:

```
this.fg.text = String.fromCharCode(Math.random() * 26 + 97);
```

This selects a random character, which is then fed into a dynamic text box as its text property, that sits on the stage in place of the graphic in **nug**. Remember to embed the outlines for the font, or you won't see anything. I also changed the depth limit to 10 so that the letters weren't too cluttered to read.

comp004c

For this iteration, I removed the letter code that I added last time and replaced the graphic with a simple translucent square with its registration point in the bottom-right corner. The first code change that I made was to the **init** function:

```
rscale = Math.random() * 9 + 88;
rrot = Math.random() * 3 - 1;
```

comp004d

There is very little change to this iteration, but it makes some totally different and really beautiful images. The only change to the code is that I reduced the depth limit to 50. I also changed the graphic to a vertical blue bar, a little to the right of the registration point.

comp004e

Again, I kept to the basic idea of the last experiment, only changing the graphic to a text string with the word "further" in it. All the code is exactly the same as the previous version.

comp004f

I kept to a similar basic setup once more, changing the scale and rotation code in **init** and the **nug** graphic. Here's the code change:

```
rscale = Math.random() * 5 + 94;
rrot = 137.5;
```

The graphic is now a set of increasingly smaller circles heading off to the right from the registration point.

comp004g

A bit of a change this time. Now instead of the graphic being directly on the **nug** clip, it's inside another movie clip called **node** that is placed onto **nug** and given the instance name **node**. The graphic in **node** is 32 frames of a filled cross in a different color every frame. There is also a **stop** action on frame 1. In **init**, I've added some code:

```
mothernug.node.gotoAndStop(Math.floor
➥ (Math.random() * mothernug._totalframes + 1));
mothernug.node._alpha = 20;
```

This code selects a random frame—and therefore color—in **node**, and sets its alpha to 20. I also changed the code in **iterate** to add a **for** loop to give each **nug** children. Here's the complete new code for that function:

```
function iterate() {
    if (this.depth<6) {
        var children:Number = Math.random() * 2 + 1;
        for(var n = 0; n<children; n++){
            var newnug:MovieClip = this.attachMovie
            ➥ ("nug", "newnug" + n, n);
            var rot:Number = Math.random() * 360;
            newnug._x = 50 * Math.cos
            ➥ (Math.PI / 180 * rot);
            newnug._y = 50 * Math.sin
            ➥ (Math.PI / 180 * rot);
            var scale:Number = 50 + Math.random() * 50;
            newnug._xscale = scale;
            newnug._yscale = scale;
            newnug._rotation = rot;
            newnug.depth = this.depth + 1;
            newnug.node.gotoAndStop(Math.floor
            ➥ (Math.random() * newnug.node._total
            ➥ frames + 1));
            newnug.node._alpha = 20;
            newnug.onEnterFrame = iterate;
        }
    }
    delete this.onEnterFrame;
}
```

comp004h

This iteration is similar to the previous one. I still have 32 different colored shapes in **node**, but this time they're almost the opposite of what they were. They're what's left of a square once a cross has been removed from it—just a collection of corners. I changed the code in **iterate** to give the shapes an alpha value of 80, making them a bit harder. I also altered the second frame as well. Here's what I altered:

```
if (this.depth<6) {

newnug._x = Math.random() * 100 - 50
newnug._y = Math.random() * 100 - 50
var scale:Number = 60 + Math.random() * 50;
```

comp004i

For the final iteration, I made a few changes. I set the graphic of node to be a large cross consisting of two dotted lines. I changed **iterate** so that the alpha value for **node** was 100. The only other changes I made were also in **iterate**, where I set the depth limit to 5 and removed the rotation line so that the crosses would all have the same orientation.

With a bit of experimentation, the rules underlying this construction method will allow for some very unusual results. For example, try changing the graphic to a simple line originating from the center. Also try transposing each new child somewhere further from the perimeter. You'll be surprised with just how fast and chaotic the construction method actually becomes when using "nonspherical" shapes.

[4g]   [4h]   [4i]

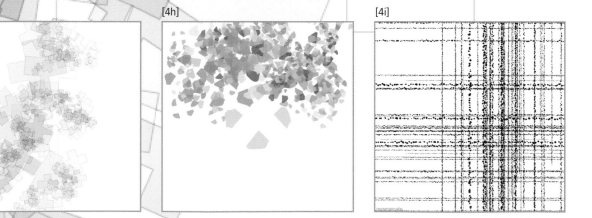

Keith Peters lives in the vicinity of Boston, MA, in the US with his wife, Kazumi, and their daughter, Kristine. He has been working with Flash since 1999, and has coauthored many books for friends of ED, including the groundbreaking *Extending Flash MX 2004: Complete Guide and Reference to JavaScript Flash* and the latest edition of *New Masters of Flash: Volume 3*.

In 2001, Keith started the experimental Flash site www.bit-101.com on which he regularly posts new, cutting-edge, open source experiments. It features fairly simple graphics, usually relying on math and scripting to build complex forms and movements, and the site recently won an award at the Flashforward 2003 Flash Film Festival in the Experimental category. In addition to the experiments on this site, Keith has produced several highly regarded Flash tutorials that have been translated into many languages and are now posted on websites throughout the world.

Keith is currently working full time on Flash development and various writing projects.

keith peters
www.bit-101.com

Dot grid

This first experiment involves a simple grid of white dots. By applying a couple of trigonometry formulas to the position of the dots in three dimensions, you can get some pretty complex behaviors. So, in keeping with the theme of this book, let's see how slight changes to the formulas can create all kinds of variations.

First, you'll create one dot, and then you'll move on to create the grid. The background is black, so the dot is just a 2×2-pixel white circle, with no outline, made into a movie clip with the instance name **dot**, and exported with the same linkage name. That's pretty much it—the rest is just code on frame 1 of the main timeline. As you can see, this code consists of the initialization of some variables, a **for** loop to attach the dots, and a function called **move** to move them:

```
var fl:Number = 200;
var xcenter:Number = 270;
var ycenter:Number = 200;
var zcenter:Number = 75;
var num:Number = 0;
for (var i=-3; i<4; i++) {
    for (var j=-3; j<4; j++) {
        var dot:MovieClip = attachMovie("dot",
        ➥ "dot" + num, num);
        dot.x = i * 40;
        dot.y = 100;
        dot.z = j * 40;
        dot.zpos = dot.z + zcenter;
        dot.scale = fl / (fl + dot.zpos);
        dot.xheight = 10;
        dot.zheight = 10;
        dot.xspeed = 10;
        dot.zspeed = 10;
        dot.xangle = dot.x;
        dot.zangle = dot.z;
        dot.onEnterFrame = move;
        num++;
    }
}
function move() {
    var xwave:Number = Math.sin(this.xangle *
    ➥ Math.PI / 180) * this.xheight;
    var zwave:Number = Math.sin(this.zangle *
    ➥ Math.PI / 180) * this.zheight;
    this.ypos = this.y + xwave + zwave;
    this.xangle += this.xspeed;
    this.zangle += this.zspeed;
    this._x = this.x * this.scale + xcenter;
    this._y = this.ypos * this.scale + ycenter;
    this._xscale = this._yscale = this.scale *
    ➥ 100;
}
```

The key variables

fl = The focal length, or how deep the field of vision is.

xcenter = The horizontal center of the screen.

ycenter = The vertical center of the screen.

zcenter = The midpoint for the depth of the screen.

y = The camera position. A position of 0 is ground level.

x = The horizontal spacing between dots.

z = The depth spacing between dots.

zpos = The current depth of the dot.

scale = The current position of the dot according to the focal length.

xheight and **zheight** = Initialize variables for the height positions of the dot wave.

xspeed and **zspeed** = Initialize variables for the speed of the dot wave.

xangle and **zangle** = Variables for dot spacing on the wave.

xwave and **zwave** = Variables for working out the current dot position on the wave.

ypos = The current dot position on the wave.

i and **j** = Loop counters for rows and columns, respectively.

num = The counter to name the duplicate dots.

The previous code creates a series of 49 dots and assigns them **x** and **z** values in a grid pattern. Take a look at the result in **exp1.swf**. The code in the **move** function uses the **x** and **z** coordinates as the horizontal position and depth. It then calculates a moving sine wave along the x-axis and another along the z-axis, and uses these waves to calculate the **y**, or height, of each dot. Then it plots the perspective of each dot and its screen **_x** and **_y** positions and scale.

In each of the following iterations (with the exception of the final one), I've returned to the original code (found in **exp1.fla**) to apply changes between experiments, rather than accumulating the changes as I progress.

exp1-1
By changing these values in the **for** loop, the wave gets more pronounced, like a rough sea:

```
dot.xheight = 15;
dot.zheight = -15;
```

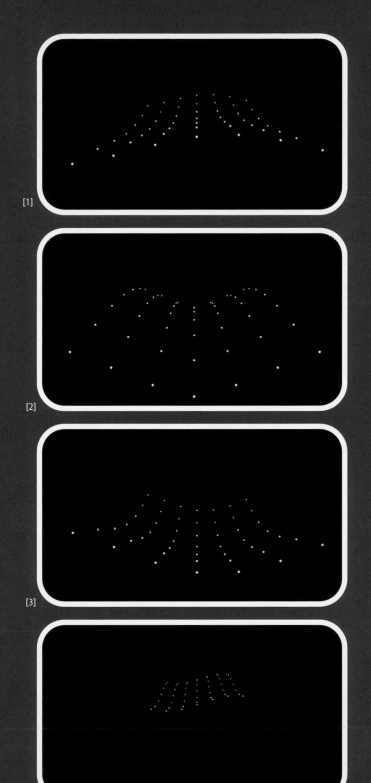

[1]

exp1-2
Using the following values, you'll get a wave with opposite pulses on the **x** and **z**, because **Math.abs** converts all the negative values to positive ones. I also reversed the **zspeed**. It gives a "breathing" effect.

```
dot.xheight = 25;
dot.zspeed = 10;
dot.xangle = Math.abs(dot.x);
```

exp1-3
I tried something different this time, taking control away from the code and giving it to the mouse, thus making it interactive. First, set the other variables back to their original states, and then add these two lines to the bottom of the **move** function:

```
this.xheight = this.zheight =
➡ (200 - _root._ymouse) / 5;
this.xspeed = this.zspeed =
➡ (_root._xmouse - 270) / 10;
```

Now just move the mouse around and watch the results.

[2]

exp1-4
For this experiment I took the **zpos** and **scale** lines out of the **for** loop and then put them back at the top of the **move** function:

```
this.zpos = this.z + zcenter;
this.scale = fl / (fl + this.zpos);
```

This allows the z-motion and perspective to take place in real time. Then add this to the bottom of the **move** code to update the motion:

```
this.z += 5;
if(this.z > 1000){
   this.z = -200;
}
```

[3]

This makes the grid swim off into the screen. Then when it gets really far away, you move it back in front of the screen so that it looks like another grid swimming past you.

[4]

exp1-5

Here, I went off on a different tangent again. This time, rather than applying the wave to the y-axis, I applied it to the x- and z-axes instead. This gives a strange shimmering effect like a calm lake. I also added some code to make the mouse control the speed of the shimmer. Replace the **move** function with this:

```
function move() {
    var xwave:Number = Math.sin(this.xangle *
    ➡ Math.PI / 180) * this.xheight;
    var zwave:Number = Math.sin(this.zangle *
    ➡ Math.PI / 180) * this.zheight;
    this.xpos = this.x + xwave;
    this.zpos = this.z + zwave + zcenter;
    this.scale = fl / (fl + this.zpos);
    this.xangle += this.xspeed;
    this.zangle += this.zspeed;
    this._x = this.xpos * this.scale + xcenter;
    this._y = this.y * this.scale + ycenter;
    this._xscale = this._yscale = this.scale *
    ➡ 100;
    this.zspeed = (_root._ymouse - 200) / 5;
    this.xspeed = (_root._xmouse - 270) / 5;
}
```

exp1-6

Move back to the original code again for this next strange effect. First, change the values of **xheight** and **xspeed** to **2** in the **for** loop:

```
dot.xheight = 2;
dot.xspeed = 2;
```

Then alter the **xwave** line in the **move** function so that it uses the tangent of **xangle** instead of the sine:

```
var xwave:Number = Math.tan(this.xangle *
➡ Math.PI / 180) * this.xheight;
```

This effect looks to me like eerie dismembered fingers playing an invisible piano.

exp1-7

As usual, return to the original code, and simply add these lines to the **move** function:

```
zcenter = zwave * 5 + 100;
this.zpos = this.z + zcenter;
this.scale = fl / (fl + this.zpos);
```

This updates the scale every frame for a pulsing effect.

exp1-8

Finally, change the preceding code slightly so that the pulses are affected by the **xwave** rather than the **zwave**:

```
zcenter = xwave * 5 + 100;
```

There are many properties to play about with in this code. The simplest thing to start with is the speed and height in the **for** loop. Make **xspeed** high and **zspeed** low, and **xheight** low and **zheight** high, and you'll start to get the idea of what's going on. Don't forget to try fractional numbers and negative numbers.

Next, go down to the **xangle** and **yangle** variables. These are the wave's initial angles, so if you set either one to a constant number (say **0**), then the whole row will move as one. By setting these variables to **x** and **z**, as I did at first, each point will be different. Try setting them to different combinations, such as these two:

```
xangle=x+z;      xangle=x+z;
zangle=x+z;      zangle=x-z;
```

Here are a couple of combinations where I've also changed some of the other factors:

```
xheight=10;      xheight=Math.sqrt(z*z+x*x)/2;
zheight=-10;     zheight=Math.sqrt(z*z+x*x)/5;
xspeed=10;       xspeed=10;
zspeed=-10;      zspeed=10;
xangle=x-z;      xangle=z/2;
zangle=x-z;      zangle=z/2;
```

Of course, this is all pseudo-code for simplicity, and you would need to prefix it with the object name **dot** where applicable.

You could spend all night on this alone. But there's even more stuff to play with in the **move** function. For instance, you can change the sine functions easily to cosine without much noticeable difference, but give it a try with **tan** like I did in **exp1-6.fla** to see the dramatic difference it makes. To counteract the craziness, it's best to lower the speed and height of the axis that you're experimenting on.

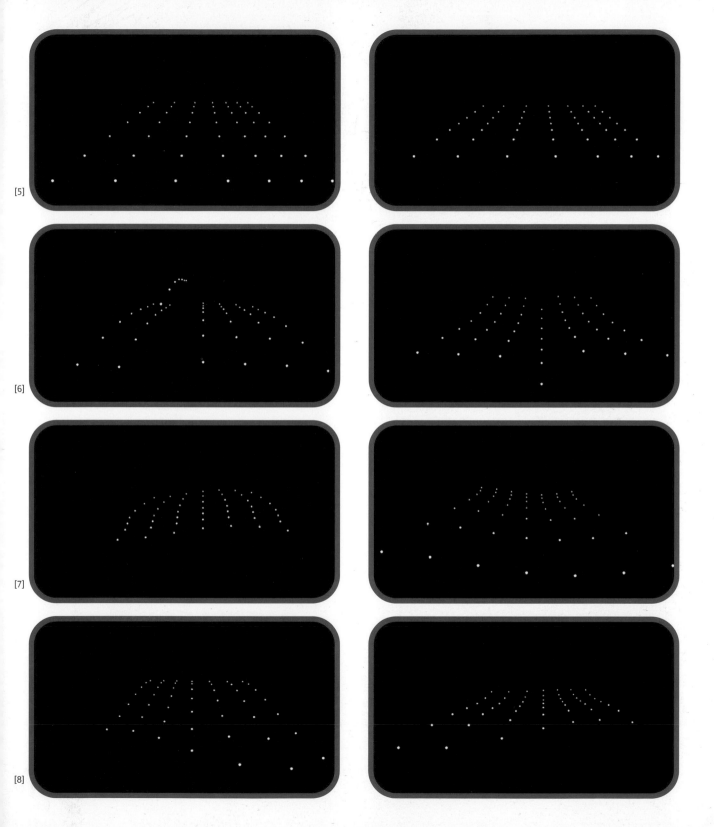

[5]

[6]

[7]

[8]

Fractal folia

For my next experiment, I want to delve into some recursion to create a fractal tree. This is where you have a function that calls itself, or in Flash terms you can have a movie clip with a copy of itself inside of it. Now if you directly try to drag an object from the Library into itself, Flash is going to complain, so you're going to trick it by using **attachMovie**. It's important to realize that Flash is complaining for a good reason here; you need to impose a limit on your recursion so that Flash doesn't try to go to infinity and beyond, and crash.

The base file of this experiment is **exp2.fla**. To build it from scratch, start by creating a new movie clip named **target**. Leave it completely blank and go back to the main movie. Now create another new movie clip named **line**, and draw a 100-pixel vertical hairline that has the registration point at its bottom end. Then drag a copy of **target** out of the Library, place it exactly at the top of the line, and give that instance of **target** the name **t1**. This is where you'll attach your movie copy. Next, go into the Library and give the **line** clip the linkage identifier **line**. Now on to the code.

All the code will be on the main timeline, as usual. Start off by initializing a couple of variables and creating your first line:

```
var count:Number = 0;
var limit:Number = 6;
var line:MovieClip = attachMovie("line",
➥ "line" + count, count++);
line._x = 250;
line._y = 400;
line.level = 0;
grow(line);
```

As you can see, the last line of code feeds the newly created **line** to a function called **grow**. This will take care of adding new lines to whatever **line** movie clip is fed to it.

Each time you attach a movie in a deeper level, you'll increase a variable called **level** by 1 so that you can check if you've surpassed your **limit**. If not, you'll attach two copies of **line** to the **target** movie clip, **t1**. Then you'll scale and rotate them a bit. Here's the code for the **grow** function:

```
function grow(line) {
  if (line.level < limit) {
    line.t1.attachMovie("line", "line" + 1, 1);
    line.t1.line1.level = line.level + 1;
    line.t1.line1._xscale =
    ➥ line.t1.line1._yscale = 50;
    line.t1.line1._rotation = -45;
    grow(line.t1.line1);

    line.t1.attachMovie("line", "line" + 2, 2);
    line.t1.line2.level = line.level + 1;
    line.t1.line2._xscale =
    ➥ line.t1.line2._yscale = 50;
    line.t1.line2._rotation = 45;
    grow(line.t1.line2);
  }
}
```

Test the movie to see a nice, conventional but basic, fractal tree. It's far from realistic, but it's good to play around with.

exp2-1

For the first iteration of this experiment, I tried changing a few of the scale and rotation variables. I created a fernlike curve where the branches grow only from one side of the tree by changing these two lines:

```
line.t1.line1._xscale = line.t1.line1._yscale = 60;
line.t1.line1._rotation = -20;
```

exp2-2

By changing these values again for both lines, you get something more akin to grass, or maybe a weeping willow:

```
line.t1.line1._xscale = line.t1.line1._yscale = 50;
line.t1.line1._rotation = 20;
line.t1.line2._xscale = line.t1.line2._yscale = 80;
line.t1.line2._rotation = 30;
```

exp2-3

When you get tired of manually playing with the numbers, and you have a feel for how the variables affect the tree, you can take another step toward realism by creating random numbers for the number of branches and the rotation.

You'll need to determine in advance the maximum and minimum branches that can be formed on each iteration. Say the number is between 1 and 4, and add this line to the **grow** function, right after the initial **if** statement:

```
var branch:Number = Math.random() * 3 + 1;
```

Next, you need to create a rotation value that will be between –30 and +30. Here's the revised code for **grow** in full:

```
function grow(line) {
  if (line.level < limit) {
    var branch:Number = Math.random() * 3 + 1;
    for(var i=0;i<branch;i++){
      var newLine:MovieClip =
      ➥ line.t1.attachMovie("line", "line" + i, i);
      newLine.level = line.level + 1;
      var scale:Number = 50;
      newLine._xscale = scale;
      newLine._yscale = scale;
      newLine._rotation = Math.random() * 60 - 30;
      grow(newLine);
    }
  }
}
```

Now, if you run the movie, you'll have a random tree every time.

Rather than rerunning the movie every time you want to generate a new tree, it's easier to make it happen at a mouse-click by placing all the initial code inside an **onMouseUp** handler:

```
onMouseUp = function(){
  count = 0;
  limit = 6;
  var line:MovieClip = attachMovie("line",
  ➥ "line" + count, count++);
  line._x = 250;
  line._y = 400;
  line.level = 0;
  grow(line);
};
```

This just starts the process fresh each time the mouse is clicked and released.

exp2-4

At the moment, the trees look a little more like umbelliferous wild chervil, but you can change this by giving them a random scale. Change the **scale** line to see what I mean:

```
var scale:Number = Math.random() * 10 + 50;
```

exp2-5

I experimented with the scale and rotation a bit more, and expanded them both to get these crazy trees:

```
var scale:Number = Math.random() * 30 + 50;
newLine._rotation = Math.random() * 180 - 90;
```

[1]

[2]

[3]

[4]

[5]

exp2-6

For this iteration I decided to make a radical change. Returning to the precraziness of `exp2-4.fla`, I added some animation to the tree. First, I reduced the number of levels to make the animation run more smoothly by setting the `limit` to `4`. Next, I added the following code toward the end of the `grow` function, just before the final call to `grow(newLine)`:

```
line.angle = 0;
line.onEnterFrame = function(){
   this.angle += 5;
   var rad:Number = this.angle * Math.PI / 180;
   this.t1._rotation = Math.sin(rad) * 60;
};
```

This sets the rotation of the branches along a sine wave, changing every frame to give you a tree that will sway from one side to the other in a virtual wind.

Try substituting rotation for scale to get some dancing trees—see `exp2-6a.fla` for an example.

[6]

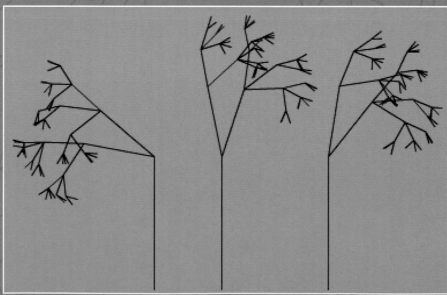

[6a]

158

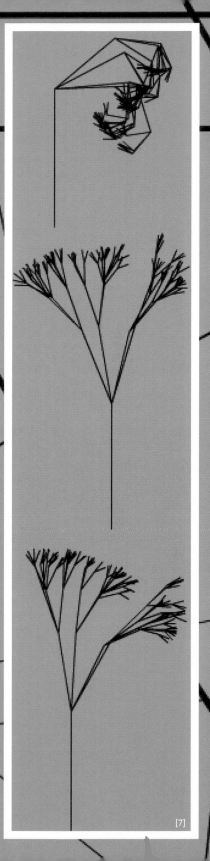

exp2-7

Here I changed the rotation so that it's controlled by the mouse instead of being on a sine curve. The **onEnterFrame** handler for **line** is now just this:

```
line.onEnterFrame = function(){
  this.t1._rotation = (_root._xmouse - 200) / 2;
};
```

exp2-8

I quite liked the effect of mouse control on the rotation, so I tried applying it to the scale as well by adding this line to the **onEnterFrame** handler:

```
this._xscale = this._yscale = (400 - _root._ymouse) / 2;
```

I love the way this iteration of the experiment goes totally out of control when you move the mouse to the extremes.

The key values to play around with to get some cool effects are the **limit** variable, and the scaling and rotation properties. Making the scale and rotation different for **line1** and **line2**, as you did in **exp2-1.fla**, can make some nice, lopsided trees. Don't forget to fool around with negative scale factors as well. Note that you shouldn't make **limit** too high or you'll be waiting forever for your tree to finish growing. Of course, there's no need to limit yourself to just a few branches either, but again, don't go too wild or Flash may crash!

[7]

159

Wire-frame organic

I make use of the trigonometric functions in Flash a great deal, as they're vital to any rotation and 3D functions and very useful for creating fluid, undulating motion. You'll make use of them for the latter purpose here to create some weird and wonderful wormlike wireframe structures.

First, make a movie clip with a shape inside it—any shape will do. I started with a simple black hairline circle, with no fill, that's 30 pixels in diameter. Try different shapes later for interesting results. Name this instance **shape** and set it to export with the same linkage name. You have the following code on frame 1:

```
var xspeed:Number = 1.32;
var yspeed:Number = .56;
var xradius:Number = 100;
var yradius:Number = 100;
var xangle:Number = 0;
var yangle:Number = 0;
var i:Number = 0;
var rot:Number = 0;

onEnterFrame = function () {
  var shape:MovieClip = attachMovie("shape",
➥ "shape"+ i , i++);
  xangle += xspeed;
  yangle += yspeed;
  var xrad:Number = xangle*Math.PI/180;
  var yrad:Number = yangle*Math.PI/180;
  shape._x = Math.sin(xrad)*xradius+270;
  shape._y = Math.cos(yrad)*yradius+200;
  shape._rotation = rot++;
  shape._alpha = 10;
  shape._xscale = Math.sin(xrad)*100;
  shape._yscale = Math.sin(yrad)*100;
};
```

The key variables

xspeed and **yspeed** = The speed at which the angles will change
xradius and **yradius** = The overall size of the worm's playing field
xangle and **yangle** = The current angle at which the worm is traveling
xrad and **yrad** = The worm's current angle converted into radians

Basically, the shape moves up and down on a sine wave, and back and forth on a cosine wave, leaving a trail behind it. The speed values control the wavelength of those two waves, and if you make them the same you should get a circle.

The first key values to play with are **xspeed** and **yspeed**. I find that setting them as decimal figures between 0.5 and 1.5 works well. Higher numbers will give you discrete shapes. Lower numbers will cause the shapes to blend together, making a smoother overall form. Very slow speeds will also make the resulting shape much darker and will, of course, take longer to draw. Also note that if you use numbers that are exact multiples, such as 0.6 and 1.2, or 0.5 and 1.5, the shapes will double back on each other quickly.

The next things to investigate are the last two lines in the **onEnterFrame** function:

```
shape._xscale = Math.sin(xrad)*100;
shape._yscale = Math.sin(yrad)*100;
```

I have **_xscale** using the sine of **xrad** and **_yscale** using the sine of **yrad**, but try substituting **cos** for one or both of them, or maybe try using **xrad** for both values. You'll see that this tends to control the "twistiness" of the shape.

You could, of course, investigate other things, such as making each shape rotate a bit faster or slower, or in a different direction. One last idea is to remove old shapes after a certain amount of time, creating the effect of a worm moving along. You can do this simply by adding these lines somewhere in the **onEnterFrame** function:

```
if(i > 100){
  i = 0;
}
```

To start, let's stick with 100 circles moving around the screen. The following sections outline a few other things I tried.

exp3-1

First I experimented by increasing the speed of rotation, and I was pleasantly surprised. I just changed this line to give some beautiful shapes:

```
shape._rotation = rot += 6;
```

exp3-2

In this iteration I played around with the scale instead. First, I changed the speed values as follows:

```
var xspeed:Number = .5;
var yspeed:Number = 2;
```

Then I changed the last two lines of the **onEnterFrame** function:

```
shape._xscale = Math.tan(xrad)*100;
//shape._yscale = Math.sin(yrad)*100;
```

Notice that I've just commented out the **_yscale**, creating a strange effect that ends up making a pair of ostrichlike creatures.

exp3-3

I changed a few more variables here to come up with a wider shape, a bit like a huge crumpled inner tube. Here are the changes to the initial code:

```
var xspeed:Number = .83;
var yspeed:Number = .52;
var xradius:Number = 200;
var yradius:Number = 100;
```

Here are the changes to **onEnterFrame**:

```
shape._rotation = rot += 2;
shape._xscale = Math.sin(xrad)*50 + 80;
shape._yscale = Math.cos(yrad)*50 + 80;
```

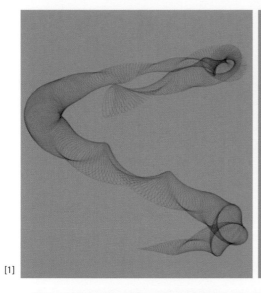
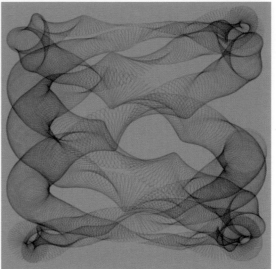

[1]

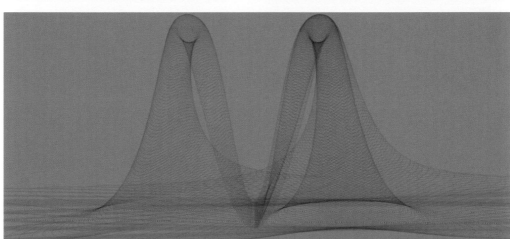

[2]

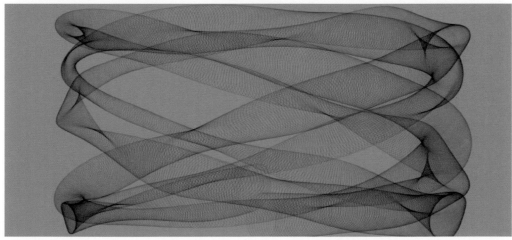

[3]

exp3-4

For this iteration, I just put the code back in to delete the circles after a while:

```
if(i > 50){
   i = 0;
}
```

I also changed the **shape** graphic to add another, smaller red circle inside the original one. This seemed to give the resultant effect an even more organic appearance.

exp3-5

Here I kept the same shape as in the last experiment, but I took out the code I added to keep the worm 50 circles long. I also sped up the rotation and experimented with a fixed **_xscale**:

```
shape._rotation = rot += 10;
shape._xscale = 50;
```

This shape leaves a nice trail, and if you leave it long enough, it will pretty much fill its bounding rectangle.

exp3-6

For the final iteration, I decided to go a different way. I changed the graphic to a simple black-and-white radial gradient filled circle. I kept the 10% alpha so that it resembles a pale sphere instead of a ring. The main change, though, is in the code where I decided to use the **_y** position of the mouse to control the scale of the shape.

Here are the changes to the initial code:

```
var xspeed:Number = .56;
var yspeed:Number = 1.32;

var scale:Number = 100;
```

I've created a new variable called **scale** that I'll use to change the scale of the shape. I initialized it to 100 so that it starts at full size. Here are the changes to the **onEnterFrame** function:

```
//shape._rotation = rot += 10;
scale += (_root._ymouse / 2 - scale) / 20;
shape._xscale = scale;
shape._yscale = scale;
if(i > 100){
   i = 0;
}
```

Notice here that I've commented out the rotation line. I don't need the shape to rotate because it will only ever be a circle. I update the new **scale** variable to the position of the mouse, and then set both **_xscale** and **_yscale** to equal **scale**. With a little experimentation and deft mouse-wobbling, you can create some really organic shapes.

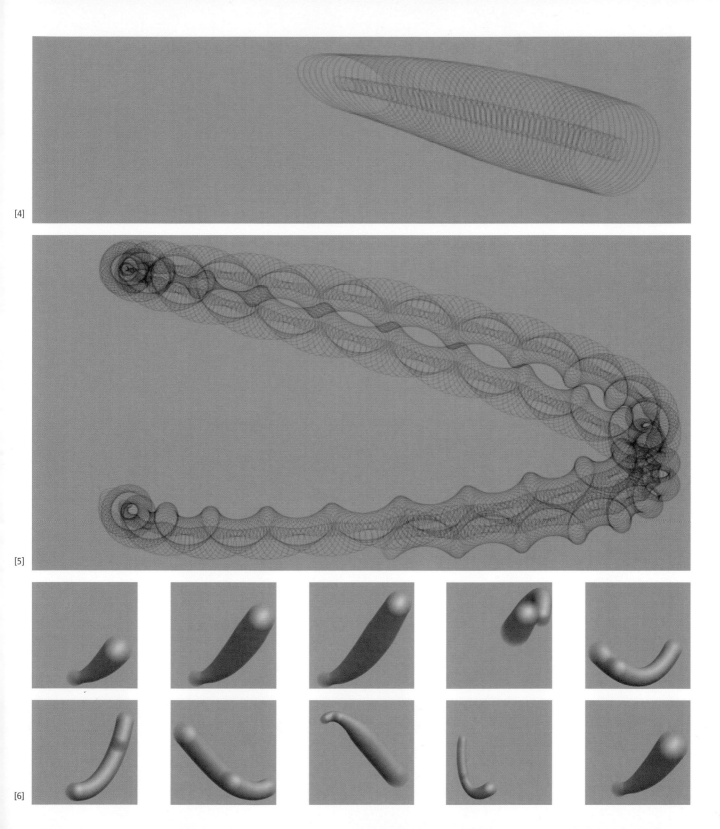

[4]

[5]

[6]

Hungry AI

Now for the fourth and final experiment. I always wanted to create some kind of artificial intelligence (AI) program, and here was my chance. My little creatures have simple behavioral characteristics. They eat until they're full, and then they go off and rest for a while. When they're hungry again, they look for some more food. I also created the perfect food for them—it gradually depletes as it's eaten, but when it's all gone, more magically reappears.

First, the easy part: the food. Make a movie clip with a simple filled shape (I made mine a circle). It's important that the shape is centered on the screen so that the creatures can find it and feed from it properly. Put an instance of the shape on the stage and name it **food**. The actions that I've added to this food element are pretty simple, and I put them on the main timeline (see **exp4.fla**):

```
food.onEnterFrame = function() {
  if (this._xscale < 10) {
    this._xscale = this._yscale = 100;
    this._x = Math.random() * 500 + 20;
    this._y = Math.random() * 360 + 20;
  }
};
```

Simply translated, when the food is depleted, it goes back to full size and is randomly positioned somewhere else on the screen.

Now for the creature. It's another movie clip that's exported with the same linkage name (I called mine **skeet**). I made a protozoan with a pointy proboscis, and he's 15 pixels high and 6 pixels wide. You can, of course, make whatever shape you like, but note that the point of attack (i.e., the mouth) should be at the registration point.

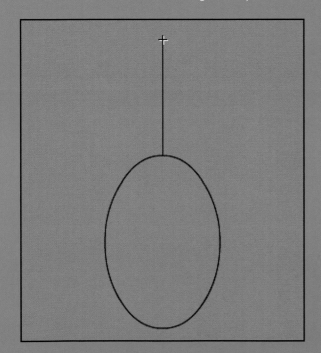

There's a bit more code in this experiment than the other experiments, but I tried to make it pretty logical and included a lot of descriptive comments in the FLA. As usual, the code is on the main timeline and in this case is split into two sections, one for initializing:

```
var skeet:MovieClip = attachMovie("skeet",
➥ "skeet", 0);
skeet._x = Math.random()*500+20;
skeet._y = Math.random()*360+20;
skeet.capacity = 10;
skeet.speed = 10;
skeet.ate = 0;
skeet.onEnterFrame = eat;
```

and one for the action:

```
function eat() {
  if (this.full) {
    this.xdist = this.xrest - this._x;
    this.ydist = this.yrest - this._y;
    this.ate -= .2;
    if (this.ate < 1) {
      this.full = false;
    }
  } else {
    this.xdist = _root.food._x - this._x;
    this.ydist = _root.food._y - this._y;
  }
  var angle = Math.atan2(this.ydist, this.xdist);
  this._rotation = angle * 180 / Math.PI + 90;
  if (_root.food.hitTest(this._x, this._y,
➥ true) && !this.full) {
    _root.food._xscale -= .5;
    _root.food._yscale -= .5;
    this.ate++;
    if (this.ate > this.capacity) {
      this.full = true;
      this.xrest = Math.random() * 200 - 100 +
      ➥ this._x;
      this.yrest = Math.random() * 200 - 100 +
      ➥ this._y;
    }
  } else {
    this._x += this.xdist / this.speed;
    this._y += this.ydist / this.speed;
  }
  this._xscale = 40 + this.ate * 10;
};
```

Test it to see the little creature in action.

The key variables

capacity = The amount that the creature can eat before it's full
ate = The current amount of food in the creature
full = Boolean variable set to **true** if the creature has eaten to its full capacity
speed = The speed of the creature (a higher number means slower movement)
xrest and **yrest** = A random resting spot for the satiated creature
xdist and **ydist** = A distance variable used for both the distance from the creature to the food and the distance from the creature to its rest position
angle = Variable used to turn the creature to face either the food or its rest position

It basically works like this: if the creature is full, then it heads to its rest position and works off some of that food until it's hungry again. When the creature is hungry, it turns to face the food and moves toward it. Once the creature arrives at the food, it eats until it's full again and then turns and heads off to another random rest position, where it repeats the cycle. During this time, you scale the creature to give a visual representation of how much it's eaten. Don't forget that you're also scaling the food and constantly checking to see if it's all gone, and then replacing and repositioning it.

exp4-1

There's a lot of useful material in this file, and a lot of answers to some common code questions, such as how to orient an object with its direction of motion, how to incorporate easing, and how to use **hitTest**. Obvious things to experiment with are the initialization variables: how much can the creature eat, and how fast can it move? The variables used within the **eat** function offer a whole range of possibilities. Here are a few off the top of my head:

```
this.ate -= .2;
```

Change the preceding variable to make the creature get hungry faster or slower.

These next values determine how fast the creature eats the food:

```
_root.food._xscale -= .5;
_root.food._yscale -= .5;
```

This determines how quickly the creature gets full:

```
this.ate++;
```

You could change the value to **ate+=.5** or **ate+=2**, for example.

Play with the following numbers to determine where the creature goes to sleep it off.

```
this.xrest = Math.random() * 200 - 100 + this._x;
this.yrest = Math.random() * 200 - 100 + this._y;
```

This is just the starting point, and I think you could plug all kinds of more complex behavior into these spots.

Now for the tour de force. Because of the modularity of the code, you can easily have more than one creature on the screen at once. Just wrap the initial code in a **for** loop, and make a couple of slight changes to the **attachMovie** line:

```
for(var i=0;i<10;i++){
    var skeet:MovieClip = attachMovie("skeet",
    ➥ "skeet" + i, i);
    skeet._x = Math.random()*500+20;
    skeet._y = Math.random()*360+20;
    skeet.capacity = 10;
    skeet.speed = 10;
    skeet.ate = 0;
    skeet.onEnterFrame = eat;
}
```

This will give you ten little protozoan vampires swarming on their food. Gets a bit creepy, huh?

exp4-2

Next, I messed around with the creatures' speed and eating habits. These changes make some nice, mellow creatures who rest a long way from the food source:

```
skeet.speed = 50;

this.ate -= .1;
this.xrest = Math.random() * 500 - 250 + this._x;
this.yrest = Math.random() * 500 - 250 + this._y;
```

exp4-3

For this next iteration, I pretty much reversed the previous experiment, making some rather voracious little things.

```
skeet.speed = 3;

this.ate -= 1;
this.xrest = Math.random() * 100 - 50 + this._x;
this.yrest = Math.random() * 100 - 50 + this._y;
```

exp4-4

For this iteration, I went back to the same code as in `exp4-1.fla`, but I changed the `food.onEnterFrame` code as follows:

```
food.onEnterFrame = function() {
    if (this._xscale < 10) {
        this._xscale = this._yscale = 100;
        this._y = 400;
    }
    this._x += (_root._xmouse - this._x) / 10;
    this._y += (_root._ymouse - this._y) / 10;
};
```

This means that I control the position of the food with the mouse, and the creatures will still attempt to get the food, following it around the screen until they can feed.

exp4-5

Here I added some more code into the **eat** function. The new code block goes underneath the current food scaling block:

```
// push food
root.food._x += this.xdist / 30;
root.food._y += this.ydist / 30;
```

Now when the creatures feed, they'll push the food away from them as they scrabble to get at it.

exp4-6

For the final iteration, I kept the creature code from `exp4-5.fla`, but I changed the code in the `food.onEnterFrame` function to this:

```
food.onEnterFrame = function() {
    if (this._xscale < 10) {
        this._xscale = this._yscale = 100;
        this._x = Math.random() * 500 + 20;
        this._y = 400;
        this.ytarget = Math.random() * 300;
    }
    this._y += (this.ytarget - this._y) / 10;
};
```

This means that the food will appear from the bottom of the screen at a random position on the x-axis, and it will head for a random position on the y-axis. Whether or not the food makes it to that random position depends on how hungry the creatures are. Still, it's good to make them work for their prize.

There are lots of things that you can do here. Simply changing the graphics is a good start—I kind of like my minimalist creatures, but you can make them as realistic as you like. You can even add animation to each stage of their lives: eating, sleeping, and moving. Also alter the code to give the creatures different movement patterns, or introduce obstacles to their world that they have to navigate around. The next step might be breeding them. Start off with one and perhaps use the amount of food that the creature has eaten as a factor to determine when it divides into two separate creatures. You could also think about adding a predator to their world, maybe initially just something that chases them that they have to avoid. The possibilities for these creatures are endless, and their lives are in your hands.

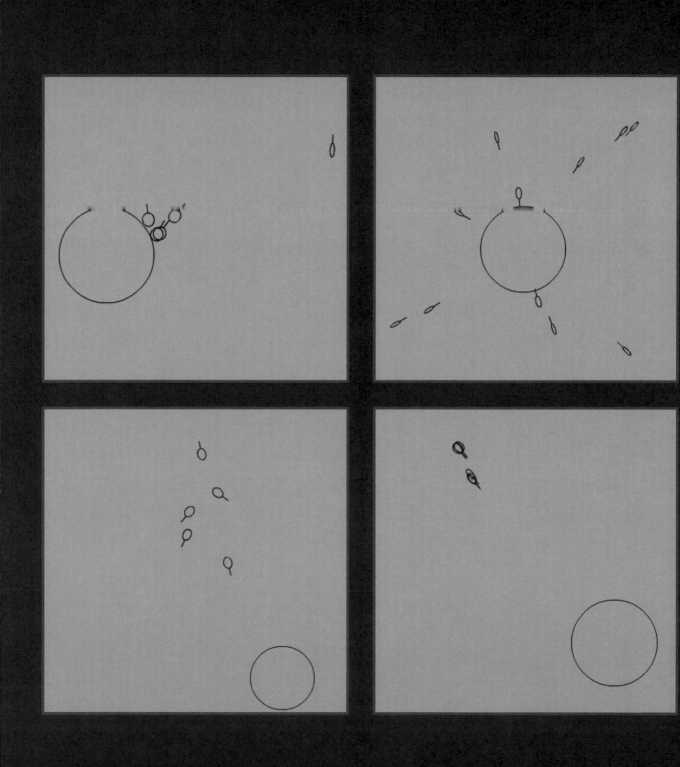

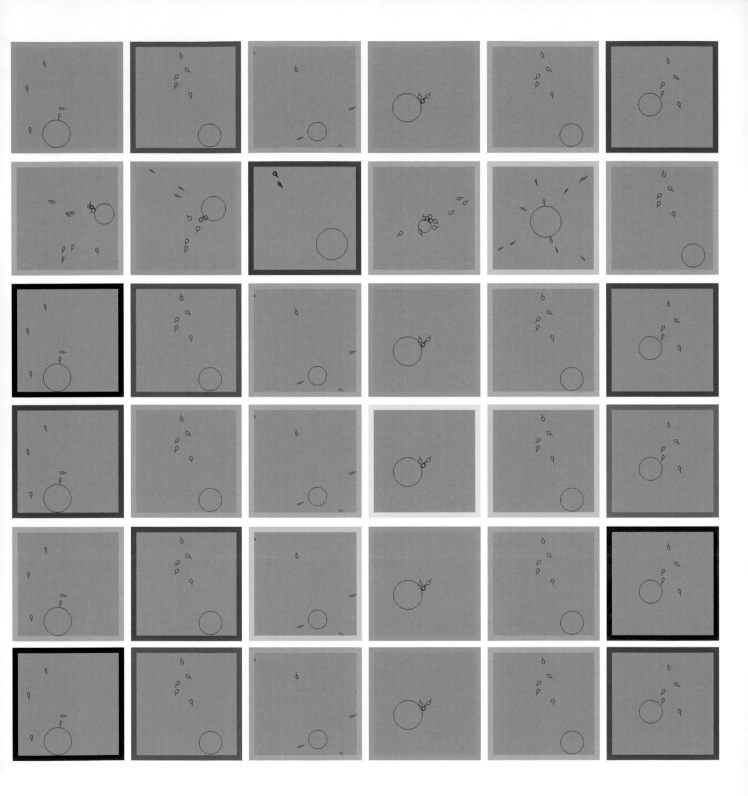

I'm not American and I don't live in London, I just work in the UK as a web developer for cash. My site for this week is pinderkaas.com, and this is my life so far:

Acorn Electron, BBC Micro Model B, Spectrum 48k, ZX Spectrum +, Dragon 16k, Atari ST 520, Amiga 1200, 286, 386SX 25Mhz, 386DX, Pentium 166Mhz, iMac 400, Power Mac G4 450Mhz.

My ambitions were to be a palaeontologist, or a milkman (so I could sit at home, eat fish fingers, and watch *Moonlighting*).

One day I will learn how to tune my guitar.

The first inspirational thing that comes to mind is train journeys. I love sitting, writing, thinking, and watching the country slide by. The next thing that comes to mind is art, and music, and computer games, and comics – especially Cerebus, and Pokemon, and keyboards, guitars, films, video cameras, digital cameras, 16mm film, Pyssla beads, clip art, cheese – the food kind, beetroot, Polaroid cameras, Kinder toys, Sim City, Populous, Chrono Trigger (and probably Chrono Cross if only they'd release it over here), Jackie Chan, Louis Barlow, John McIntyre, Ian MacKaye, Howe Gelb, Pokey the horse, BASIC, Eddie Izzard, Art Adams, Bill Sienkiewicz, the adverts in old Marvel comics, HTML, JavaScript prompt boxes, the Fetch and printy dogs, motorways at night, Nigel Slater, Repton, the Casio SK-1, Paul Auster, the sea air early in the morning, trees, texture, Like a Velvet Glove Cast in Iron, clouds, typewriters, Guiseppe Penone, David Hockney, Norman McLaren, stickers, soft-boiled eggs, fuzzy felt, cat dancing, Robert Pollard and his wet suitcase, elephants, Karl Bez, Franz Kafka, Charles Bukowski, Chilly Gonzales, grasses, and personalized license plates.

Tomorrow it'll probably be rocks.

ken jokol

Growing lines

I like watching things grow and change. The university I attended had these really unreliable S-VHS cameras, which had the added bonus that they could shoot a frame or so every few minutes. Perfect for filming the passing of time, or so I thought, but as with all cheap analog video cameras and record button presses, tape tends to rewind itself every now and again. Ignoring this factor, I went ahead and set up one of these cameras so that it ran overnight. It was set up to look out of my third-floor window, pointed at the green opposite. I was hoping to get a sunrise time-lapse reminiscent of those that you see in high-quality nature documentaries. True to the nature of video and the weary old camera, though, it messed up and I got a 3-second clip of night. Oh, well.

THE SAME GREEN... A DIFFERENT DAY...

Luckily, when I want to watch something change in Flash, I can. I like to see the seams and how something is built brick by brick. I'd much rather see a shape being drawn in a slow, clunky manner than being presented with a polished composition that hides some of the much-required production detail. For this chapter, I thought I'd build something in Flash that grows bit by bit and changes from a square into an elongated rectangle.

Have a look at **pre_lines.swf**, my initial proof-of-concept test file. You'll notice that very little happens in it—a shape just grows—but however dull it looks, it forms the basis of the following experiments.

The file is more complicated than it looks, but only a little. It's actually made up of a long line of 10x10-pixel squares, each colored half blue and half red. (OK, so it's not quite half and half, but who's counting?) All these squares are instances of the movie clip **q**, which is exported from the Library with the linkage name **q**.

The movie clip is then attached and positioned by this short code on the first frame of the root:

```
for (var i=0; i<40; i++) {
  var q:MovieClip = attachMovie("q", "sq" + i, i);
  q._x = 275;
  q._y = i * 10;
  q._xscale = q._yscale = 40;
  q.onEnterFrame = function(){
    this._xscale += 10;
  };
}
```

This code simply copies the movie clip and places the copy 10 pixels below the original, so that you get the appearance of one continuous shape. It then assigns an **onEnterFrame** handler to make the square expand horizontally on every frame.

lines01

First, I decided to add some rotation to the root code so that the shape begins to flower:

```
q._rotation = i * 10;
```

This produces a really interesting pattern, and if you leave it long enough you can see the logic behind making the colors not quite half and half, as the red begins to outgrow the blue. Try moving the square away from the registration point to get different effects.

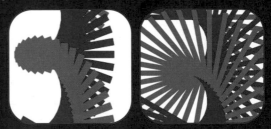

lines02

Next, I experimented with the transparency of the squares by adding this code to the **onEnterFrame** handler:

```
this._alpha -= 1;
if(this._alpha < 20){
  this._alpha = 20;
}
```

Now the squares become more and more transparent as they grow, but I added an **if** statement as a cut-off to stop them from fading out completely.

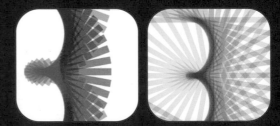

lines03

Continuing with my alpha experiments, I removed the code that I just added to **onEnterFrame**, and instead put this script in the **for** loop:

```
q._alpha = (40 - i) * 2.5;
```

This initializes a set alpha for each square, so the squares fade out from top to bottom.

lines04

In this iteration, I took out the previous alpha code and reduced the number of squares to produce one smooth arc. I also added to the **y** position of each square to center the arc on the screen. To achieve this, I modified these two lines in the **for** loop:

```
for (var i=0; i<19; i++) {
q._y = i * 10 + 100;
```

Another interesting effect to try here is to add an outline to the square (don't set it to hairline) so that as the square grows, the outline will get thicker and thicker until it completely covers the original square.

lines05

I decided to experiment with larger numbers with this next iteration. I wanted 360 movie clips growing on the screen. Normally, this isn't the best idea for a processor with this kind of frame rate, but I had an idea in my head, so I went ahead and did it anyway. Resisting the urge to push the frame rate up, and reveling as I do in lo-fi and rough aspects of design, I set the SWF quality to low for better performance and those beautifully jagged edges. Sometimes limitations are there for a reason. Here's the **for** loop that makes it happen:

```
for (var i=0; i<360; i++) {
  var q:MovieClip = attachMovie("q", "sq" + i, i);
  q._x = 100;
  q._y = i * 10;
  q._xscale = q._yscale = 18.5;
  q._rotation = i;
  q.onEnterFrame = function(){
    this._xscale += 10;
  };
}
```

If you run this SWF and let it go for a while, you'll see where the number 360 comes into effect. I also made my square slightly smaller by lowering the **_xscale** and **_yscale**, and I changed its color and x-position. By setting the rotation to a very low amount, the resulting curve created by all the duplicated shapes is almost flat, but it creates a kind of rough, distorted, moiré-like pattern as the lines intersect at certain places. If anyone makes anything dirtier from this, please let me know. I like dirt.

lines06

Sometimes the simplest equations can give spookily good results. I continued with the previous code but tried various multipliers for the rotation, so the relevant new code is basically as follows:

```
q._rotation = i * x;
```

Here, **x** is my multiplier amount. Rather than just pick numbers out of thin air, I arrived at them by dividing 360 by different amounts, so if you use the numbers 2 through 5, you get the results 180, 120, 90, and 72. Try plugging these into the preceding code to see the difference they make. My personal favorite magic number for rotation is 88, so try that too. You'll find these various iterations in the five files named **lines06a.fla** to **lines06e.fla**.

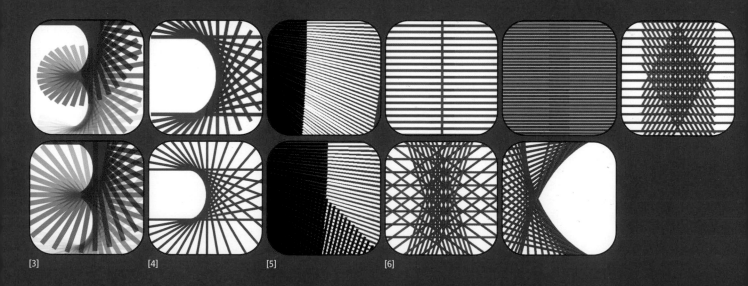

[3]   [4]   [5]   [6]

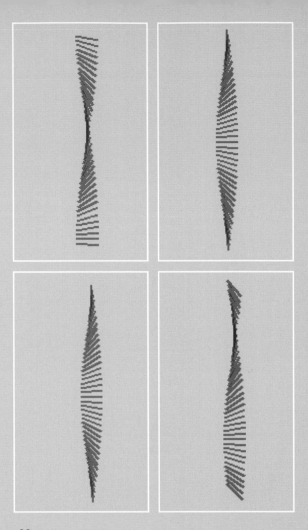

lines07

So far you've seen the square increase in the **_xscale** but not the **_yscale**, so in this SWF the square does just that, but it increases disproportionately to the **_xscale**. I added this line of code to the **onEnterFrame** function:

```
this._yscale += 1;
```

It's worth mentioning that from now on, the square is set at 50% alpha to add a little more of a visual effect when the shapes overlap. I also set up some basic values in the **for** loop: **_rotation** is set to **i*10**, and the number of squares is set to **40**. The increase begins like an invisible transformation and becomes apparent only when the shapes are at a significant size. And, of course, you'll see that I've changed the movie clip graphics when you run the movie.

lines08

In this iteration, I took out the **_yscale** and played around with rotation again, but this time I set the rotation in **onEnterFrame** so the squares are continuously spinning. I also limited the **_xscale** so that the squares only grow to a set size before stopping and just spinning in waves. The last thing I did was to set the rotation in the root to **i*9**. I arrived at this figure by dividing 360 by the number of squares (40) to get 9. Here's the new **onEnterFrame** code:

```
q.onEnterFrame = function(){
  this._xscale += 10;
  if(this._xscale >= 100){
    this._xscale = 100;
  }
  this._rotation += 10;
};
```

This reminds me of one of those amazing wooden wave machines that they always have in children's science programs. I also achieved some nice effects by reducing the size of the square for thinner lines and moving the square off-center so that the registration point is on its left side.

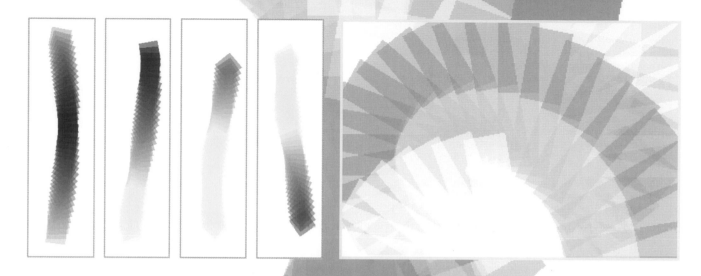

lines09

I now decided to add some color into the mix. First, I made my square chunkier, removing the line that scales it down, because I want a bit more bulk and blending when the colors overlap. Here's the complete new code:

```
_quality = "low";
for (var i=0; i<40; i++) {
  var q:MovieClip = attachMovie("q", "sq" + i, i);
  q._x = 275;
  q._y = i * 10;
  q._rotation = i * 4.5;
  q._alpha = 50;
  q.me = new Color(q);
  q.metr = new Object();
  q.onEnterFrame = function(){
    this._xscale += 10;
    if(this._xscale >= 100){
      this._xscale = 100;
    }
    this._rotation += 10;
    this.metr.rb = Math.abs(this._rotation);
    this.metr.gb = Math.abs(this._rotation * 2);
    this.metr.bb = Math.abs(this._rotation / 2);
    this.me.setTransform(this.metr);
  };
}
```

This sets the colors depending on rotation so you get a nice wave of color flooding it from top to bottom. Another thing you can try is setting the colors in the **for** loop so that they stay the same rather than cycling.

lines10

I took this color effect one stage further, so that rather than a static, predefined set of colors, the colors now change as the squares grow. Here's the **onEnterFrame** code:

```
q.onEnterFrame = function(){
  this._xscale += 10;
  this._yscale += 1;
  this.metr.rb = this._xscale / 2;
  this.metr.gb = this._yscale;
  this.metr.bb = this._y / 2;
  this.me.setTransform(this.metr);
};
```

By making the colors based on different attributes, the color range is a little different. Because of the slight changes in **_y**, the colors are banded.

lines11

Now for a few simple, short deviations from the original SWFs. For those who love their distortion, I've started you off with **lines11.swf**, which defies a considerable amount of the good-taste Flash work that you'll see out there on the Web. Here's the code for the root:

```
_quality = "low";
for (var i=0; i<1000; i++) {
  var q:MovieClip = attachMovie("q", "sq" + i, i);
  q._x = i * Math.random() * 5 + 100;
  q._y = i;
  q._xscale = q._yscale = 40;
  q.onEnterFrame = function(){
    this._xscale += 10;
  };
}
```

With **lines11a.swf**, I added one line to create this eye-destroying effect:

```
q._rotation = i * 10;
```

lines12

In this iteration, the shape drawn is a circular sunburst with wild colors. Here's the **for** loop:

```
for (var i=0; i<100; i++) {
  var q:MovieClip = attachMovie("q", "sq" + i, i);
  q._x = 275;
  q._y = i + 150;
  q._xscale = q._yscale = 40;
  q._rotation = i * 10 + 100;
  q.onEnterFrame = function(){
    this._xscale += 10;
  };
}
```

I changed the square into a circle and played around with the colors to produce **lines12a.swf** through **lines12c.swf**.

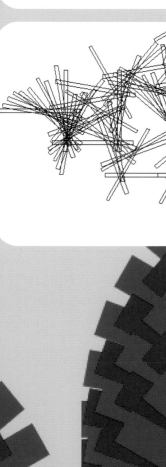

lines13

For the final couple of experiments I played around with just using outlines and a bit of randomization code. Check out **lines13.fla** and **lines13a.fla**.

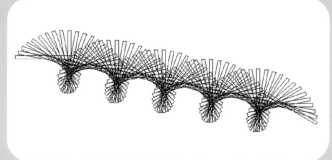

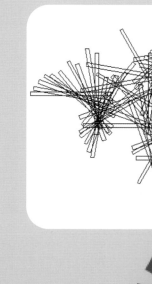

Generative Grid

I'm a little bit of a creative automation freak. My usual intention is to make something in Flash, make a million amendments to it, and then take screenshots of every permutation and layer and edit them in Photoshop. It never actually turns out that way because I get stuck making new SWFs in Flash, but it's a good way to keep me churning out fresh experiments.

In this section, I'm going to dabble in generating some simple graphics based on a straightforward grid structure created with a couple of **for** loops. I chose an 8x8 grid to begin with, reminiscent of the old-school Spectrum days, when I'd painstakingly sit with a ruler and a pile of paper creating my own fonts and typing in all sixty-four 0s and 1s that made up each character (and to what end?).

I'm going to avoid using the **Color** object this time and try to stick to composition. The concentration here is on generative design and approaches to manipulating a simple grid structure. Sometimes limitations can force you to look at and approach something in a different way.

blocks01

I started off with a basic 50x50-pixel square movie clip, with the registration point in the top-left corner, in the Library of **blocks01.fla** with the linkage name **sq**. I then attached the following code to frame 1 of the root:

```
var count:Number = 1;
for (var i=0; i<8; i++) {
  for (var x=0; x<8; x++) {
    var sq:MovieClip = attachMovie("sq", "sq"
    ➥ + count, count);
    sq._x = x * 50;
    sq._y = i * 50;
    sq._alpha = i * 12;
    count++;
  }
}
```

Here, I simply have a pair of nested **for** loops to create an 8x8 grid. I then alter the alpha of each row to achieve a gradient effect.

blocks02

In this iteration of the experiment, the alpha gradient is applied using the formula **x*i**, which results in a diagonal slope of color from the top left to bottom right:

```
sq._alpha = i * x;
```

Because each block is a 50x50-pixel square and the code is positioning the squares using 50 as a multiplier, they never overlap or infringe on one another—but great things can happen when they do. Try setting the size of the squares to be a little smaller, say 40×40, and the squares will overlap and give a little more depth because of the alpha layering (see, for example, **blocks02a.swf**).

blocks03

In this SWF, the same rules apply as before, but I introduced a few different shapes to change the general design and to give that square a break. I placed a triangle on frame 2 and a blank frame on frame 3 of the movie clip, with a **stop** action on the first frame. I then applied the following code to the **for** loop to toggle between these three frames, and added a little rotation to them:

```
sq.gotoAndStop(Math.floor(Math.random() * 3 + 1));
sq._rotation = 90 + Math.random() * 4;
```

Try using different shapes, or just move the shapes around inside the movie clip. You'll get different results depending on whether the registration point is at the top left of the shape or in the center.

[1]

[2]

[3]

176

blocks04

So far the output has pretty much stayed within a rigid gridlike structure, but if I add a few lines of code, the grid becomes unfixed—or so it appears. In this SWF, I've added a simple amount of rotation to the **for** loop, and voilà!—falling tiles:

```
sq._rotation = Math.random() * 360;
```

blocks05

At the moment, each square follows a universal pattern of some sort (excluding the randomness that I've used), but by using the **count** variable to affect various properties, I can quickly make a difference. I changed these lines in the **for** loop:

```
sq._alpha = (i * x) + 20;
sq._rotation = count;
```

I also tried the following couple of tricks with **count**. First, I tried passing the **count** variable to the new **sq** clip and setting the rotation in an **onEnterFrame** handler in the for loop as follows (see **blocks05a.fla**):

```
sq.count = count;
sq.onEnterFrame = function(){
  this._rotation += this.count / 10;
};
```

This produced some pretty weird uniformity after a while (try speeding this up with a higher frame rate and a lower quality setting). The next thing I tried was this:

```
sq.count = count;
sq.onEnterFrame = function(){
  this._yscale += this.count / 10;
};
```

In **blocks05b.fla**, the blocks grow fastest at the bottom right and slowest at the top left, producing some interesting patterns.

blocks06

Here the shapes grow in **_xscale** and **_yscale**, but their direction is reversed when they reach a set size each way. Initially, the pattern is chaotic, but after a little while you can see some waves:

```
var count:Number = 1;
for (var i=0; i<8; i++) {
  for (x=0; x<8; x++) {
    var sq:MovieClip = attachMovie("sq",
    ➥ "sq" + count, count);
    sq._x = x * 30 + 50;
    sq._y = i * 30 + 50;
    sq._alpha = i * x;
    sq.addMeAmount = count / 20;
    sq.addMe = -count / 20;
    sq.onEnterFrame = function(){
      if(this._xscale < 0){
        this.addMe = this.addMeAmount;
      }
      if(this._xscale > 100){
        this.addMe = -this.addMeAmount;
      }
      this._yscale += this.addMe;
      this._xscale += this.addMe;
    };
    count++;
  }
}
```

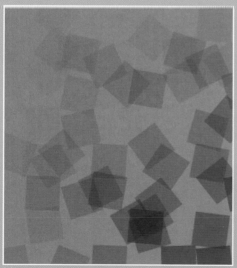

[4]

[5]

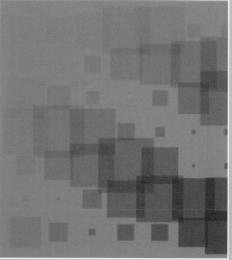

[6]

blocks07

This SWF produces a cascade of squares dripping from top to bottom. I made a slight amendment to the main **for** loop to change the **_y** position of each square depending on its duplicated number (**count**):

```
var count:Number = 1;
for (var i=1; i<9; i++) {
  for (x=1; x<9; x++) {
    var sq:MovieClip = attachMovie("sq", "sq"
    ➥ + count, count);
    sq._x = x * 40
    sq._y = i * (count / x);
    sq._alpha = 20;
    count++;
  }
}
```

I also made a few other small modifications: I changed the loop counters to run from 1 to 9 rather than 0 to 8, so that I didn't get any divide-by-zero errors, and I reduced the **_x** position slightly to squash the squares up a bit toward the top right. I also set the alpha to 20.

blocks08

I took a bit of a radical departure here. I've already mentioned my fascination with 8-bit characters, so I stepped it up to code some basic pixel-style characters. I upgraded to a 10x10 square grid (shame on you, pixel boy!), and my square movie clip is now 40x40 pixels. Here's the new code for the root:

```
var pixel:Array = new Array(12,13,16,17,21,24,
➥ 25,28,33,34,35,36,43,46,51,52,53,54,55,56,
➥ 57,58,61,63,66,68,71,73,76,78,81,88);
var count:Number = 0;
for (x=0; x<10; x++) {
  for (var i=0; i<10; i++) {
    var sq:MovieClip = attachMovie("sq", "sq"
    ➥ + count, count);
    sq._x = i * 40
    sq._y = x * 40;
    sq._alpha = i * 10;
    sq._visible = false;
    for(var a=0; a < pixel.length; a++){
      if(count == pixel[a]){
        sq._visible = true;
      }
    }
    sq.addMe = 1;
    sq.onEnterFrame = function(){
      if(this._alpha < 0){
        this.addMe = 1;
      }
      if(this._alpha > 100){
        this.addMe = -1;
      }
      this._alpha += this.addMe;
    };
    count++;
  }
}
```

Each number in the array refers to a position in the grid, and each single number can be thought of as a pair. So 12 is actually 1 and 2—the first number represents the column, and the second number represents the row. These numbers are then picked up in the inner **for** loop:

```
sq._visible = false;
for(var a=0; a < pixel.length; a++){
  if(count == pixel[a]){
    sq._visible = true;
  }
}
```

This code just initializes every clip as invisible and then turns on the ones that it's told to in the array. To save you a little time, I've made a simple drawing application called **blocks_draw.swf** for recording a shape's values to be entered into this code.

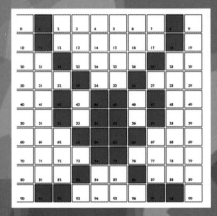

Calculating and typing the code by hand isn't exactly the most therapeutic process, but with the cut-and-paste ability of the drawing application and the ease of increasing the size of the grid, you'll be making cross-stitch patterns in no time!

blocks09

Building on the last experiment, I decided to generate a random pattern over half of the canvas and mirror it in the other half. This is now set instead of the old pixel array in the main code:

```
var pixel:Array = new Array();
for(var a = 0; a < 25; a++){
  pixel[a] = Math.floor(Math.random() * 50);
  pixel[a + 25] = 100 - pixel[a] - 1;
}
```

Try increasing the number of blocks in a tighter grid to make more abstract patterns.

blocks10

In this last experiment, I set up a couple of lines of code to change the alpha depending on **count**:

```
var total:Number = Math.floor(count / 10) +
➥ count % 10;
sq._alpha = total * 8;
```

You can take this code in a number of different directions now. You can bring in the **Color** object. Yes, I know I've resisted it throughout, but for generative design, color is an essential component. The best rule I've found, though, is to stick to three colors and apply these to the objects. Or you could just go crazy and set each object totally randomly. Also, you can experiment with modularity. The SWFs that I've made are confined to the main stage and aren't modular. Nest the grids, and you can make new and intriguing patterns by replicating or duplicating these grids. Another idea, if you want to take the design to a different level, would be to give your grid code a modular structure. Make things modular if you want to take something to a different level. In addition, you can just forget about coding and try different shapes—it's simple but effective.

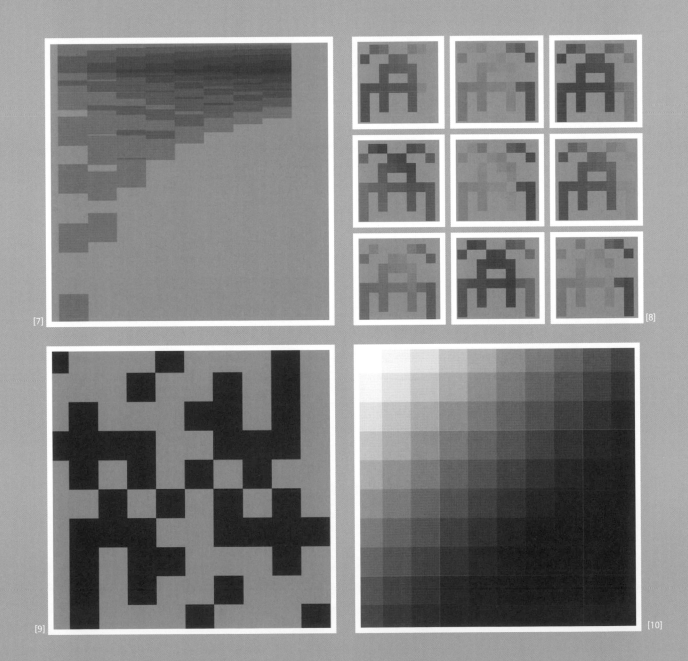

[7]

[8]

[9]

[10]

Colorsuck

For this experiment, I wanted to play about with the **Color** object, and also try and make use of **hitTest** because I'm always complaining about how annoying it is to get it to work exactly how I want it to. I came up with the simple idea of having three colored squares (red, green, and blue) moving around the screen and sucking color out of each other whenever they touch.

The initial experiment is based on a movie clip in the Library of **colorsuck01.fla** named **square**. It's exported with the same name and has its ActionScript 2.0 Class field in the Linkage Properties dialog box set to **ColorSuckA**. An external ActionScript file named **ColorSuckA.as** is in the same folder as the FLA. This is an ActionScript 2.0 class file that gives the square several new properties and methods to change its color and move around the stage. Here are the contents of that file:

```
class ColorSuckA extends MovieClip {
    private var xspeed:Number;
    private var yspeed:Number;

    public var me:Color;
    public var metr:Object;

    public function ColorSuckA(){
        init();
    }
    private function init(){
        this._x = Math.random() * 400;
        this._y = Math.random() * 400;
        me = new Color(this);
        metr = {rb:0, gb:0, bb:0};
        xspeed = Math.random() * 20 - 10;
        yspeed = Math.random() * 20 - 10;
    }
    public function onEnterFrame(){
        if (_x>400) {
            xspeed = Math.random() * 10;
            xspeed *= -1;
            yspeed = Math.random() * 10;
        }
        if (_x<0) {
            xspeed = Math.random() * 10;
            yspeed = Math.random() * 10;
        }
        if (_y>400) {
            yspeed = Math.random() * 10;
            yspeed *= -1;
            xspeed = Math.random() * 10;
        }

        xspeed = Math.random() * 10;
        yspeed = Math.random() * 10;
```

On the main timeline of **colorsuck01.fla** is the following code, which attaches the movie clips, sets their initial colors, and then uses an **onEnterFrame** handler to check for the collisions and perform additional color changing:

```
attachMovie("square", "block1", 0);
attachMovie("square", "block2", 1);
attachMovie("square", "block3", 2);

block1.metr = {rb:255, gb:0, bb:0};
block1.me.setTransform(block1.metr);

block2.metr = {rb:0, gb:255, bb:0};
block2.me.setTransform(block2.metr);

block3.metr = {rb:0, gb:0, bb:255};
block3.me.setTransform(block3.metr);

onEnterFrame = function(){
    if (block1.hitTest(block2)) {
        block1.metr.rb -= 5;
        block1.metr.gb += 5;
        block1.me.setTransform(block1.metr);

        block2.metr.gb -= 5;
        block2.metr.rb += 5;
        block2.me.setTransform(block2.metr);
    }
    if (block1.hitTest(block3)) {
        block1.metr.rb -= 5;
        block1.metr.bb += 5;
        block1.me.setTransform(block1.metr);
        block3.metr.bb -= 5;
        block3.metr.rb += 5;
        block3.me.setTransform(block3.metr);
    }
    if (block2.hitTest(block3)) {
        block2.metr.gb -= 5;
        block2.metr.bb += 5;
        block2.me.setTransform(block2.metr);
        block3.metr.bb -= 5;
        block3.metr.gb += 5;
        block3.me.setTransform(block3.metr);
    }
};
```

As you can see, **block1** sucks color from blocks 2 and 3, **block2** sucks color from blocks 1 and 3, and **block3** sucks color from blocks 1 and 2.

The key variables

xspeed and **yspeed** = Variables to control the speed of each block. They're set to a random value when the block is initialized, and they're set again whenever the block hits a wall.
me = The **Color** object, which is used to control the color of the block.

The class code is really quite simple. I create a new **Color** object, and set an initial random speed and direction. Each block then bounces around the screen (using hard-coded values for the screen dimensions).

The main timeline code is constantly checking to see if any block is in contact with either of the other two blocks. If a block is in contact with another block, then 5 is subtracted from the block's original color, and 5 is added to its new color. Say, for example, that **block1** (red) has just come into contact with **block2** (green). **block1** loses 5 red and gains 5 green, and **block2** loses 5 green and gains 5 red. It's easy to understand once you see it in motion. And that's it: colorsuck.

One strange thing that I discovered after running this code was the correlation that appears between RGB and CMYK. I've never really studied color theory before, so this all came as quite a surprise to me.

colorsuck02

Here, I changed the blocks so that they were affected by only one other color rather than by both, so 1 is affected by 3, 2 is affected by 1, and 3 is affected by 2. This means that rather than changing to new colors, the blocks just swap colors.

colorsuck03

In this iteration, I wanted the blocks to leave trails behind them so they'd leave patterns of changing colors. I did this by simply duplicating a similar movie clip behind each square as it moved. This is done in a new class, **ColorSuckB**, and you can see that the **square** clip is now assigned this class as its ActionScript 2.0 Class (via Linkage). This new class adds one line to the top of the previous class:

```
public var count:Number;
```

This line simply defines a new public variable, **count**, that will be used to name the newly attached clips. In the main timeline code, **count** is set to **1** for the first block, **2000** for the second, and **4000** for the third. This ensures that the new clips will be at different depths. The main change to the class comes in the **onEnterFrame** function, where I added the following to the end of the code:

```
var newBox:MovieClip = _root.attachMovie
➥ ("winky", "box"+count, count);
newBox._x = _x;
newBox._y = _y;
var newCol = new Color(newBox);
newCol.setTransform(metr);
count++;
```

Here, I attached a new copy of another clip, which I exported from the Library with the linkage name **winky**, and set its position and color to that of the moving block. Although this clip has the same graphics as **square**, I need to make it another movie clip so that it doesn't inherit the code of **ColorSuckB**. It doesn't hurt to set this to low quality for a bit more speed, and try to make the squares smaller so you can see more of the lines.

colorsuck04

In this iteration, I changed the block into a diagonal line (so that it effectively still takes up the same area as the square as far as **hitTest** is concerned, because I'm using the bounding box). The ActionScript 2.0 Class linkage is now set to the **ColorSuckC**. This new class adds another property, **trail**, to specify which movie clip it should leave behind it. It also adds some code to rotate itself and its copies, giving a nice effect when the lines intertwine and the colors flow through the gaps. Here are the new/updated lines in **ColorSuckC.as**:

```
public var trail:String;

var newBox:MovieClip = _root.attachMovie(trail,
➥ "box"+count, count);

newBox._rotation = this._rotation = count;
```

[3]

[4]

colorsuck05

I wanted to try and add alpha to the mix. I began by adding a new circle clip to the Library with similar behavior to the line clips. The difference is that whenever the circle hits a line, it gains alpha instead of sucking color. It's exported from the Library with the name **biff**, and it has **ColorSuckC** as its ActionScript 2.0 Class. A single copy of **biff** is attached and set up in a way similar to the lines:

```
attachMovie("biff", "biff", 3);
```

In the **onEnterFrame** function on the main timeline, a hit test is made from **biff** to each of the blocks:

```
biff.metr = {rb:0, gb:0, bb:0, ab:-255};
biff.me.setTransform(biff3.metr);
biff.count = 10000;
biff.trail = "circleCopy";
biff._visible = false;
```

Don't worry if you don't see anything to begin with. The circle starts off invisible and then fades in subtly, in a ghostly fashion, when it hits a line. You could also try altering the circle's speed so that it gets faster as it sucks color as well.

colorsuck06

Originally, I had intended to use the alpha ball to suck the alpha out of the lines, but I kind of liked the effect it made, so I removed the lines altogether and replaced them with three alpha balls. Remember that they start off invisible. It reminds me of a Rothko painting—you stare at it to see if you can see a difference in the textures, and think you can, but there's nothing there. It's just your mind expecting to see something and visualizing it.

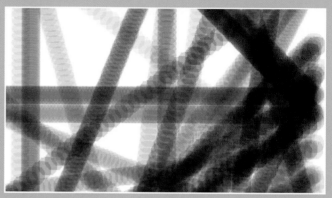

colorsuck07

I played around for a while with different shapes and colors, and then I decided to try adding sounds as well. I created a set of three simple sounds in SoundEdit (you can use any sound editor) and gave them linkage names of **s1**, **s2**, and **s3**.

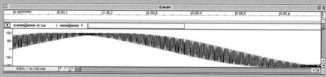

I then added a few lines of code to the new class, **ColorSuckD** (which I'll use for the remainder of this section). First, I added a couple of new variables and a line in the **init** function:

```
public var snd:Sound;
public var soundcount:Number = 100;

snd = new Sound(this);
```

And then I added a setter function to assign the sound link and a function to play the sound:

```
public function set soundLink(link:String):Void {
  snd.attachSound(link);
}
public function playSound(){
  snd.setVolume(soundcount--);
  snd.start();
  if(soundcount == 0){
    soundcount = 100;
  }
}
```

This code just creates a new **Sound** object and attaches the given sound from the Library to it. I also defined a new variable, **soundcount**, which will control the volume of the sound. So for **block2**, I have **block2.soundLink = "s2"** and so on.

Now I needed to add some code to the **onEnterFrame** loop to play the sound and change the colors:

```
onEnterFrame = function(){
  if(block1.hitTest(block2)){
    block1.metr.ab += 1;
    block1.me.setTransform(block1.metr);
    block1.playSound();

    block2.metr.ab += 1;
    block2.me.setTransform(block2.metr);
    block2.playSound();
  }
  if(block1.hitTest(block3)){
    block1.metr.ab += 1;
    block1.me.setTransform(block1.metr);
    block1.playSound();

    block3.metr.ab += 1;
    block3.me.setTransform(block3.metr);
    block3.playSound();
  }
  if(block2.hitTest(block3)){
    block2.metr.ab += 1;
    block2.me.setTransform(block2.metr);
    block2.playSound();

    block3.metr.ab += 1;
    block3.me.setTransform(block3.metr);
    block3.playSound();
  }
};
```

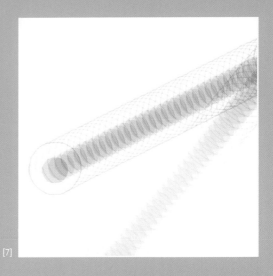

[7]

All this does is run the movie clip's **playSound** method, in which I set the sound volume and start it playing whenever two shapes collide. I also reduced the sound volume so that the sound fades out as it repeats and gives new and different sound combinations depending on the volume. Lastly, there's a simple **if** statement to check if the sound has gone all the way down to 0 and reset it to 100 when it does. You may also want to increase the size of the shape so that the sounds appear more often.

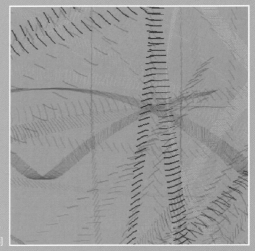

[8]

colorsuck08
I just started experimenting here with different sounds and different shapes. I reset the colors to RGB and added a bit of rotation.

colorsuck09
Again, this is just a collection of different sounds and shapes, but it produces some beautiful movies.

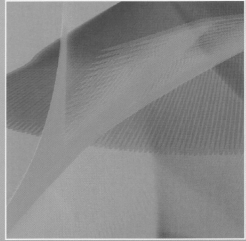

[9]

colorsuck10

I added a few more objects, one for each of my eight sounds, and set them going. I set all the clips in a loop, rather than eight separate code blocks, and I also changed the color code slightly to give each one a random color:

```
for(var i=1;i<=8;i++){
    var block:MovieClip = attachMovie("biff",
    ➥ "block"+i, i);
    var a:Number = Math.random() * 255;
    var b:Number = Math.random() * 255;
    var c:Number = Math.random() * 255;
    block.metr = {rb:a, gb:b, bb:c, ab:-255};
    block.me.setTransform(block.metr);
    block.count = 1000 * i;
    block.trail = "circleCopy";
    block.soundLink = "s"+i;
}
```

colorsuck11

For this iteration I recorded some new sounds of a slowed-down voice speaking numbers on a Mac.

colorsuck12

Again, this is just a change in the sounds being played. If you can't work out what they're saying, it's the three syllables of pinderkaas. (Obviously . . .)

colorsuck13

More sounds again—this time a few notes recorded straight from a guitar. Sometimes it's even quite tuneful.

colorsuck14

For the final iteration, I created a set of new sounds, and I also made a background object that's affected by the following code:

```
var a:Number = Math.random() * 255;
var b:Number = Math.random() * 255;
var c:Number = Math.random() * 255;
var me = new Color(back);
var metr:Object = {rb:a, gb:b, bb:c, ab:-255};
me.setTransform(metr);
```

As you can probably tell by now, this code just sets the background to a random color when the movie starts. This has to be my favorite experiment out of all of them—it has beautiful sounds and colors, and it makes beautiful pictures.

I spent hours playing with new shapes and sounds for this, but I won't bore you by detailing them all. Go create your own and enjoy!

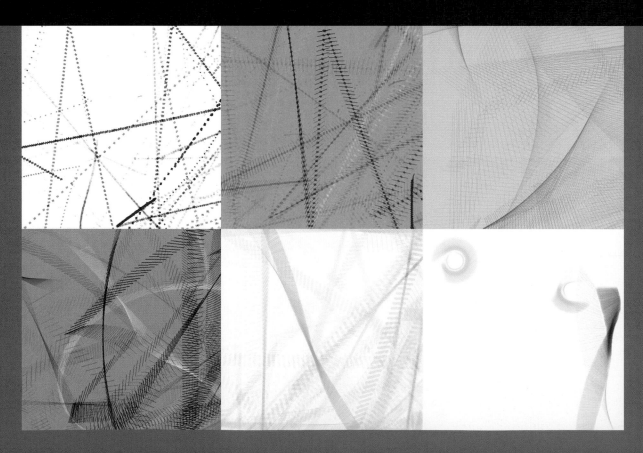

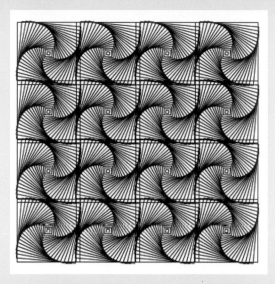
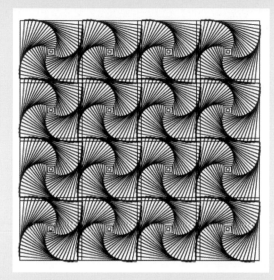

Squares

This experiment is the ultimate in simplicity: a static picture inspired by spirographs and old computer magazines. I think, though, that this is one of the most absorbing things I've created in a long time, just because it's so easy to customize. I change the graphic a tiny bit, I get a new picture. I change one number in the code, I get a new picture.

When I first started playing with this, I just sat for hours tweaking things, making tiny changes, and loving what came out. I made whole series of differences—adding the **Color** object here, a bit of animation there, or a liberal sprinkling of invisible rollovers—but when it came down to choosing which ones I'd put in the book, I came right back to the most basic static images because I love their simplicity. I'll run through a few of the iterations that I liked, but I'd prefer it if you just completely ignore all that I've written and go off and enjoy creating your own.

I'm sure you'll all have seen this first one before. It's just the good old rotating, shrinking square.

```
var d:Number = 0;
for (var b=1; b<5; b++) {
  for (var a=1; a<5; a++) {
    for (var i=0; i<20; i++) {
      d++;
      var square:MovieClip =
      ➥ attachMovie("square", "square"+d, d);
      square._x = 50*a;
      square._y = 50*b;
      square._rotation = i * 5;
      square._xscale = 100 - i * 5;
      square._yscale = 100 - i * 5;
    }
  }
}
```

This code sits on the main timeline in **square01.fla**. In the Library is a movie clip with a simple graphic outline of a 100x100-pixel square. This movie clip has the linkage name **square**.

The code is basically just a set of three nested **for** loops: the first to count loops down the screen, the second to count loops across the screen, and the last to actually control the meat of the code—duplicating, positioning, and sizing the individual movie clips.

The key variables

d = The overall counter of the number of times the innermost loop loops, and therefore the number of new movie clips that are attached onto the screen. It's used to name the new movie clips, but it can also be thrown into other parts of the code to create different effects for each movie clip.

a and **b** = The two outer loops. They're used as counters for the number of times the inner loop is run across and down the screen. They're used for positioning the movie clips later on.

i = The counter for the inner loop. The amount of times that the movie clip is duplicated for each position across and down the screen.

square02

By changing the square for a circle and setting it slightly off-center, I got a simple spirograph pattern:

```
var d:Number = 0;
for (var b=1; b<2; b++) {
  for (var a=1; a<2; a++) {
    for (var i=0; i<100; i++) {
      d++;
      var square:MovieClip = attachMovie
      ➥ ("square", "square"+d, d);
      square._x = 200 * a;
      square._y = 200 * b;
      square._rotation = i * 5;
      square._xscale = 105;
      square._yscale = 105;
    }
  }
}
```

For what it's worth, you could just as easily remove the scaling lines from this one. I left them in only to save retyping them later on.

square03

Here, I made the circle smaller (20x20) and set it even further off-center. Then I changed the inner **for** loop to the following, bringing scale back into it:

```
for (var i=0; i<200; i++) {
  d++;
  var square:MovieClip = attachMovie
  ➥ ("square", "square"+d, d);
  square._x = 200 * a;
  square._y = 200 * b;
  square._rotation = i * 45;
  square._xscale = 100 - i * 2;
  square._yscale = 100 - i * 2
}
```

square04

For this experiment, I substituted the circle for a gradient-filled ellipse and messed with the scale a bit more to create this slightly ammonite-like shape:

```
square._rotation = i * 11;
square._xscale = 100 - i / 2;
square._yscale = 100 - i * 2
```

square05

I replaced the ellipse with a simple off-center black-and-white gradient-filled circle, and changed the code slightly to this:

```
var d:Number = 0;
for (var b=1; b<3; b++) {
  for (var a=1; a<3; a++) {
    for (var i=0; i<150; i++) {
      d++;
      var square:MovieClip = attachMovie
      ➥ ("square", "square"+d, d);
      square._x = 150 * a;
      square._y = 150 * b;
      square._rotation = Math.round
      ➥ (Math.pow(a, b));
      square._xscale = 100 - i / a;
      square._yscale = 100 - i / b;
    }
  }
}
```

I love the way that the same small piece of code creates four completely different shapes. By moving the circle closer to the center so that it's only a little off to one side, you get a really strange effect, almost like a cone being peeled open from the top.

square06

I changed the graphic again, this time to three small black triangles, and altered the code slightly to create this image of chaotic combs:

```
var d:Number = 0;
for (var b=1; b<6; b++) {
  for (var a=1; a<6; a++) {
    for (var i=0; i<10; i++) {
      d++;
      var square:MovieClip = attachMovie
      ➥ ("square", "square"+d, d);
      square._x = 60 * a;
      square._y = 60 * b;
      square._rotation = Math.round
      ➥ (Math.pow(a, b));
      square._xscale = 100 - i * a;
      square._yscale = 100 - i * b;
    }
  }
}
```

[2]

[3]

[4]

[5]

[6]

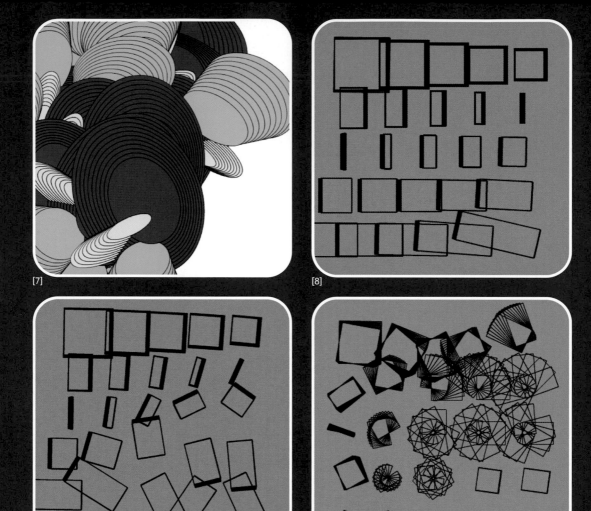

[7]

[8]

[9]

[10]

square07

By simply changing the graphic for a set of three overlapping, filled ellipses, I arrived at this piece. It reminds me of 1970s wallpaper—but that could just be me.

square08

For this piece, I changed the graphic back to the original simple square, but moved it a little off-center. I also changed the following lines of code to give a strange collection of patterns:

```
square._rotation = Math.round(Math.pow(a, b) / d);
square._xscale = 100 - d;
square._yscale = 100 - d / b;
```

square09

Here, I changed one line of code slightly, and the squares appear to fall away into chaos as they approach the bottom-right corner:

```
square._rotation = Math.round(Math.pow(a, b));
```

square10

Finally, here's what I consider to be one of the nicest of the series. By simply changing a couple of the lines of code again

```
square._rotation = Math.round(Math.pow(a, b) * d);
square._xscale = 100 - d / a;
```

I was able to create 25 different shapes, all from that one simple piece of ActionScript.

Ty Lettau is currently Senior Interactive Designer at Macromedia's Experience Design Group. Before this, he co-founded the Fourm Design Studio. Ty also operates www.soundofdesign.com, which serves as a collection of all of his corporate work as well as explorations. His interactive work has earned four Flashforward Flash Film Festival and two SXSW nominations. He has been featured in numerous design publications and has co-authored several Flash books. Ty has taught Advanced Flash, Interface Design, and Information Design courses at MIAD and UW-Milwaukee. He recently entered into the world of typography by launching a digital type foundry at foundry.soundofdesign.com.

Inspiration is in everything. If you look for it, you'll find it.

ty lettau
www.soundofdesign.com

Lines

This experiment begins with the file **lines01.fla**. This project consists primarily of the **LineClip** movie clip and a dynamically created mask movie clip. **LineClip** is the main graphic in the movie—it's just a 100-pixel vertical purple line with the center point at **x=50, y=50**, exported from the Library with the linkage name **LineClip**. This is what you'll attach later. First, you need to attach some initialization code to the first frame of the root:

```
//  ─────────
// Movie parameters
//  ─────────
_highquality = false;
Stage.scaleMode = "noScale";
fscommand("fullscreen", "true");
//  ──────────────
// Move the mask to a level higher
// than the attached clips so it is always in front.
//  ──────────────
Mask.swapDepths(1);
createEmptyMovieClip("lines", 0);
lines.setMask(mask);
```

The following code comes next:

```
lines.setMask(mask);
var C:Number = 0;
onEnterFrame = function(){
  if (_root.C < 300) {
    //  ──────────────
    // Continually duplicate the "Line" clip.
    //  ──────────────
    C++;
    var line:MovieClip = lines.attachMovie("LineClip", "Line" + C, C);
    //  ──────────────
    // Parameters of duplicates
    //  ──────────────
    line._x = C * 2;
    line._y = 100;
    line._xscale = 100;
    line._yscale = Math.random() * 200;
    line._rotation = lines["Line" + (C - 1)]._rotation + Math.random() * 50 - 25;
    line._alpha = Math.random() * 50;
  }
};
```

The key variables

C = A counter that simply counts from 0 to 300. It's the only variable here.

You need **C** for several things. First, it allows you to give each instance of **LineClip** a unique name. As you attach **LineClip**, you're adding the **C** value to the end of its name each time. So when **C** is 124, the new movie clip is named **Line124**. You also use **C** to determine the depth that each duplicate is placed onto. When you attach the new instance, you store a reference to it in the temporary variable **line**. This just makes things easier to type.

First, you set the **_x** position to **C*2**, so as the **C** value increases, it will move the movie clips across the stage. The **_y** position stays at 100 for each movie clip. The **_xscale** will stay at 100, but the **_yscale** is set to a random value.

You use the same naming convention for the `_rotation` value, but you add `C - 1` to the end of the name. This will give you the second most recent movie clip (that is, the one created two frames ago). So this means that you're adding a random number to the last movie clip's `_rotation`, which makes the movie clips form an uneven spiral. Lastly, set the `_alpha` to another random number.

The `onEnterFrame` function is where you'll make most of the changes, and each iteration will build upon the preceding changes.

lines02
All you're doing in this iteration is creating less of a `_rotation` by decreasing the range of the random number:

```
line._rotation = lines["Line" + (C - 1)]._rotation +
➥ Math.random() * 10 - 5;
```

lines03
For this version, you're adding the following `onEnterFrame` handler to each new `line` movie clip:

```
line.onEnterFrame = function(){
   this._rotation += 3;
};
```

This will give your lines some motion as a whole.

[3]

lines04
Now back to the main `onEnterFrame` code:

```
line._rotation = lines["Line" + (C - 1)]._rotation +
➥ Math.random() * 100 - 50;
```

You're changing the rotation line again to give a greater random range. The other change that you're making is to the `LineClip` clip. I've edited it by setting the registration point to be at the very top. Now when it's rotated, it will behave differently.

[4]

lines05
For this iteration, you simply remove the `line.onEnterFrame` code to see what the new rotation settings look like when they're static.

[5]

lines06

By having the _x position set to C*2, and knowing that the stage is 600 pixels wide, you can tell that a movie clip has reached the edge of the screen when C equals 300. When this happens, you can set the next instance's _x position back to 0 to start it off again from the left. To do this, you add in two new variables. You need to temporarily maintain the counter variable, so you replace C with a new variable, D, which you then use in the counter loop. Now C will still count, meaning that your naming and depth values stay usable, but you have another counter variable that you can reset without compromising your original naming counter. You also have X, which will now represent the _x position that you used C for before. So D and X count with C to start off with, but when they get to 300, D and X reset to 0, while C keeps on counting. Here's the full new code for the onEnterFrame function:

```
onEnterFrame = function(){
  if (_root.D < 300) {
    C++;
    D++;
    X++;
    var line:MovieClip = lines.attachMovie
    ➥ ("LineClip", "Line" + C, C);
    line._x = X * 2;
    line._y = 100;
    line._xscale = 100;
    line._yscale = Math.random() * 200;
    line._rotation = lines["Line" + (C - 1)]
    ➥ ._rotation + Math.random() * 100 - 50;
    line._alpha = Math.random() * 50;
  } else {
    D = 0;
    X = 0;
  }
};
```

The result is that when the counter hits 300 and the last clip is placed on the right of the stage, the very next clip gets set to 0, or the far left of the stage. All new duplicates then pile on top of the old ones in a new iteration of lines.

lines07

Here, I edited LineClip, making its height 2,000 pixels. Now the line will extend to the edge no matter where it is.

lines08

Now let's make a few changes to get something totally different. You're going to go back to the C counter, but this time you're going to use it as a way to remove movie clips. In the last iteration, you purposely preserved the C value as incremental. This time you're going to reset it after it hits 100. With a few modifications to the parameters, such as an _x position and _rotation relative to the last duplicate, you'll get something new and interesting. Also, you need to move the registration point of LineClip so that it's in the center. Lastly, you apply two constraints so that if the duplicate goes past 100 to the left, it locks to 100; or if it goes past 500 to the right, it locks to 500. This just keeps everything on the stage. Go back to the onEnterFrame code from line04.fla and make the following changes:

```
onEnterFrame = function(){
  if (C < 100) {
    C++;
    var line:MovieClip = lines.attachMovie
    ➥ ("LineClip", "Line" + C, C);
    line._x = lines["Line" + (C - 1)]._x +
    ➥ Math.random() * 120 - 60;
    line._y = 100;
    line._rotation = lines["Line" + (C - 1)]
    ➥ ._rotation + Math.random() * 30 - 15;
    line._alpha = Math.random() * 50;
    if(line._x < 100){
      line._x = 100;
    }
    if(line._x > 500){
      line._x = 500;
    }
  } else {
    C = 0;
  }
};
```

lines09

Let's apply one last feature to the file: the function of polarity. First, delete the **onEnterFrame** function—you don't need it anymore. Next, edit **LineClip** and rotate the graphic by 45 degrees. As for the code, replace the **onEnterFrame** function you just deleted with a **for** loop to make 21 instances of **LineClip**, place them across the stage, and assign an **onEnterFrame** handler to each that introduces a mouse interactivity element:

```
for(var i=0;i<21;i++){
    var line:MovieClip = lines.attachMovie
    ➥ ("LineClip", "Line" + i, i);
    line._x = 100 + i * 15;
    line._y = 100;
    line._alpha = Math.random() * 50;
    line.onEnterFrame = function(){
        var N1X:Number = this._x;
        var N1Y:Number = this._y;
        var N2X:Number = _root._xmouse;
        var N2Y:Number = _root._ymouse;
        var DX:Number = N2X - N1X;
        var DY:Number = -(N2Y - N1Y);
        var A:Number = Math.atan2(DY, DX) *
        ➥ 180 / Math.PI;
        var R:Number = ((A < 0 ? 360 + A : A) *
        ➥ 1000) / 1000;
        this._rotation = -R;
    };
}
```

N1X and **N1Y** mark the point **A**, and **N2X** and **N2Y** mark the point **B**. **DX** and **DY** are the distances on each axis between the two points. You can then use these values to arrive at an angle. If you draw a line from the movie clip (**A**) to the cursor (**B**), then this will find the angle perpendicular to that line. Now set the newly attached **line** movie clip to this angle (represented by **R**). Also set the **_alpha** to a random value.

lines10

You can click into **LineClip** now and do anything to the graphics. Let's add two more lines inside to make a more complex pattern. At this point, you can do just about anything, and it will result in a large change in the final result. Go crazy!

Orbits

The basic setup for this series of experiments, starting with **orbits01.fla**, looks very similar to the last one: the **LineClip** movie clip consisting of the standard 100×100-pixel, 45-degree line, exported from the Library with the same linkage name. But look a little closer and you'll see that **LineClip** has been edited and converted to a simple 30-frame alpha tween, followed by a **removeMovieClip()** action.

Now for the ActionScript that controls this movie. On frame 1 of the root timeline, you start off with the same parameter and mask definitions that you saw in the previous experiment, followed by this new code:

```
var C:Number = 0;
var MX:Number = 0;
var MY:Number = 0;
onEnterFrame = function () {
    // ————————————————
    // Continually duplicate the "Line" clip.
    // ————————————————
    C++;
    var line:MovieClip = lines.attachMovie("LineClip", "Line"+C, C);
    // ——————————————
    // Parameters of duplicates
    // ——————————————
    line._x = _root.Follow._x;
    line._y = _root.Follow._y;
    line._xscale = lines["Line"+(C-1)]._x-Follow._x;
    line._yscale = lines["Line"+(C-1)]._y-Follow._y;
    // —————————-
    // Elasticity Engine
    // —————————-
    var OX:Number = _root._xmouse;
    var OY:Number = _root._ymouse;
    MX = (MX*.96)+(OX-Follow._x)*.13;
    MY = (MY*.96)+(OY-Follow._y)*.13;
    Follow._x += MX;
    Follow._y += MY;
};
```

The key variables
C = A counter
OX = The mouse's **_x** position
OY = The mouse's **_y** position

Check out the resulting effect of this code in **orbits01.fla**. This is just your basic mouse trail, but with a twist. Each duplicated line attaches one of its endpoints to the last line and the other endpoint to a new location. The lines then fade out and are ultimately removed.

The speed in the elasticity engine is controlled by a fixed number, which in this case is 0.13. The value 0.96 equates to friction. The result of this code is an elastic string, which responds to the mouse movement. The mouse position is taken by **OX** and **OY** and fed into the **MX** and **MY** equations, which output new **_x** and **_y** positions for the **Follow** movie clip.

orbits02

For the first iteration, I've gone into **LineClip** and dragged both end keyframes from frame 30 to frame 90. Make sure you expand the motion tween as well when you try it yourself. All this does is make the life of the movie clip longer, giving a different visual result.

Let's also change the origin point for the elastic code in the **onEnterFrame** code. Make the origin the direct opposite of where the mouse is:

```
var OX:Number = 600 - _root._xmouse;
var OY:Number = 200 - _root._ymouse;
```

orbits03

Here, you'll put the **LineClip** keyframes back to frame 30. You'll also change the same lines of code again. This time, add a random value to the mouse location. You'll still have very fluid movement, but it won't be as controlled:

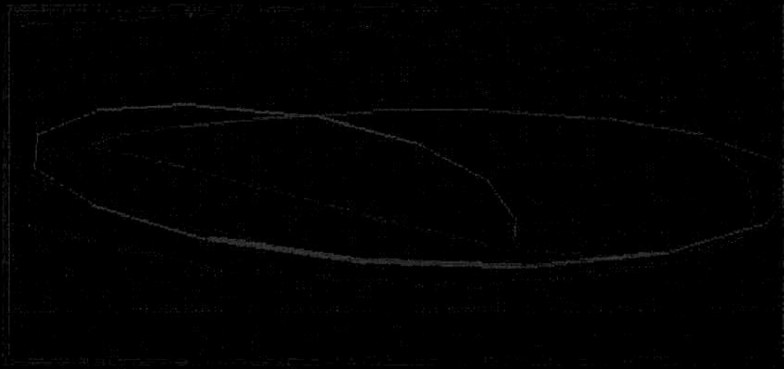

```
var OX:Number = _root._xmouse + Math.random() * 100 - 50;
var OY:Number = _root._ymouse + Math.random() * 100 - 50;
```

[2]

orbits04

Again, let's put the **LineClip** ending keyframes back to frame 90, to see what a longer string will do with the new random feature.

[3]

orbits05

For the final experiment, you'll make one more adjustment to the **LineClip** movie clip. You'll add keyframes at frame 40 and frame 50, and set the **_alpha** of **LineClip** at both frames to 0. At frame 89, you'll bring the alpha back up to 100.

These examples make good use of Flash's scripting and tweening capabilities. Try playing around with more tween, or alter some of the code variables to see what you can achieve. You may want to try altering the visual movie clip to create different effects.

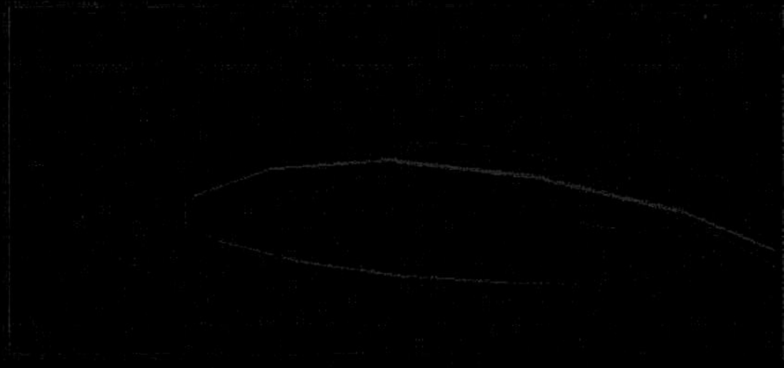

[4]

Terra

The setup for this experiment is similar to that in the **Lines** and **Orbits** experiments. **LineClip** is just a 100-pixel-wide green line that's centered on the screen. You export this from the Library with the linkage name **LineClip**.

Here are the basic parameters of the movie and the function that produces the duplicate clips. They go on frame 1 of the root:

```
_highquality = false;
Stage.scaleMode = "noScale";
fscommand("fullscreen", "true");
Mask.swapDepths(1);
createEmptyMovieClip("lines", 0);
lines.setMask(mask);
var C:Number = 0;
var D:Number = 0;
var X:Number = 0;
onEnterFrame = function(){
  if (D < 300) {
    C++;
    D++;
    X++;
    var line:MovieClip = lines.attachMovie("LineClip", "Line" + C, C);
    line._x = X * 2;
    if(C > 1){
      line._y = lines["Line" + (C - 1)]._y + Math.random() * 10 - 5;
    } else {
      line._y = 100;
    }
    if (line._y < 0) {
      line._y = 0;
    }
    if (line._y > 200) {
      line._y = 200;
    }
  } else {
    D = 0;
    X = 0;
  }
};
```

The key variables

C = The counter used to name the clip and define depths
D = The counter used in the loop
X = A counter used to control the **_x** position

This code is very similar to the initial code of the **Lines** experiment, so I won't repeat all the details here. To summarize, the code simply counts, attaches, and positions the **LineClip** instances across the stage. You have three counters in this experiment: **C**, **D**, and **X**. The **C** counter continuously increases, whereas the **D** and **X** counters reset when they get to 300. This allows you to use **X** to control the **_x** position. **D** assumes the role of being the counter in the loop, and **C**'s purpose is to name the clips and their associated depths.

terra02

In the **onEnterFrame** function, add these two lines just above the bottom two **if** statements:

```
lines["Line" + (_root.C - 1)]._x += Math.random() * 50 - 25;
lines["Line" + (_root.C - 1)]._y += Math.random() * 50 - 25;
```

Adding these two lines will take each duplicate after it is created and give it a more random location.

terra03

Now let's change that code again. Remove the two lines you just added and change the **_y** to use the mouse location instead. Also, you're going to change the depth that you set the duplicates to. Rather than using the counter, let's use a random value. This will cause the duplicates to be replaced in a random pattern. For example, if a duplicate is placed at 128, the next time the random value is 128, that last duplicate will disappear to make room for the new one. The result is a disintegrating look:

```
var line:MovieClip = lines.attachMovie("LineClip", "Line" + C, Math.random() * 300);

line._y = _root._ymouse;
```

Now you have a ribbon that you can control.

terra04

Go into the **LineClip** movie clip and set the width of the line to 20 in the Info or Properties panel, and set the center point at **x=10**, **y=0**. Now you have a narrower ribbon. Moving the mouse fast gives a strange pattern of marks.

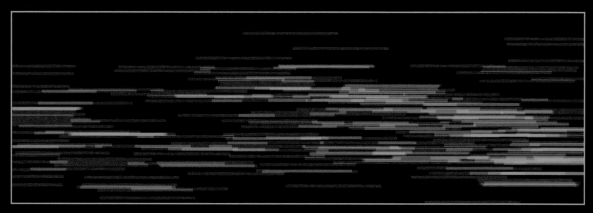

terra05

Let's change back the depth counter, and then apply some code that was used in the **Orbits** experiment. You need to go into **LineClip** and make it the 100x100-pixel diagonal line that you used earlier. The four new lines of code you add for this example place and scale the object. Also, the added **if** statement simply gets rid of the line that is drawn when the duplicates flip back to 0 to start over at the left of the stage. Otherwise, you get a long line that goes all the way from right to left. Here's the code in full:

```
var  C:Number = 0;
var  D:Number = 0;
var  X:Number = 0;
onEnterFrame = function(){
  if (D < 300) {
    C++;
    D++;
    X++;
    var line:MovieClip = lines.attachMovie
    ➡ ("LineClip", "Line" + C, C);
    line._x = X * 2;
    line._y = _root._ymouse;
    line._xscale = lines["Line" +
    ➡ (C - 1)]._x - X * 2;
    line._yscale = lines["Line" + (C - 1)]._y
    ➡ - _root._ymouse;
    if (line._y < 0) {
      line._y = 0;
    }
```

```
    if (line._y > 200) {
      line._y = 200;
    }
  } else {
    D = 0;
    X = 0;
  }
  if(D == 1){
    line._visible = false;
  }
};
```

terra06

This next iteration happened by accident. I changed one value but forgot to change the other, and the result was very interesting:

```
if(C > 1){
  line._y = lines["Line" + (C - 1)]._y +
  ➡ Math.random() * 10 - 5;
} else {
  line._y = 100;
}
```

Note also that if **C** isn't greater than 1, you set the **_y** property of **line** to 100, so that the first instance is centered vertically.

terra07

Let's keep playing with the combinations of this code. Try setting the **_xscale** with a **_y** value:

```
line._xscale = lines["Line" + (C - 1)]._x - _root._ymouse;
```

terra08

Lastly, let's go into **LineClip** and make a keyframe at frame 30. Set the **_alpha** of this line to 0, and then add a motion tween with a 1-degree counterclockwise (CCW) rotation so that you have a rotation and alpha fade effect. Now, as the movie clips duplicate, they will form new patterns.

[7]

[8]

Polarity

As usual, the basic setup of this movie (**polarity01.fla**) is identical to the previous experiments. I won't go into detail with it all, because you've done it all before, but here's a quick recap.

The **LineClip** movie clip is just a 10×10-pixel diagonal orange line with its center point at 0,0. This is what you'll be attaching later, so give it the linkage name **LineClip**. Next, you'll start with the usual code on the first frame of the root:

```
_highquality = false;
Stage.scaleMode = "noScale";
fscommand("fullscreen", "true");
Mask.swapDepths(1);
createEmptyMovieClip("lines", 0);
lines.setMask(mask);
```

Finally, write the **onEnterFrame** function to attach and position the lines and give them their own **onEnterFrame** handlers:

```
var C:Number = 0;
onEnterFrame = function(){
  if(C < 300){
    C++;
    var line:MovieClip = lines.attachMovie
    ➡ ("LineClip", "Line" + C, C);
    line._x = Math.random() * 600;
    line._y = Math.random() * 200;
    line._alpha = Math.random() * 50;
    line.onEnterFrame = function(){
      var N1X:Number = this._x;
      var N1Y:Number = this._y;
      var N2X:Number = _root._xmouse;
      var N2Y:Number = _root._ymouse;
      var DX:Number = (N2X - N1X);
      var DY:Number = -(N2Y - N1Y);
```

```
      var A:Number = Math.atan2(DY, DX) * 180
      ➡ / Math.PI;
      this._rotation = -Math.floor((A < 0 ?
      ➡ 360 + A : A) * 1000) / 1000;
    }
  } else {
    C = 0;
  }
};
```

The key variables

N1X = The **_x** value of point A
N1Y = The **_y** value of point A
N2X = The **_x** value of point B
N2Y = The **_y** value of point B
DX = The distance on the x-axis between points A and B
DY = The distance on the y-axis between points A and B

These variables perform the same angle calculation function as they did back in **lines09.fla**. Now set the **LineClip** movie clip **_rotation** property such that it will rotate itself based on the mouse location.

In this code, you'll again use **C** as the sole counter. It defines the loop length, names the clips, and defines the depths that the clips sit on.

To start off with, set the **_x** position and the **_y** position to a random number. Use the proportions of the stage (600×200) as your random range.

polarity02

For the next iteration, try altering the line graphic within **LineClip**. Add a few more lines in this movie clip by copying the line and pasting a new one, or even creating a nested movie clip and placing it wherever you want. Different line patterns will yield different results when you run the SWF. I chose to make a 4×2 grid of the lines, with the lines 10 pixels apart.

polarity03

For this version, you're going to control the positions of the duplicates a bit more. I've also taken the opportunity to change the line graphic again—back to a single line, but rotated this time.

You need to place the first line at a particular location on the stage. You'll do this by placing the line at 300,100 if **C** isn't more than 1. You'll also change a few more lines after that:

```
if(C > 1){
  line._x = lines["Line" + (C-1)]._x +
  ➥ Math.random() * 60 - 30;
  line._y = lines["Line" + (C-1)]._y +
  ➥ Math.random() * 60 - 30;
} else {
  line._x = 300;
  line._y = 100;
}
if(line._x < 0){
  line._x = 0;
}
if(line._x > 600){
  line._x = 600;
}
if(line._y < 0){
  line._y = 0;
}
if(line._y >200){
  linc._y = 200;
}
```

Change the **_x** and **_y** position to locate where the last duplicate was placed, and then to place the next one within 30 pixels from it on each axis. The four **if** statements are merely constraints to keep the movie clips from being placed off the stage.

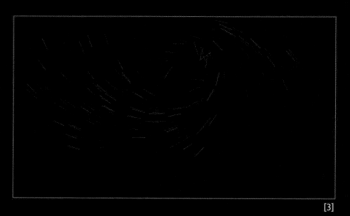

[3]

polarity04

Now let's look at the **onEnterFrame** code. Add a bit more structure by reducing the amount that the duplicates can jump from one to the next by changing the following lines:

```
line._x = lines["Line" + (C-1)]._x + Math.random() * 20 - 10;
line._y = lines["Line" + (C-1)]._y + Math.random() * 20 - 10;
```

polarity05

You'll try something new here: delete **onEnterFrame**. Go into **LineClip** and change the line graphic to be at 0,0. Now go back to the root, and replace the former **onEnterFrame** with a double set of **for** loops that create a grid of movie clips 16 pixels apart.

This will give you a clear view of how the polarity code actually functions, and it will also reveal some very nice patterns.

polarity06

Right after you set the rotation of each clip, add a couple more lines to change its scale:

```
this._xscale = DX;
this._yscale = DY;
```

Here you add something that will set the scale based on the distance from the mouse to the movie clip.

polarity07

The last iteration started out as a bit of a mistake, but it created an interesting effect. Sometimes surprises or happy accidents like this can work out nicely. You'll now try to do what I originally intended for the last one. Go into the line graphic and make it a 20-pixel vertical line, and set the center point to 0,0. Now it will react properly.

[5]

[6]

[7]

polarity08

This time, go back into the main **onEnterFrame** and change the code again:

```
line._xscale = Math.random() * 1200;
line._yscale = Math.random() * 1200;
```

Now you have a more chaotic pattern again.

polarity09

You'll change that clip event one last time. Check out the Library of **polarity09.fla** and notice that the instance of **LineClip2** inside **LineClip** has the instance name **center**. I've also added the following line to the **for** loop code:

```
line.center._rotation = Math.random() * 360;
```

Now your movie clips have the polarity code, but since they start out with random rotations, the pattern fields are gone. As in all the experiments, a slight change in the code can have a drastic impact on the final effect.

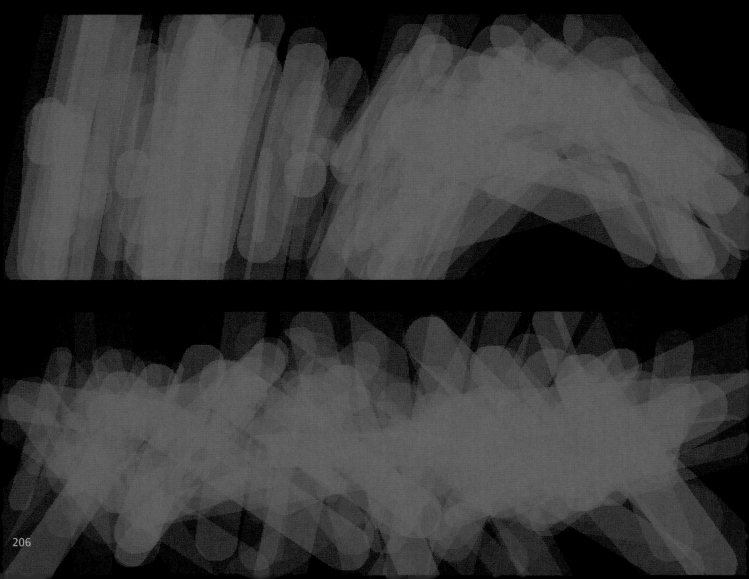

I was born in 1979, and graduated from the department of Computer Science at Moscow State University. During my time there, I researched different methods of texture compression. I'm interested in computer graphics, image processing, 3D visualization, and creating and playing computer games.

I sometimes think Flash is the best application in the world.

When it came to creating an effect for this book, I started thinking about the amount of 3D and text effects created in Flash and I thought about combining the two. The result was a 3D shape using text as the texture. Taking this a little further and knowing that the best text effects can be manipulated by the user, I set out to create a dynamic application. The result is on display in this chapter, along with a couple of other 3D experiments.

pavel kaluzhny

kaluzhny.nm.ru

Balls

This movie consists of three separate pieces. One is the FLA file itself, **balls_0.fla**. The others are external ActionScript 2.0 class files named **Ball.as** and **Line.as**. The class files contain properties and methods that give the individual elements (the lines and balls) their special behavior.

First let's take a look at the FLA file. The Library contains two movie clips: **Line** and **PointShape**. They're both set to export with the same linkage name and are assigned the ActionScript 2.0 classes, **Line** and **Ball**. Now let's take a look at the code on the timeline of this movie:

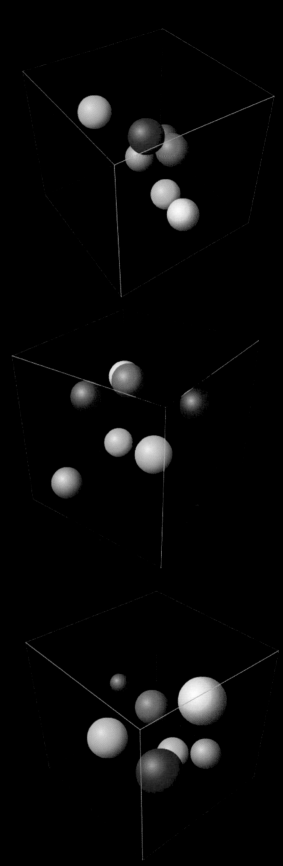

```
var ax:Number = 0;
var ay:Number = 0.4;
var cos2:Number = Math.cos(ax);
var sin2:Number = Math.sin(ax);
var cos1:Number = Math.cos(ay);
var sin1:Number = Math.sin(ay);

var pline:Array = new Array();
pline[0]  = [ 1,  1,  1,    1,  1, -1];
pline[1]  = [ 1,  1, -1,    1, -1, -1];
pline[2]  = [ 1, -1, -1,    1, -1,  1];
pline[3]  = [ 1, -1,  1,    1,  1,  1];
pline[4]  = [-1,  1,  1,   -1,  1, -1];
pline[5]  = [-1,  1, -1,   -1, -1, -1];
pline[6]  = [-1, -1, -1,   -1, -1,  1];
pline[7]  = [-1, -1,  1,   -1,  1,  1];
pline[8]  = [ 1,  1,  1,   -1,  1,  1];
pline[9]  = [ 1,  1, -1,   -1,  1, -1];
pline[10] = [ 1, -1, -1,   -1, -1, -1];
pline[11] = [ 1, -1,  1,   -1, -1,  1];

var bnum:Number = 7;
var lnum:Number = 12;

for (var i=0; i<bnum; i++) {
   attachMovie("PointShape", "ball"+i, i+1000, {id:i});
}
for (i=0; i<lnum; i++) {
   attachMovie("Line", "line"+i, i, {pline:pline[i]});
}

onEnterFrame = function () {
   adjustAngles();
   for (var i=0; i<bnum-1; i++) {
      var ball1:MovieClip = this["ball" + i];
      for (var j=i+1; j<bnum; j++) {
         ball1.checkCollision(this["ball" + j]);
      }
   }
};

function adjustAngles(){
   ax += 0.02;
   ay = 0.4 + 0.3 * Math.cos(ax / 2.3);
   cos1 = Math.cos(ay);
   sin1 = Math.sin(ay);
   cos2 = Math.cos(ax);
   sin2 = Math.sin(ax);
}
```

This code sets up some points to draw the lines to, and it creates a couple of angles that continuously change, causing the objects in the movie to rotate. It also attaches several instances of the line and ball clips, and then cycles through the ball clips, checking to see if any one collided with any other.

Now we get to the class files. The first is the **Line** class, which just takes care of rotating the lines around in a 3D space:

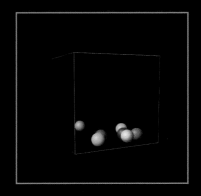

```
class Line extends MovieClip {
   public var pline:Array;

   private var pnt1:Object;
   private var pnt2:Object;
   private var LS:Number = 10;
   private var VPf:Number = 60;
   private var cx:Number = 320;
   private var sx:Number = 10;
   private var cy:Number = 240;
   private var sy:Number = 10;

   public function Line(){
      init();
   }

   private function init(){
      pnt1 = new Object();
      pnt2 = new Object();
   }

   public function onEnterFrame() {
      pnt1.x = pline[0] * LS;
      pnt1.y = pline[1] * LS;
      pnt1.z = pline[2] * LS;
      pnt2.x = pline[3] * LS;
      pnt2.y = pline[4] * LS;
      pnt2.z = pline[5] * LS;
      rotate(pnt1);
      rotate(pnt2);
      _x = cx + sx * pnt1.x * VPf / (VPf - pnt1.z);
      _y = cy - sy * pnt1.y * VPf / (VPf - pnt1.z);
      _xscale = cx + sx * pnt2.x * VPf / (VPf - pnt2.z) - _x;
      _yscale = cy - sy * pnt2.y * VPf / (VPf - pnt2.z) - _y;
      swapDepths(int( (pnt1.z + pnt2.z) * 3000) + 100000);
      gotoAndStop(int( (pnt1.z + pnt2.z + 20) / 4));
   }
   private function rotate(p:Object):Void  {
      var y = p.y;
      var z = p.z;
      p.z = _parent.cos2 * z - _parent.sin2 * p.x;
      p.x = _parent.sin2 * z + _parent.cos2 * p.x;
      p.y = _parent.cos1 * y - _parent.sin1 * p.z;
      p.z = _parent.sin1 * y + _parent.cos1 * p.z;
   }
}
```

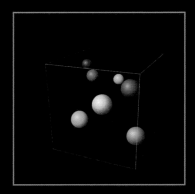

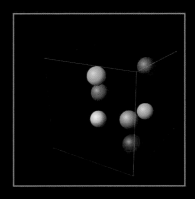

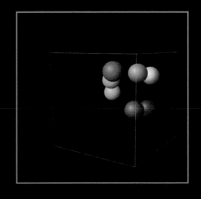

Then there is the `Ball` class:

```
class Ball extends MovieClip {
    public var x:Number;
    public var y:Number;
    public var z:Number;
    public var vx:Number;
    public var vy:Number;
    public var vz:Number;

    public var radius:Number = 2;
    public var mass:Number = 1;
    public var id:Number = 0;
    public var gravity:Number = 0;
    public var friction:Number = 1;

    private var pnt:Object;
    private var LS:Number = 10;
    private var VPf:Number = 60;
    private var cx:Number = 320;
    private var sx:Number = 10;
    private var cy:Number = 240;
    private var sy:Number = 10;

    public function Ball(){
        init();
    }

    private function init(Void):Void {
        gotoAndStop(id % _totalframes + 1);
        x = Math.random() * 16 - 8;
        y = Math.random() * 16 - 8;
        z = Math.random() * 16 - 8;
        vx = (Math.random() * 16 - 8) / 10;
        vy = (Math.random() * 16 - 8) / 10;
        vz = (Math.random() * 16 - 8) / 10;
        pnt = new Object();
    }

    public function getDist(sibl:MovieClip):Number {
        var dx:Number = x - sibl.x;
        var dy:Number = y - sibl.y;
        var dz:Number = z - sibl.z;
        return Math.sqrt(dx * dx + dy * dy + dz * dz);
    }

    public function onEnterFrame() {
        vy -= gravity;
        vy *= friction;
        x += vx;
        y += vy;
        z += vz;
        if (x < -LS + radius) {
            vx *= -1;
            x = -LS + radius;
        }
```

```
        if (x > LS - radius) {
            vx *= -1;
            x = LS - radius;
        }
        if (y < -LS + radius) {
            vy *= -1;
            y = -LS + radius;
        }
        if (y > LS - radius) {
            vy *= -1;
            y = LS - radius;
        }
        if (z < -LS + radius) {
            vz *= -1;
            z = -LS + radius;
        }
        if (z > LS - radius) {
            vz *= -1;
            z = LS - radius;
        }
        pnt.x = x;
        pnt.y = y;
        pnt.z = z;
        rotate();
        var k = VPf / (VPf - pnt.z);
        _x = cx + sx * pnt.x * k;
        _y = cy - sy * pnt.y * k;
        _xscale = sx * radius * 2 * k;
        _yscale = sy * radius * 2 * k;
        this.swapDepths(int(pnt.z * 1000) + 100000);
    }

    private function rotate(Void):Void   {
        var y = pnt.y;
        var z = pnt.z;
        pnt.z = _parent.cos2 * z - _parent.sin2 * pnt.x;
        pnt.x = _parent.sin2 * z + _parent.cos2 * pnt.x;
        pnt.y = _parent.cos1 * y - _parent.sin1 * pnt.z;
        pnt.z = _parent.sin1 * y + _parent.cos1 * pnt.z;
    }

    function checkCollision(ball2:MovieClip)
    ➥ :Void {
        var dist:Number = getDist(ball2);
        var maxDist:Number = radius +
        ➥ ball2.radius;
        if (dist < maxDist) {
            var ratio:Number = maxDist / dist;
            x = ball2.x + (x - ball2.x) * ratio;
            y = ball2.y + (y - ball2.y) * ratio;
            z = ball2.z + (z - ball2.z) * ratio;
            if (mass == ball2.mass) {
                var tmp:Number = vx;
                vx = ball2.vx;
                ball2.vx = tmp;
```

```
            tmp = vy;
            vy = ball2.vy;
            ball2.vy = tmp;

            tmp = vz;
            vz = ball2.vz;
            ball2.vz = tmp;

    } else {
        var totalMass:Number = mass +
        ➡ ball2.mass;

        var tmp:Number = vx;
        vx = (ball2.mass * (2 * ball2.vx - vx) +
        ➡ mass * vx) / totalMass;
        ball2.vx = vx + tmp - ball2.vx;
```

```
            tmp = vy;
            vy = (ball2.mass * (2 * ball2.vy - vy)
            ➡ + mass * vy) / totalMass;
            ball2.vy = vy + tmp - ball2.vy;

            tmp = vx;
            vz = (ball2.mass * (2 * ball2.vz - vz)
            ➡ + mass * vz) / totalMass;
            ball2.vz = vz + tmp - ball2.vz;
        }
    }
}
```

This experiment models the physics of solid interaction. Each solid ball has a mass and radius. On the collision of two balls, the first ball changes its position, and changes its velocity and the second ball's velocity. Figure 1, over the page, illustrates this step by step.

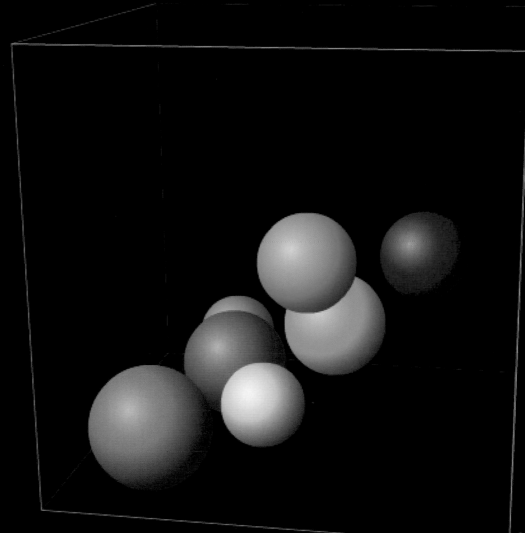

The key variables and functions

The main timeline variables and functions are as follows:

ax, **ay** = The two directions of camera rotation around the box (see Figure 2, opposite).
sin1, **cos1** = The sine and cosine of **ay**.
sin2, **cos2** = The sine and cosine of **ax**.
bnum = The number of balls.
lnum = The number of lines. (The lines are **(A,B)**, **(B,C)**, **(C,D)**, **(D,A)**, **(E,F)**, **(F,G)**, **(G,H)**, **(H,E)**, **(A,E)**, **(B,F)**, **(C,G)**, and **(D,E)**. See Figure 2 for details.)

Here are relevant variables and functions from the **Line** class:

VPf = The distance from the camera (the viewpoint) to the center (0, 0, 0).
cx, **cy** = The coordinates of image center on the screen.
sx, **sy** = The image scale coefficients for **x** and **y**.
rotate(p) = The function to rotate point **p** around **Oy** to an angle defined by **cos2** and **sin2**, and then rotate the point around **Ox** to an angle defined by **cos1** and **sin1**.
LS = The line scale factor.
pline = An array of line coordinates. Each element contains the first and second point of the line.

The **Ball** class variables and functions are as follows (as well as the following, the **Ball** class contains many of the same variables as listed under **Line**):

radius = The ball radius.
mass = The ball mass.
pnt = A temporary object.
getDist(sibl) = The return distance between this ball and the **sibl** ball. **sibl** is another **Ball** movie clip that is compared to this ball in the **_root onEnterFrame** function.
onEnterFrame()= The function to change the clip parameters (**_x**, **_y**, **_xscale**, **_yscale**), change the movie clip depth, and change the 3D location of the ball on each frame.

Many of the parameters just mentioned may be changed in this experiment. For example, if **LS** is set to 15, then the box will be larger. If **vx**, **vy**, and/or **vz** are changed in the function **onEnterFrame**, then the balls will fly into space due to the gravitational force. It is possible to create laws of gravity between balls, and so on.

In the files **balls_1.fla** to **balls_8.fla**, you'll find some iterations of this basic effect. Have a look at the variables I've altered in each file and see what the impacts are on the end result. Note that each file uses the same class files, and only the code in the FLA has changed. Obviously, you're not limited to the changes I've made, nor is there any reason that you couldn't start making changes to the classes themselves. After studying my iterations, try changing some variables of your own and see what the effects are.

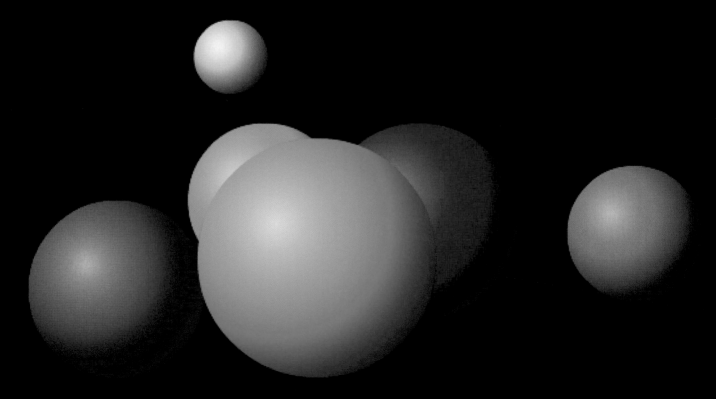

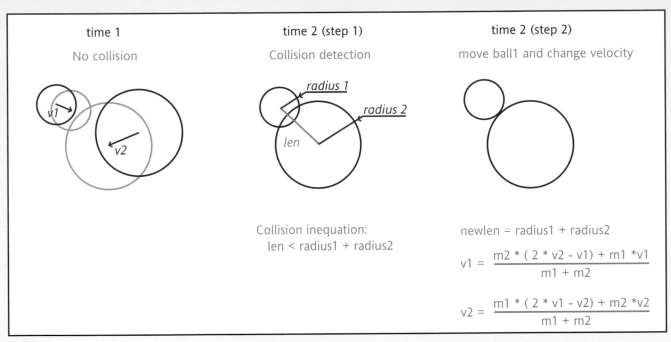

time 1
No collision

time 2 (step 1)
Collision detection

radius 1

radius 2

len

time 2 (step 2)
move ball1 and change velocity

Collision inequation:
len < radius1 + radius2

newlen = radius1 + radius2

$$v1 = \frac{m2 * (2 * v2 - v1) + m1 * v1}{m1 + m2}$$

$$v2 = \frac{m1 * (2 * v1 - v2) + m2 * v2}{m1 + m2}$$

Figure 1

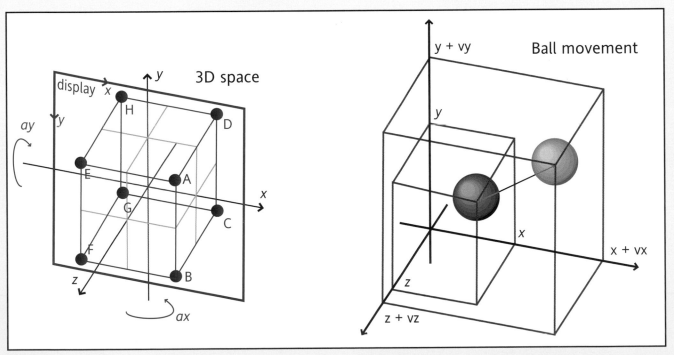

3D space

display *x*

y

ay

H   D

E   A

G

C

F

B

z

ax

Ball movement

y + vy

y

x

x + vx

z

z + vz

Figure 2

Rings

In this experiment, you'll create a crazy 3D effect involving a sphere moving through a horizontal circle made up of vertical circles. Clear enough? Take a look at `Ring_0.swf` for a sneak peek. Turning your attention to the source file, `Ring_0.fla`, the Library of this movie contains a movie clip named `Ball` and another named `3Dring`. `Ball` is exported and given the linkage name and ActionScript 2.0 class name `Ball`. `3DRing` is exported as `3DRing` and has the ActionScript 2.0 class name `Ring`. Within the `Ball` clip lives a clip given instance name `S`. The movie `3DRing` itself contains another movie clip called `C`. The `C` clip contains a ring shape that forms the basis of the end visual effect.

Frame 1 of the root timeline contains the following code, which is the only code on the main stage itself:

```
for (var i=0; i<5; i++) {
    var ball:MovieClip = attachMovie("Ball", "B"
    ➥ + i, i);
    ball.timer = -i * 10;
}
```

There are also two external ActionScript class files, `Ball.as` and `Ring.as`. Here is the code for `Ball.as`:

```
class Ball extends MovieClip {
    private var rnd1:Number;
    private var rnd2:Number;
    private var rnd3:Number;
    private var rnd4:Number;
    private var rnd5:Number;
    private var VPf:Number = 150;
    private var centerx:Number = 320;
    private var centery:Number = 240;
    private var pnt:Object;
    private var pnt0:Object;
    private var pnt1:Object;
    private var pnt2:Object;
    private var R0:MovieClip;
    private var R1:MovieClip;
    private var R2:MovieClip;
    private var S:MovieClip;
    public var timer:Number;

    public function Ball(){
        init();
    }
    private function init(){
        rnd1 = 10 + Math.random() * 10;
        rnd2 = 10 + Math.random() * 10;
        rnd3 = 10 + Math.random() * 10;
        rnd4 = 7 + Math.random() * 7;
        rnd5 = 7 + Math.random() * 7;
        pnt = new Object();
        pnt0 = new Object();
        pnt1 = new Object();
```

```
        pnt2 = new Object();
        _xscale = 100;
        _yscale = 100;
        attachMovie("3DRing", "R0", 0);
        attachMovie("3DRing", "R1", 1);
        attachMovie("3DRing", "R2", 2);
        S.SetPos = function(px:Number, py:Number,
        ➥ scale:Number):Void {
            this._xscale = scale * 100;
            this._yscale = scale * 100;
            this._x = px;
            this._y = py;
        }
}

function Prf(p:Object) {
    p.x = centerx + p.x * VPf / (VPf - p.z);
    p.y = centery - p.y * VPf / (VPf - p.z);
}
function rot (p:Object, cos1:Number,
➥ sin1:Number, cos2:Number, sin2:Number) {
    var x:Number = p.x;
    p.x = cos1 * x - sin1 * p.y;
    var y:Number = sin1 * x + cos1 * p.y;
    p.y = cos2 * y - sin2 * p.z;
    p.z = sin2 * y + cos2 * p.z;
}

function Set3DPos(x:Number, y:Number,
➥ z:Number, a1:Number, a2:Number) {
    pnt.x = x;
    pnt.y = y;
    pnt.z = z;

    pnt0.x = 1;
    pnt0.y = 0;
    pnt0.z = 0;

    pnt1.x = 0;
    pnt1.y = 1;
    pnt1.z = 0;

    pnt2.x = 0;
    pnt2.y = 0;
    pnt2.z = 1;

    var cos1:Number = Math.cos(a1);
    var sin1:Number = Math.sin(a1);
    var cos2:Number = Math.cos(a2);
    var sin2:Number = Math.sin(a2);

    rot(pnt0, cos1, sin1, cos2, sin2);
    rot(pnt1, cos1, sin1, cos2, sin2);
    rot(pnt2, cos1, sin1, cos2, sin2);

    pnt0.x += x;
    pnt0.y += y;
```

```
        pnt0.z += z;

        pnt1.x += x;
        pnt1.y += y;
        pnt1.z += z;

        pnt2.x += x;
        pnt2.y += y;
        pnt2.z += z;

        Prf(pnt);
        Prf(pnt0);
        Prf(pnt1);
        Prf(pnt2);

        R0.SetPos(pnt.x, pnt.y,
    ➥ pnt0.x - pnt.x, -pnt0.y + pnt.y,
    ➥ pnt1.x - pnt.x, -pnt1.y + pnt.y);
        R1.SetPos(pnt.x, pnt.y,
    ➥ pnt1.x - pnt.x, -pnt1.y + pnt.y,
    ➥ pnt2.x - pnt.x, -pnt2.y + pnt.y);
        R2.SetPos(pnt.x, pnt.y,
    ➥ pnt2.x - pnt.x, -pnt2.y + pnt.y,
    ➥ pnt0.x - pnt.x, -pnt0.y + pnt.y);

        S.SetPos(pnt.x, pnt.y, VPf / (VPf - z));

        this.swapDepths(int(z * 10 + 5000));
    }
    public function onEnterFrame(){
        timer++;
        Set3DPos(56 * Math.cos(timer / rnd1 + 2),
            56 * Math.cos( timer / rnd2 ),
            56 * Math.cos(timer / rnd3 + 1),
            timer / rnd4,
            timer / rnd5);
    }
}
```

Here's the **Ring.as** code:

```
class Ring extends MovieClip{
    private var R:MovieClip;
    private var clr:Color;

    public function Ring(){
        init();
    }
    private function init(){
        clr = new Color(this);
    }

    public function SetPos (px:Number, py:Number,
    ➥ a1:Number, b1:Number, a2:Number, b2:Number) {
        var k1:Number = Math.atan2(b2 - a1, a2 + b1);
        var k2:Number = Math.atan2(b2 + a1, a2 - b1);
        var alpha:Number = 0.5 * ( k1 + k2 );
        var phy:Number = 0.5 * ( k1 - k2 );
        if ( Math.sin(k1) == 0 || Math.sin(k2) == 0 ) {
            var sx:Number = 0.5 * ((a2+b1) /
            ➥ Math.cos(k1) + (a2-b1) / Math.cos(k2));
            var sy:Number = 0.5 * ((a2+b1) /
            ➥ Math.cos(k1) - (a2-b1) / Math.cos(k2));
        } else {
            var sx:Number = 0.5 * ((b2-a1) /
            ➥ Math.sin(k1) + (b2+a1) / Math.sin(k2));
            var sy:Number = 0.5 * ((b2-a1) /
            ➥ Math.sin(k1) - (b2+a1) / Math.sin(k2));
        }
        _rotation = phy * (-180) / Math.PI;
        _xscale = sx * 100;
        _yscale = sy * 100;
        _rotation = alpha * (-180) / Math.PI;
        _x = px;
        _y = py;
    }

}
```

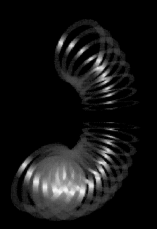
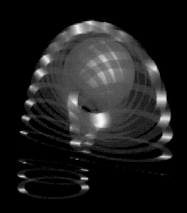
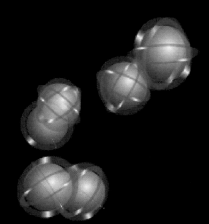

The code starts by creating five instances of the **Ball** movie clip. Each ball moves itself separately, and the trace of each ball is a Lissajous figure. **Ball** attaches to itself three rings, which spin around the ball. Figure 3 shows the ring's transformation from movie clip coordinate space to 3D space. You need three points to locate one ring, but you need only four points to locate three rings, as Figure 3 shows. Only four points are projected. This isn't a precision 3D projection, but it certainly *looks* like a 3D projection.

The key variables and functions
Let's look at the variables and functions of the **Ball** class first.

rnd1, **rnd2**, **rnd3** – The x, y, and z parameters used for the Lissajous figure. **RndN** is the scale factor used on the **timer** counter when it's put into the **cos()** equation.
rnd4, **rnd5** = The rotation speed of the ball.
VPf = The distance from the camera (viewpoint) to the 3D shape.
centerx, **centery** = The coordinates of the image center on the screen.
pnt, **pnt0**, **pnt1**, **pnt2** = Temporary 3D points (object **this** x, y, and z properties).
Prf(p) = A function that projects a point **p(x, y, z)** to the plane **Oxy** from **ViewPoint(0,0, VPf)**, and then returns the result to itself as **p(x, y)**.
rot(p, cos1, sin1, cos2, sin2) = A function to rotate the point **p** around **Ox** to an angle defined by **cos1** and **sin1**, and then rotate point **p** around **Oz** to an angle defined by **cos2** and **sin2**.
Set3DPos(x, y, z, a1, a2) = A function that moves the movie clips **R0**, **R1**, **R2**, and **S**.
x, **y**, **z** = The ball center coordinates.
a1, **a2** = The ball rotation.

Next up are the interesting **Ring** class variables and functions.

SetPos(px, py, a1, b1, a2, b2) = A function to change clip parameters (_rotation, _xscale, _yscale, _x, _y)
px, **py** = Screen coordinates of a ring (shape center at point **a**; see Figure 3)
(px+a1, py+b1) = The screen coordinates of a ring (point **b**; see Figure 3)
(px+a2, py+b2) = The screen coordinates of a ring (point **c**; see Figure 3)
k1, **k2**, **alpha**, **phy**, **sx**, **sy** = Temporary variables in the function body

Figure 3

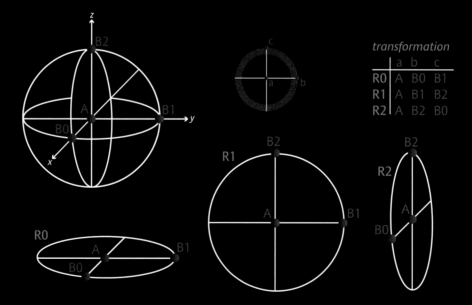

This is a nice little vehicle for some great effects. By playing with the variables, you can take these effects and move them to another level. Check out some of the iterations that I've prepared, available with this chapter's source code files. A good example is in **Ring_4.fla**; here you'll see how the basic model can easily be developed into something quite stunning. Also note that there are a few different versions of the class files used to create different effects.

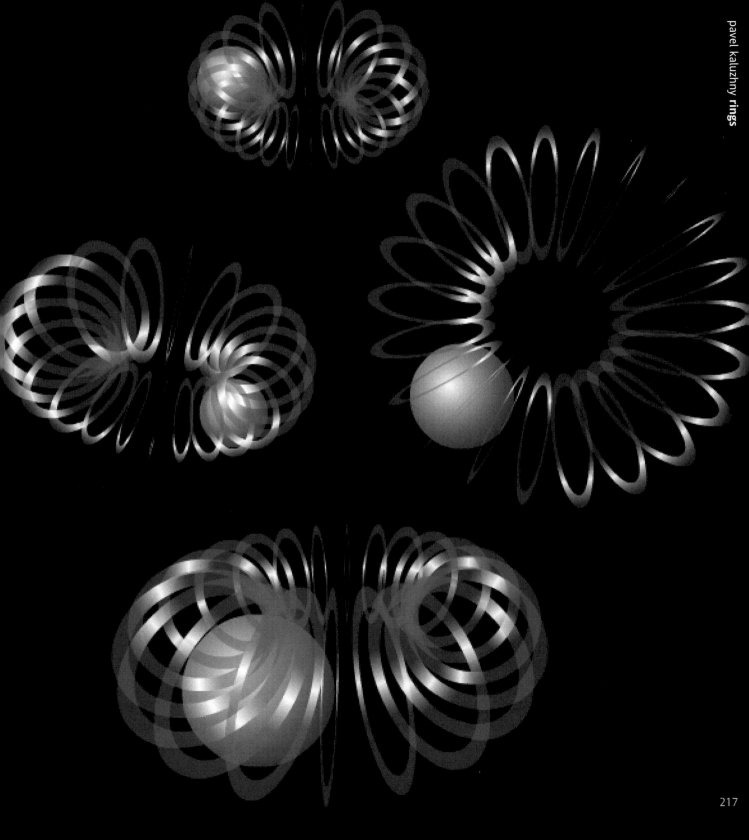

3D Text

This effect will create the illusion of 3D text, which you'll map over a surface or animate. You can see the results of the code listed here in the file **txt_I_0.swf**. Let's look at what its associated FLA consists of.

The Library of **txt_I_0.fla** contains two important movie clips: **Text3D** and **Char3D**. **Char3D** is exported from the Library and assigned an ActionScript 2.0 class—both the linkage and class names are also **Char3D**. **Text3D** is similarly set up. Finally, there's another clip called **Char** that contains a dynamic text field named **tf**. **Char3D** contains an instance of **Char**, named **charClip**, and **Text3D** is empty.

Let's examine the code that creates this great effect, starting with the code that sits in frame 1 of the timeline:

```
inputText = "You may type  any\n";
inputText += "text. This is\n";
inputText += "3D-shape of text\n";
inputText += "and other symbols.\n";
inputText += "cool text effect\n";
inputText += "freedom of mind ;-)\n";
attachMovie("Text3D", "text" ,0);
text._x = 320;
text._y = 240;
text.text = inputText;
```

That's all the code for the main timeline. The rest of the code is contained in two external class files, **Char3D.as** and **Text3D.as**.

This is the code for the **Text3D** class:

```
class Text3D extends MovieClip {
  private var VPf:Number = 260;
  private var sclx:Number = 20;
  private var scly:Number = 20;
  private var pnt0:Object;
  private var pnt1:Object;
  private var pnt2:Object;
  private var timer:Number = 0;
  private var str:String;
  private var numChars:Number = 0;
  private var xoffset:Number = 8;
  private var yoffset:Number = 4;

  public function Text3D(){
    init();
  }

  private function init(Void):Void {
    pnt0 = new Object();
    pnt1 = new Object();
    pnt2 = new Object();
    if(str != undefined){
      setText();
    }
  }
```

```
private function makeShape(u:Number,
➡ v:Number, p:Object):Void {
  p.x = (u - xoffset) * 20;
  p.y = (yoffset - v) * 14 + Math.cos
  ➡ (Math.sqrt((u - xoffset) *
  ➡ (u - xoffset) + (3 - v) * (3 - v)) / 2
  ➡ + timer / 4) * 36;
  p.z = (v - yoffset) * 20;
}
private function projectPoint(p:Object):Void {
  p.x = p.x * VPf / (VPf - p.z);
  p.y = -p.y * VPf / (VPf - p.z);
}

public function setText(Void):Void   {
  for(var prop in this){
    if(typeof this[prop] == "movieclip"){
      this[prop].removeMovieClip();
    }
  }
  var x:Number = 0;
  var y:Number = 0;
  var num:Number = 0;
  for(var i=0; i<str.length; i++ ) {
    var ch:String = str.charAt(i);
    if (ch > " ") {
      var theChar:MovieClip = attachMovie
      ➡ ("Char3D", "char" + num, num);
      theChar.u = x;
      theChar.v = y;
      theChar.charClip.tf.text = ch;
      num++;
      x++;
    } else if (ch == " ") {
      x++;
    }
    if (ch < " ") {
      y += 1.5;
      x = 0;
    }
  }
  numChars = num;
}

function onEnterFrame (Void):Void {
  timer++;
  for (var i=0; i < numChars; i++ ) {
    var theChar:MovieClip = this["char" + i];
    makeShape(theChar.u, theChar.v, pnt0);
    makeShape(theChar.u, theChar.v + 1, pnt1);
    makeShape(theChar.u + 1, theChar.v, pnt2);

    var c:Number = (int(128 + (pnt0.y +
    ➡ pnt0.z * 0.7) * 3) & 0xFF);
```

```
      c = (c << 16) | (c << 8) | 0xFF;
        theChar.clr.setRGB(c);
        projectPoint(pnt0);
        projectPoint(pnt1);
        projectPoint(pnt2);
        theChar.setPos(pnt0.x, pnt0.y,
        ➥ pnt1.x-pnt0.x, -pnt1.y+pnt0.y,
        ➥ pnt2.x-pnt0.x, -pnt2.y+pnt0.y);
      }
    }
    public function set text(txt:String){
      str = txt;
      setText();
    }
    public function get text():String {
      return str;
    }
  }
}
```

Here's the code for the **Char3D** class:

```
class Char3D extends MovieClip {
  private var charClip:MovieClip;
  public var clr:Color;

  public function Char3D(){
    init();
  }

  private function init(){
    clr = new Color(this);
  }

  public function setPos (px, py, a1, b1, a2, b2) {
    var k1:Number = Math.atan2(b2 - a1, a2 + b1);
    var k2:Number = Math.atan2(b2 + a1, a2 - b1);
    var alpha = 0.5 * ( k1 + k2 );
    var phy   = 0.5 * ( k1 - k2 );
    if ( Math.sin(k1) == 0 || Math.sin(k2) == 0 ) {
      var sx = 0.5 * ((a2 + b1) / Math.cos(k1) +
      ➥ (a2 - b1) / Math.cos(k2));
      var sy = 0.5 * ((a2 + b1) / Math.cos(k1) -
      ➥ (a2 - b1) / Math.cos(k2));
    } else {
      var sx = 0.5 * ((b2 - a1) / Math.sin(k1) +
      ➥ (b2 + a1) / Math.sin(k2));
      var sy = 0.5 * ((b2 - a1) / Math.sin(k1) -
      ➥ (b2 + a1) / Math.sin(k2));
    }
    charClip._rotation = phy * -180 / Math.PI;
    _xscale = sx * 100 / 24;
    _yscale = sy * 100 / 24;
    _rotation = alpha * -180 / Math.PI;
    _x = px;
    _y = py;
  }
}
```

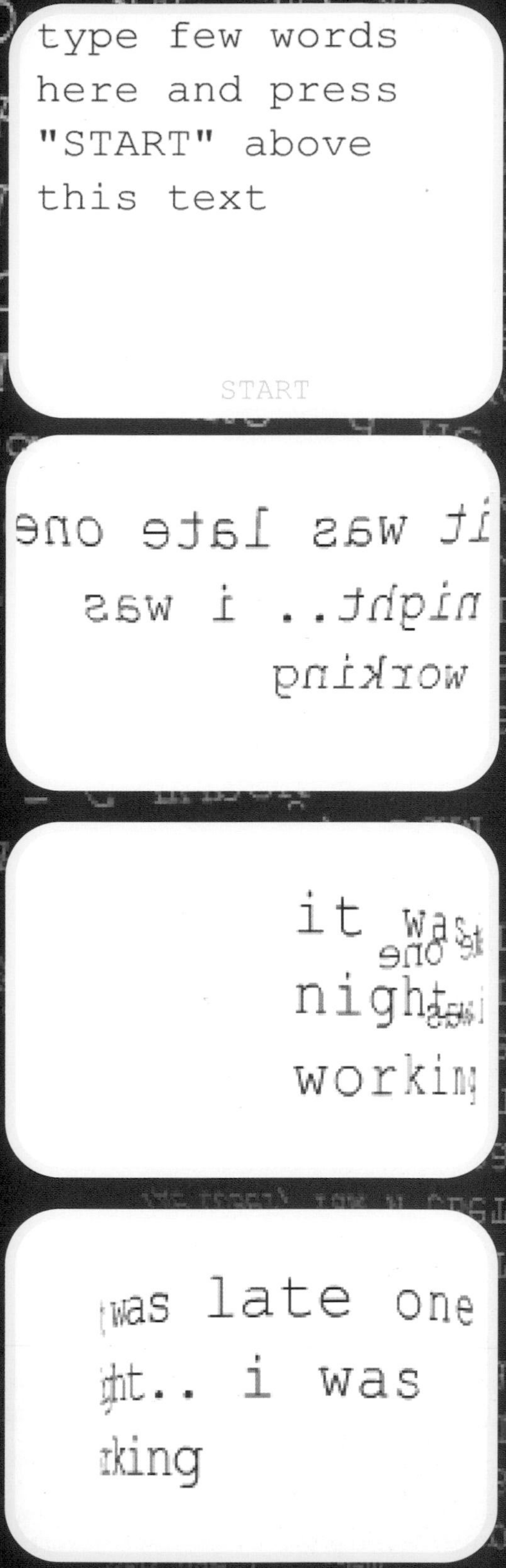

The code just divides the input text into the single characters. Each symbol gets put into an instance of **Char3D** and has text field space coordinates and 3D space coordinates (see Figure 4). **Text3D** updates parameters on the enter frame. Each symbol transforms itself, as you can see at the bottom of Figure 4.

Figure 4

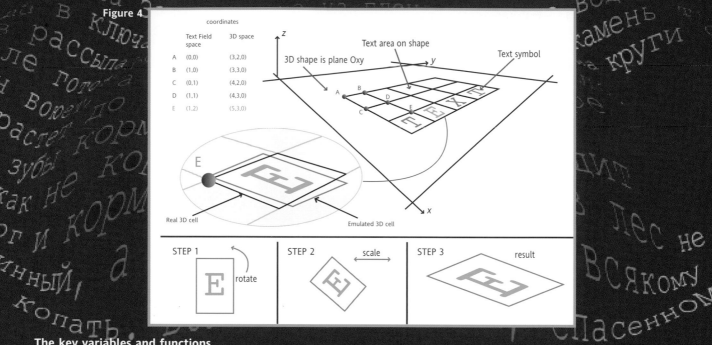

The key variables and functions

inputText = The main text for effect, available for changing. (This is the only root variable.)

The relevant **Text3D** class variables and functions are as follows:

VPf = The distance from the camera (or viewpoint) to the 3D shape.
pnt0, **pnt1**, **pnt2** = Temporary 3D points (object **this** x, y, and z properties).
makeShape(u, v, p) = A function to determine the 3D shape. The function takes the **(u, v)** coordinates of text field space and returns point **p** in 3D space. Figure 4 shows coordinate points in text field space compared to the coordinates in 3D space.
projectPoint(p) = A function that projects point **p(x, y, z)** to the plane **Oxy** from the viewpoint **(0,0, VPf)**, and returns the result to itself: **p(x, y)**.
setText (str) = A function that creates or updates symbols. First it removes all old objects, and then it attaches new instances of **Char3D**. Variables **x** and **y** are **u** and **v** coordinates in text field space.
onEnterFrame() = A function that draws the image. It changes each symbol's parameters.

The **Char3D** variables and functions are as follows:

clr = A color or symbol
setPos(px, py, a1, b1, a2, b2) = A function to change the clip parameters (**_rotation**, **_xscale**, **_yscale**, **_x**, **_y**)
px, **py** = The screen coordinates of a symbol (top-left corner)
(px+a1, py+b1) = The screen coordinates of a symbol (top-right corner)
(px+a2, py+b2) = The screen coordinates of a symbol (bottom-left corner)
k1, k2, alpha, phy, sx, sy = Temporary variables in the function's body

You can expand on this initial idea by making simple code changes. Take a look at my sample files for inspiration—you'll soon see how diverse the output can be just by changing a few variables here and there. Note that I have several versions of the class file to create the different effects. You can even create a SWF where you enter the text you'd like to transform into the file, and the movie displays it on a 3D wave for you (see, for example, **txt_IV_0.swf**).

JD Hooge has a broad range of design and interactive development experience. After earning a B.F.A. in Communication Design from the Milwaukee Institute of Art & Design, he co-founded the Fourm Design Studio. JD started www.infourm.com and continues to design fonts for www.miniml.com, a digital type foundry. JD currently works as a designer for Second Story Interactive Studios in Portland, Oregon.

jd hooge
www.gridplane.com

Terraforming

The set of four experiments that I describe in this chapter contain all of the controls you'll need to alter the values in them in real time. That isn't to say that you can't go in and fiddle with the code—I'll give you some suggestions for that later—but there should be enough here to keep you busy for a while. And, of course, each movie contains custom-made slider controls, so you can also look at the source code to get an idea about how they're structured and incorporated into the overall experiment.

There are three layers on the main timeline: **code**, **objects**, and **grid**. The **code** layer contains the majority of the code for the movie, but there's also some code in an external class file called **Points.as** (as well as in the **Slider.as** component script). The **objects** layer contains the interface elements of the movie: all of the sliders, buttons, and labels. The **grid** layer contains a movie clip with a grid in it—it's wrapped in a movie clip so you can control the alpha of it with a slider, allowing you to fade it in and out.

I'll explain the main areas of code here and look at what they do, but be sure to check the FLA for the layout of the controls and the construction details of the buttons and movie clips.

Here's the code for frame 1 of the root timeline (see **exp_1.fla**):

```
// =============== initialize a few things
fscommand ("allowscale", "false");
fscommand ("fullscreen", "true");
_quality = "LOW";
bar1.value = 15;
bar2.value = 50;
var lineCount:Number = 0;
// =============== attach points and lines
for (var i=1; i<10; i++) {
    var point:MovieClip = attachMovie
    ➡ ("pointclip", "point"+i, i*1000);
    point.display = i;
}
```

```
// =============== draw and connect lines
onEnterFrame = function() {
    var line:MovieClip = createEmptyMovieClip
    ➡ ("line" + lineCount, lineCount);
    line.moveTo(point1._x, point1._y);
    for (i=2; i<10; i++) {
        var col:Number = (90 << 16) | (190 << 8) |
        ➡ (70 + i * 20);
        line.lineStyle(1, col, 100);
        line.lineTo(this["point" + i]._x,
        ➡ this["point" + i]._y);
    }
    line.onEnterFrame = function(){
        this._alpha-=2;
        if(this._alpha < 1){
            this.removeMovieClip();
        }
    };
    lineCount++;
    if(lineCount > bar3.value){
        lineCount = 0;
    }
};
// =============== set up the controls
bar4.onChanged = function(){
    grid._alpha = this.value;
};
autorunBtn.onRelease = function(){
    for (i=1; i<10; i++) {
        var point:MovieClip = _root["point" + i];
        point.auto = !point.auto;
    }
};
labelBtn.onRelease = function(){
    for (i=1; i<10; i++) {
        var point:MovieClip = _root["point" + i];
        point.label._visible =
        ➡ !point.label._visible;
    }
};
```

The other important piece of code is in the **Point.as** class file:

```
class Point extends MovieClip {
  public var display:Number;
  public var label:MovieClip;
  public var auto:Boolean = false;

  private var i:Number = 0;
  private var xn:Number = 0;
  private var yn:Number = 0;
  private var x:Number = 0;
  private var y:Number = 0;
  private var timer:Number = 0;
  private var pointBtn:Button;

  public function Point(){
    init();
  }
  private function init(){
    _x = 200;
    _y = 0;
    label._visible = false;

    pointBtn.onPress = function() {
      this._parent.startDrag(true,
      ➥ this._parent._x + 1, 0,
      ➥ this._parent._x + 1, 300);
    }
    pointBtn.onRelease =
    ➥ pointBtn.onReleaseOutside = function(){
      this._parent.stopDrag();
    }
  }
```

```
  public function onEnterFrame(){
    if(Math.abs(this._xmouse) > 20 ||
    ➥ Math.abs(this._ymouse) > 10){
      // set accel and elast equal to their
      // sliders
      var accel:Number = _parent.bar1.value / 100;
      var elast:Number = _parent.bar2.value / 100;
      if(i < timer && Math.abs(_y - yn) > 3) {
        i++;
      } else {
        // When i catches up with timer,
        // set new destinations for all points
        if (!auto) {
          yn = 140;
        } else {
          yn = (Math.random() * 5 + 1) * 60;
        }
        xn = -50 + display * 50;
        i = 0;
        timer = Math.random() * 20 + 10;
      }

      // position _x
      _x -= x = (x + (_x - xn) * accel) * elast;

      // position _y
      _y -= y = (y + (_y - yn) * accel) * elast;
    }
  }
}
```

The rest of the code is just the slider code in the **Slider.as** file, so I won't go into that here. Take a look in the file to see what it does.

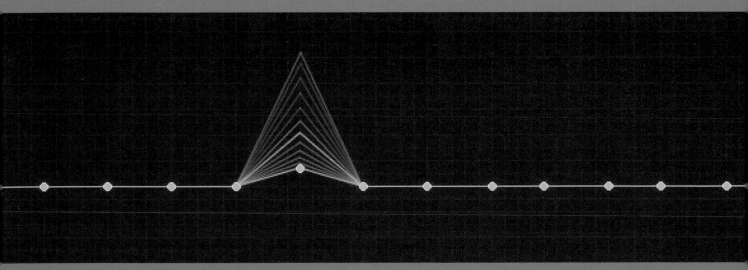

The key variables and functions

On the main timeline are the following variables and functions:

auto = A toggle for the auto-run button. **true** means it's off; **false** means it's on.

timer = The time it takes for a point to change direction, updated as a random number later on.

bar1 = The acceleration slider.

bar2 = The elasticity slider.

bar3 = The number of trails slider.

bar4 = The grid alpha slider.

pointclip = The linkage name of **clip_Point** in the Library.

onEnterFrame = A function to draw the new lines.

In the **Points.as** class, the interesting code elements are as follows:

label = A toggle for the point labels. **true** means they're there; **false** means they're not.

display = The variable name assigned to a dynamic text box inside **clip_Point** to display the number of the point, assigned as a variable when the point is created.

onEnterFrame = A function to update the position of the current point.

accel = The value of the acceleration slider.

elast = The value of the elasticity slider.

yn = The **y** destination of the point. If auto-run isn't on, then it's automatically set to the center; otherwise, it's a random value.

xn = The **x** destination of the point. Each point has a fixed x-position.

So, here is how it works. First, you create several points (attached from the Library) and place them in a row. You then create an empty movie clip and use it to draw lines from the first point through all the rest.

On the next frame, you do the same thing with a new movie clip. When enough line clips have been created, the next one takes the place of the first. The creation and removal of these line movie clips is what gives the trailing effect. You can either drag the point around yourself or set it to auto-run, meaning that the points will automatically keep moving to random positions, leaving you free to play about with the various sliders.

The primary script (on frame 1 of the main timeline) does the following:

1. Attaches all the points

2. Connects the points with the lines

3. Fades the lines

4. Colors the lines

5. Handles changes to the controls

The **Points** class file essentially moves the points based on random calculations.

I have given default values for the controls that create a very fluid motion. However, there are many different aspects that you could change to get different types of motion. For instance, if you turn **accel** way down and **elast** way up, you'll start to get images resembling terraforms. If you turn up the amount of lines created, you'll increase this effect. Try changing the RGB values in the primary script or removing the graphic of the point to just leave the traced lines moving around the screen. Another thing to try is setting the x-position to a similar random value to the y-position so that the lines can travel all around the screen.

Trailing lines

This experiment is similar to the last one, but with some distinct differences. Run **exp_2.swf** to see what I mean. This time, rather than having all of the points along one horizontal line, there's an axis in the center of the screen and one point on each arm of the axis. I've also changed some of the sliders: there isn't an auto-run toggle for this experiment—it's always on. And there's an additional slider that controls the timer variable so you can set how often the points move. The setup on the main stage of the FLA is also similar, except I've added a new layer containing a background movie clip. This clip simply fades the background in when the movie begins.

As before, I'll attach all the main code on frame 1 of the root timeline, and then give an explanation of what each section does and how it all works together.

Here's the code for the first frame of **exp_2.fla**:

```
// ==============  initialize a few things
fscommand ("allowscale", "false");
fscommand ("fullscreen", "true");
_quality = "LOW";
bar1.value = 10;
bar2.value = 77;
bar3.value = 15;
bar4.value = 35;
bar5.value = 15;
var lineCount:Number = 0;
// ==============  attach points and lines
for (var i=1; i<5; i++) {
    var point:MovieClip = attachMovie("pointclip", "point"+i, i*1000);
    point.display = i;
}
// ==============  draw and connect lines
onEnterFrame = function() {
    var line:MovieClip = createEmptyMovieClip("line" + lineCount, lineCount);
    line.moveTo(point1._x, point1._y);
    for (i=2; i<5; i++) {
        var col:Number = (90 << 16) | (190 << 8) | (70 + i * 20);
        line.lineStyle(1, col, 100);
        line.lineTo(this["point" + i]._x, this["point" + i]._y);
    }
    line.onEnterFrame = function(){
        this._alpha-=2;
        if(this._alpha < 1){
            this.removeMovieClip();
        }
    };
    line.lineTo(point1._x, point1._y);
    lineCount++;
    if(lineCount > bar3.value){
        lineCount = 0;
    }
    // ==============  run timer based on random value
    timer = Math.random() * 20 + bar5.value;
};
// ==============  set up the controls
bar4.onChanged = function(){
    grid._alpha = this.value;
};
labelBtn.onRelease = function(){
    for (i=1; i<10; i++) {
        var point:MovieClip = _root["point" + i];
        point.label._visible = !point.label._visible;
    }
};
```

As before, there's an external **Point.as** class file, though it's a bit different from the last one:

```
class Point extends MovieClip {
    public var display:Number;
    public var label:MovieClip;
    public var auto:Boolean = true;

    private var i:Number = 0;
    private var xn:Number = 0;
    private var yn:Number = 0;
    private var x:Number = 0;
    private var y:Number = 0;
    private var timer:Number = 0;
    private var pointBtn:Button;

    public function Point(){
        init();
    }
    private function init(){
        _x = 200;
        _y = 0;
        label._visible = false;

        pointBtn.onPress = function() {
            this._parent.startDrag(true,
            ➡ this._parent._x + 1, 0,
            ➡ this._parent._x + 1, 300);
        };
        pointBtn.onRelease =
        ➡ pointBtn.onReleaseOutside = function(){
            this._parent.stopDrag();
        }
    };
```

```
    public function onEnterFrame(){
        if (i<_parent.timer) {
            i++;
        } else {
            // When i catches up with timer,
            // set new destinations for all 4
            // points
            if (display == 1) {
                // point 1
                yn = (Math.random() * 7 + 1) * 20;
                xn = _parent.xaxis._x;
            } else if (display == 2) {
                // point 2
                yn = _parent.yaxis._y;
                xn = (Math.random() * 7 + 12) * 20;
            } else if (display == 3) {
                // point 3
                yn = (Math.random() * 7 + 12) * 20;
                xn = _parent.xaxis._x;
            } else if (display == 4) {
                // point 4
                yn = _parent.yaxis._y;
                xn = (Math.random() * 7 + 1) * 20;
            }
            i = 0;
        }
        // =================
        var accel:Number = _parent.bar1.value / 100;
        var elast:Number = _parent.bar2.value / 100;
        // position _x
        _x -= x = (x + (_x - xn) * accel) * elast;
        // position _y
        _y -= y = (y + (_y - yn) * accel) * elast;
    }
}
```

And finally, there's the slider code in **Slider.as**, which hasn't changed.

The key variables and functions

On the main timeline and in **Point.as** are the following elements:

bar1 = The acceleration slider.

bar2 = The elasticity slider.

bar3 = The timer slider.

bar4 = The number of trails slider.

bar5 = The grid alpha slider.

pointclip = The linkage name of **clip_Point** in the Library.

onEnterFrame = A function to draw the new lines.

timer = The time it takes for a point to change direction.

label = A toggle for the point labels. **true** means they're there; **false** means they're not there.

display = The variable name assigned to a dynamic text box inside **clip_Point** to display the number of the point, assigned as a variable when the point is created.

onEnterFrame = A function to update the position of the current point.

accel = The value of the acceleration slider.

elast = The value of the elasticity slider.

yn = The **y** destination of the point, set to a random value along the axis.

xn = the **x** destination of the point, set to a random value along the axis.

The experiment works like this: first, you create four points (attached from the Library). Two are placed on the x-axis, and two are placed on the y-axis. You then create an empty movie clip and draw lines between the four points. On each frame, a new movie clip is created with lines to the new positions of the points. The old lines fade out and are eventually replaced by new ones, so they create a trail behind the main moving line.

The primary script (on frame 1 of the main timeline) does the following:

1. Attaches all the points
2. Connects the points with the lines
3. Fades the original lines
4. Colors the lines
5. Handles changes to the controls

And again, the **Points** class in **Point.as** moves the points based on random calculations.

As before, I've given default values for the controls to create a fluid motion. However, there are many different aspects that you could change to get different types of motion. I suggest that you mess around with the controls for a good amount of time, because there are many possible variations. Things you could do manually include replacing the line-drawing code to use different colors, alphas, or widths.

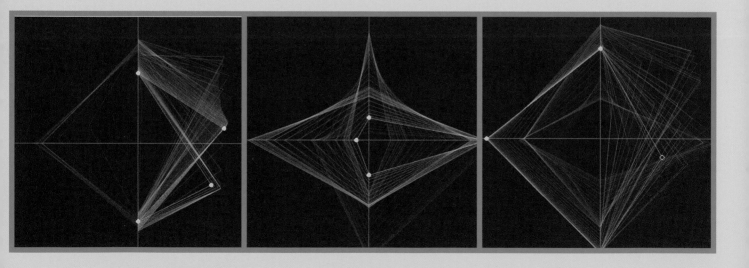

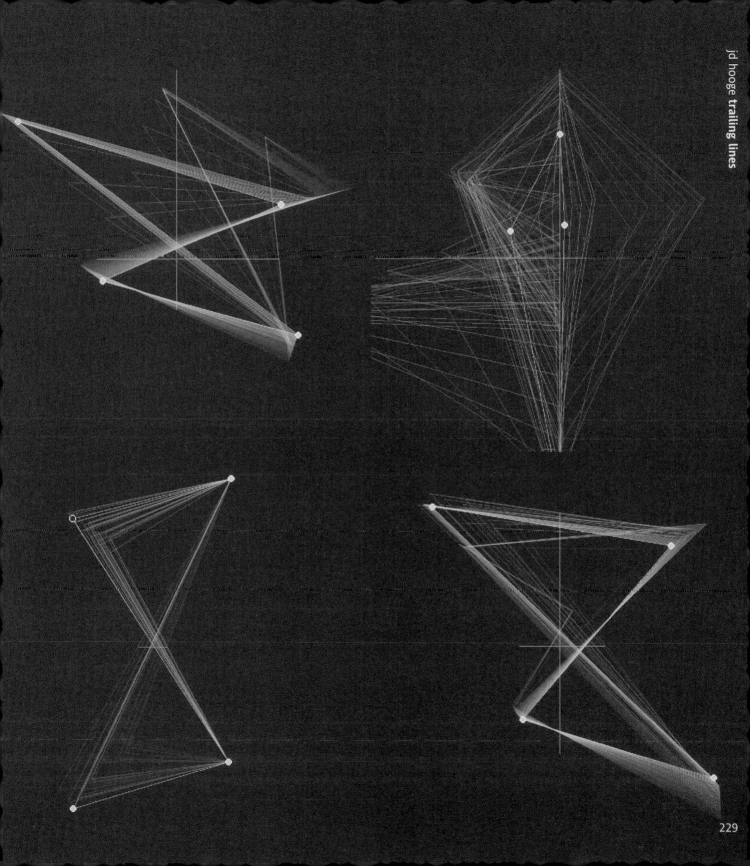

Elastic waves

This is a completely new effect, but it's based on some principles similar to the previous experiments. This time, rather than setting up trails of fading lines behind the originals, you're setting the points up in a line of vertical pairs and joining each point in a pair together with a line. The points can then move along the y-axis depending on some bounds put upon them by the user with some new sliders on the left side of the screen. If this experiment is set to auto-run, then the expanding and contracting pairs will produce waveforms that can then be controlled with the sliders. The waves will move back and forth along the screen, bouncing back off each side and causing splashes of repercussions in the next wave.

The basic layer setup is the same as before, but on the **objects** layer there are some new sliders on the left side clustered around a bar. The leftmost sliders control the base point of the wave—that is, the line that they oscillate around—and they'll return to the point at which they become still. To see the effect of this line, try turning off auto-run and then moving the sliders. The sliders on the right side of the bar control the peak destination of the wave. The points can go above or below this point depending on the acceleration, but this will be the average. These new controls are all contained in a new component called **Slider2**. As before, the **Slider2.as** class file contains the code that makes this component work. (The **Slider.as** file you've been using for the right sliders remains the same.)

The main code for this experiment is in the same places as the other experiments, so I'll list it here as I've done previously. To start with, here's the code from the first frame of the main timeline (**exp_3.fla**):

```
// ============== initialize a few things
fscommand ("allowscale", "false");
fscommand ("fullscreen", "true");
_quality = "LOW";

var num:Number = 39;
var half:Number = 19;
var over:Number = 0;
var counter:Number = 0;
var plus:Number = 0;
var minus:Number = 0;
var go:Boolean = true;
var toggle:Boolean = true;

bar1.value = 15;
bar2.value = 90;
bar4.value = 35;

// ============== attach points and lines
for (var i=1; i<half + 1; i++) {
  var point:MovieClip = attachMovie
  ➥ ("pointclip", "point"+i, i*1000);
  point._x = 200;
  point._y = 120;
  point.display = i;
}
```

```
for (var i=half + 1; i<num; i++) {
  var point:MovieClip = attachMovie
  ➥ ("pointclip", "point"+i, i*1000);
  point._x = 200;
  point._y = 180;
  point.display = i;
}
createEmptyMovieClip("lines", 0);


// ============== draw and connect lines
onEnterFrame = function() {
  lines.clear();
  for (i=1; i<=half; i++) {
    var col:Number = (90 << 16) | (190 << 8)
    ➥ | (140 + i * 20);
    lines.moveTo(this["point" + i]._x,
    ➥ this["point" + i]._y);
    lines.lineStyle(1, col, 100);
    lines.lineTo(this["point" + (i+half)]._x,
    ➥ this["point" + (i+half)]._y);
  }
  if (toggle) {
    over = counter;
  }
  if (counter < 0) {
    plus = 1;
    minus = half;
    counter = plus;
  }
  if (plus < half) {
    minus = half;
    plus++;
    go = true;
  } else {
    minus—;
    go = false;
  }
  if (go) {
    counter = plus;
  } else {
    counter = minus;
  }
};
// ============== set up the controls
bar4.onChanged = function(){
  grid._alpha = this.value;
};
autorunBtn.onRelease = function(){
  toggle = !toggle;
  if(!toggle){
    counter = 0;
    over = 0;
  }
};
```

Here's the code that's in **Point.as**:

```
class Point extends MovieClip {
  public var display:Number;
  public var label:MovieClip;
  public var auto:Boolean = true;

  private var i:Number = 0;
  private var xn:Number = 0;
  private var yn:Number = 0;
  private var x:Number = 0;
  private var y:Number = 0;
  private var timer:Number = 0;
  private var pointBtn:Button;

  public function Point(){
    init();
  }
  private function init(){
    label._visible = false;

    pointBtn.onPress = function() {
      this._parent.startDrag(true, this._parent._x +
      ➥ 1, 0, this._parent._x + 1, 300);
    };
    pointBtn.onRelease = pointBtn.onReleaseOutside =
    ➥ function(){
      this._parent.stopDrag();
    };
  }

  public function onEnterFrame(){
    // set accel and elast equal to their sliders
    var accel:Number = _parent.bar1.value / 100;
    var elast:Number = _parent.bar2.value / 100;

    // set destinations and heights for all points
    if (display<20) {
      if (_parent.over == display) {
        yn = _parent.slider2.dest1;
      } else {
        yn = _parent.slider2.static1;
      }
    } else {
      if (_parent.over == display-19) {
        yn = _parent.slider2.dest2;
      } else {
        yn = _parent.slider2.static2;
      }
    }
    if (display<20) {
      xn = 50 + (display * 20);
    } else {
      xn = 50 + (display - _parent.half) * 20;
    }
    // ==================
    // position _x
    _x -= (_x - xn) * .5;
    // position _y
    _y -= y = (y + (_y - yn) * accel) * elast;
  }
}
```

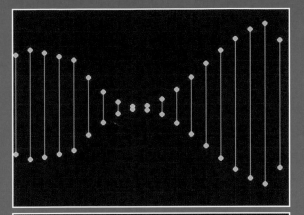

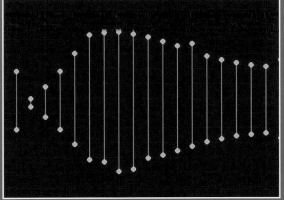

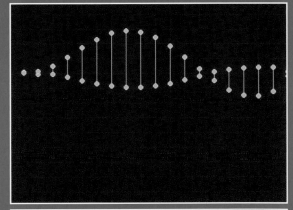

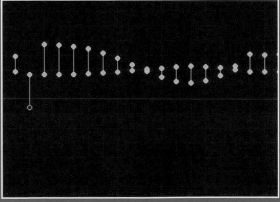

The key variables and functions

On the main timeline you'll see the following variable elements:

num = The total number of points
half = Half of the total number of points (therefore, the number of points on each row)
bar1 = The acceleration slider
bar2 = The elasticity slider
bar3 = The grid alpha slider
toggle = The auto-run toggle
pointclip = The linkage name of **clip_Point** in the Library
onEnterFrame = A function to draw the lines
sequence = A function to calculate the wave pattern

In **Slider2**, you have the following to play with:

dest1 = The value of the top destination arrow position
dest2 = The value of the bottom destination arrow position
static1 = The value of the top static arrow position
static2 = The value of the bottom static arrow position

And in **Points.as**, you have the following:

display = The number of the current point.
onEnterFrame = A function to update the position of the current point.
accel = The value of the acceleration slider.
elast = The value of the elasticity slider.
yn = The **y** destination of the point.
xn = The **x** destination of the point. This is currently a fixed position.

Here's how it works. You create two rows of points (attached from the Library dynamically). After that, you create an empty movie clip, with which you draw lines that connect the points, and then move the points along the y-axis. You control the static position of the points as well as the position that they'll bounce up or down to. You also run a calculation that counts up to 20 and then back down, over and over again. You tell the points where to bounce based on this sequence to get the wave pattern effect.

The primary script (on frame 1 of the main timeline) does the following:

1. Attaches all the points

2. Connects the points with lines

3. Colors the lines

4. Calculates the wave pattern number sequence

5. Handles changes to the controls

The **Point** class file simply moves the points based on the controls.

Once more, I've given default values for the controls to give a good wave pattern. As per usual, the easiest way to make a quick difference is to alter the graphics. There are also many code changes that you can make, ranging from simple color changes to big alterations to scale, position, and bounce.

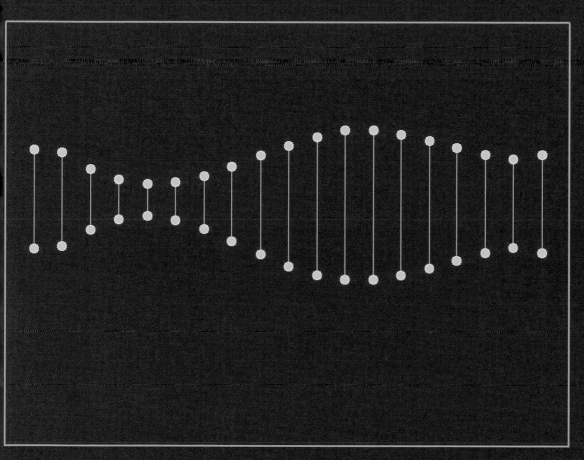

AUTO RUN ● ON/OFF

ACCEL
○

ELASTIC
○

GRID
○

Phantom shapes

This experiment takes some of the elements from the earlier movies in this series and combines them to create something completely new. You're still using points and lines, but this time you're rotating one point around in a circle and duplicating a low-alpha shape after it. This shape runs through a quick tween, and then fades out and removes itself. Because the line is spinning quite quickly, you get a really nice morphing effect, in which the shapes overlap each other, resulting in a strange, amorphous blob. The controls that the user has allow the alteration of the radius of the circle that the line spins in, the number of shapes in the trail, and whether or not the line and circle are displayed.

The layer setup is slightly different from the other experiments. There are four layers here called **Code**, **Controls**, **Main Clip**, and **Diameter**. **Main Clip** contains an instance of the **clip_Main** movie clip in the center of the stage with the instance name **main**. **Controls** contains the sliders and other interface components, in the top-right corner of the stage. **Diameter** contains a copy of **clip_Circle** in the center of the stage with the instance name **circle**. The main code is on the first frame of the main timeline—you can find this code in **exp_4.fla**. The only other code, to control the sliders, is found in **Slider.as**, as in all previous experiments.

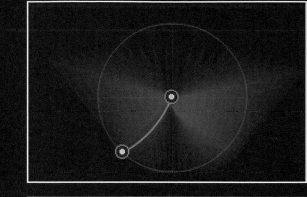

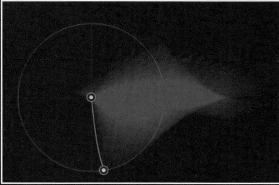

Here's the primary script that sits on frame 1 of the root:

```
_quality = "LOW";
fscommand("fullscreen", "true");
fscommand("allowscale", "false");
var skeleton:Boolean = true;
var degrees:Number = 0;
var j:Number = 0;
var Angle:Number;
var radius:Number;

// ============== Attach line and points
attachMovie("lineclip", "line", 1000);
attachMovie("pointclip", "point1", 2000);
attachMovie("pointclip", "point2", 3000,
➡ {_x:main._x, _y:main._y});
// ============== function setAngle;
function setAngle () {
  Angle = degrees * (Math.PI / 180);
  degrees += 4;
}
// ============== function drawPoints;
function drawPoints () {
  point1._x = main._x + radius *
  ➡ Math.cos(Angle);
  point1._y = main._y + radius *
  ➡ Math.sin(Angle);
}
// ============== function drawLine;
function drawLine () {
  line._x = point1._x;
  line._y = point1._y;
  line._xscale = point2._x - point1._x;
  line._yscale = point2._y - point1._y;
}
// ============== function drawShapes;
function drawShapes () {
  if (j < bar2.value) {
    j++;
  } else {
    j = 0;
  }
```

```
  // Attach the shapes;
  for (var i=1; i<2; i++) {
    var shape:MovieClip = attachMovie
    ➡ ("shapeclip", "L" + i + "_" + j, j + (i + 2));
    // Set the color of the shapes
    var R:Number = 70;
    var G:Number = 150;
    var B:Number = 100 + j;
    new Color(shape).setRGB(R << 16 | G << 8 | B);
  }
  // Set the position, scale, and alpha of the
  // shapes;
  for (i=1; i<2; i++) {
    shape = this["L"+i+"_"+j]
    shape._x = line._x;
    shape._y = line._y;
    shape._xscale = line._xscale;
    shape._yscale = line._yscale;
    shape._alpha = 50;
  }
}
// ============== End
skeletonBtn.onRelease = function(){
  skeleton = !skeleton;
  // Toggle skeleton elements on/off;
  circle._visible = skeleton;
  main._visible = skeleton;
  point1._visible = skeleton;
  point2._visible = skeleton;
  line._visible = skeleton;
};
bar1.onChanged = function(){
  radius = this.value * 1.5;
  circle._xscale = circle._yscale = this.value
  ➡ * 1.5;
  main.axis._xscale = main.axis._yscale =
  ➡ this.value * 1.5;
};
bar1.value = 60;

onEnterFrame = function(){
  setAngle();
  drawPoints();
  drawLine();
  drawShapes();
};
```

The key variables and functions

bar1 = The radius slider

bar2 = The number of shapes slider

skeleton = The toggle for displaying the line and circle

radius = The radius of the circle, used for scaling the **diameter** clip on the stage

degrees = The initial rotation of the line

lineclip = The linkage name of **clip_Line** from the Library

pointclip – The linkage name of **clip_Point** from the Library

shapeclip = The linkage name of **clip_Shape** from the Library

setAngle = A function to convert the **degrees** value into radians and then update it

drawPoints = A function to position the two points (center and outer) on the stage

drawLine = A function to position and scale the line connecting the points

drawShapes = A function to attach a new shape to the stage and set its color, position, scale, and alpha

The experiment works like this. You create two points (attached from the Library), and you then create a line (also attached from the Library) and connect the points with it.

Next, you run a calculation that moves one point around a specified radius. You create the shapes by attaching a new clip each time the frame loops. These shapes are positioned in the same spot as the line, and they don't move, so they create a great fading trail behind the line.

The primary script (on frame 1 of the main timeline) does the following:

1. Sets up the controls

2. Attaches the two points and one line (**clip_Point**, **clip_Line**)

3. Positions and scales the points and lines

4. Attaches the shapes (**clip_Shape**)

5. Sets the color, position, scale, and alpha of the shapes

I suggest you first try changing the **clip_Shape** movie clip. You could create different shapes or simply change the tween that already exists there. Also, changing the color of that clip or the color of the background can make a significant difference.

My name is Manuel Tan but almost everybody calls me Manny. I currently work for a design shop called The Fin Company here in New York. In my spare time I update my site www.uncontrol.com. It deals with programmatic movement in Flash. Uncontrol is the place for me to experiment with motion and behaviors through code. I've been published in a few books like *New Masters of Flash: The 2002 Annual*, *72 DPI*, and *Young Guns NYC III* as well as exhibiting works at OFFF in Barcelona and ADC in New York. I was recently involved in the Biennial at Tirana and was exhibited locally at the Deitch Gallery in Soho, NY. When I'm not doing Flash stuff I build Bandai models, mountain bike, and grow my herbal plants on my windowsill.

I find that the best way to understand something is to try and recreate it to the best of my abilities. Sometimes I am able to recreate it perfectly for what I want it to do, while other times I fall flat on my face. My computer is filled with hundreds of iterations of experiments that don't work but it's no big deal, I just move on and try to make something else work. Eventually, after a few cigarettes, a few more cups of coffee, and a fresh perspective, I'll come back and try to solve it again – primarily just because I don't like leaving things unfinished and undone. The good thing is that I have enough screwed up work lying around to last me for a long while. I try and get into the mindset of code, understanding why it works and especially why it doesn't work.

manuel tan
www.uncontrol.com

Color blend

Open experiment_a.swf and play around with it. The buttons at the top change the shape of the lines, and the slider bars control the spread of the lines. The movie consists of two main types of graphical elements: the line movie clip that you use to duplicate, which sits in the Library with the linkage name line_link, and the various interface elements.

All of the interesting experiment code is contained on the main timeline of experiment_a.fla (apart from the interface code, which you can find in the external .as files). I'll list the code in full here, including code comments along the way, and then walk through its creation and function afterward.

```actionscript
_quality = "LOW";
// ───────────────────────
// FOR loop variables
// ───────────────────────
var z_objects:Number = 6;
var y_objects:Number = 6;
var x_objects:Number = 6;
var counter:Number = 1;
// ───────────────────────
// creates objects and assigns color to each object
// ───────────────────────
for (var z = 1; z<=z_objects; z++) {
  for (var y = 1; y<=y_objects; y++) {
    for (var x = 1; x<=x_objects; x++) {
      // ───────────────────────
      // creates objects and assigns color to each object
      // ───────────────────────
      attachMovie("line_link", "line_"+counter, counter);
      var wing_color_spot_01:Color = new Color(this["line_"+counter]);
      var new_color_spot_01:Object = {rb:(x*51)-51, gb:(y*51)-51, bb:(z*51)-51, aa:25};
      wing_color_spot_01.setTransform(new_color_spot_01);
      // ───────────────────────
      counter++;
    }
  }
}
// ───────────────────────
// initialize sinusoid variables
// ───────────────────────
var slider_speed:Number = 5;
var slider_radius:Number = 100;
var slider_offset:Number = 200;
var slider_increment:Number = 1;
// ───────────────────────
// initialize master buttons
// ───────────────────────
var color_status:Number = 1;
```

```
master_button_1.num = 1;
master_button_1.onRelease = masterChoice;
master_button_2.num = 2;
master_button_2.onRelease = masterChoice;
master_button_3.num = 3;
master_button_3.onRelease = masterChoice;
master_button_4.num = 4;
master_button_4.onRelease = masterChoice;
function masterChoice() {
  color_status = this.num;
  nav_square.gotoAndStop(this.num);
}
onEnterFrame = function () {
  // ──────────────────────
  // grabs data from slider bars
  // ──────────────────────
  var data_y:Number = nav_vertical.value;
  var data_x:Number = nav_horizontal.value;
  var slider_radius:Number = data_x;
  // ──────────────────────
  // start of position script
  // ──────────────────────
  var counter:Number = 1;
  for (var z = 1; z<=z_objects; z++) {
    for (var y = 1; y<=y_objects; y++) {
      for (var x = 1; x<=x_objects; x++) {
        // ──────────────────────
        // changes line style
        // ──────────────────────
        this["line_"+counter].gotoAndStop(color_status);
        // ──────────────────────
        // computes sinusoid variables
        // ──────────────────────
        var slider_increment_offset:Number = (z/x*y*10);
        var slider_sin:Number = Math.sin((slider_increment+
        ➥ slider_increment_offset)/Math.PI/slider_speed)
        ➥ *slider_radius+slider_offset;
        // ──────────────────────
        // plots points from variables including offsets
        // ──────────────────────
        this["line_"+counter]._x = (y*2)+(z*12)+slider_sin-50;
        this["line_"+counter]._y = (x*(data_y/3))-data_y+200;
        // ──────────────────────
        counter++;
      }
    }
  }
  slider_increment++;
};
```

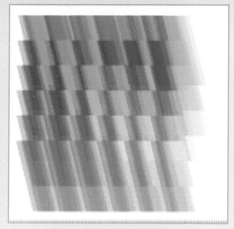

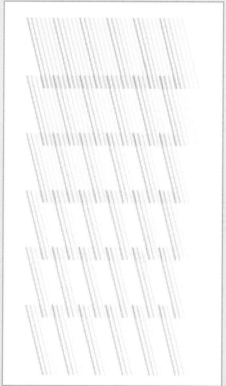

As you can see, I commented as many code areas as I could to better explain some of the parts, so be sure to check through it if you get confused. One of the first things I saw with the script was an easy way of generating the hexadecimal color chart. There are three primary color values used to create the range of colors (red, green, and blue; RGB), and there are six main increments of each primary color (00, 33, 66, 99, CC, and FF). The embedded `for` loops allow me to cycle through all of the RGB values. Each one loops six times, giving a total of 256 iterations. I decided to pull these three loop counter values out of the loop, so if I use the `for` loops again for a different number of iterations, I only have to make a change in one place. You can find these variables at the top named `z_objects`, `y_objects`, and `x_objects` to coincide with the counter variable for each loop (z, y, and x).

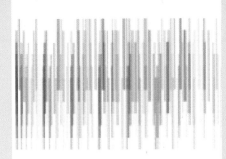

Before I begin adding color to an object, I need to first create an object to add the color to. I didn't want to use the `duplicateMovieClip` action because I feel it clutters the stage unnecessarily. Instead, I opted for the `attachMovie` method. I used a simple counter, called `counter`, to create the names and level of each new clip. The last thing I did (which wasn't vital, but was aesthetically pleasing) was change the spacing of the color value lines to make the code easier to read. Here's the end result:

```
// FOR loop variables
// ─────────────────────
var z_objects:Number = 6;
var y_objects:Number = 6;
var x_objects:Number = 6;
var counter:Number = 1;
// ─────────────────────
// creates objects and assigns color to each object
// ─────────────────────
for (var z = 1; z<=z_objects; z++) {
  for (var y = 1; y<=y_objects; y++) {
    for (var x = 1; x<=x_objects; x++) {
      // ─────────────────────
      // creates objects and assigns color to each object
      // ─────────────────────
      attachMovie("line_link", "line_"+counter, counter);
      var wing_color_spot_01:Color =
      ➥ new Color(this["line_"+counter]);
      var new_color_spot_01:Object = {rb:(x*51)-51,gb:(y*51)-51,
      ➥ bb:(z*51)-51, aa:25};
      wing_color_spot_01.setTransform(new_color_spot_01);
      // ─────────────────────
      counter++;
    }
  }
}
```

This is all just for preparation. Now I have to actually make it move in the `onEnterFrame` function. I think it would have been great to have just placed these objects on a simple grid pattern, and I would have done so if it weren't for my desire to make the objects in this experiment move back and forth. A smooth and realistic way to do this is to use **sinusoidal movement**, which simply means the oscillating object will accelerate and decelerate from one point to another using the sine and cosine functions. I started by reusing the same loop structure from the previous batch of code to cycle through all the objects. I replaced the scripts inside the `for` loops with these lines:

```
this["line_"+counter]._x = (x*10);
this["line_"+counter]._y = (y*5) + (z*40);
```

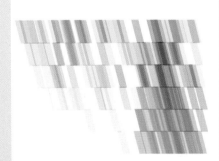

The numbers multiplied with the variables are completely arbitrary. I used them to spread out all the objects so I could see them. The next thing to do is add the sinusoids (I love using that word; it reminds me of a toy I played with when I was a kid). Think of the sinusoids as moving along the perimeter of a circle at a constant speed. If you completely disregard the y-axis, the object will move in a similar fashion to a carousel pole at eye level. There are many ways of writing this equation. I prefer this one because it's simple:

```
var slider_sin:Number = Math.sin
➥ (slider_increment/Math.PI/slider_speed)
➥ *slider_radius + slider_offset;

slider_increment++;
```

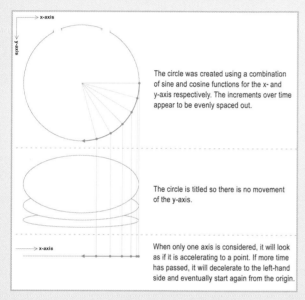

x-axis

y-axis

The circle was created using a combination of sine and cosine functions for the x- and y-axis respectively. The increments over time appear to be evenly spaced out.

The circle is titled so there is no movement of the y-axis.

x-axis

When only one axis is considered, it will look as if it is accelerating to a point. If more time has passed, it will decelerate to the left-hand side and eventually start again from the origin.

To use this, I needed to initialize a bunch of variables such as speed, radius, and offset. I added these variables to the code earlier. If you don't understand the reasoning behind this, that's OK. To reuse the carousel analogy, these variables will determine how fast you are spinning around, how close you are to the center of the carousel, and where the carousel is placed. You can get a better idea of what these variables do if you change these numbers around. The last variable, called slider_increment, probably doesn't look too familiar. It's a counter script that generates all the values for the oscillating movement. I linked this variable to the x-axis and originally came up with this:

```
this["line_"+counter]._x = slider_sin;
```

When I tested the code, all the objects moved at the same time. That was pretty boring, so I figured I needed to offset/separate them. The easiest and most logical way to separate them is to have each object along a row start at a different time. To go back to the earlier carousel analogy, at the moment the carousel effectively has only one pole. All I want to do now, then, is disperse poles for a more even carousel. To do this in the code, I replaced the slider_increment value with something else that's unique to each character. I decided to integrate the x, y, and z values into an equation:

```
var slider_increment_offset:Number = (z/x*y*10);
var slider_sin:Number = Math.sin
➥ ((slider_increment+slider_increment_offset)
➥ /Math.PI/slider_speed)*slider_radius+
➥ slider_offset;
```

That code looks pretty complex, and to be honest, I don't know exactly how it translates into the current moving thingy. This is where I threw my math book out the door and opted to create something that looked good through trial and error. My only prerequisite was to use all three values. I used the same trial-and-error technique to create these final scripts between the for loops:

```
this["line_"+counter]._x = (y*2) + (z*12) +
➥ slider_sin-50;
this["line_"+counter]._y = (x*(data_y/3)) -
➥ data_y + 200;
```

While I was building this, I also wanted to make it interactive, so I created two slider bars that gave me values. These sliders are controlled by ActionScript 2.0 classes, which you can find in the files HorizontalSlider.as and VerticalSlider.as. The values generated by these sliders are dumped into two variables called data_x and data_y to represent the horizontal and vertical axes. data_x is used to change the radius of the carousel, while data_y is used to evenly spread out the objects along the horizontal focal point.

The last bit of code changes the style of the object. I just made four simple styles and placed them on four frames in the line movie clip. The following code targets a specific frame:

```
_this["line_"+counter].gotoAndStop(color_status);
```

That's it for the first experiment. Give the carousel a whirl and see what you think. Try adding some new shapes to the line clip and seeing what effects you can make—but to be honest, I don't recommend drawing a full carousel horse, or anything too complex, because things would probably get messy.

Spinner

Take a look at experiment_b.swf. The top-left buttons and the sliders perform similar functions to the buttons and sliders in the previous experiment, but there are two new sets of buttons. The middle set controls the position of the shapes, and the top-right set controls the scale of the shapes, giving them perspective. The shapes have changed, too. Now instead of a series of different colored lines, there are three layers of squares, with a grid of nine squares in each layer. The layers appear to move around each other depending on the position of a focal clip that's moving around a circle in the center of the screen. The best way to understand the experiment is just to watch it—you'll see what I mean if you do so. The code, like the last experiment, is all on the main stage, except for the code in the external class files. Here's the main code in its entirety:

```
_quality = "LOW";
// ———————————————————————
function convert_array_to_3d(point_name, xx, yy, zz) {
    // ———————————————————————
    // master points
    // ———————————————————————
    var x:Number = 0;
    var y:Number = 1;
    var z:Number = 2;
    var focal_point_x:Number = master_point_00._x;
    var focal_point_y:Number = master_point_00._y;
    var pivot_point_x:Number = master_point_0._x;
    var pivot_point_y:Number = master_point_0._y;
    // ———————————————————————
    // 3d plotting function
    // ———————————————————————
    this[point_name]._x = (pivot_point_x-focal_point_x)*(zz/1000+1)
    ➥ +xx*(zz/1000+1)+focal_point_x;
    this[point_name]._y = (pivot_point_y-focal_point_y)*(zz/1000+1)
    ➥ +yy*(zz/1000+1)+focal_point_y;
}
// ———————————————————————
// initialization of all the variables for the nav
// ———————————————————————
color_status = 1;
scale_increment = 10;
// ———————————————————————
// FOR loop variables
// ———————————————————————
z_objects = 3;
y_objects = 3;
x_objects = 3;
counter = 1;
// ———————————————————————
// creates objects and assigns color to each object
// ———————————————————————
for (z=1; z<=z_objects; z++) {
  for (y=1; y<=y_objects; y++) {
    for (x=1; x<=x_objects; x++) {
      // ———————————————————————
      // creates objects and assigns color to each object
      // ———————————————————————
      attachMovie("square_link", "square_"+counter, counter);
      wing_color_spot_01 = new Color(this["square_"+counter]);
      new_color_spot_01 = {rb:255-(x*102-51), gb:255-(y*102-51), bb:255-(z*102-51), aa:50};
      wing_color_spot_01.setTransform(new_color_spot_01);
      // ———————————————————————
      counter++;
    }
  }
}
```

```
// ───────────────────────────
// initialize sinusoid variables
// ───────────────────────────
slider_speed = 2;
slider_increment = 1;
slider_offset = 200;
// ───────────────────────────
// initialize master buttons
// ───────────────────────────
var color_status:Number = 1;
master_button_1.num = 1;
master_button_1.onRelease = masterChoice;
master_button_2.num = 2;
master_button_2.onRelease = masterChoice;
function masterChoice() {
  color_status = this.num;
  nav_square.gotoAndStop(this.num);
}
onEnterFrame = function () {
  // ───────────────────────────
  // data from nav sliders
  // ───────────────────────────
  data_x = nav_horizontal.value;
  data_y = nav_vertical.value;
  // ───────────────────────────
  // scales gray circle
  // ───────────────────────────
  circle._xscale = data_x;
  circle._yscale = data_y;
  // ───────────────────────────
  // moves master_point_00 around circle using data from nav sliders
  // ───────────────────────────
  master_point_00._x = Math.cos(slider_increment/Math.PI/slider_speed)*data_x+slider_offset;
  master_point_00._y = Math.sin(slider_increment/Math.PI/slider_speed)*data_y+slider_offset;
  slider_increment++;
  // ───────────────────────────
  // start of position script
  // ───────────────────────────
  counter = 1;
  for (z=1; z<=z_objects; z++) {
    for (y=1; y<=y_objects; y++) {
      for (x=1; x<=x_objects; x++) {
        // ───────────────────────────
        // changes line style
        // ───────────────────────────
        this["square_"+counter].gotoAndStop(color_status);
        // ───────────────────────────
        // takes given data and parses it through 3d engine function
        // ───────────────────────────
        convert_array_to_3d("square_"+counter,
        ➡ (x+nav_position.x_offset)*nav_scale.xscale_offset, (y+nav_position.y_offset)
        ➡ *nav_scale.yscale_offset, (z+nav_position.z_offset)*nav_scale.zscale_offset);
        // ───────────────────────────
        counter++;
      }
    }
  }
};
```

I created a simple, one-point perspective 3D engine function a while back, and I thought that this code would work pretty well in the present experiment. The function is called `convert_array_to_3d`, and it takes the x-, y-, and z-coordinates of a 3D point and converts them onto a Cartesian plane.

The 3D engine function requires four variables to position an object: the name of the object, its x-position, its y-position, and its z-position, in that order. If you look in the `onEnterFrame` code, between the `for` loops, I put each variable on its own line, making it easier to read. For this script to work, you also need to know where two specific points are: the absolute coordinates (0,0,0) and the focal point on the horizon. These are taken care of by two objects on the main stage called `masterpoint_0` and `masterpoint_00`.

From my experience, the script tends to get messy when you use extreme numbers along the z-axis. For example, if you want to set a point 1,000 pixels into the distance or –1,000, it will flip up and over the event horizon (at least I think that's what it's called—I saw too many sci-fi films to remember properly) and land on some weird spot. I specifically built this script to handle smaller numbers. I arbitrarily decided that the maximum distance around the absolute point would be between –200 and 200 on all axes.

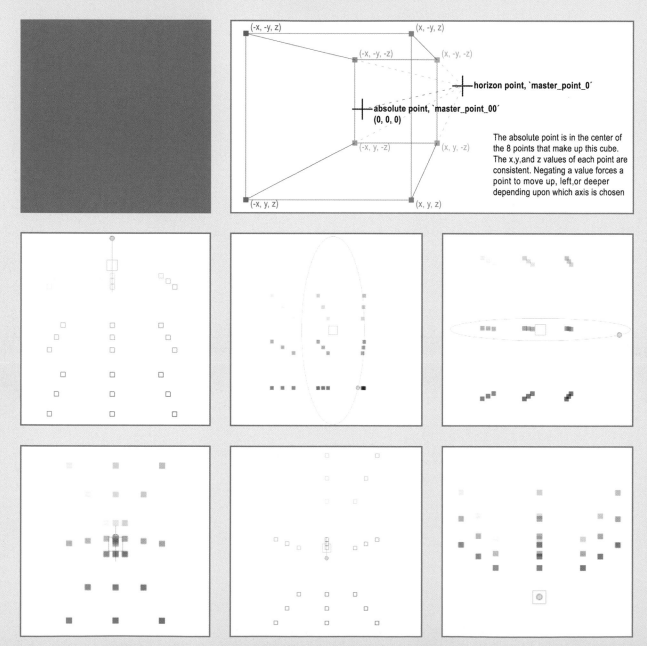

(-x, -y, z)   (x, -y, z)

(-x, -y, -z)   (x, -y, -z)

┼ horizon point, `master_point_0´

┼ absolute point, `master_point_00´
(0, 0, 0)

(-x, y, -z)   (x, y, -z)

(-x, y, z)   (x, y, z)

The absolute point is in the center of the 8 points that make up this cube. The x, y, and z values of each point are consistent. Negating a value forces a point to move up, left, or deeper depending upon which axis is chosen

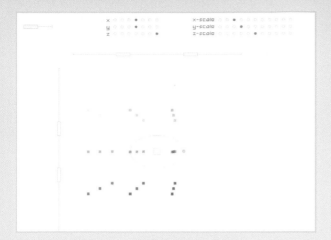
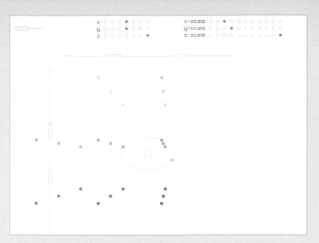

As explained earlier, the initial `for` loops are there to create the objects needed, as well as define a specific color. The `for` loops in the `onEnterFrame` code are there to cycle through all the given points: the inner loop establishes the horizontal coordinates, the middle loop controls the vertical movement, and the outer loop controls the depth. There are two sets of variables that create the cube. The first set deals with the translation, or positioning, of the objects as a whole, and these are labeled as `x_offset`, `y_offset`, and `z_offset`. These variables are set by the `nav_position` component, and they're properties of that component. Adding them to the x, y, and z variables repositions them. The second set deals with scaling as a whole, and they're labeled `xscale_offset`, `yscale_offset`, and `zscale_offset`. They're also properties of the `nav_scale` component. Multiplying them by the x, y, and z variables scales them. Here's an example that changes the position and scaling along the z-axis:

```
(z+nav_position.z_offset)*nav_scale.zscale_offset
```

You'll notice that `z_offset` is executed first and then `zscale_offset`. There's a precise and mathematical explanation for it, but all that information escaped from my head after I moved on to college and discovered beer. To get to this point, I kept messing around, mixing and matching simple math functions until I got it to work. If you feel like taking a look inside the `ScaleChooser` and `PositionChooser` class files, you'll see where the radial button navigation is created and initialized, and right at the top you can see where I initialized the actual variables needed to make this work.

That's basically all there is to the position and scaling of the objects as a whole. Let's now move on to making them oscillate.

The only thing I move to make oscillate is the focal point or `masterpoint_00` position. Using the example from the first experiment, I have this:

```
master_point_00._x = Math.sin(slider_increment/
 ➡ Math.PI/slider_speed)*slider_radius +
 ➡ slider_offset;
slider_increment++;
```

You should know what each variable does from the previous example. This script will only oscillate on the x-axis. I wanted to make it move along a circle using both the x- and y-axes, so I added this:

```
master_point_00._x = Math.sin(slider_increment/
 ➡ Math.PI/slider_speed)*slider_radius +
 ➡ slider_offset;
master_point_00._y = Math.cos(slider_increment/
 ➡ Math.PI/slider_speed)*slider_radius +
 ➡ slider_offset;
slider_increment++;
```

The trick to making an object move around in a circle is to have one axis use the sine function while the other axis uses the cosine function. For our purposes, I don't think it really matters which axis goes with which trigonometry function, so you should go with what you feel comfortable with. The only value that changes is the radius of the circular orbit. The trick is that the radius of both the x- and y-axes can be different, so I swapped `slider_radius` from the two lines and replaced it with a unique variable. I duplicated the same navigation bars from the previous example to provide data for this experiment. Here's the final code:

```
master_point_00._x = Math.cos(slider_increment/
 ➡ Math.PI/slider_speed) * data_x + slider_offset;
master_point_00._y = Math.sin(slider_increment/
 ➡ Math.PI/slider_speed) * data_y + slider_offset;
slider_increment++;
```

The last thing to do is create a circular path for `master_point_00` to follow. I just made a simple circular outline, and I scaled that circle based on the radius data:

```
circle._xscale = data_x;
circle._yscale = data_y;
```

There are a few more little pieces left, but since I explained them already in the first experiment, just refer to the relevant source files to see how everything fits together in this experiment.

245

Fluid dynamics

This experiment is similar to the last one, but rather than having a grid of squares, I have a wave of squares. Check out `experiment_c.fla` to see the effect. The other major change in this experiment is that instead of the focus spinning around a circle, it's now controllable by the user. Try dragging the focus around the screen and seeing the difference it makes. Another new addition is a line clip that's used to join the squares to heighten the impression of a wave. You can also remove the squares altogether and just have a wave made up of lines. As per usual, the majority of the code is on the main timeline, but there's also some code for the interface buttons in an external class file, `PositionChooser.as`. (Note that the class has changed a bit to make a new type of component.)

Here's the code on the main timeline:

```
_quality = "LOW";
// ————————————————————
var color_status:Number = 1;
var line_status:Number = 1;
var xscale_offset:Number = 30;
var yscale_offset:Number = 30;
var zscale_offset:Number = 100;
var scale_increment:Number = 10;
var counter:Number = 1;
// ————————————————————
master_button_1.onRelease = changeShape;
master_button_2.num = 2;
master_button_2.onRelease = changeShape;
master_button_3.num = 3;
master_button_3.onRelease = changeShape;
function changeShape() {
  nav_square.gotoAndStop(this.num);
  color_status = this.num;
}
master_button_4.num = 1;
master_button_4.onRelease = changeLine;
master_button_5.num = 2;
master_button_5.onRelease = changeLine;
function changeLine() {
  nav_line.gotoAndStop(this.num);
  line_status = this.num;
}
master_point_00.btn.onPress = function() {
  this._parent.startDrag(false, 0, 0, 400, 400);
};
master_point_00.btn.onRelease = function() {
  this._parent.stopDrag();
};
master_point_0.btn.onPress = function() {
  this._parent.startDrag(false, 0, 200, 400, 200);
};
master_point_0.btn.onRelease = function() {
  this._parent.stopDrag();
};
function convert_array_to_3d(point_name, xx, yy,
➥  zz) {
  // ————————————————————
  // master points
  // ————————————————————
```

```
var x:Number = 0;
var y:Number = 1;
var z:Number = 2;
var focal_point_x:Number = master_point_00._x;
var focal_point_y:Number = master_point_00._y;
var pivot_point_x:Number = master_point_0._x;
var pivot_point_y:Number = master_point_0._y;
// ————————————————————
// 3d plotting function
// ————————————————————
this[point_name]._x =
➥  (pivot_point_x-focal_point_x)*(zz/1000+1)+xx*
➥  (zz/1000+1)+focal_point_x;
this[point_name]._y = (pivot_point_y-
➥  focal_point_y)*(zz/1000+1)+yy*
➥  (zz/1000+1)+focal_point_y;
}
// ————————————————————
function line_blue_link(start_point, end_point,
➥  line_name, line_depth) {
  var line:MovieClip = attachMovie
  ➥  ("line_blue_link", "line_"+line_name,
  ➥  line_depth);
  line._x = this[start_point]._x;
  line._y = this[start_point]._y;
  line._xscale = this[end_point].
  ➥  _x-this[start_point]._x;
  line._yscale = this[end_point].
  ➥  _y-this[start_point]._y;
  line._alpha = 50;
}
function line_grey_link(start_point, end_point,
➥  line_name, line_depth) {
  var line:MovieClip = attachMovie
  ➥  ("line_grey_link", "line_"+line_name,
  ➥  line_depth);
  line._x = this[start_point]._x;
  line._y = this[start_point]._y;
  line._xscale = this[end_point].
  ➥  _x-this[start_point]._x;
  line._yscale = this[end_point].
  ➥  _y-this[start_point]._y;
  line._alpha = 50;
}
function removeline(line_name) {
  removeMovieClip("line_"+line_name);
}
// ————————————————————
// removes objects and blue lines
// ————————————————————
function removeObjects() {
  var line_depth:Number = 0;
  for (var z = 1; z<=10; z++) {
    for (var y = 1; y<=10; y++) {
      for (var x = 1; x<=10; x++) {
        removeMovieClip(this
        ➥  ["square_"+x+"_"+y+"_"+z]);
        removeline("line_"+line_depth);
        // ————————————————————
        counter++;
        line_depth++;
      }
```

```
        }
      }
    }
// ─────────────────────────────
// creates objects and assigns color to each
// object
// ─────────────────────────────
function createObjects() {
  for (var z = 1; z<=nav_objects.z_objects; z++) {
    for (var y = 1; y<=nav_objects.y_objects; y++) {
      for (var x = 1; x<=nav_objects.x_objects;
      ➡ x++) {
        // ─────────────────────────────
        // creates objects and assigns color to
        // each object
        // ─────────────────────────────
        var square:MovieClip =
        ➡ attachMovie("square_link",
        ➡ "square_"+x+"_"+y+"_"+z, counter);
        var wing_color_spot_01:Color = new
        ➡ Color(square);
        new_color_spot_01 = {rb:255-(x*102),
        ➡ gb:255-(y*102), bb:255-(z*102), aa:50};
        wing_color_spot_01.setTransform
        ➡ (new_color_spot_01);
        // ─────────────────────────────
        counter++;
      }
    }
  }
}
createObjects();
// ─────────────────────────────
// initialize sinusoid variables
// ─────────────────────────────
var slider_speed:Number = 4;
var slider_radius:Number = 15;
var slider_increment:Number = 1;
onEnterFrame = function () {
  // ─────────────────────────────
  // initialize counter variables
  // ─────────────────────────────
  var counter:Number = 1;
  var line_depth:Number = 100;
  // ─────────────────────────────
  // start of position script
  // ─────────────────────────────
  for (var z = 1; z<=nav_objects.z_objects; z++) {
    for (var y =1; y<=nav_objects.y_objects; y++) {
      for (var x = 1; x<=nav_objects.x_objects;
      ➡ x++) {
        // ─────────────────────────────
        // changes line style
        // ─────────────────────────────
        this["square_"+x+"_"+y+"_"+z]
        ➡ .gotoAndStop(color_status);
        // ─────────────────────────────
        // creates data
        // ─────────────────────────────
        var slider_offset_y:Number = (y*10)-25;
        var slider_offset_z:Number = (z*100);
```

```
        slider_radius =
        ➡ 15*((nav_objects.y_objects-y+1)*.25);
        var slider_increment_offset:Number =
        ➡ z*20;
        var slider_cos:Number = Math.cos
        ➡ ((slider_increment+slider
        ➡ _increment_offset)/
        ➡ Math.PI/slider_speed)*slider_radius+
        ➡ slider_offset_y;
        var slider_sin:Number = Math.sin
        ➡ ((slider_increment+slider_increment
        _offset)/Math.PI/slider_speed)
        ➡ *slider_radius+slider_offset_z;
        // ─────────────────────────────
        // takes given data and parses it
        // through 3d engine function
        // ─────────────────────────────
        convert_array_to_3d
        ➡ ("square_"+x+"_"+y+"_"+z, (x*10)-10,
        ➡ slider_cos, slider_sin);
        // ─────────────────────────────
        // creates and removes blue lines
        // ─────────────────────────────
        if (z != 1) {
          if (line_status == 1) {
            line_blue_link
            ➡ ("square_"+x+"_"+y+"_"+z,
            ➡ "square_"+x+"_"+y+"_"+Number(z-1),
            ➡ "line_"+line_depth, line_depth);
          } else {
            removeline("line_"+line_depth);
          }
        }
        // ─────────────────────────────
        counter++;
        line_depth++;
        // ─────────────────────────────
      }
    }
  }
slider_increment++;
// ─────────────────────────────
// draws gray line
// ─────────────────────────────
line_grey_link("master_point_0",
➡ "master_point_00", "line_"+line_depth,
➡ line_depth);
};
```

A while ago, I saw a math/physics website that taught **fluid dynamics**—in other words, how objects move underwater. There was even an interactive model written in Java of how particles move in water. The interesting thing was that the particles move in a circular motion, almost like they're in orbit. The site showed a series of particles equally spaced out vertically and horizontally. Rows of particles moved at the same rate, but at different increments. Columns of particles had varying radiuses. The top row had large radiuses, while the bottom row barely moved. Inspired by the preceding experiments' scripts, I decided to try to interpolate this with sinusoidal motion, by controlling the radius, speed, and increment of circles across a given area. It would have been easy to stick with two dimensions and replicate the movement, but I'm a glutton for punishment. I wanted to move it into a 3D environment, specifically along the y- and z-axes. On top of that, I wanted to connect the points with a line.

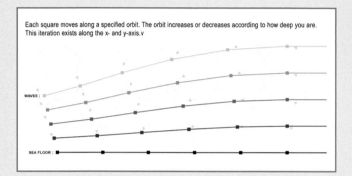

Each square moves along a specified orbit. The orbit increases or decreases according to how deep you are. This iteration exists along the x- and y-axis.v

WAVES :

SEA FLOOR :

So where the heck to start? First, I extrapolated as much data as I could from the previous experiment. I placed the `for` loops first to build and color the points. I then placed another set of `for` loops in the onEnterFrame code to work with the `convert_array_to_3d` function. The main difference so far is that before, I used the counter to name all the objects, but since this time I needed to target specific points, I instead used the x, y, and z variables as a naming convention. Another thing I did was add the base sinusoidal motion into the loop from the previous example, as shown here:

```
var slider_cos:Number = Math.cos
➡ (slider_increment/Math.PI/slider_speed)
➡ *slider_radius+slider_offset;
var slider_sin:Number = Math.sin
➡ (slider_increment/Math.PI/slider_speed)
➡ *slider_radius+slider_offset;
convert_array_to_3d
    (
        "square_"+x+"_"+y+"_"+z,
        (x*10)-10,
        slider_cos,
        slider_sin
    );
```

Subtracting 10 allowed me to start the 3D array at the x=0 point along the 3D space. `slider_cos` deals with the y-movement, and `slider_sin` deals with the z-movement. Let's look at `increment_offset` first. Since `increment_offset` deals with particles along the z-axis, I used the z variable to change values. I also needed to change the radius of each particle orbit so it grows bigger as it goes higher. I did this with the y variable. To save time, I also changed `slider_offset` to make the movement along the y- and z-axes more dramatic:

```
var slider_offset_y:Number = (y*10) - 25;
var slider_offset_z:Number = (z*100);
slider_radius = 15*((nav_objects.y_objects
➡ - y + 1)*.25);
var slider_increment_offset:Number = z*20;
var slider_cos:Number = Math.cos
➡ ((slider_increment+slider_increment_offset)
➡ /Math.PI/slider_speed)*slider_radius +
➡ slider_offset_y;
var slider_sin:Number = Math.sin
➡ ((slider_increment+slider_increment_offset)
➡ /Math.PI/slider_speed)*slider_radius +
➡ slider_offset_z;
convert_array_to_3d
    (
        "square_"+ x + "_" + y + "_" + z,
        (x*10) - 10,
        slider_cos,
        slider_sin
    );
```

Everything looks good so far, except for `slider_radius`, which looks pretty monstrous. That equation was done with some **bodging** (a term I learned from the TV show *Junkyard Wars* that essentially means fitting a square peg in a round hole using the maximum amount of force). I'm not going to try to explain it; I'm just glad it works.

So now that I had the points, I just needed to connect them with lines. I created another function called `line_blue_link` that draws a simple blue line between two points. All I need is a starting object, an ending object, the line name, and the line depth. It almost looks like an `attachMovie` method, but bigger. Since I was just connecting the z-coordinates, I offset the z-index by 1 to connect it to the previous line:

```
if (z != 1) {
    line_blue_link ("square_"+ x + "_" + y + "_"
    ➡ + z, "square_"+ x + "_" + y + "_" + Number
    ➡ (z-1), "line_"+line_depth, line_depth);
}
```

Since there are no values when the z-index is 0, I just put a quick Boolean condition in to stop it before z goes past 1.

One big thing I wanted to do was dynamically change the number of points and lines created. The best way to do this was through the `x_objects`, `y_objects`, and `z_objects` variables. These are properties of `nav_objects`. When you change the variables, it calls the `createObjects` function, which reorders all the `for` loops and re-creates the appropriate number of objects. The only problem is that sometimes you have an excess of objects on the screen. The best way to get around this is to remove all the other objects on the screen before you create them. You can do this by having the component call the `removeObjects` function first.

The last things to implement are the style changes of the points and the style changes of the lines. You already know where to change the style of the points. For the lines, it's the same as wiping the graphics out and starting from scratch again. Here's the final `line` script:

```
if (z != 1) {
  if (line_status == 1) {
    line_blue_link ("square_"+ x + "_" + y + "_"
    ➥ + z, "square_"+ x + "_" + y + "_" + Number
    ➥ (z-1), "line_"+line_depth, line_depth);
  } else {
    removeline ("line_"+line_depth);
  }
}
```

There are a couple of things left to do, but they're pretty simple, so I'll leave you to figure them out. If you want to change things, start by fiddling with the graphics, and then head into the code and get your hands dirty.

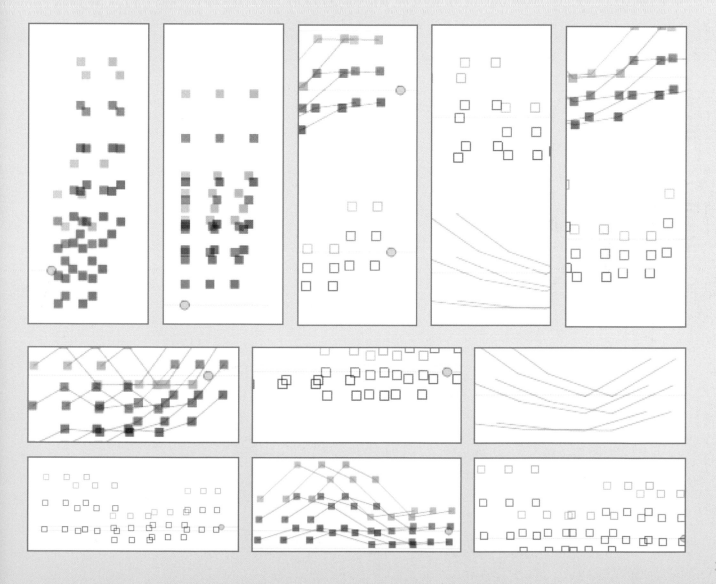

Vortex vase

Staying with the 3D engine, I modified it again to create this new—and fairly cool—effect. I now have a spinning 3D vortex that I can alter in a number of ways. Take a look at `experiment_d.fla` and see what you think. You can move the sliders on either side of the vortex up and down, as well as from side to side, to alter the size of it. The central slider is the midpoint, and the vortex will flare out at either side of it. The only buttons that you haven't encountered before are the `offset` buttons. These control the distance between the first and last points that make up the spout. Clicking the far-right button will give you a perfect, closed vortex, and the further left you go, the more open the vortex will become. Try it out to see the difference it makes. The majority of the code is on the main stage, but there's also some important code in the external class files, `HorizontalSlider.as`, `CircleButton.as`, and `PositionChooser.as`. These files have been altered somewhat from the previous experiments to produce the behaviors required for this file.

Here's the code on the main timeline:

```
_quality = "LOW";
// ——————————————————
var color_status:Number = 1;
var line_status:Number = 1;
// ——————————————————
function convert_array_to_3d (point_name, xx,
➡ yy, zz) {
    // ——————————————————
    // master points
    // ——————————————————
    var x:Number = 0;
    var y:Number = 1;
    var z:Number = 2;
    var focal_point_x:Number = master_point_00._x;
    var focal_point_y:Number = master_point_00._y;
    var pivot_point_x:Number = master_point_0._x;
    var pivot_point_y:Number = master_point_0._y;
    // ——————————————————
    // 3d plotting function
    // ——————————————————
    this[point_name]._x = (pivot_point
➡ _x-focal_point_x)*(zz/1000+1)+xx*
➡ (zz/1000+1)+focal_point_x;
    this[point_name]._y = (pivot_point
➡ _y-focal_point_y)*(zz/1000+1)+yy*
➡ (zz/1000+1)+focal_point_y;
}
// ——————————————————
master_button_1.num = 1;
master_button_1.onRelease = changeShape;
master_button_2.num = 2;
master_button_2.onRelease = changeShape;
master_button_3.num = 3;
master_button_3.onRelease = changeShape;
function changeShape(){
    nav_square.gotoAndStop(this.num);
    color_status = this.num;
}
//
master_button_4.num = 1;
master_button_4.onRelease = changeLine;
master_button_5.num = 2;
master_button_5.onRelease = changeLine;
function changeLine(){
    nav_line.gotoAndStop(this.num);
    line_status = this.num;
}
//
master_point_00.btn.onPress = function(){
    this._parent.startDrag(false, 0, 0, 400, 400);
};
master_point_00.btn.onRelease = function(){
    this._parent.stopDrag();
};
```

```
function drawline (start_point, end_point,
➡ line_name, line_depth) {
  var line:MovieClip = attachMovie("line_link",
  ➡ "line_"+line_name, line_depth);
  line._x = this[start_point]._x;
  line._y = this[start_point]._y;
  line._xscale = this[end_point]
  ➡ ._x - this[start_point]._x;
  line._yscale = this[end_point]
  ➡ ._y - this[start_point]._y;
  line._alpha = 50;
}
function removeline (line_name) {
  this["line_"+line_name].removeMovieClip();
}
// ──────────────────────────
// FOR loop variables
// ──────────────────────────
var z_objects:Number = 5;
var y_objects:Number = 8;
var x_objects:Number = 1;
var counter:Number = 1;
// ──────────────────────────
// creates objects and assigns color to each
// object
// ──────────────────────────
for (var z=1; z<=z_objects; z++) {
  for (var y=1; y<=y_objects; y++) {
    for (var x=1; x<=x_objects; x++) {
      // ──────────────────────────
      // creates objects and assigns color to
      // each object
      // ──────────────────────────
      var square:MovieClip = attachMovie
      ➡ ("square_link", "square_"+ x +
      ➡"_" + y + "_" + z, counter);
      var wing_color_spot_01:Color = new
      ➡ Color(square);
      new_color_spot_01 =
        {
          rb:255 - (x*102),
          gb:255 - (y*102),
          bb:255 - (z*102),
          aa:50
        };
      wing_color_spot_01.setTransform
      ➡ (new_color_spot_01);

      // ──────────────────────────
      counter++;
    }
  }
}
// ──────────────────────────
// initialize sinusoid variables
// ──────────────────────────
```

```
var slider_speed:Number = 5;
var slider_offset:Number  = 0;
var slider_increment:Number = 1;
//
onEnterFrame = function(){
  // ──────────────────────────
  // initialize counter variables
  // ──────────────────────────
  var counter:Number = 1;
  var line_depth:Number = 100;
  // ──────────────────────────
  // start of position script
  // ──────────────────────────
  for (var z=1; z<=z_objects; z++) {
    for (var y=1; y<=y_objects; y++) {
      for (var x=1; x<=x_objects; x++) {
        // ──────────────────────────
        // changes line style
        // ──────────────────────────
        this["square_"+ x + "_" + y + "_" +
        ➡ z].gotoAndStop (color_status);
        // ──────────────────────────
        // creates data
        // ──────────────────────────
        // parabola variables
        var xx:Number = y -
        ➡ (100-vertical_bar.y_value)*.05;
        var aa:Number =
        ➡ (vertical_bar.x_value-15)*.075;
        var bb:Number = 4;
        var cc:Number = 5;

        // sinusoid variables
        var slider_radius:Number = (aa*xx*xx)
        ➡ + (bb*(xx))  + (cc);
        var slider_increment_offset:Number =
        ➡ counter * nav_offset.value;
        var slider_cos:Number = Math.cos
        ➡ ((slider_increment+slider
        ➡ _increment_offset)/Math.PI/slider
        ➡ _speed)*slider_radius+slider_offset;
        var slider_sin:Number = Math.sin
        ➡ ((slider_increment+slider
        ➡ _increment_offset)/Math.PI/slider
        ➡ _speed)*slider_radius+slider_offset;
        // ──────────────────────────
        // takes given data and parses it
        // through 3d engine function
        // ──────────────────────────
        convert_array_to_3d
          (
            "square_"+ x + "_" + y + "_" + z,
            slider_sin,
            (y*-25)+112.5,
            slider_cos
          );
```

```
//  ————————————————
// creates and removes blue lines
//  ————————————————
if (y != 1) {
    if (line_status == 1) {
        drawline ("square_"+ x + "_" +
        ➡ y + "_" + z, "square_"+ x +
        ➡ "_" + Number(y-1) + "_" + z,
        ➡ "line_"+line_depth,
        ➡ line_depth);  line_depth++;
    } else {
        removeline ("line_"+line_depth);
        line_depth++;
    }
}
//  ————————————————
counter++;
line_depth++;
//  ————————————————
        }
    }
}
slider_increment++;
//  ————————————————
// draws or removes line to connect all top
// and bottom points
//  ————————————————
if (line_status == 1) {
    drawline ("square_1_1_1", "square_1_1_2",
    ➡ "line_"+line_depth, line_depth);
    line_depth++;
    drawline ("square_1_1_2", "square_1_1_3",
    ➡ "line_"+line_depth, line_depth);
    line_depth++;
    drawline ("square_1_1_3", "square_1_1_4",
    ➡ "line_"+line_depth, line_depth);
    line_depth++;
    drawline ("square_1_1_4", "square_1_1_5",
    ➡ "line_"+line_depth, line_depth);
    line_depth++;
```

```
//
    drawline ("square_1_8_1", "square_1_8_2",
    ➡ "line_"+line_depth, line_depth);
    ➡ line_depth++;
    drawline ("square_1_8_2", "square_1_8_3",
    ➡ "line_"+line_depth, line_depth);
    line_depth++;
    drawline ("square_1_8_3", "square_1_8_4",
    ➡ "line_"+line_depth, line_depth);
    line_depth++;
    drawline ("square_1_8_4", "square_1_8_5",
    ➡ "line_"+line_depth, line_depth);
    line_depth++;
} else {
    removeline ("line_"+line_depth);
    line_depth++;
    removeline ("line_"+line_depth);
    line_depth++;
    removeline ("line_"+line_depth);
    line_depth++;
    removeline ("line_"+line_depth);
    line_depth++;
    removeline ("line_"+line_depth);
    line_depth++;

    removeline ("line_"+line_depth);
    line_depth++;
    removeline ("line_"+line_depth);
    line_depth++;
    removeline ("line_"+line_depth);
    line_depth++;
    removeline ("line_"+line_depth);
    line_depth++;
    removeline ("line_"+line_depth);
    line_depth++;
}
};
```

Halfway through building the third experiment, I wanted to see how a particle moved around the y-axis in 3D space. I had already created the framework in the previous experiments; all I had to do was create a new form. I didn't have a clue as to what I was making, but I just kept on changing and adding things until it resembled what you see here. I decided to use parabolic motion, which is an equation my high-school teachers drilled into my skull in math class. This made all the difference in making this fourth experiment. Before I describe it, though, let's examine the steps it took to get there.

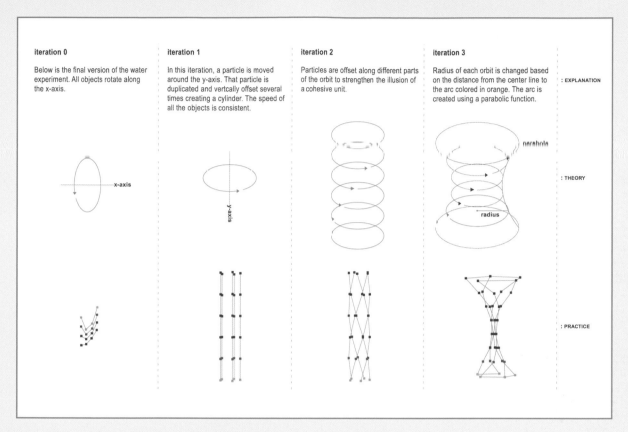

iteration 0

Below is the final version of the water experiment. All objects rotate along the x-axis.

iteration 1

In this iteration, a particle is moved around the y-axis. That particle is duplicated and vertcally offset several times creating a cylinder. The speed of all the objects is consistent.

iteration 2

Particles are offset along different parts of the orbit to strengthen the illusion of a cohesive unit.

iteration 3

Radius of each orbit is changed based on the distance from the center line to the arc colored in orange. The arc is created using a parabolic function.

: EXPLANATION

: THEORY

: PRACTICE

Using the previous experiment as a boilerplate, I placed the x_, y_, and z_object variables, as well as the new code for the creating and coloring for loops, at the beginning of the file. I simplified the script in the onEnterFrame code from the third experiment, and this time I switched around the order in the convert_array_to_3d function so that it would rotate and spin around the y-axis:

```
var slider_increment_offset:Number = counter * nav_offset.value;
var slider_cos:Number = Math.cos((slider_increment+slider_increment_offset)/Math.PI/slider_speed)*
➤ slider_radius+slider_offset;
var slider_sin:Number = Math.sin((slider_increment+slider_increment_offset)/Math.PI/slider_speed)*
➤ slider_radius+slider_offset;
convert_array_to_3d
  (
    "square_"+ x + "_" + y + "_" + z,
    slider_sin,
    (y*-25)+112.5,
    slider_cos
  );
```

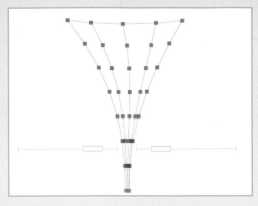

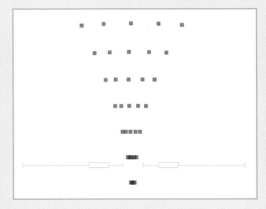

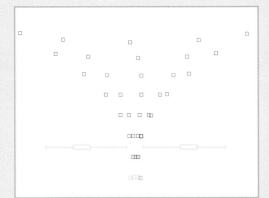

As in the third experiment, I increased y just so it's easier to use. I also added a slider increment because I wanted to offset the points again. The only difference is that I used the return value from the `nav_offset` component (the top-right set of buttons). So, what I have here is something that looks like a rotating cylinder. Next, I wanted to dynamically change the radius of each orbit by using another script. The variable being changed is `slider_offset`, and the script uses the parabolic function. If you remember high-school math class, you should remember this polynomial equation:

```
y=ax^2 + bx + c
```

Variables x and y plot the points, while a, b, and c are constants. I just took this equation and converted it into ActionScript:

```
var xx:Number = y - (100-vertical_bar.y_value)*.05;
var aa:Number = (vertical_bar.x_value-15)*.075;
var bb:Number = 4;
var cc:Number = 5;

var slider_radius:Number = (aa*xx*xx) + (bb*(xx)) + (cc);
```

This looks pretty straightforward, with the exception of the xx variable. A parabolic line assumes that the values of meta-x and meta-y are still variables, so it solves for all points along a Cartesian plane, creating a smooth, curved line. For this script to work, I needed to create the points along one axis to create the values of the second. So if I knew, for example, that meta-y was equal to 10, I could easily figure out the value of meta-x and the position of that on the plane. xx creates those initial variables, while `slider_radius` gives its corresponding value. xx is made more complex with the addition of the y and `vertical_bar.dragger._y` variables used to properly space out the meta-y values. The thing that I had a hard time understanding was that the values used for the parabola don't represent the plotted points for the 3D function, nor are they coordinate points for positioning movie clips. They're used primarily as a step in a process that takes data and converts it. I used the "meta-" term in hopes of clarifying the differences between this and the already existing x and y values.

That's pretty much the bulk of the script. There are other functions here, such as `drawline` and `removeline`, that are used to connect or to remove lines, but I explained them in the earlier experiments.

There are plenty of other parts of this and the other experiments that I didn't explain—for example, how data is being pushed from the slider bars to the function, and how to set up the symbols and Library elements. I also could have gone line by line through some of the predefined functions and explained them. But all I really wanted to do was show you the key features of each experiment. Explaining every little thing seems redundant and only insults your intelligence. (That and I just didn't feel like writing about it.)

I hope you got something out of these experiments and explanations, and I hope they inspire you in making your own.

Michael Brandon Williams has many years of mathematics and computer science study in his c.v. In the past his mathematics focus has been single and multivariable calculus, real analysis, linear algebra, ordinary differential equations, elementary combinatorics, and number theory. His computer science experience is based on programming design, object-oriented programming, and problem solving. His goal is to pursue a Ph.D. in Mathematics. In his spare time, he helps run the math forum at Were-Here (www.were-here.com) under the name of ahab, and works for Eyeland Studios (www.eyeland.com) as a games programmer.

Flipping through any math book, from analytic geometry to calculus, you can usually find a section dealing with mathematics in three dimensions. In geometry you see shapes such as spheres and cylinders, and define geometric objects such as vectors. In calculus you discuss the calculus of surfaces, their rates of change in various directions and the volume underneath. The pictures in these books grab everyone's attention no matter how complex the mathematics become. The continuous, wireframe surfaces are sensational sights, sometimes mimicking the very terrain we see in the countryside. These amazing eye candies are what I wanted to create in Flash. I wanted to develop a program so that I could simply change one equation, the function of the surface itself, and create that beautiful wireframe representation of a surface that I had seen in countless textbooks. I also wanted to be able to change the range of x- and y-values graphed and the angle at which I viewed the graph. I would then use that program to discover the different possibilities of three-dimensional graphs and see what kind of incredible forms would arise. This is that program.

brandon williams

This is a slightly different experiment, in both style and presentation, from those you've seen so far, but it's the logical conclusion to this book. It's a full-function graph plotter in Flash—you select the function and away you go, dynamically plotting your graph. Check out **base.swf** to see some ready-made functions. Just select the one that you want and click the Plot button.

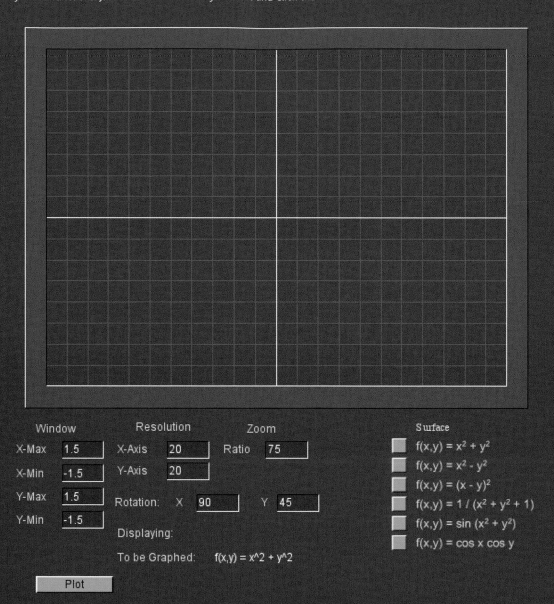

To demonstrate the workings of this mini application, you're going to delve into the code and get your hands dirty building the bare bones of the plotter. The code for this experiment is longer than that for other experiments in this book, but don't let that put you off—it's well worth the extra effort. Rather than having a separate section for the key variables and functions, I've instead heavily commented the code, so you should be able to easily follow along and get a good idea of what's going on. I give a more thorough explanation of the functionality after each code listing.

Let's start with the main stage of **basicEffect.fla**. The only thing that I have here is one layer called **actions**. The **actions** layer contains the code to create a new graph, which in turn relies on a separate ActionScript 2.0 class. This class, which makes all of the calculations, is contained in an external class file called **Graph.as**. Without further ado, here's the code for the **actions** layer:

```
// set up a new graph — initial settings here are for a parabaloid in a 20x20 square region
my_graph = new Graph (10, -10, 10, -10, 20, 20, 15, -45, 20, 275, 200);

my_graph.plot ();
```

More important, here is the **Graph** class code, which will help to clarify what the previous parameters relate to. Again, note that I've included helpful descriptions of various elements throughout this code in comment format:

```
class Graph {
    private var x_max:Number;
    private var x_min:Number;
    private var y_max:Number;
    private var y_min:Number;
    private var num_points_x:Number;
    private var num_points_y:Number;
    private var zoom:Number;
    private var increment_x:Number;
    private var increment_y:Number;
    private var origin_x:Number;
    private var origin_y:Number;
    private var rotate_x:Number;
    private var rotate_y:Number;
    private var sin_x:Number;
    private var cos_x:Number;
    private var sin_y:Number;
    private var cos_y:Number;
    private var points:Array;
    private var trans:Number = Math.PI/180;
    //
    // graph object — draws a new graph
    // PARAMETERS
    // equation - a function reference that returns a value when passed two others ("x" and "y")
    // x_max, x_min, y_max, y_min - dimensions of the window for the graph
    // num_points_x, num_points_y - number of points to be plotted along the x- and y-axes
    // zoom - a ratio of how much to zoom in ... adjusting this makes graphs easier to view
    // rotate_x, rotate_y - orientation of graph
    // center_x, center_y - the origin as it should appear on Flash's Stage
    function Graph(x_max:Number, x_min:Number, y_max:Number, y_min:Number, num_points_x:Number,
➥ num_points_y:Number, zoom:Number, rotate_x:Number, rotate_y:Number, origin_x:Number,
➥ origin_y:Number) {
        // rectangular region that surface will be drawn over (domain) — D = {(x, y) | x_min < x <
        // x_max, y_min < y < y_max}
        this.x_max = x_max;
        this.x_min = x_min;
        this.y_max = y_max;
        this.y_min = y_min;
        // number of points to be placed along the x- and y-axes
        this.num_points_x = num_points_x;
        this.num_points_y = num_points_y;
        // zoom ratio
        this.zoom = zoom;
        // increments to go along the x- and y-axes
        this.increment_x = (this.x_max-this.x_min)/this.num_points_x;
        this.increment_y = (this.y_max-this.y_min)/this.num_points_y;
        // position of the origin
        this.origin_x = origin_x;
        this.origin_y = origin_y;
```

```actionscript
        // orientation of graph on the x- and y-axes
        this.rotate_x = rotate_x;
        this.rotate_y = rotate_y;
        // sine and cosine of rotation angles
        sin_x = Math.sin(this.rotate_x*trans);
        cos_x = Math.cos(this.rotate_x*trans);
        sin_y = Math.sin(this.rotate_y*trans);
        cos_y = Math.cos(this.rotate_y*trans);
    }
    //
    // stretches "mc" to connect point (x1, y1) and (x2, y2) — "mc" should be the full path to the
    // movie clip
    private function draw_line(mc:MovieClip, x1:Number, y1:Number, x2:Number, y2:Number) {
        mc._x = x1;
        mc._y = y1;
        mc._xscale = x2-x1;
        mc._yscale = y2-y1;
    }
    //
    // multivariable function that depends on both "x" and "y" — mess with the return value to
    // render different surfaces
    // NOTE: when using trigonometric functions, multiply the expression within the parentheses by
    // "trans" to change degrees into radians
    private function function_xy(x:Number, y:Number) {
        return (4*Math.sin((x*y-x*x+y*y)*trans));
    }
    //
    // plots a 3D surface z = f(x, y)
    public function plot() {
        // get the position of the points on the surface
        calculate_points();
        // connect all the points with lines — to create the grid
        draw_grid();
    }
    //
    // connects all the points with lines to create the grid
    private function draw_grid() {
        // the position of the two points a line will connect
        var x1:Number;
        var y1:Number;
        var x2:Number;
        var y2:Number;
        //
        _root.clear();
        _root.lineStyle(1, 0x00ff00, 100);
        // loop through and connect all the lines going vertical
        for (var j = 1; j<num_points_x+1; j++) {
            for (var k = 0; k<=num_points_y; k++) {
                // find the two points the line is to connect
                x1 = points[j][k].perspective_x;
                y1 = points[j][k].perspective_y;
                x2 = points[j-1][k].perspective_x;
                y2 = points[j-1][k].perspective_y;
                // connect the two points with the line
                _root.moveTo(x1, y1);
                _root.lineTo(x2, y2);
            }
        }
        //
        // loop through and connect all the lines going horizontal
        for (var j = 0; j<=num_points_x; j++) {
            for (var k = 1; k<=num_points_y; k++) {
```

```
            // find the two points the line is to connect
            x1 = points[j][k].perspective_x;
            y1 = points[j][k].perspective_y;
            x2 = points[j][k-1].perspective_x;
            y2 = points[j][k-1].perspective_y;
            //
            // connect the two points with the line
            _root.moveTo(x1, y1);
            _root.lineTo(x2, y2);
        }
    }
}
//
// calculates the position of the points to be rendered
private function calculate_points() {
    // 2D array of objects that holds the position of every point
    points = new Array();
    //
    // loop through the x-values
    for (var j = 0; j<=num_points_x+1; j++) {
        // add another dimension to the array
        points[j] = new Array();
        // loop through the y-values
        for (var k = 0; k<=num_points_y; k++) {
            // create a new object in the array's element to keep track of the ordered triplet (x,y,z)
            points[j][k] = new Object();
            // calculate the ordered triplet
            points[j][k].x = index_to_coord("x", j);
            points[j][k].y = index_to_coord("y", k);
            points[j][k].z = function_xy(points[j][k].x, points[j][k].y);
            // change the point from Flash's coordinate system to a real math rectangular system
            exchange_point(j, k);
            // rotate the point around the x- and y-axes
            rotate_point(j, k);
            // zoom into graph
            scale_point(j, k);
            // add perspective to point
            perspective_point(j, k);
            // translate point to the origin
            translate_point(j, k);
        }
    }
}
// changes index values (j, k) of an array to coordinates (x, y) on the graph
private function index_to_coord(determine:String, index:Number) {
    return (index*this["increment_"+determine]+this[determine+"_min"]);
}
```

```actionscript
//
// changes the window of the graph
public function change_window(x_max:Number, x_min:Number, y_max:Number, y_min:Number,
➡ z_max:Number, z_min:Number) {
  // update the window dimensions
  this.x_max = Number(x_max);
  this.x_min = Number(x_min);
  this.y_max = Number(y_max);
  this.y_min = Number(y_min);
  // update the increments along the x- and y-axes
  increment_x = (this.x_max-this.x_min)/num_points_x;
  increment_y = (this.y_max-this.y_min)/num_points_y;
}
// changes the number of points to be plotted along the x- and y-axes
public function change_num_points(num_points_x:Number, num_points_y:Number) {
  // update the number of points to be placed along the x- and y-axes
  this.num_points_x = Number(num_points_x);
  this.num_points_y = Number(num_points_y);
  // update the increments along the x- and y-axes
  increment_x = (this.x_max-this.x_min)/this.num_points_x;
  increment_y = (this.y_max-this.y_min)/this.num_points_y;
}
//
// changes the zoom ratio
public function change_zoom(zoom:Number) {
  this.zoom = Number(zoom);
}
//
// changes the rotation angles
public function change_rotation(rotate_x:Number, rotate_y:Number) {
  this.rotate_x = Number(rotate_x);
  this.rotate_y = Number(rotate_y);
  // update the sine and cosine of the rotation angles
  calculate_sine_cosine();
}
//
// changes a point from Flash's coordinate system to a real math rectangular system
private function exchange_point(a:Number, b:Number) {
  // the ordered triplet of the point
  var x:Number;
  var y:Number;
  var z:Number;
  // get the ordered triplet
  x = points[a][b].x;
  y = points[a][b].y;
  z = points[a][b].z;
  // change from Flash's system to rectangular
  points[a][b].x = y;
  points[a][b].y = z;
  points[a][b].z = x;
}
//
// rotates a point (passed as an Object) by "a" and "b" on the x- and y-axes
private function rotate_point(a:Number, b:Number) {
  // ordered triplet to be rotated
  var x:Number;
  var y:Number;
  var z:Number;
  // temporary rotated coordinates
  var rx1:Number;
  var ry1:Number;
  var rz1:Number;
```

```
    var rx2:Number;
    var ry2:Number;
    var rz2:Number;
    // get ordered triplet
    x = points[a][b].x;
    y = points[a][b].y;
    z = points[a][b].z;
    // rotate point on y-axes
    rx1 = x*cos_y-z*sin_y;
    ry1 = y;
    rz1 = z*cos_y+x*sin_y;
    // rotate point on x-axes
    rx2 = rx1;
    ry2 = ry1*cos_x-rz1*sin_x;
    rz2 = rz1*cos_x+ry1*sin_x;
    // update the values in the position array
    points[a][b].x = rx2;
    points[a][b].y = ry2;
    points[a][b].z = rz2;
}
//
// scales the graph — appears to "zoom"
private function scale_point(a:Number, b:Number) {
    points[a][b].x *= zoom;
    points[a][b].y *= zoom;
    points[a][b].z *= zoom;
}
//
// changes an ordered triplet to an ordered pair
private function perspective_point(a:Number, b:Number) {
    // used for perspective — distance from the viewer's eye to the screen
    var D:Number = 500;
    // perspective ratio — used for changing an ordered triplet to an ordered pair
    var perspective_ratio:Number;
    // if point is in front of view calculate position of screen
    if (points[a][b].z>-D) {
        // calculate the perspective ratio
        perspective_ratio = D/(points[a][b].z+D);
        // calculate the position of the point on the screen
        points[a][b].perspective_x = perspective_ratio*points[a][b].x;
        points[a][b].perspective_y = perspective_ratio*points[a][b].y;
    } else {
        // point is behind user so it should not be drawn
        points[a][b].perspective_x = null;
        points[a][b].perspective_y = null;
    }
}
//
// translates the point to make the origin where the user specifies
private function translate_point(a:Number, b:Number) {
    points[a][b].perspective_x = origin_x+points[a][b].perspective_x;
    points[a][b].perspective_y = origin_y-points[a][b].perspective_y;
}
//
// calculates the sine and cosine of the rotation angles
private function calculate_sine_cosine() {
    sin_x = Math.sin(rotate_x*trans);
    cos_x = Math.cos(rotate_x*trans);
    sin_y = Math.sin(rotate_y*trans);
    cos_y = Math.cos(rotate_y*trans);
}
```

Theory, explanation, and discussion

To understand the **Graph** class, you must first understand multivariable functions. The level of theory covered in this short explanation is elementary to say the least; it's material that could have been covered in a middle-school algebra class.

In algebra, a function of **x** took every **x** in its domain and assigned to it a **y** value. When you plotted many **x** and **y** ordered pairs, you eventually saw a graph forming—anything from a parabola to a sine curve. For a function of **x** and **y**, also called a **multivariable function**, you assign a **z** value for every combination of **x** and **y** in the function's domain. Once you have the **x**, **y**, **z** ordered triplet, you plot the point by moving **x** units along the x-axis, **y** units along the y-axis, and **z** units along the z-axis. After plotting more and more of these ordered triplets, a 3D graph takes shape.

I thought that this could be programmed quite easily in Flash. First, I would define the range of **x** and **y** values that I wanted to graph. Then, I would simply loop through all of the different combinations of **x** and **y** values in that range and assign them a **z** value by plugging **x** and **y** into a multivariable function. However, a slight problem arose: how would I keep track of all these numbers? I opted for a 2D array. The indices of the array would be the number of points graphed along the x- and y-axes, then for every element in the 2D array I would have an object with variables for the **x**, **y**, and **z** position of the point, as well as the position of the point when perspective is added.

After I calculated the ordered triplet of the points, I still wasn't entirely done, as I had a few coordinate transformations that I wanted to put the points through. I translated, rotated, and scaled the points before I finally calculated them with perspective. The translation simply shifts the graph to the center of the screen, since Flash's origin is at the top left of it. The rotation allows me to view the graph from different angles, and the scale allows me to zoom in and out of the graph so that I can have more precision.

When the points were initially calculated, transformed, and then projected onto the computer screen for perspective, I was ready to render the graph. Because I wanted the surface to be a wire-frame object, I used the drawing API in Flash to draw lines connecting two points. I then looped through the graph's range of **x** values to connect all the lines that run horizontally, and through the range of **y** values to connect all the lines that run vertically. Once the lines were drawn, the rendering was complete, and I beheld a wondrous 3D graph in Flash.

In what follows, I'll present a rundown of some of the important functions and the part they play in the experiment.

Because there had to be a lot of interaction between the graph and the user (resolution, zoom, orientation, etc.), I created a specific **Graph** class with its own associated methods—these methods, in turn, would be invoked elsewhere in the movie and script. A **Graph** object, which is an instance of the class, holds all the important variables: the ranges of the **x** and **y** values to be graphed, the number of points to be graphed along the x- and y-axes, the rotation of the graph, the sine and cosine of the rotation angles, and other values. These variables would then be used in the functions that I was going to create in the class.

The first function I created, called **draw_line**, was for connecting two points with a line. The function is passed the x- and y-positions of the two points, and it draws the line using the drawing API.

The next function is the multivariable function that I talked about earlier, **function_xy**. This requires an input of **x** and **y**, and it then returns the value of the mathematical function. It is this return value that you'll want to mess around with to create different surfaces.

The next series of functions take care of the task of when the user wants to change one of the rendering parameters, such as the number of points to be plotted along the x- and y-axes. These functions take care of when the user wants to change the dimensions of the viewing window, the number of points to be plotted along the x- and y-axes, the zoom amount, and the rotation angles of the graph. They are **change_window**, **change_num_points**, **change_zoom**, and **change_rotation**.

When calling the function that updates the rotation angles, another function is called to find the sine and cosine of the angle. This function is called **calculate_sine_cosine**.

The next series of functions do all of the coordinate transformations. One is for the rotation, one is for zooming, one is for translating, and the last one is for changing an ordered triplet into an ordered pair. However, these functions don't operate on all of the points; rather, they operate on only one. The specific point to be transformed is passed to each function by the means of two variables, **a** and **b**. These variables are the indices of where the point can be found in the position array. For reference, these functions are named as follows: **rotate_point**, **scale_point**, **perspective_point**, and **translate_point**.

A problem I ran into at one point was that the rotation of the graph was a little awkward. After racking my brain for a few hours, I figured that it was because I set up the 3D coordinate system in Flash a little differently from how it is usually achieved in mathematics. In Flash, I have the x- and y-axes as usual and the z-axis coming out at you. In math, the x-axis comes toward you, the y-axis goes off to the sides, and the z-axis goes up and down. Therefore, I simply wrote a function to change the points to the math coordinate system. This function is called **exchange_point**.

The next function is the big one. **calculate_points** calculates the position of all of the points to be connected with lines. It loops through the number of points along the x- and y-axes so that it can index the array that keeps track of the position of the points. But, if you remember, to use the multivariable function, you were to give the function two values: **x** and **y**. Those values were positions of points in the x-y plane, and when they were plugged into the multivariable function you got a z-position. You can't, however, plug in indices of an array and get the z-position. Therefore, you must change the index values to actual x- and y-positions—for this, I employed an **index_to_coord** function, logically enough! After the indices are changed to coordinates, you calculate the z-positions, and finally you go through all the coordinate transformations. These two functions are called **calculate_points** and **index_to_coord**.

The last function in the rendering process is the one that connects the points with lines, **draw_grid**. The function handles this in two parts: first, it connects all the lines running vertically, and then it connects all the lines going horizontally.

Finally, you have a few functions left that just tie up some loose ends. One function, **plot**, is called when you want to plot a new surface. This function first calls the function that removes the old lines, then it calls the function that calculates the position of all the points, and finally it calls the function that draws all the lines.

That's pretty much it, really. If you like, you can alter this experiment to add a GUI, as I have with **base.swf**. This is basically just a wrapper with some prebuilt functions on it that lets you input and plot your own functions without having to go deep into the code. Check out the FLA for some ideas on how to do this. It's mostly just code attached to buttons from the main timeline, but you'll also need to make a couple of changes to the main code, add some equations to plot, and add another parameter to the **Graph** class constructor. You'll see these changes in **base.fla**. Note that in order to preserve the original **Graph** class, the class used in **base.fla** is named **Graph2** (and, accordingly, the relevant code is found in **Graph2.as**).

To add even more depth to the terrain generated, you could also use the **Color** object. By making the lines that connect points with small z-positions a little darker, you could make it seem as if the crevices are getting little light, whereas the tops of the hills are of a brighter shade and getting plenty of light.

Here are some parameters to try for the graph function. This covers the first nine parameters, and I've left the last two—the x and y origin—the same so that the origin is always the center of the screen. These go in the **actions** layer of **basicEffect.fla**, or you can enter them "manually" into the appropriate boxes if you're using **base.fla** as a start point:

x_max, x_min, y_max, y_min, num_points_x,
num_points_y, zoom, rotate_x, rotate_y

1.5, –1.5, 1.5, –1.5, 30, 30, 175, 90, 0
2, –2, 2, –2, 30, 30, 50, –90, 0
180, –180, 180, –180, 30, 30, 1, –20, 0
3, –3, 3, –3, 30, 30, 70, –35, 0
20, –20, 20, –20, 20, 20, 5, –60, 0
10, –10, 10, –10, 15, 15, 15, –45, 20

Try different combinations of these parameters with different surface models—you'll soon be getting some very interesting results. Good luck!

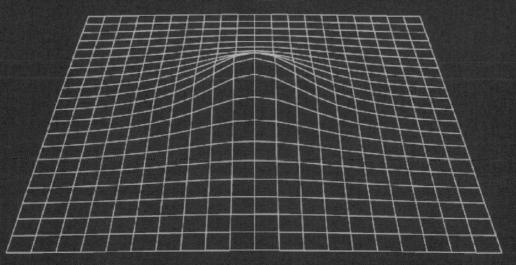

TANGENTS

www.potatoland.org

www.flong.com

www.kettering.edu/~drussell/demos.html

www.parasolpress.com/lewitt_2.html

www.turux.org

www.spacefuture.com/archive/inhabiting_artificial_gravity.shtml

www.sodaplay.com

http://dbn.media.mit.edu

www.georgehart.com/sculpture/sculpture.html

http://processing.org/exhibition/

www.ertdfgcvb.ch

www.signwave.co.uk

www-groups.dcs.st-andrews.ac.uk/~history/Java/index.html

www.jodi.org

www.muzeumsztuki.lodz.pl/images/bridget_riley.htm

www.cleoag.ru

www.numeral.com/appletsoftware/online.html

www.noodlebox.com/bitsandpieces/main.htm

www-ai.ijs.si/eliza/eliza.html

www.red3d.com/cwr/boids/

www.rhizome.org

http://mathworld.wolfram.com/LogarithmicSpiral.html

www.serv.net/Java/SineRule.html

www.tygh.co.uk/tan/tan.htm

http://acg.media.mit.edu

www.re-move.org

www.robertpenner.com

www.modifyme.com

www.wireframe.co.za

www.arseiam.com

www.dextro.org

www.sylloge.com/5k/entries/176/1.html

www.numeral.com/artwork.html

www.red3d.com/cwr/steer

http://acg.media.mit.edu/people/golan

http://astronomy.swin.edu.au/pbourke/fractals/fracintro

http://users.shore.net/~ndm/symbols/symbols.html

www.mcs.surrey.ac.uk/Personal/R.Knott/Fibonacci/phi3DGeom.html

www.kevlindev.com

www.moonstar.com/~nedmay/chromat/fibonaci.htm

www.flight404.com

www.easylife.org/386dx

www.nst.ing.tu-bs.de/schaukasten/fourier/en_idx.html

www.jhu.edu/~signals/fourier2

www-groups.dcs.st-andrews.ac.uk/~history/Curves/Curves.html

www.math.ubc.ca/~feldman/demos/pendulum.html

http://mathworld.wolfram.com/topics/AnimatedGIFs.html

www.rhizome.org/object.rhiz?2793

www.toxi.co.uk

http://yugop.com

www.pitaru.com

www.noodlebox.com/classic/window.html

www.auto-illustrator.com

www.math.ubc.ca/~feldman/demos/demo9.html

friendsofed.com/forums

Join the friends of ED forums to find out more about our books, discover useful technology tips and tricks, or get a helping hand on a challenging project. *Designer to Designer*™ is what it's all about—our community sharing ideas and inspiring each other. In the friends of ED forums, you'll find a wide range of topics to discuss, so look around, find a forum, and dive right in!

Books and Information

Chat about friends of ED books, gossip about the community, or even tell us some bad jokes!

Flash

Discuss design issues, ActionScript, dynamic content, and video and sound.

Web Design

From front-end frustrations to back-end blight, share your problems and your knowledge here.

Site Check

Show off your work or get new ideas.

Digital Imagery

Create eye candy with Photoshop, Fireworks, Illustrator, and FreeHand.

ArchivED

Browse through an archive of old questions and answers.

HOW TO PARTICIPATE

Go to the friends of ED forums at **www.friendsofed.com/forums**.

Visit **www.friendsofed.com** to get the latest on our books, find out what's going on in the community, and discover some of the slickest sites online today!

friendsof

DESIGNER TO DESIGNER™

an Apress® company

FOUNDATION
Flash MX 2004

Kristian Besley
and Sham Bhangal

1-59059-303-0 $29.99 [US]

FOUNDATION
ActionScript for Flash MX 2004

Sham Bhangal

1-59059-305-7 $34.99 [US]

FOUNDATION
Dreamweaver MX 2004

Craig Grannell
David Powers
George McLachlan

1-59059-308-1 $34.99 [US]

FOUNDATION
Mac OS X Web Development

Phil Sherry

1-59059-336-7 $34.99 [US]

FOUNDATION
Swift 3D

Honeycutt
Halligan
McBee
Shank
Spencer
Mousthasan

1-59059-210-7 $34.99 [US]

EXPERIENCE THE
DESIGNER TO DESIGNER™
DIFFERENCE

Fireworks MX 2004
ZERO TO HERO

Joyce J. Evans
Charles E. Brown

1-59059-306-5 $34.99 [US]

Paint Shop Pro 8
ZERO TO HERO

Sally Beacham
Ron Lacey

1-59059-238-7 $24.99 [US]

Windows
Movie Maker 2
ZERO TO HERO

Jon Bounds
John Buechler
Jon Bichsel

1-59059-149-6 $24.99 [US]

FLASH MX
MOST WANTED
EFFECTS & MOVIES

SHAM BHANGAL BRAD CORBIN DAVID DOULL
KEITH PETERS ADAM PHILLIPS JORDAN STONE
WebMeGroup + Digital Motion TODD YARD

1-59059-224-7 $39.99 [US]

FLASH 3D CHEATS
MOST WANTED

Aral Balkan Josh Dura Anthony Eden
Brian Monnone James Dean Palmer
Jared Tarbell Todd Yard

1-59059-221-2 $39.99 [US]

FLASH MX 2004
GAMES MOST WANTED

KRISTIAN BESLEY SHAM BHANGAL
ANTHONY EDEN BRAD FERGUSON BRIAN MONNONE
KEITH PETERS GLEN RHODES STEVE YOUNG

1-59059-236-0 $39.99 [US]

ILLUSTRATOR CS
MOST WANTED
TECHNIQUES AND EFFECTS

MATT KLOSKOWSKI

1-59059-372-3 $39.99 [US]

PHOTOSHOP
MOST WANTED
MORE EFFECTS AND DESIGN TIPS

colin smith
al ward

1-59059-262-X $49.99 [US]

Extending
Flash MX 2004
Complete Guide and Reference to JavaScript Flash

Keith Peters and Todd Yard

1-59059-304-9 $49.99 [US]

EXTREME
CS
PHOTOSHOP CS
PROFESSIONAL DESIGN AND ADVANCED ILLUSTRATION TECHNIQUES

By Matt Kloskowski

1-59059-428-2 $39.99 [US]

Object-Oriented
Flash MX 2004

PETER ELST
WILLIAM DROL

1-59059-399-5 $44.99 [US]

New Masters of Flash
Volume 3

OLA BERGMAN
BILLY BUSSEY
ANTHONY EDEN
DANNY FRANZREB
KRISTIN HENRY
NATHALIE LAWHEAD
SIMONE LEGNO
TODD MARKS
SHANE MIELKE
KEITH PETERS
ADAM PHILLIPS
OLIVER SHAW
JARED TARBELL

FOREWORD BY
SHAM BHANGAL

INTRODUCTION BY
BRENDAN DAWES

1-59059-314-6 $59.99 [US]

New Masters of Photoshop
Volume 2

1-59059-315-4 $59.99 [US]

Cascading
Style Sheets
SEPARATING CONTENT FROM PRESENTATION

Second Edition

Owen Briggs, Steven Champeon, Eric Costello, and Matt Patterson

1-59059-231-X $39.99 [US]

Constructing
Usable Shopping Carts
DESIGNING AND BUILDING GREAT E-COMMERCE APPLICATIONS

Clifton Evans, Jody Kerr, and Jon Stephens

1-59059-408-8 $34.99 [US]

Apache Essentials
Install, Configure, Maintain

DARREN JAMES HARKNESS

1-59059-355-3 $39.99 [US]

WEB STANDARDS SOLUTIONS
The Markup and Style Handbook

Dan Cederholm

1-59059-381-2 $29.99 [US]

Macromedia
Dreamweaver MX 2004
Design Projects

Rachel Andrew
Craig Grannell
Allan Kent
Christopher Schmitt

1-59059-409-6 $39.99 [US]